MUSSOLINI'S
EARLY DIPLOMACY

Mussolini's Early Diplomacy

BY ALAN CASSELS

Princeton University Press

Princeton, New Jersey 1970

For Nancy

Preface

MUSSOLINI came to power in 1922 pledged to fulfill a certain task in foreign affairs: to assuage the national pride of those Italians who believed their country had been slighted in the Paris peace settlement after World War I. The conviction that Italy's victory in the war had been "mutilated" at Paris was widespread between 1919 and 1922, and the Liberal ministers of the day were freely denounced as *rinunciatari* (renouncers). Actually Italy's material interests were not seriously hurt in the peace treaties. For this reason Gaetano Salvemini called Italy, after Molière, the *malade imaginaire*. But the nationalist grievance was all the more potent for being mythical.

"Our preoccupation is primarily with matters of foreign policy," Mussolini declared in 1921. He was well aware that he had ridden to power on a wave of nationalist dissatisfaction. He seemed conscious, too, of the fact that, if he did not play the patriotic hero, he might be supplanted by another. It was not until 1921 that Mussolini emerged as chief nationalist spokesman. Hitherto, this role had belonged to the romantic poet, Gabriele D'Annunzio, whose legionnaires had for 18 months occupied the town of Fiume, "in the name of the Italian people." Even after gaining office Mussolini kept a wary eye on his rival. He heaped flattery and honors on D'Annunzio and provided him with a gatekeeper to ward off unwelcome tourists. The gatekeeper, in addition, was a Fascist police spy who reported sedulously to the Duce. In February 1923 Mussolini seized the opportunity to consolidate his position as undisputed nationalist leader by fusing the Nationalist party with the *Partito nazionale fascista* (P.N.F.).

The difficulty in raising Italy's international stature was to devise a strategy for achieving it. With the opening of this century Italy had begun to gravitate toward the Anglo-

PREFACE

French orbit, a process that had culminated in the Treaty of London, April 26, 1915, whereby Italy entered World War I. It was a moot point whether Mussolini could gain the diplomatic victories he promised within the framework of the wartime alliance. After all, it was the British and the French who were responsible for the "mutilated victory." The temptation for Mussolini to strike out in new directions would be great. Some sort of collaboration with the defeated powers, eager to revise the 1919 settlement, could not be ruled out. Furthermore, it was problematical whether mere diplomatic successes, if they could be won, would satisfy the Italian hypernationalists. Or would Mussolini resort to military adventures? Ultimately he chose the alternatives of war and alliance with Hitlerian revisionism. The momentous events of 1935-43, when this occurred, have understandably and properly received the lion's share of attention given to Fascist Italian foreign policy. This book, by contrast recounts Mussolini's first and relatively unpublicized efforts to bring fresh vigor and perhaps a new direction to Italian diplomacy. The international situation in which Fascist Italy operated in the mid-1920s was patently different from that of a decade later. (The obvious and crucial difference lay in the change from a vanquished Germany in one period to a rampant, nationalistic Germany in the other.) Yet Mussolini was expected to live up to his chauvinist propaganda from the first moment he took office. And he tried to do so. In several of its characteristics early Fascist diplomacy signaled the disastrous course Mussolini would follow in the 1930s.

Something of a subplot to the main theme concerns the permanent officials of the Italian Ministry of Foreign Affairs. Many observers, both within and without Italy, set great store by the ability of these career diplomats to restrain Mussolini from rash adventures. Hence the degree of *fascistizzazione* of the foreign ministry served as a rough indicator of Mussolini's deviation from traditional Italian diplomacy.

I have divided the narrative of Fascist Italy's early foreign policy into four phases. The first six months or so after the March on Rome in October 1922 were largely taken up with problems left over from World War I, especially the negotiation of a peace treaty with Turkey and the climax of the Franco-German quarrel over reparations. The Duce had his own ideas on these matters, but the old guard at the foreign ministry were able to keep him fairly well in check. Also, in the sensitive Adriatic question Mussolini pleased his diplomats by assuming at the outset a remarkably moderate approach.

The second phase began in the summer of 1923 when Mussolini began to assert himself. The island of Corfu was occupied for a month and Fiume gained outright. In his campaign to win the latter, Mussolini explored the possibility of working with German nationalist elements. Next he turned to schemes to bring about a special relationship with such disparate states as Spain and Soviet Russia. And in the spring of 1924 he set in motion plans which pointed to a colonial venture in Asia Minor. However, all this came to an abrupt halt on June 10, 1924 with the murder of the Socialist deputy, Giacomo Matteotti. The crime, laid at Mussolini's door, paralyzed the Fascist regime.

In its third phase early Fascist diplomacy became passive and conciliatory, which was particularly apparent in the case of Albania, a territory long designated by Italian nationalists as an Italian sphere of influence. Yet for months Mussolini declined to intervene in the Albanian civil war, although it threatened to bring to power an anti-Italian faction supported by Yugoslavia. With his troubles at home Mussolini sought to make friends abroad, not fresh enemies. Thus he made his peace with the League of Nations, whose principles he despised. Similarly, although he regarded

France as Italy's natural rival, he encouraged talk of a settlement of all issues outstanding between Paris and Rome. But it was the British government with which Mussolini established the closest rapport and from which he derived the most comfort. The return of the Conservatives to office in London in November 1924 saw the start of an Anglo-Italian entente focused mostly on colonial affairs. But it also supplied a kind of guarantee that Mussolini would behave like a "good European"; for instance, it was partly to oblige Great Britain that Italy signed the Locarno Pacts in October 1925.

During 1925 Mussolini recovered from the Matteotti affair to fasten a veritable dictatorship on Italy. This freed his hands anew for a forceful foreign policy. A fourth stage of Fascist diplomacy was ushered in symbolically by the appointment of the P.N.F. hierarch, Dino Grandi, as undersecretary for foreign affairs in May 1925. Within the next two years several prominent career diplomats, who had agreed to serve Mussolini in 1922 in order to curb him, resigned their posts in despair. Proclaiming 1926 to be his Napoleonic year, the Duce opened it with a furious altercation with Berlin over the fate of Germans living in the Italian Alto Adige. In the meantime, his position in the Albanian question changed drastically. Mussolini now seized every opportunity to implant Italian influence in Tirana. In this he succeeded to the extent of establishing a virtual Italian protectorate over Albania, albeit at the cost of a grievous breach with Yugoslavia. Elsewhere in the Balkans Mussolini tried vainly to sponsor a novel diplomatic grouping, which would have embraced both the victorious and defeated nations of World War I. Fundamentally Mussolini's purpose in the Balkans was to substitute Italian for French influence. Indeed, on the international scene it was becoming increasingly apparent that he regarded France as the main obstacle to the fulfillment of Italian nationalism. So in 1926 Franco-Italian relations went rapidly down-hill. Especially bitter was the quarrel over the exiles from Fascist Italy (*fuorusciti*) in Paris. Mussolini's emphasis on the *fuorusciti* question was indicative of his growing disposition to see international politics in ideological terms and to think of Fascism as an exportable commodity.

This book ends in early 1927, by which time the years of indecision in Fascist foreign policy were over. During 1926 Mussolini's foreign policy took firm shape; in both the main and peripheral themes of this book a climax and a resolution were reached. First, the areas in which Italian national prestige would be sought and the general diplomatic strategy followed were mapped out. Second, the permanent officials of the foreign ministry were effectively pushed aside. In about four and a half years, then, Italian foreign policy had assumed a distinct Mussolinian tinge. Within this span the Duce adequately demonstrated his willingness to use unorthodox as well as conventional diplomacy, force and threat in addition to pacific negotiation, and to cultivate traditional allies and new revisionist friends alike. By the new year 1927 the shape of things to come in the 1930s was beginning to emerge.

THE PRIME SOURCE of information on Fascism's early diplomacy consists of *I documenti diplomatici italiani,* series vii (1922-35). The period between the March on Rome and the new year 1927 is covered in the first four volumes of the series; I have also used a few items from Volume V. This documentary collection, still many years from completion, is compiled largely from the archives of the Ministry of Foreign Affairs in Rome. The selection and editing is done by the *Commissione per la pubblicazione dei documenti diplomatici italiani,* a body of Italian scholars working under government auspices. The end product is almost beyond cavil, an indispensable research tool.

One or two other documentary sources deserve mention. A mass of enemy records captured by the Allies at the end of World War II are available in microfilm or photostat form. Most of the Italian records in this category concern Italy in World War II, but do provide occasional information about the 1920s. They may be found in the National Archives, Washington, D.C., and in St. Antony's College, Oxford, where a superior index compiled by F. W. Deakin is attached. The German records, both departmental correspondence and such collections of private papers as the *Nachlass* Stresemann, have more to say on the twenties and have proved invaluable in examining the vital question of Italo-German relations; they are accessible in the National Archives and the Foreign Office library in London. Central to Mussolini's early foreign policy was the Anglo-Italian entente; useful information on this subject has been obtained from the British Foreign Office files, which include Sir Austen Chamberlain's private papers, and the British cabinet minutes. These are open for scrutiny in the Public Record Office, London.

Memoir material on Fascist Italy's early diplomacy is not plentiful, and some of it is misleading. By far the most comprehensive and honest account is by Raffaele Guariglia, *Ricordi, 1922–1946*. Other reminiscences fill gaps in certain topics, principally Mussolini's Balkan policy. In addition, *I documenti diplomatici italiani* contain some revealing extracts from unpublished memoirs concerning Italo-German relations.

With the Fascists' accession to power Mussolini himself took over the post of foreign minister. Consequently nearly all diplomatic correspondence was addressed to him, or went out with his approval. Yet on the score of the limits of human energy alone, much of this paperwork must have been routinely processed by Mussolini's secretariat and not seen at all by the Duce. Obviously this is an important point in evaluating Mussolini's personal influence on Italian foreign policy. Therefore, I have tried to ascribe to Mussolini only his authentic acts and thoughts, using internal documentary evidence as a guide. Sometimes a telegram was drafted in Mussolini's hand—information helpfully supplied by the editors of *I documenti diplomatici italiani*— or the aggressive first-person style betokens Mussolini's authorship. To indicate that a piece of correspondence from abroad actually came to the Fascist leader's notice, there is Mussolini's own marginalia or his reply to the document in question. All in all, to isolate and define the Mussolinian touch has not proved an impossible task.

Much of Chapters 6 and 14 has been published in the *Journal of Modern History*, xxxv (June 1963), and some of Chapter 8 in the *American Historical Review*, LXIX (April 1964). I would like to thank the editors of these journals for permission to reproduce this material here. Of those librarians who have rendered me assistance over the past few years, I express particular gratitude to the staffs of the Public Record Office in London and of the Diplomatic, Legal, and Fiscal branch of the National Archives in Washington, D.C. I am also indebted to the Historical Office of the U.S. State Department for its permission to use certain records when they were classified. Among the several scholars who have extended help, I am especially grateful to Professors Howard M. Ehrmann and Gerhard L. Weinberg of the University of Michigan. Their advice and encouragement at the outset of this study were invaluable. Above all my appreciation goes to my wife, both for her patience and for her more positive contribution in the form of critical appreciation.

Alan Cassels

McMaster University
Hamilton, Ontario, Canada
July 1969

Contents

Abbreviations

ADAP   Germany, *Akten zur Deutschen Auswärtigen Politik, 1918-1945*: Serie B, 1925-1933. Vols. I-III (1925-1926). Göttingen, 1966 and continuing. Citation is by volume and document number.

B.D.   British documents. Foreign Office files (including annual reports on Italy compiled by the British embassy in Rome and Sir Austen Chamberlain's papers) and cabinet minutes. Public Record Office, London.

DBFP   Great Britain, *Documents on British Foreign Policy, 1919-1939*: Series IA, 1925-1929. Edited by W. N. Medlicott, D. Dakin, and M. E. Lambert. Vols. I-II (1925-1927). London, 1966 and continuing. Citation is by volume and document number, except for material in appendices which is referred to by page number.

DDB   Belgium, Académie royale de Belgique. *Documents diplomatiques belges, 1920-1940: La Politique de sécurité extérieure.* Edited by C. de Visscher and F. Vanlangenhove. 5 vols. Brussels, 1964-1966. Citation is by volume and document number.

DDI   Italy, Ministero degli affari esteri. *I documenti diplomatici italiani*: Settima serie, 1922-1935. Edited by R. Moscati and G. Carocci. Vols. I-V (1922-1927). Rome, 1953 and continuing. The documents in this important collection are arranged and numbered in chronological order; a few are paraphrased in footnotes. Save for the latter where page and footnote are quoted, reference to actual documents is by number.

G.D.   German documents (Auswärtiges Amt). "World War II Collection of Seized Enemy Records." Microcopy T-120. National Archives, Washington, D.C. Numerals refer to serial, container and frame(s) in that order. This collection contains the Stresemann papers which are designated when cited.

It.D.   Italian documents. "World War II Collection of Seized Enemy Records." Microcopy T-586. National Archives, Washington, D. C. Numerals refer to filming job, container and frame (s); there are no serial numbers.

These records are drawn chiefly from Mussolini's private secretariat and from the files of the Ministry of Foreign Affairs and the Ministry of Popular Culture. (This last, the propaganda ministry, was not formally constituted until 1937 but came to serve as a depository for many documents from an earlier period.) The departmental source of each document is indicated in the footnotes.

LNOJ   League of Nations. *Official Journal.* 20 vols. Geneva, 1920-1939. Many of the League's records are printed in the *Official Journal's* 194 special supplements.

OO   B. Mussolini. *Opera omnia.* Edited by E. and D. Susmel. 32 vols. Florence, 1951-1961.

State Dept. files   U. S. Department of State. Decimal Files. National Archives, Washington, D.C.

USFR   U. S. Department of State. *Papers Relating to the Foreign Relations of the United States.* Washington, D.C.

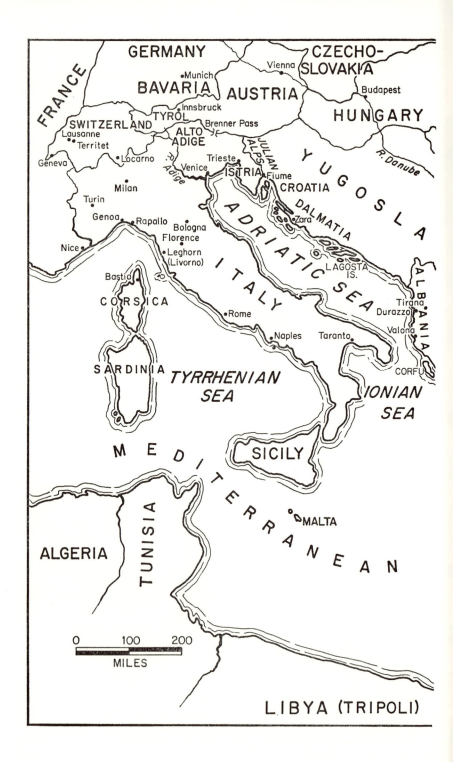

SOVIET
RUSSIA

BESSARABIA

RUMANIA

Bucharest •

BLACK
SEA

Belgrade •

BULGARIA

Sofia •

V I A

Constantinople •

G R E E C E

Salonika •

T U R K E Y

• Janina

STRAITS

AEGEAN
SEA

ANATOLIA

Athens •

SMYRNA

ADALIA

DODECANESE

CASTELLORIZZO IS.

RHODES IS.

CYPRUS

CRETE

SUDAN

RED SEA

YEMEN

ARABIA

R. Nile

R. Gash

ERITREA

Adowa •

SEA

Lake
Tsana

FRENCH SOMALILAND

Djibuti •

BRITISH
SOMALILAND

Addis
• Ababa

CYRENAICA

EGYPT

ETHIOPIA
(ABYSSINIA)

JUBALAND

ITALIAN
SOMALILAND

• Jarabub

KENYA

MUSSOLINI'S
EARLY DIPLOMACY

Introduction
The Reception of Fascism

Italy's Foreign Service

THE ITALIAN ministry which took office on October 31, 1922, in the midst of the March on Rome was dominated by Benito Mussolini. The Fascist leader not only became president of the Council of Ministers and minister of the interior but in pooh-bah fashion also assumed, pro tem, direction of the foreign ministry. Yet the government was not completely Fascist; only 4 of 14 ministers in the council belonged to the Fascist party. The coalition indicated that to achieve power Mussolini had relied on non-Fascist support, open and covert, and that he might continue to seek non-Fascist cooperation at the outset of his administration. Church and monarchy in Italy, although guarded in their utterances, managed to imply approval of Fascism. More openly, the Bolshevik-haunted industrialists and landowners supplied Mussolini's movement with money. In parliament the doyen of the Liberals, Giovanni Giolitti, had on occasion seen fit to encourage Fascism, while the Nationalist party could be counted on to vote with the Fascists, especially on foreign policy. But those called on to associate most closely with Mussolini, not merely in terms of an aloof toleration or vague conservative empathy but on the basis of daily contact and practical execution of Fascist policy, were the Italian bureaucrats. Within this category the most influential group, and one with a considerable esprit de corps, was the Italian Ministry of Foreign Affairs lodged in the Palazzo della Consulta.

With only one or two exceptions the Consulta officials agreed to serve the new regime and the new foreign minister. Their motives were varied. Some who depended on their bureaucratic posts for their livelihood took an apolitical attitude and insisted that Mussolini's accession to power represented a regular rotation of governments. On the other hand, most in the upper echelons of the Consulta enjoyed wealth and social position enough to be independent of their jobs, and were therefore free to reject Fascism. But of course these conservative aristocrats saw in Fascist "discipline" a bulwark of the established order and their own privileged status; for this reason they could condone the violence that attended Mussolini's rise to power. Fascism was thus necessary and tolerable to an entire class. Said one Italian diplomat: "If His Majesty accepts Mussolini, I do not see why I too should not accept him."[1]

To be fair, however, it appears that less personal and more disinterested motives for acquiescence in the new order were present in the Consulta. As a body the Italian foreign ministry was highly patriotic, and, like most Italian patriots in 1922, subscribed to the notion of a postwar "mutilated victory."[2] Italy was cheated out of her just rewards because of timid Italian diplomacy which was a consequence of Italy's internal weakness. On both counts Mussolini offered a remedy for the national malaise. At the cost of some loss of liberty he offered to impose order at home on which to base a strong foreign policy. Abroad, Mussolini, with his penchant for bluster, might be used as a bogey man to win concessions from allies large and small. Such in fact was the Consulta's plan. Yet it should be emphasized that the Consulta officials, in keeping with their conservative temper, were cautious and deeply attached to the traditional forms of international relations. Moreover, they were well aware of Italy's limited diplomatic power and feared the pos-

[1] Quoted in P. Quaroni, *Ricordi di un ambasciatore* (Milan, 1954), p. 18.
[2] The limited value of what Italy sought but failed to win in 1919 is cogently presented by G. Salvemini, *Mussolini diplomatico, 1922-1932*, rev. ed. (Bari, 1952), Chap. 1, "La malata immaginaria."

sibility of miscalculation and rashness on the part of Mussolini. Therefore they undertook to tame as well as exploit him. Raffaele Guariglia, the most articulate of the Italian diplomats to defend his association with Fascism, wrote in his *Ricordi* 25 years later: "To present to the world the Man [Mussolini] as capable of bringing new strength to our country, but without transgressing the bounds of international life . . . this was the task which seemed indispensable for the good of the country to . . . the handful of Consulta functionaries who collaborated. . . . . I chose collaboration readily not because I was convinced of the absolute good and utility of the new regime . . . but out of fear of the fatal consequences that its sudden collapse might have on the international position of the country and in the hope that its consolidation, proceeding gradually with the elimination of its defects, would bring advantages to Italian interests."[3]

This was the same calculated risk taken by the parliamentarians who gambled that Mussolini would grow more constitutional with time and the responsibilities of office. But beyond that, Italy's self-confident diplomats played for higher stakes in the larger game of world politics.

That the foreign ministry was so nearly unanimous in its acceptance of Fascism was due largely to the commanding personality of its secretary general after 1920, Salvatore Contarini. Despite his eccentricity and frequent irascibility, Contarini's adroitness in handling the minutiae of diplomacy and his clear vision of the world situation had won him a considerable reputation at home and abroad. His disgust with Italy's inferior postwar status had led him before the March on Rome into a cordial relationship with elements not far removed from Fascism, namely, the Nationalist party and the popular nationalist hero, Gabriele D'Annunzio. It was not surprising that such a man might

[3] Guariglia, *Ricordi, 1922-1946* (Naples, 1950), pp. 14-16.

5

regard Mussolini—professionally advised and controlled
—as an advantage to Italy. Not only did Contarini agree
to remain as secretary general, but his rapport with Mussolini in November 1922 was close enough to cause rumors
that Contarini had been offered the post of foreign minister itself. With Contarini in the Fascist fold it was unlikely
that many Consulta officials would refuse to serve the new
regime.[4]

But Mussolini was taking no chances. In his early dealings
with Italy's career diplomats he trod a middle path between
fulfilling his function as a new broom and indicating his
moderation and tractability. On one hand, the vague hint
was thrown out that recruitment to the Italian foreign service might be based less on birth and more on competitive
examination, while, as the symbolical end of an era, the
Ministry of Foreign Affairs was moved from the secluded
Palazzo della Consulta to the garish Palazzo Chigi on one
of Rome's busiest corners, where Mussolini might harangue
Romans at will.[5] On the other hand, the unpopularity of
these measures with the career diplomats was more than offset by other gestures of sweet reasonableness. In his first
appointments to high office Mussolini was conciliatory in
the extreme. It may be that he offered the foreign ministry
not only to Contarini but also to Sidney Sonnino, Italy's
wartime foreign minister. But with both men refusing the
offer—if it was made—the Duce was able to take the foreign
affairs portfolio himself—reluctantly. Also at the cabinet

[4] R. De Felice, *Mussolini: Il fascista*, I (Turin, 1966), pp. 375-76;
H. S. Hughes, "Early Diplomacy of Italian Fascism, 1922-1932," in *The
Diplomats*, ed. G. Craig and F. Gilbert (Princeton, 1953), pp. 216-17;
Legatus [R. Cantalupo], *Vita diplomatica di Salvatore Contarini*
(Rome, 1947), pp. 73-78; R. Moscati, "La politica estera del fascismo:
l'esordio del primo ministero Mussolini," *Studi Politici*, II (Sept. 1953),
400-405; P. Quaroni, *Valigia diplomatica* (Milan 1956), pp. 15-22;
D. Varé, *Laughing Diplomat* (New York, 1938), pp. 232-34.
[5] *OO*, XIX, 7; Guariglia, *Ricordi*, p. 25; Q. Navarra, *Memorie del
cameriere di Mussolini* (Milan, 1946), p. 13.

level two newcomers were General Armando Diaz at the Ministry of War and Admiral Paolo Thaon di Revel at the Ministry of Marine; both were war heroes, idols of the Nationalist party, and eminently respectable conservatives in the eyes of Italy's diplomatic corps. The important position of *chef de cabinet* went to a young aristocrat and former secretary to three former Italian foreign ministers, Giacomo Paulucci de' Calboli, who romantically liked to be called Barone Russo. The choice was a surprise Mussolinian caprice, but at least Barone Russo came from the same background as the old guard of the foreign service. Most reassuring of all was Mussolini's dispensing of the offices of the Ministry of Foreign Affairs itself. In addition to the retention of Secretary General Contarini, all the important posts at home and abroad were filled by career diplomats and politicians of the pre-Fascist era. In particular, the two key embassies of London and Paris were offered to, and accepted by, respectively, the Marquis Tomasi della Torretta and Baron Camillo Romano Avezzana. The former was an erstwhile foreign minister himself and confidant of Contarini; the latter was no less experienced in foreign affairs and was associated politically with the former Liberal premier, Francesco Nitti. In addition, Mussolini tried to persuade the well-known Liberal editor of the *Corriere della Sera*, Luigi Albertini, to take the embassy in Washington. Albertini declined because of ill health and interest in his newspaper; Mussolini chose in his stead Gelasio Caetani, a prominent member of the Nationalist party.[6]

But the Duce's efforts to allay apprehension did not stop with appointments in the traditional style. During his first few weeks of office he showed a willingness to shed his Fascist black shirt and don the conventional statesman's attire. Wearing this civilian dress, he took to visiting King Vic-

[6] N. Beyens, *Quatre ans à Rome, 1921-1926* (Paris, 1934), p. 133; Moscati, *Studi Politici*, II (1953-54), 404-408.

7

tor Emmanuel III every Monday and Thursday morning like a true constitutional head of government and monarchist.[7] On the latter score Mussolini was suspect in the foreign ministry because he had been a republican up to May 1921, and had only come out openly for the monarchy on the eve of the March on Rome. In the privacy of the Palazzo Chigi he showed his ability to accommodate still further by submitting meekly to lessons at the hands of the permanent officials in deportment, protocol, and the technicalities of running a foreign ministry. Mussolini seemed an assiduous student; a young diplomat who observed the educative process considered that "in a rather short space of time he became an excellent functionary."[8] The old-guard officials appeared to have every reason to congratulate themselves on their decision to collaborate with Fascism. Mussolini proved at first a deceptively easy tiger to tame.

While the majority of Italian career diplomats succumbed to Mussolini's charms, there remained a few who refused to traffic with Fascism either out of conscience or a fear of the ruin Fascism could bring to Italy. For the most part these recalcitrants were minor officials, but they also included two figures from the higher echelons of the diplomatic service. The ambassador to Germany, Alfredo Frassati, a follower of Giolitti, resigned his post and quietly but firmly refused to take up another under Mussolini.[9] The resignation of Carlo Sforza from the Paris embassy was more spectacular. As one of a procession of postwar Italian foreign ministers, Sforza was renowned for his attempted rapprochement with Yugoslavia, epitomized in the Treaty of Rapallo of November 12, 1920. Not without reason, Sforza feared that Mussolini intended to overturn this policy. Sforza's telegram of resignation was bitter; it ex-

[7] Navarra, *Memorie*, pp. 13-14.
[8] M. Donosti [M. Luciolli], *Mussolini e l'Europa* (Rome, 1945), p. 13.
[9] *DDI*, I, Nos. 6, 67.

8

pressed his ideological opposition to Fascism and forecast that Mussolini's foreign policy would be "a mere summary of sentiments and resentments." Then, to crown the insult, Sforza released his extremely frank message to the press. Contarini, who hoped to induce Mussolini to imitate Sforza's Adriatic policy, begged Sforza to withdraw his resignation and criticism. "Your action . . . will create," he wrote, "on the one hand, serious complications with Belgrade and, on the other, will make it more difficult in Italy to guide Fascism along the path of moderation." Sforza retracted so far as to offer to represent Italy on an ad hoc basis at the forthcoming international conference to arrange a peace settlement with Turkey. Mussolini, however, was not beguiled by this condescension. Sforza came to Rome, nonetheless, and two interviews with Mussolini were arranged; but they proved strained and useless.[10] Sforza returned to Paris and a kind of voluntary exile. Because of his international reputation, Sforza's action became a talking point outside Italy. A senior French diplomat summed up the prevailing opinion: "Sforza's resignation . . . will be regrettable. For us Sforza's remaining would be a security."[11] The affair was an unfortunate corollary to the campaign, deemed necessary and promoted by Contarini, to win for the new Fascist regime the confidence and respect of foreign powers.

Europe's Opinion

In 1922 it was difficult to appraise Fascism because its leader boasted of having no set policy. On his first appearance before parliament as president of the Council of Ministers, Mussolini proclaimed: "Before achieving this position, we were asked on all sides for a program. It is not pro-

[10] *DDI*, No. 2 and note 17; Navarra, *Memorie*, pp. 10-11. For Sforza's own version see his *Pensiero e azione di una politica estera italiana* (Bari 1924), p. 283, and his *L'Italia dal 1914 al 1944 quale io la vidi,* 3rd ed. (Verona, 1946), p. 172.
[11] P. Cambon, *Correspondance* (Paris, 1940-46), III, 421.

grams, alas, which are lacking in Italy: only men and the will to apply programs. All the problems of Italian life, all, I say, have been solved on paper, but the will to translate them into facts is lacking. This will, firm and decisive, is represented by the government today."[12] To be sure, Mussolini had persistently advertised his preeminent concern for foreign affairs.[13] But the specifics of his foreign policy were impossible to deduce from Mussolini's inconsistent statements in the newspaper he owned, *Popolo d'Italia*, before taking office. His sudden and suspicious conversion to the cause of Italian intervention in the World War was notorious. After the war he had vacillated between calls for the strict application of the Versailles Treaty and proposals for reviewing its reparations and colonial provisions. On the sensitive subject of the Adriatic, Mussolini had been in the van of those claiming "sacred" Dalmatia and Fiume for Italy. But he had given only moral support to D'Annunzio's Fiume coup, and Sforza's Treaty of Rapallo, which secured neither Dalmatia nor Fiume, had at first won the approbation of the *Popolo d'Italia*. But as popular criticism of the treaty spread, Mussolini reversed himself again and rejoined the hue and cry after the *rinunciatari*. From this record of patent opportunism little was to be gleaned about future intentions.[14] Moreover, until the summer of 1922 Mussolini was no more than one agitator among many in a restless Europe; outside Italy little attention was paid to his utterances on foreign policy or anything else.

Notwithstanding this lack of precise knowledge, a certain disquiet was felt throughout Europe over Mussolini's

[12] *OO*, XIX, 18.

[13] G. Rumi, "Fascismo nelle origini e i problemi di politica estera," *Movimento di Liberazione in Italia*, No. 75 (April 1964), 3-7. Cf. Mussolini's remark in a press interview, June 27, 1921: "Our preoccupation is primarily with matters of foreign policy" (*OO*, XVIII, 13).

[14] E. Di Nolfo, *Mussolini e la politica estera (1919-1933)* (Padua, 1960), Chap. 1, *passim*.

arrival in office. Clearly the Duce was an extreme chauvinist, and would have no compunction about upsetting
the international status quo. The impression was rein-
forced by his last speech before taking office, to the Fascist
congress in Naples on October 24, 1922, by which time
Europe was aware that this was the probable next premier
of Italy speaking. In violent language Dalmatia was declared
to be unredeemed and, in culmination of several weeks of
anti-British propaganda, the foreigner was enjoined to
leave the Mediterranean under the slogan: "The Mediterranean for the Mediterraneans!"[15] The words were well
heeded in British quarters, while Sforza cited the speech as a
decisive factor in his resignation.[16] After the March on
Rome it was reported that Turkey and Egypt looked to
Fascist Italy for assistance in warding off British imperialism, while defeated Hungary hoped for Mussolini's friendship on the basis of a common hatred of the Slavs.[17] However, to the satisfied nations, weary of wartime and postwar
strife, Italian restlessness coupled with the Fascist doctrine
of force, was ominous.

To set minds outside Italy at ease was not difficult. The
circumstances were propitious. In the first place, Mussolini
was not the most immediate danger to international stability in 1922. The real danger lay in the near breakdown
of the Franco-German reparations settlement. By comparison, the menace of Mussolini was a small, distant cloud in
the sky and tended to be discounted accordingly. Second,
the prevailing European temper was conservative. The fall
of the Liberal leader, David Lloyd George, and the creation
of the Conservative government, first under Andrew Bonar
Law and then Stanley Baldwin, was a sign of the times in
Britain. In France the ministry of Raymond Poincaré was

[15] *OO*, XVIII, 453-61.
[16] *OO*, XIX, 3-4; *DDI*, I, No. 3.
[17] *DDI*, I, Nos. 26, 34, 41.

11

a manifestation of right-wing nationalism. And in Germany control of the Weimar Republic was gradually passing from social democratic to more conservative hands. No matter how much Mussolini might protest that his movement was revolutionary and not reactionary, friend and foe alike outside Italy viewed it as decidedly conservative.[18] Fascism thus suited the mood of the times. Consequently Mussolini's claim that he represented the only "dike" against the red tide of bolshevism in Italy and perhaps elsewhere was widely accepted throughout Europe. This was reflected by those conservative barometers, the international money markets, where a fast rise in the value of the lira followed the March on Rome.[19] Although in reality the threat of a Bolshevik coup in Italy had long since passed by 1922—if indeed it had ever seriously existed—this fact was obscured by a barrage of Fascist propaganda. In the deliberately confused atmosphere the fact that the bulk of the Italian power structure appeared to accept Mussolini at his anti-Bolshevik face value took on added importance, for it was to responsible Italian opinion that a somewhat perplexed Europe first looked for a judgment on Fascism. Seizing on this, Contarini and the other diplomats, who were personally well known and respected in the chancelleries of Europe, exerted their influence to the utmost in Mussolini's favor.[20] For further endorsement by those whose opinion counted outside Italy, Mussolini could depend on the goodwill of most of the foreign diplomats in Rome. In particular, Camille Barrère, French ambassador since 1898, supported Fascism so openly that he incurred the suspicion of having intrigued to bring Mussolini into office. Almost as well known was the sympathy of the British ambassador,

[18] Right-wing groups in such diverse places as Bavaria, Portugal, Sweden, Hungary, and Poland took heart from the March on Rome (*DDI*, I, Nos. 24, 31, 45, 69, 223).

[19] *DDI*, I, Nos. 30, 36, 37.

[20] Guariglia, *Ricordi*, p. 13; Legatus, *Vita di Contarini*, p. 74.

Sir Ronald Graham, who privately advised his government: "If Mussolini is going to prove the regenerator of Italy, it will be very useful to have him on our side." And the American ambassador, Richard Washburn Child, showed his colors by writing at a later date Mussolini's autobiography for him.[21]

Mussolini's accession to power, then, provoked an ambivalent frame of mind outside Italy. On one hand, there was a rational apprehension that Fascist foreign policy must be a threat to the peace, on the other a predisposition to regard Fascism through rose-colored glasses. That the latter view came to predominate was due largely to Mussolini's early skillful moves. As calculated, the appointment of respected diplomats to the chief ambassadorial posts was appreciated abroad. As early as November 1, 1922 Mussolini had a cordial exchange of views with British ambassador Graham, during which he airily dismissed his recent Anglophobe statements: "Those are things which one says when one has no responsibility, but forgets as soon as one has." Graham was relieved and reassured.[22] In his early public statements to the press Mussolini proclaimed his intention to continue Italian cooperation with the British and French, who by historical tradition and their victorious position at the end of World War I, acted as arbiters of European opinion.[23] Mussolini's first policy statement to the Italian parliament as president of the Council of Ministers was awaited with interest. Made on November 16 to the Chamber of Deputies, the statement was a mixture, with something for everybody. There were soothing

[21] E. Serra, *Barrère e l'intesa italo-francese* (Milan, 1950), p. 354; B.D., E12084/27/44; and *DDI*, I, No. 79; B. Mussolini, *My Autobiography*, foreword by R. W. Child (New York 1928).

[22] I. Kirkpatrick, *Mussolini: A Study in Power* (New York, 1964), pp. 191-92.

[23] *OO*, XIX, 7-9. See also Mussolini's assurances of cooperation sent by telegram to Bonar Law and Poincaré (*OO*, XIX, 377).

words to calm anxiety abroad, next to threat and bombast for nationalistic consumption at home. Thus a promise to honor obligations already contracted by Italy, clearly a reference to the Treaty of Rapallo, was juxtaposed to the general law: "Treaties are neither eternal nor irreparable; they are only chapters in history." While the intention to work with the Allies was repeated, Mussolini demanded in return more respect for Italy's claims—"niente per niente" was his aphorism. If these claims were not met, warned Mussolini, Italy, "resuming her freedom of action, will take care of her interests with other policies."[24] Although the speech won few converts to Fascism, it apparently made no fresh enemies either. Everyone read his own views into Mussolini's jumble.[25]

But of course Mussolini was going to be judged by his deeds, not his words. Within a few weeks of taking office he was given the opportunity to demonstrate his verbal resolve to continue Italy's traditional policy in collaboration with the Allies. During the fall of 1922 steps were taken toward an international conference for a Near Eastern peace settlement, due to open in Lausanne on November 20. All the Allies of World War I deemed a united front essential in the face of a resurgent nationalistic Turkey, possibly backed by Soviet Russia freed of her civil war incubus. To dramatize the importance of the occasion and the firm and united purpose of the Allies, the British foreign secretary, Lord Curzon, and Poincaré, who headed both the French government and foreign ministry, decided to attend the opening of the Lausanne Conference. They were imitated by sundry premiers and foreign ministers of lesser Allied states. Would Mussolini, too, preserve the united Allied front, and make the token journey to Lausanne?

24 *OO*, XIX, 17-20.
25 E. Di Nolfo, "Opinione pubblica europea e l'ascesa al potere di Mussolini," *Il Mulino*, III (Oct. 1954), 635-37.

At first Mussolini was reluctant; but Contarini and Barone Russo believed attendance would further Mussolini's diplomatic education, and in the end the Fascist leader yielded.[26] In going to Lausanne, Mussolini was concerned less with Allied unity than with Italian prestige. Curzon, en route to Lausanne, stopped in Paris to discuss the Near Eastern situation with Poincaré. Mussolini was unable to attend these talks and the Italian ambassador in Paris gained admittance only with difficulty. Mussolini suspected a secret Anglo-French accord on the Near East. To reassert Italian parity with Britain and France, therefore, the Duce, before leaving Rome on the morning of November 19, sent a telegram to Curzon and Poincaré, demanding that a pre-conference meeting of the three major Allied foreign ministers be held, not at Lausanne itself, but at the nearby village of Territet, which was on Mussolini's route from Italy.[27]

Poincaré was incensed at this effrontery, but Curzon was more amused than angry. In a hard-headed way, Curzon was prepared to allow Mussolini his gesture of independence provided the substance of cooperation was not impaired. As the Lausanne Conference was more vital to British than to French interests, Curzon was able to prevail on Poincaré.[28] Together they went on to Territet, where they held a private conversation with Mussolini on the evening of the 19th. Later that evening the three foreign ministers traveled to Lausanne for the opening of the conference the next day. Actually Italy gained little lasting profit from Mussolini's Territet gambit and confidential exchange with Curzon and Poincaré. But in the short run Mussolini appeared to have achieved the near impossible;

[26] Moscati, *Studi Politici*, II (1953-54). 411.
[27] *DDI*, I, Nos. 118, 124, 128.
[28] H. Nicolson, *Curzon: The Last Phase* (London, 1934), pp. 288-89. Apparently Curzon did not scorn Mussolini as an upstart, as was once imagined, but promptly recognized him as an important figure to be won over to the British side (Kirkpatrick, *Mussolini*, pp. 198-200).

at one and the same time he had shown his willingness to continue the traditional Anglo-French-Italian entente in the eastern Mediterranean, and had compelled Europe's two most influential statesmen to bow to his whim. The deference shown to Mussolini by Curzon and Poincaré set the tone for the rest of the European diplomatic community.

If Britain dared not antagonize Fascist Italy out of Near Eastern considerations, neither could France affront Mussolini because of the state of the reparations question. By the fall of 1922 the German reparations settlement was proving itself unworkable. In British eyes Germany's inability to pay called for a reduction of her reparations burden. The French view was that Germany's refusal to pay justified enforcing the settlement by the most stringent sanctions. The collection of the full sum of reparations from Germany was the cardinal point, even the obsession, of Poincaré's foreign policy, and he needed Fascist Italy's support in countering British leniency. Mussolini was well aware of this; soon after taking office he ingratiated himself with Poincaré by making Germanophobe statements to the effect that Germany must be made to pay her entire legal debt. In fact, during November 1922 a tacit agreement seemed to be reached between Paris and Rome: France would place no obstacles in the way of the new Fascist regime's entry into international society; Poincaré would present his bill for the favor when the showdown on reparations was reached.[29]

These diplomatic maneuvers left their mark on European opinion at large through the medium of the press. Newspaper reaction to the March on Rome was fairly predictable. Socialist and radical journals were uncompromisingly hostile to Mussolini; the right-wing press admired him

---

[29] *OO*, XIX, 9, 34. For appraisals of the tacit Franco-Italian bargain at this time, see *DDI*, I, No. 130; [F. Charles-Roux], "La France et l'Italie dès armistices à Locarno," *Revue des Deux Mondes* (March 1, 1926), pp. 194-96.

uncritically. But the majority of Europe's newspapers fell between the two extremes. Representing middle-of-the-road opinion, at first they voiced common repugnance at Mussolini's castor oil methods in Italy and fear of his hypothetical violence in the international sphere. On the other hand, they generally preferred Fascism to the logical socialist alternative, and recognized that the March on Rome was a fait accompli which no amount of moral disapproval could reverse. Beset by such conflicting emotions moderate press opinion was slow to take a firm stand for or against Mussolini. In the latter part of November, however, it began to warm toward the new Italian government. In London the *Daily Telegraph* and the *Economist* dropped their caution and took to rationalizing away their fear of Fascism. Across the channel the reputable *Matin* and the popular *Petit Parisien* became sudden admirers of the new Italy. In thus discovering sympathy for Mussolini the moderate European newspapers did no more than reflect, deliberately or not, the amiability of Whitehall and the Quai d'Orsay toward Fascist Italy dramatically manifested at Territet. Middle-of-the-road press opinion continued to be wary of Mussolini. But by the end of November 1922 this had come to be mitigated by goodwill and optimistic expectations, an attitude characterized by an Italian writer as "una benevola aspettativa."[30]

After his first month in office Mussolini could, and did, feel pleased with his record. No state had regarded this accession to office as other than a routine change of Italian parliamentary government; the question of diplomatic recognition of the new regime had not been raised. Mus-

---

[30] E. Anchiere, "L'esordio della politica estera fascista," *Il Politico,* xx (Sept. 1955), 211. Cf. Di Nolfo, *Il Mulino,* iii (1954), 638-47; E. Fasano Guarini, "Il 'Times' di fronte al fascismo (1919-1932)," *Rivista Storica del Socialismo* (May-Dec. 1965), pp. 166-70; C. Vivanti, "La stampa francese di fronte al fascismo (1922-1925)," *Rivista Storica del Socialismo* (Jan.-April 1965), pp. 52-73.

solini's social acceptance by the diplomatic community had been sealed by Curzon and Poincaré. A policy of conciliation tinged with only verbal threats and of traditional cooperation with the Anglo-French bloc seemed to be paying rich dividends. In his euphoria Mussolini was prepared to continue on this line. He intimated his future good behavior and restraint to the Italian Senate on November 27: "I do not intend to conduct a foreign policy of adventure, nor one of renunciation. In this field miracles are not to be expected because one cannot change in a half-hour speech, no matter how dramatic, a policy that derives from many elements and a long period of time. I believe that, in foreign policy, one must keep as an ideal the maintenance of peace; it is a beautiful ideal especially after four years of war."[31] Mild words indeed for Mussolini, and welcome ones to a dozen chancelleries. Unhappily, within a few weeks Mussolini's affability was to disappear as he was forced to come to grips with the reality, and not merely the superficiality of international relations.

[31] *OO*, XIX, 48.

PHASE ONE

October 1922 to June 1923

1. The Lausanne Conference

A Mandate and Economic Privileges

COINCIDENTALLY Mussolini entered office at the moment that a climax was approaching in each of two outstanding international problems left over from World War I. One was the question of negotiating a definitive Near Eastern peace treaty; the other concerned the implementation of the postwar reparations settlement. Together they provided a convenient and early test of Fascist Italy's diplomatic mettle.

At the end of the First World War the Allied victors considered it both politic and practicable to subject Germany's Turkish ally to the same fate as Germany's Austro-Hungarian partner—partition of her empire. This was achieved on paper in August 1920 when the Allies forced the Sultan to accept the Treaty of Sèvres and the Tripartite Accord. While the treaty was notable for the transformation of the more remote regions of the Turkish empire into independent Arab states and British and French mandates, the accord delineated areas of what was left of Turkey as spheres of French and Italian economic influence. For their modest share of the spoils the Italians were constrained to pay a price. In 1912, during the war to wrest Libya from the Turks, Italy had occupied the Dodecanese Islands off the Turkish coast. After the war was over, Italy kept the islands to insure that Turkey would fulfill the terms of the peace settlement. But it was not generally anticipated that Italy would return the islands, regardless of what conditions Turkey met. In fact, by Article VIII of the Treaty of London of 1915, which brought Italy into the First World War, Great Britain and France accepted "Italy's entire sovereignty over the Dodecanese Islands." Despite the change from Turkish to Italian administration, the population and culture of the Dodecanese re-

21

mained overwhelmingly Greek, a factor that sprang into prominence with the attention paid to self-determination by wartime propaganda. When after the war Greece was designated by Lloyd George to achieve the final humbling of the Turks, the Dodecanese seemed a suitable reward for this service. Even before Italy's share of the Turkish empire was defined by Sèvres and the Tripartite Accord, agreement was reached under British supervision to cede the Dodecanese to Greece; such was the essence of the Tittoni-Venizelos Accord of July 29, 1919.

The delicate balance of the transactions, however, was upset when, contrary to expert prediction, Turkey, under the revivifying direction of Kemal Ataturk, proceeded to drive the Greeks into the sea. France and Italy hastened to placate this new force. France recognized the Kemalist government and even supplied it with arms, while Italy recalled her troops from Adalia, where they had been sent to prevent the Greeks from garnering all the prestige and profit from Turkey's expected collapse. By the fall of 1922 the Allies precariously controlled the Straits and Constantinople. Sèvres and the Tripartite Accord were dead; a new Near Eastern settlement required not dictation but negotiation; for this the Allies needed to repair their disunited front. In the circumstances the Italians had no compunction about declaring their intention to retain the Dodecanese in lieu of their gains under the now defunct plans for Turkish partition. Yet despite the need for harmony among the major Allies, on October 15 Britain, still backing her Greek client, sent a note of some asperity to Rome, calling on Italy to honor her pledge to yield the islands.[1] The note was still unanswered and the impasse unresolved when Mussolini came to power on October 31, 1922.

Previously the Fascist and Nationalist parties had criticized unceasingly Italy's inferior status within the postwar

[1] Guariglia, *Ricordi*, p. 19.

alliance. The Near Eastern question presented the new Mussolini government with an immediate opportunity to see what it could do about raising Italian prestige. As far as the Dodecanese were concerned, Fascist goals were shared by the foreign ministry officials. Indeed, the Italian retort to Britain's note of October 15, although one of the first diplomatic documents to bear Mussolini's signature (it was dated November 3), was composed by Secretary General Contarini.[2] The arguments used were hardly original. A review of the historical and juridical bases of Italy's occupation of the Dodecanese was followed by a bland insistence that the Dodecanese formed part of the overall Near Eastern problem. Therefore, only if Britain could secure for Italy the position in Turkish Anatolia promised by Sèvres and the Tripartite Accord would Italy evacuate the islands. The note contained a hint that an appeal to ethnic principles in the Dodecanese case could only set a precedent inimical to all Allied colonial ambitions in the Near East. But the general tenor of the note was not threatening. Italy gave every assurance of a desire to cooperate with and support Britain in the negotiation of a Near Eastern peace settlement.[3] This mixture of diplomatic tact and firmness, markedly different from the Fascist government's public bombast, had its effect in the right quarters. Lord Curzon, the British foreign secretary, described Contarini's note as "statesmanlike." Curzon's admiration was expressed more concretely in a statement of Britain's minimum terms for a Near Eastern peace treaty, which was sent to the Italian government in mid-November. Under the heading "Aegean Islands," the statement said that "these must be handed over by Turkey to the Allies whereupon they will be dis-

[2] The task was first entrusted to Guariglia who in 1922 was considered one of the foreign ministry's more able young diplomats. Apparently overcome by the importance of the task, he bungled it, whereupon Contarini stepped in and drafted the note (*ibid.*, pp. 19-20).

[3] *DDI*, I, No. 70.

posed of in a manner acceptable to the latter."[4] In other words, for the sake of a united Allied front against Turkey, Britain agreed to leave Italy for the time being in de facto possession of the Dodecanese. If the matter was not settled definitively, both London and Rome were aware that the longer the Italian administration of the islands continued, the more difficult it would be to end it. Thus Fascist Italy won an early and not inconsiderable victory, although the actual battle was fought and won by the professionals in the Palazzo Chigi.

But the shelving of the Dodecanese question was not clear-cut and spectacular enough to be of use to Fascist propaganda. Besides, Mussolini's Near Eastern ambitions went far beyond the Dodecanese. On November 4, the fourth anniversary of Italy's success at the Battle of Vittorio Veneto, Mussolini issued a patriotic message to Italians living in the Near East, recalling the days when that part of the world lived under the Roman empire and later under the Italian city states. Also portentous was Mussolini's speech of November 16 to the Chamber of Deputies, which, made only one day after Britain agreed to let the Dodecanese matter rest, demanded still further Allied consideration of Italian interests.[5] As the Near Eastern peace negotiations developed, it turned out that Mussolini had two objectives: first, an Italian mandate; *what* mandate was never specified, but probably Mussolini hoped to substitute Italian control for British in Iraq. Second, he wanted Italy's participation in Anglo-French economic enterprises in the Near East, to compensate for the vanished expectations of the Tripartite Accord. Such had also been the aim of some of Mussolini's predecessors, but the enunciation of the demands—for a mandate in particular— had been preempted by the Fascists and Nationalists before

4 *DDI*, I, Nos. 92, 120.
5 *OO*, XIX, 20, 406.

the March on Rome. Whether Italy could afford the expense of running a mandated territory and whether she had enough capital for investment abroad were questions not touched on by Fascist propaganda.

The professionals of Italy's foreign ministry were distinctly skeptical of the value and the attainability of Mussolini's ambitions. Before leaving the Paris embassy, Sforza spoke for the professionals. He warned the new Fascist premier that British and French complaints of the troubles of mandate administration were no indication that the British and French were ready to yield part of their burden to Italy. As for economic privileges in the Near East, Sforza granted that France, although not Britain, might be pressed into signing an agreement for some sort of economic cooperation with Italy. But he was convinced France would execute such an agreement only indifferently.[6] As events were to show, Sforza was right, but Mussolini remained to be convinced. On the other hand, the Duce did follow Sforza's cautionary advice to the extent that he made no specific reference in public to a Near Eastern mandate and economic privileges, but awaited the opening of the Lausanne Peace Conference on November 20.

It was appropriate that the Duce should journey to Lausanne to present Fascism's special Near Eastern demands. Moreover, as noted, even those in the Ministry of Foreign Affairs who did not share all of Fascism's expansive ideas approved such a trip. It seemed necessary, not merely to further Mussolini's diplomatic education, but to maintain Italy's place within the alliance. Curzon and Poincaré, it was reported, had reached an accord of their own on the Near Eastern question, a circumstance potentially dangerous to Italian interests. The internal condition of Italy had prevented Mussolini from traveling to London and Paris to confer with the British and French

[6] *DDI*, I, Nos. 18, 21.

foreign ministers. The best thing for him was to make the short trip to Lausanne on the eve of the conference and clarify Italy's Near Eastern position and expectations by a meeting with Curzon and Poincaré before the conference formally opened. Mussolini himself, once he made up his mind to attend, anticipated a startling diplomatic coup brought about by his own personal magnetism.

On the 19th, then, Mussolini rode north by train in company with Contarini, Barone Russo, Guariglia, and other officials who intended to protect the Fascist premier from his own impetuosity and from the wiles of the "old foxes" of European diplomacy.[7] But Mussolini had two surprises in store for his advisers. The first was the above-mentioned demand that Curzon and Poincaré meet him at Territet for a pre-conference discussion. Presumably emboldened by this *succès d'estime* and by the presence at Territet of numerous blackshirts *"fort affairés,"* as French General Maxime Weygand observed,[8] Mussolini sprang his next surprise. In a display of contempt for his diplomatic advisers he insisted on conversing tête-à-tête with Curzon and Poincaré. For a half-hour the three talked alone, with Mussolini relying on his French, which, although he had once taught the language as a schoolmaster, was far from perfect. From this bizarre encounter emerged a joint communiqué which spoke of a "common resolution to settle in a spirit of the most cordial friendship and on a basis of perfect equality among the Allies all questions to be treated at the Conference of Lausanne."[9] Contarini at once had misgivings. Equality for Italy was promised, true, but only in those matters under discussion at Lausanne. Neither mandates, an economic agreement in lieu of the Tripartite Accord nor the final disposition of the Dodecanese, appeared on the

[7] Guariglia, *Ricordi*, p. 21.

[8] Weygand, *Mémoires* (Paris, 1950-57), II, 193.

[9] *OO*, XIX, 420-22; *DDI*, I, No. 138.

conference agenda. The Anglo-French promises might turn out to be mere words.[10] But this subtlety was lost on Mussolini.

Further talks with Curzon and Poincaré during the first two days of the conference were conducted with the assistance of professional advisers, and Mussolini's contribution was little more than "Je suis d'accord."[11] But his outward good spirits were undisturbed. On the evening of November 21, as he prepared to return to Italy, Mussolini told the press: "Steps have been taken toward the concrete realization of the pact of equality among the Allies." He informed King Victor Emmanuel in a similar vein: "I have the impression that this last conversation represents a notable step toward the concrete realization of a position of equality in the eastern basin of the Mediterranean."[12] It remained for the Lausanne Conference to reveal whether Mussolini had by some miracle indeed wrung real concessions from Britain and France, or whether, as Contarini suspected, the "old foxes" had won after all.

In Mussolini's eyes an Italian mandate was the most prestigious trophy he could bring back from Lausanne. Even before leaving Switzerland he sought to put in motion the wheels that would transform the pledge of inter-Allied parity into a mandate for Italy. In a message to Della Torretta, his ambassador in London, Mussolini explained how Curzon, faced with the threat of Italian defection from the united Allied front, had capitulated and granted that the recognition in principle of an Italian mandate be embodied in an exchange of notes between the British Foreign Office and the Italian embassy in London. Della

[10] Guariglia, *Ricordi*, p. 21. Guariglia also makes the shrewd comment that the recognition of Italian equality was in itself insulting, as it implied that, without such a specific statement, Italy would indeed be an inferior partner.

[11] Nicolson, *Curzon*, p. 290.

[12] *OO*, XIX, 37; *DDI*, I, No. 141.

Torretta was instructed to accomplish this as soon as possible. The ambassador's démarche, however, immediately exploded Mussolini's hopes. Sir Eyre Crowe, permanent undersecretary in charge of the Foreign Office during Curzon's absence at Lausanne, denied all knowledge of any project for an exchange of notes. But he allowed Della Torretta in confidence to read a telegram from Curzon in which the British foreign secretary described his meetings with Mussolini. According to this account, Curzon had turned aside Mussolini's request for an Italian mandate with the observation that mandates were not under discussion at Lausanne. Instead, Curzon had suggested that if Italy had "any concrete and definite proposals" to make on the subject, she should submit them to Whitehall for consideration. Mussolini had inflated Curzon's noncommittal remarks into the promise of an Italian mandate to be formalized by an exchange of notes.[13]

The misunderstanding may have been due simply to Mussolini's lack of fluency in French and his diplomatic inexperience. Contarini did in fact rebuke his foreign minister for neglecting "a memorandum which ought to have been but was not presented" to Curzon.[14] On the other hand, although Mussolini exuded optimism in general after the exchanges at Territet and Lausanne, his public statements on the specific question of mandates were singularly reticent. The most he would say to the press was: "I cannot say much but I believe that, even in the question of mandates, Italian rights will be recognized." Asked whether some Near Eastern mandates would survive the demise of the Treaty of Sèvres, he replied enigmatically: "I don't know; maybe not."[15] Such indecisiveness was not typical of the brash, boastful Fascist leader. It is entirely plausible that Mussolini knew full well that Curzon had not made

[13] *DDI*, I, Nos. 145, 166.　[14] *DDI*, I, No. 219.　[15] *OO*, XIX, 38-39.

28

a mandate promise. But having led both himself and others to believe that something big was to be expected from his visit to Lausanne, he was forced to save face by claiming that the spectacular had been achieved. If his bluff was called by the British, Mussolini could pretend in diplomatic circles that failure was due, not to his own shortcomings, but to Curzon's duplicity.

After the evaporation of Curzon's "promise," one obvious stratagem was left to Mussolini if he wished to continue the struggle for a mandate. This was to carry out the threat to resume freedom of action in the Near Eastern question. So Mussolini resolved. The first matter of substance to be negotiated at Lausanne was the Straits. Britain's time-honored policy of leaving the Straits in Turkish hands and closed to warships was predicated on the existence of a friendly Turkey and a strong and expansionist Russia. By 1922 the reverse was true. An Anglophobe new Turkey and a weak, perhaps defenseless, new Russia caused London to urge that the straits be internationalized, demilitarized, and opened to all ships. Naturally Turkey and Soviet Russia were opposed. Mussolini was assured by his naval and military experts that Italian strategic interests would not be hurt if Britain did not get her way in the Straits.[16] The Fascist premier's inclination was expressed in a telegram, which he drafted himself, instructing the Italian delegation at Lausanne to cease its cooperation with the Allies. The Palazzo Chigi tried to thwart the Duce's impetuosity, and in fact seems to have prevented the sending of Mussolini's first message and substituted a circumspect injunction to Italy's representatives in Lausanne, London, and Paris to "adopt an attitude of reserve which will induce [the Allies] to take into account the importance of our collaboration."[17] But Mussolini was not to be denied and apparently conveyed

[16] *DDI*, I, p. 100, n. 3.   [17] *DDI*, I, p. 123, n. 2, and No. 198.

his original intention to the Marquis Camillo Garroni who, since Mussolini's departure from Lausanne, had headed the Italian delegation there. On the morning of December 4 Garroni visited Curzon and bluntly stated that unless Italy's desire for a mandate was met she would be found in the Russo-Turkish camp on the Straits issue. At the best of times Curzon possessed little respect for Garroni, whom he liked to describe as "the turtle." Faced with this experiment in diplomatic blackmail, the British foreign secretary grew apoplectic. Eventually recovering his speech and composure, he dared Garroni to carry out his threat, and remarked that the Italian exit from Allied councils in 1919 was an unfortunate precedent to imitate.[18]

There loomed the contingency Italy's professional diplomats had remained in office to forestall—a radical departure from traditional foreign policy. Not merely was the Palazzo Chigi unenthusiastic about a mandate; it saw Italy's longstanding aim in the Dodecanese Islands jeopardized by the threatened breach with the Allies. Contarini, while generally a Russophile, never put Russian friendship ahead of the British alliance. Garroni, too, let it be known that his action in bringing pressure on Curzon might be to the Duce's taste but not to his own. Not normally a fearless bureaucrat, Garroni took his courage in his hands when he sought to dissuade Mussolini. He warned that Italy would find little support at Lausanne for an anti-British stand on the Straits question. Even Turkey might be won over to the British scheme of internationalization. Then Italy could find herself alone except for the dubious company of Soviet Russia. In the very telegram describing his stormy interview with Curzon, Garroni begged Mussolini not to break the united Allied front, but instead to accept in good faith Curzon's one conciliatory gesture regarding mandates, namely, "to consider as rapidly as possible such precise

---

[18] Nicolson, *Curzon*, pp. 303-304.

formulas as might be submitted."[19] The moment of decision in the mandate crisis came five weeks after Mussolini had assumed power. In those first weeks in office Mussolini could still be restrained at crucial moments by his career diplomats. On December 5, the day after the presentation of Italy's ultimatum, Mussolini gave in, and Garroni was authorized to support the Anglo-French position on the Straits.[20] Ostensibly the professionals were in command at the Palazzo Chigi.

The issue of an Italian mandate was now dead; what remained was an anticlimax. But because Curzon had stated he was open to practical suggestions, Contarini left for Lausanne to see what he could salvage. He achieved nothing. Curzon was in an exceedingly bad humor, insisting again that London, not Lausanne, was the place to discuss mandates.[21] So Della Torretta and Crowe in the British capital wrestled further with the problem throughout December. Whitehall, although keen for Italian investment in British mandated territories, remained adamant against an Italian territorial or administrative stake. Della Torretta reported continuing British criticism of the costs of the Iraqi mandate, which might result in withdrawal at a later date.[22] But in effect the ambassador, realizing Italy's suit was hopeless, was providing consolation, illusory if need be, to keep Mussolini quiet. Indeed, one gets the impression that the participants in the talks at the British Foreign Office conducted them not in anticipation of any accord but to put a more favorable face on Mussolini's actions.

Mussolini himself was reduced to a policy of pinpricks. In the new year 1923, Fascist Italy sought to embarrass the Anglo-French mandate-holders at the League of Nations by championing the rights of native petitioners in the man-

[19] *DDI*, I, Nos. 178, 190, 200.
[20] *DDI*, I, No. 206 and notes.
[21] *DDI*, I, Nos. 219-20.
[22] *DDI*, I, No. 248.

dated territories.[23] Furthermore, by aligning with the United States, Italy was instrumental in delaying the full implementation of the Near Eastern mandates. However, in April, when Washington modified its opposition, Mussolini recognized that conditions were "unfavorable to the possibility of continuing resistance alone." As a final gesture he required a guarantee of the rights of Italian citizens in the mandated areas. This took the summer of 1923 to negotiate, but on September 30 Italy agreed to support at Geneva a resolution ratifying the authority of Britain and France in their Near Eastern mandates. Although he had totally given in, Mussolini was the last to admit it. With his acceptance of the Anglo-French mandates went the stipulation that it was "not prejudicial to the re-examination of the general question concerning Allied reciprocity in the eastern Mediterranean."[24] Toward the close of 1925, when a German mandate was rumored in connection with Germany's entry into the League of Nations, Fascist Italy vehemently demanded precedence.[25] And in 1927 when a Franco-Italian global detente came under discussion, the Fascist press listed a mandate as an Italian desideratum that had to be met.[26] In someone other than Mussolini such persistent but unfounded optimism might have been pathetic.

The search for the other Fascist objective in the Near East—a share of the Allied economic gains in the mold of the defunct Tripartite Accord—began along lines similar to those of the mandate struggle. Mussolini automatically assumed that the Territet and Lausanne pledges of Allied parity included economic privileges. But when the

[23] *LNOJ*, IV (1923), 298-300.
[24] *DDI*, I, No. 689; II, No. 412.
[25] *DBFP*, I, No. 121 and n. 3. Cf. ADAP, I (1), No. 274.
[26] B.D., C4176/480/22; R. Moscati, "Locarno—Il revisionismo fascista —Il periodo Grandi," in *La politica estera italiana dal 1914 al 1943* ("Edizioni Radio-televisione italiani") (Turin, 1963), p. 112.

Italian economic experts at Lausanne broached the matter they met the same negative Anglo-French attitude that had prevailed in the mandate discussions. Fascist Italy's predictable response was to threaten to break the Allied united front.[27] But here the parallel ceased. The day after Garroni's attempt to browbeat Curzon, the Quai d'Orsay indicated its willingness to help in promoting a Franco-Italian consortium for the economic exploitation of the Near East.[28] This was not altogether surprising; international politics at the close of 1922 were conditioned by an Anglo-French understanding that Britain's Near Eastern interests were to be given priority in return for recognition of France's paramount concern in the reparations problem. There is no evidence of a written or precise agreement, which was widely rumored in Germany, but the situation was too obvious to need stating.[29] By this reckoning it was France's clear duty to make the concession or bribe that would keep Italy loyal to the alliance at Lausanne. Hence the paradox that Italian pressure on the British foreign secretary produced a result in Paris.

On the other hand, France had no intention of sacrificing something for nothing in return. Before opening negotiations she made it clear that she expected Italian support for her intended decisive action in the reparations question— the occupation of the Ruhr. To this overture the Italian ambassador in Paris, Romano Avezzana, returned a guarded reply. Limited Italian backing was not out of the question, but it did depend on "equivalent advantages" for Italy.[30] Although the French seemed satisfied with this qualified assurance, they avoided any formal exchanges until the new year 1923. At this point the occupation of the Ruhr be-

[27] *DDI*, I, Nos. 154-55.
[28] *DDI*, I, No. 203.
[29] E. Rosen, "Mussolini und Deutschland, 1922-1923," *Vierteljahrshefte für Zeitgeschichte*, V (Jan. 1957), 27-28.
[30] *DDI*, I, No. 246.

came imminent and the need for Italian support urgent, so negotiations began in Paris.

The actual economic agreement was no problem. But Poincaré wanted to include a preamble stating that "recent events in Europe and the Near East have shown once more that a similarity of political interests exists between Italy and France and that it is a simple matter to render more intimate that collaboration between the two governments envisaged in the peace treaties."[31] This meant blanket Italian endorsement of France's Ruhr policy. In the mandate question Italy's career diplomats had been alarmed lest Mussolini break with the other Allies; now they feared the reverse. The Palazzo Chigi saw clearly enough Italy's need to side with France on the reparations issue, but wanted to do so circumspectly. The Duce, on the other hand, was so determined that something which could serve a propaganda purpose should emerge from his trip to Lausanne that he was liable, for an insubstantial Near Eastern gain, to obligate himself utterly and recklessly to France in an important European question. This belief was reenforced when Mussolini did not reject the French preamble outright. Therefore Romano Avezzana took pains to open Mussolini's eyes to the implications of the French formula by proposing his own, in which the phrase "similarity of political interests" was replaced by an innocuous reference to Franco-Italian "cordial relations."[32] The situation resolved itself when Poincaré, realizing Italy was not going to accept the exact wording he had proposed, declared himself ready to sign the economic agreement without any preamble at all. On February 3 there was an exchange of letters defining the terms of reference of an economic consortium, and stating that obligations under the Tripartite Accord were hereby discharged. The texts of the

[31] *DDI*, I, No. 392.
[32] *DDI*, I, Nos. 402, 406.

letters were kept secret, but their existence and purport were announced. Mussolini's longing for a public triumph had been met.[33]

But it was a modest success. After all, France had admitted Italy to partnership just because her Near Eastern interests were less than those of Great Britain. It was an economic association with Britain that Mussolini really wanted. But both Curzon at Lausanne and the Foreign Office in London clearly assumed that French concessions satisfied the lip service paid to Allied equality in communiqués from Lausanne, and so refused to consider any further Italian demands. Although his diplomats conveyed the British attitude quite plainly, Mussolini exhibited the utmost optimism. He calculated that Italy's accord with France presaged a broader economic arrangement with British involvement. Indeed, he was prepared to postpone announcement of the Franco-Italian consortium until Britain adhered to it.[34] Dissuaded from this by his professional advisers, Mussolini then confidently counted on news of the Franco-Italian agreement to induce the British to negotiate. But Whitehall used the argument that, contrary to the situation in other nations, British financiers did not obey official dictation, so the British government could not assume an economic obligation to Fascist Italy. Or if it did so, the pledge would be worthless.[35] To an authoritarian politician like Mussolini, any reference to a pluralistic society had to be mere dissembling. Ambassador Della Torretta in London, then, was constrained to keep on importuning the Foreign Office, with the result that in March the British government did in fact give token adherence to the Franco-Italian accord. The hollowness of the success was stressed in an anonymous memorandum drafted within the

[33] *DDI*, I, Nos. 312, 450, 460-62.
[34] *DDI*, I, No. 316.
[35] *DDI*, I, Nos. 317, 459, 534.

Italian foreign ministry for Mussolini's edification. The memorandum drew attention to "certain reservations" attached to Britain's commitment and estimated that Italy stood to gain little "without the specific concurrence of English financial circles." The achievement of this sine qua non was, to say the least, dubious, and the memorandum kept a discreet silence on the prospect.[36]

The Palazzo Chigi's scorn for Mussolini's "success" seemed to turn him in another direction. For this new foray he chose Giulio Montagna, at the time Italian plenipotentiary at Lausanne and by reason of his ultranationalism one of Mussolini's firmest supporters among the career diplomats. Montagna was instructed, probably privately, to contact the American observers at the peace conference.[37] Although ostensibly expressing concern for the open door in the Near East, the United States had just obtained a concession in Asia Minor—the Chester Accord. Montagna approached Joseph Grew, the United States representative at Lausanne. First he proffered somewhat unctuously Italy's approval of the Chester Accord. A few days later he informally suggested an Italo-American partnership to exploit the resources of the Near East. Not surprisingly, a startled Grew rejected the suggestion out of hand, and another of Mussolini's fantasies came to an abrupt conclusion.

Mussolini's efforts to achieve his Near Eastern ambitions were now played out, with a meager net result. An Italian mandate was no longer possible. The French and British signatures to a tripartite consortium had been wrung from reluctant governments; the reluctance was a sign that

[36] *DDI*, I, No. 694.

[37] There is no record of this in the *Documenti diplomatici italiani*, which would indicate that Mussolini was bypassing his unappreciative foreign ministry. Although Montagna himself told the Americans that he spoke without his government's authorization, it seems hardly conceivable that he was not acting on Mussolini's instructions. Information on the episode comes from J. Grew, *Turbulent Era* (Boston, 1952), I, 566-69, and from Grew's reports in State Dept. files, 767.68119/549 and 564.

promises would be honored in the breach only. In a way, Mussolini seemed to recognize this fact in his desperate overture for an economic partnership with the United States. Italy's professional diplomats, distrustful from the start of Mussolini's pet schemes in the Near East, no doubt counted on Anglo-French obstinacy to thwart them. While Fascist Italy strove vainly in London and Paris for an Oriental mandate and concessions, the Lausanne Conference pursued its work. It was at the conference that Italy's prime and by now traditional Near Eastern objective was to be secured. Title to the Dodecanese was a goal of Italian diplomacy on which both Fascists and the Palazzo Chigi agreed.[38]

The Dodecanese

Insofar as the old-guard Italian diplomats cherished dreams of Italian expansion in the Near East, they were gradualists. To them the acquisition of the Dodecanese was the first pragmatic step to be taken before any kind of Italian penetration into Asia Minor could be contemplated. Moreover, their strategy for securing the islands themselves was circumspect. By the tacit Anglo-Italian understanding reached before the Lausanne Conference opened, the conference would simply abolish Turkish sovereignty over the Dodecanese, leaving their actual administration in Italy's hands pending a final disposition after a Near Eastern peace was signed. This continuance of the status quo already favorable to Italy was accepted by the Palazzo Chigi as the most that could be won at the moment.

On the contrary, success by stealth was not Mussolini's ideal at all. The Italian governor of Rhodes considered the population of the Dodecanese disposed "to accept equably the proclamation of our sovereignty," and urged that Italy's position be regularized as soon as possible.[39] Con-

[38] Guariglia, *Ricordi*, p. 22.
[39] *DDI*, I, No. 76.

sequently Mussolini raised the matter in his talks with Curzon at Territet and Lausanne, after which he announced to the press: "The Dodecanese question no longer exists."[40] This was nonsense. As in the case of his boasts of a mandate and economic privileges, it is very possible that Mussolini knew he was merely whistling in the dark. To King Victor Emmanuel he wrote a more accurate appraisal of his understanding with Curzon: "It has been agreed that the Dodecanese question cannot form an object of discussion without Italy's wishes being taken into account."[41] But so long as Mussolini regarded his own projects for a Near Eastern mandate and economic privileges as viable ambitions, his attention turned only sporadically to Italy's conventional goal in the Dodecanese. Thus for a few months, Italian diplomats at Lausanne were left to handle the Dodecanese problem in their own way.

Events were moving in Italy's favor. For some time the Turks had been reconciled to the loss of the Dodecanese; not surprisingly they preferred their successors to be the Italians rather than the hated Greeks. In a sense, Italy had paid Turkey for the islands in 1921 by helping to sabotage the Allied attack on Kemal Ataturk. More important still, the Anglo-Greek combination, which was the chief obstacle to Italy's possession of the Dodecanese, was showing signs of disrepair by the end of 1922. In October the architect of Britain's Hellenophile policy, Prime Minister Lloyd George, fell from office. The new British government, while not anti-Greek, could be expected to take a more circumspect attitude toward Greek moves in the eastern Mediterranean. British reserve increased shortly after the opening of the Lausanne Conference when a successful coup d'état staged in Athens was followed by the summary execution of most of the ousted cabinet. London expressed its sense

40 *OO*, xix, 38.
41 *DDI*, i, No. 141.

of outrage by refusing to recognize the new Greek government for almost a year. This was far from a complete breach. Lest the impetuous Mussolini imagine that it was, and act accordingly, his diplomats assured him that, given a free choice, the British Foreign Office and Admiralty would still like to see the Greeks, bloodstains notwithstanding, in the strategically important Dodecanese.[42] Nevertheless, there existed at Lausanne a distinct Anglo-Greek *raffroidissement* which contrasted with the growth—after the unfortunate experiment in browbeating Curzon into granting an Italian mandate had been surmounted—of a friendly rapport between the British and Italian delegations. The latter development was regarded by Guariglia, a member of the Italian delegation, as a fruit of Contarini's campaign to persuade Britain of the continuity of Italy's traditional foreign policy under Fascism.[43] Despite Mussolini's clear demonstration of the new Italy's heightened expectations in the Near East, the British apparently were willing to be convinced.

The Italian representatives at Lausanne were able to take advantage of the situation. During one of his conversations with Curzon at the opening of the conference Mussolini in his euphoria had accepted the foreign secretary's formula for Turkish surrender of the Dodecanese in the peace treaty: this meant that cession would be not to Italy specifically but the Allies in general. After Mussolini's departure the Italian delegation set out to rectify his error. The British, anxious to shelve the Dodecanese question until the conference was over, offered only mild opposition (soon withdrawn) to the inclusion in the new treaty of the clause in the Treaty of Sèvres ceding the Dodecanese to Italy pending a final settlement. Garroni and Guariglia were content for the time being with the small victory, and carefully abstained from raising, even privately, the

<hr>

[42] *DDI*, I, No. 210.
[43] Guariglia, *Ricordi*, pp. 23-24.

unresolved question of full Italian sovereignty over the islands.[44]

The first session of the Lausanne Conference lasted from November 20, 1922 to February 4, 1923, when it abruptly halted as a result of Anglo-Turkish differences. Lord Curzon, eager to return to London, took to making ultimatums. The Turks, for their part, were slow, more than unwilling, to meet Curzon's demands halfway, which was enough to cause the impatient British delegation to bolt the conference. The dispute was over economic and juridical matters that were immaterial to the Dodecanese issue. The Italians could not help but regret the delay in signing the peace treaty that would recognize Italy's de facto ownership of the islands; therefore they joined the French and the American observers in desperate but futile efforts to mediate between the British and Turkish delegations.[45] Yet since the breach arose largely from a clash of personalities and did not concern the most substantive issues at Lausanne, a speedy resumption of negotiations was generally anticipated. Only a few hours after the British departure, Ismet Pasha, Turkey's plenipotentiary, expressed his willingness to accept the juridical capitulations proposed by the conference's subcommittee on minorities, which was chaired by the Italian delegate, Montagna. The Montagna formula contained the most important of Curzon's terms. Within a few days there were plans for a resumption of the conference.[46]

If the occasion for the interruption was nothing more than a tempest in a teacup, the delay itself brought a new headache for Italy. With the conference still in recess, Turkey, formerly so compliant about the Dodecanese, informed Italy that she now refused to cede one of the islands

[44] *Ibid.*, pp. 22-23; *DDI*, I, No. 421.
[45] *DDI*, I, Nos. 251, 428; Grew, *Turbulent Era*, I, 550-54; Nicolson, *Curzon*, pp. 346-48.
[46] *DDI*, I, Nos. 466, 473, 477, 512.

—Castellorizzo, of insignificant size but the most easterly of the group and only a few miles off the coast of Turkish Adalia, the region once designated by the Treaty of Sèvres and the Tripartite Accord as a zone of special Italian influence. An Italian possession within sight of the Turkish mainland, argued Ankara, would be unacceptable to Turkish public opinion.[47] Behind the diplomatic cliché the Turks planned at least a token gesture of defiance at the Mussolini brand of imperialism, which considered possession of Turkey's offshore islands merely one step on the road to penetration of Asia Minor. It was also a skillful diplomatic maneuver intended to divide the Allies. The professionals of the Palazzo Chigi tried to sell the notion that Castellorizzo had no strategic value or interest for Italy. This was partly to mollify the Turks, and partly to assuage Mussolini lest, by insisting on Castellorizzo, he lose the rest of the Dodecanese. But to no avail; Turkey remained adamant, and the Duce likewise decided, in Guariglia's words, "to hold firm at all costs out of sole concern for the prestige of the new Fascist government."[48]

Toward the end of March Curzon arranged a meeting of Allied representatives in London to coordinate policy before the Lausanne Conference resumed. Ambassador Della Torretta seized the opportunity to probe British intentions regarding Castellorizzo. Outwardly Curzon was reassuring; no change in the territorial settlements already reached at Lausanne would be permitted; Castellorizzo, therefore, was Italy's. Nevertheless, Curzon was uncertain "what the Allies and Italy should do if, agreement having been reached on all points in dispute, the Turks were to make the Castellorizzo question a sine qua non of signing the peace." This perhaps innocent musing aroused some Italian disquiet. Della Torretta was satisfied Britain would

[47] *DDI*, I, No. 591.
[48] Guariglia, *Ricordi*, p. 22.

stand by Italy. But Montagna, who assumed the leadership
of the Italian delegation at Lausanne when the conference
reopened on April 23, was forthright about his "doubt of
Curzon's loyalty."[49] Mussolini probably agreed with Montagna's suspicions. After all, he was convinced, or at least
he pretended to be convinced, that Curzon had broken his
word given at Territet and Lausanne; so why not expect
the same treatment over Castellorizzo? So Montagna was
allowed to negotiate at Lausanne on the presumption of
British unreliability. The Italian delegation was now to
try to determine Turkey's price for Castellorizzo.[50]

The Turks were delighted at the turn of events. Only a
few days after first voicing their objections to an Italian
Castellorizzo, they hinted that their veto would be lifted
if Italy undertook never to cede any of the Dodecanese to
Greece.[51] Left to themselves, the Italians would have
promised gladly, but it meant prejudging the final settlement of the Dodecanese, and this the British, still obliged to
protect Greek interests, would certainly thwart. In the
process even Italy's immediate occupation of the islands
might come in for reexamination at Lausanne. So Italy
refused the Turkish bait. Turkey then proposed another
trade to detach Italy from the other Allies: Turkey would
tolerate Italy in Castellorizzo in return for Italian support
at Lausanne of the Montagna formula for Turkish juridical capitulations. Although this might have been acceptable when the conference broke down in February, by
the time it reconvened the Allies had pledged themselves
to press for a different capitulatory regime. Despite the personal flattery contained in the Turkish offer, Montagna
expressed his indignation to Ismet Pasha at "such impractical barter by which he did not hesitate to put me in an
equivocal position vis-à-vis the Allies and to obligate me

49 *DDI*, I, Nos. 659, 743, 748; II, Nos. 14, 21.
50 *DDI*, II, No. 39.
51 *DDI*, I, No. 611.

beyond what is permissible."[52] Having failed to strike a bargain with Turkey, Montagna now asked for, and received, Mussolini's authority to try another tack. This consisted of an attempt to compel the British to bring pressure to bear on the Turks. Specifically Montagna used the tactic of temporarily withholding Italian approval of the Greco-Turkish reparations agreement reached after some difficult negotiation under British auspices.[53] Actually the stratagem was undermined by Mussolini who told the British ambassador in Rome that Montagna's obstruction was mere bluff and would end shortly, information that was promptly passed on to the British delegation at Lausanne.[54] Nevertheless, Italy's importunity impressed the British at last because, only a few hours after Montagna on May 27 threatened to hold up a reparations settlement, the Turks apparently received some sort of British injunction. That same evening Ismet Pasha promised Montagna that Turkey would renounce Castellorizzo in a formal statement to the conference. The net result of the Italo-Turkish argument was an understanding, which sprang from Italy's repeated disclaimer of strategic interest in Castellorizzo, that the island would remain unfortified.[55]

After the flurry over Castellorizzo, the Italian delegation patiently awaited the formal signing of a Near Eastern peace treaty, which came on July 24, 1923. Article XV of the Lausanne Treaty temporarily transferred to Italy "all rights and title" over the Dodecanese. Now the final disposition of the islands remained to be decided. Typically Mussolini had not wanted to wait for the signing of a treaty before broaching the question. The breakdown of the Lausanne Conference in February had tried his patience. Arguing that the difficulties at Lausanne had noth-

[52] *DDI*, II, No. 43.
[53] *DDI*, II, No. 52 and notes, and p. 38, n. 3.
[54] *DDI*, II, No. 57.
[55] *DDI*, I, No. 743; II, No. 59.

ing to do with the Anglo-Italian agreement on the islands' interim status, Mussolini had encouraged his ambassador in London to open discussion with Curzon for a final settlement. But Della Torretta's tentative overture had evoked no response.[56] Undaunted, Mussolini had promptly come up with the suggestion that the approaching visit of King George V to Rome be used to force Whitehall into a quick resolution in Italy's favor of such pending questions as the Dodecanese. Alarmed at this piece of simplistic diplomacy, Della Torretta informed Mussolini unequivocally that Curzon would not anticipate the conclusion of a Near Eastern peace treaty. The ambassador pleaded that he be allowed to judge British official and popular opinion and to select the most propitious moment to pursue a definitive Dodecanese settlement, to which Mussolini outwardly complied.[57]

But it was perhaps too much to expect that the actual signing of the Lausanne Treaty would go by without some gesture designed to bring Fascist Italy's triumph to public attention, and calculated to force the pace on the road to Italian de jure sovereignty over the Dodecanese. Abetted by the nationalist Admiral Emilio Solari, Mussolini proposed to send a fleet to take ceremonial possession of the islands. The Palazzo Chigi immediately saw how provocative this would appear to the British. Indeed, a rumor of Mussolini's plan did reach London, where it was interpreted as a veiled annexation and a breach of Italy's promise to negotiate the ultimate disposition of the Dodecanese. Mussolini desisted, but not primarily out of concern for the diplomatic complications involved. Rather, he was dissuaded by Guariglia who, if we may believe his own account, observed shrewdly that "the project seemed to manifest a comic side as our warships would go fully armed to take possession of territories which had been in our hands for over ten

[56] *DDI*, I, Nos. 495, 523.   [57] *DDI*, I, Nos. 593, 617.

years."[58] Ridicule was one reaction pretentious Fascism dared not risk.

In reality the Treaty of Lausanne assured Italy of eventual ownership of the Dodecanese—a notable Italian victory, although hardly attributable to Mussolini's diplomacy. Italy's de facto possession of the islands antedated Fascism, and so did the strategy devised to win them outright. It was entirely appropriate that the campaign for the Dodecanese, even under Mussolini, should be carried forward by the career diplomats who had launched it; what success Italy achieved at Lausanne was almost exclusively due to them. In Near Eastern affairs generally until mid-1923 their influence remained strong, even decisive.

[58] Guariglia, *Ricordi*, pp. 26-27; cf. *DDI*, II, No. 157.

2. Reparations

A Middle Road in the Ruhr Crisis

THE OTHER large international issue to confront Mussolini soon after taking office involved Germany's payment of reparations. The London schedule of payments imposed in May 1921 was proving unworkable. It had been deemed necessary to waive payments in currency during 1922. But the German economy had continued downhill and German reluctance to pay had grown. As 1922 and the partial moratorium drew to a close, the Allies were faced with a clear choice between a substantial relaxation of the London schedule and its application by force. The British preferred the former; German economic recovery was essential to that of Europe as a whole which, in turn, spelled hope and opportunity for faltering British commerce. To the French, on the other hand, a heavy reparations bill was a political weapon to depress Germany's military potential and thereby obtain a measure of that national security supposedly denied at the Paris Peace Conference. While London argued that the Germans *could* not pay, Paris felt compelled to insist that the Germans *would* not. A thorough review of the reparations tangle was in order, and was indeed the purpose of a meeting to be held in Brussels between the Allies and Germany. But first it was necessary to try to induce some harmony among the Allies themselves. Therefore, shortly after Mussolini came to power, plans were laid for a preparatory conference of Allied government heads. Mussolini at once demanded Italian participation in any Allied discussion of reparations, the same claim to equality with Britain and France that he was making in the Near Eastern question. Mussolini's right to attend was readily granted, although his plea to hold the conference on the Continent, so his absence from Italy would be as brief as possible, was denied.[1] It was for London and a further taste of diplomacy by conference, then, that Mussolini entrained on December 7, 1922, less than three weeks after his first taste of an international conference at Lausanne.

Before the March on Rome the Fascists had inclined toward a rigid position on reparations. After all, "making the Germans pay" was a cheap and easy propaganda slogan, and certainly more congenial to nationalists than the alternative of international economic cooperation offered by Lloyd George at the Genoa Conference in April 1922. Moreover, French money had been paid to Mussolini early in World War I in return for his urging in his *Popolo d'Italia* Italian intervention on the Allies' side. It does not seem too much to suggest—as does Salvemini, for instance[2]—that Paris after the war was able to buy the Duce's pro-French stand on reparations. In his first three weeks of office Mussolini, in his statements to the press, continued to assert that Germany should fulfill the London schedule.[3] But behind the scenes Mussolini's economic advisers were hard at work trying to convince him of the futility of a harsh reparations policy; what is more, they succeeded. Perhaps Mussolini was swayed by their technical arguments, or perhaps he imagined that, by moving closer to the British line on reparations, London might concede him something in the Near East. Most likely, however, he foresaw a chance to mediate among France, Britain, and Germany. On many occasions Mussolini was to aspire to the position of *arbiter mundi*. Remember that the London Conference opened two days after the Fascist bluff to break the united front at Lausanne had been called; Mussolini needed a restorative diplomatic coup such as a successful arbitration in the reparations question. Fascist Italy's decision to seek the middle ground was indicated when Mussolini en route to Lon-

[1] *DDI*, I, Nos. 176, 184.
[2] Salvemini, *Mussolini diplomatico*, p. 40.
[3] *OO*, XIX, 9, 41.

don spoke to newspaper correspondents. Certainly Germany must pay, he declared, but with the qualification: "I do not know whether the amount fixed at London is what Germany is able to pay." In general he was guarded and deliberately cryptic.[4]

Mussolini took to London the draft of a new German reparations settlement, part of it written by himself, indicating that he had made himself familiar with some of the complexities of reparations—doubtless part of his early campaign to persuade the Palazzo Chigi that he could become "a good functionary."[5] The Italian plan was based on the interrelation of reparations and inter-Allied war debt, a reasonable idea if not an original one, as Mussolini was shortly to claim.[6] The plan proposed reducing the total German reparations from the London schedule figure of 132 billion gold marks to 50 billion (approximately $32 billion and $13 billion, respectively). The latter figure was enough to cover the Allied war debt to the United States, which amounted at the end of 1922 to something under $12 billion, including interest. Italy herself stood to lose, for she could claim only 10 percent of the 13 billion to be obtained from Germany, and she owed the United States 2 billion. But then, the Italians did not expect to pay their full American debt. So it may be inferred from Mussolini's suggestion to the London Conference that German reparations be reduced even below the figure of 50 billion reichsmarks if Washington agreed to cancel a portion of the Allied war debt owed the U.S. But the major compensation under the Italian plan for the Allies' renunciation of 82 billion reichsmarks of German reparations was to be made at Britain's expense. London was asked to relinquish the bulk of $10 billion worth of war debt and interest owed

[4] *OO*, XIX, 60. On Mussolini's intent to mediate see Moscati, *Studi Politici*, II (1953-54), 419.
[5] *DDI*, I, No. 217.
[6] *OO*, XIX, 66.

by the other Allies (7 billion if the irrecoverable Russian debt were excluded), of which Italy's share was $2.5 billion.[7] This was not the wild and inconsiderate proposal it might seem. The Balfour note of August 1, 1922 had stated Britain's intention to recover only the debt necessary to meet her own obligations to the United States. During the London Conference the British were to come close to embracing the principle of Italy's proposal in an offer to carry the cancellation of debt beyond the limit set by the Balfour note, in return for a lenient German reparations settlement. The Italian project was not only economically sound but was substantially acceptable to the British, who were asked to shoulder the heaviest material burden.

Unfortunately the major difficulty was not to find a feasible economic solution which Britain would underwrite; it was to satisfy France's political demands on Germany. To placate France the Italian plan called for the resumption of reparations annuities after a two-year moratorium—a delay of four years was being widely canvassed at the London Conference—and it held out a variety of liens on the German economy as pledges of fulfillment. But by the end of 1922 France wanted immediate payment and demanded much more than the civil and economic guarantees offered by Italy. In fact, Paris had already decided that the military occupation of German territory was the only productive pledge in sight. The plan Mussolini presented to the London Conference on December 9 did not begin to meet French requirements, and so stood no real chance of adoption. Recognizing this, the conference did not so much reject

---

[7] For the text of the Italian plan see Great Britain, Parliamentary Papers, 1923, Vol. XXIV (*Accounts and Papers*, Vol. XII), Cmd. 1812, "Inter-Allied Conferences on Reparations and Inter-Allied Debts," pp. 28-31. Figures of inter-Allied indebtedness are to be found in H. Moulton and L. Pasvolsky, *War Debts and World Prosperity* (Washington, D.C., 1932), pp. 425-31; and Italy's particular debts in C. McGuire, *Italy's International Economic Position* (New York, 1926), pp. 371-80.

Mussolini's proposal as ignore it. The two premiers, Bonar Law and Poincaré, concentrated on a restatement of conventional British and French attitudes toward Germany. Neither moved the other an inch, so it was arranged to hold yet another round of Allied talks in the new year in Paris.[8] The London Conference served only to emphasize the gulf between Britain and France and the ephemeral nature of Mussolini's plan to mediate between them.

But Mussolini was nothing if not an optimist, and he left London undismayed. He was encouraged by Britain's retreat from her position in the Balfour note; this he characterized as "a great step forward." During the London Conference Bonar Law had expressed himself ready to discuss Italy's reparations proposal after its examination by the "experts"; the inference which Mussolini was anxious to draw was that the plan might emerge from such examination as a possible basis of discussion at the forthcoming Paris meeting.[9] But soon portents sufficient to disabuse even Mussolini began to appear. First, Bonar Law gave a lengthy review of the reparations situation in the House of Commons without any reference to the Italian plan.[10] Then came the news that the British, far from taking up Mussolini's proposition, intended to present their own plan at Paris.[11] The Italian ambassador in London, Della Torretta, tried to smooth things over by suggesting that Mussolini concentrate on winning support in the Reparations Commission in Paris, where the economic merits of Italy's plan might be best appreciated by the supposedly apolitical financial experts.[12] And indeed, all the Allied delegates to

[8] Great Britain, Parliamentary Papers, 1923, Vol. XXIV, *Accounts and Papers*, Cmd. 1812, pp. 60-62. For Mussolini's explanation to the conference of the pledges he envisaged, see *ibid.*, pp. 59-60.

[9] *OO*, XIX, p. 64; Great Britain, Parliamentary Papers, 1923, Vol. XXIV, *Accounts and Papers*, Cmd. 1812, p. 54.

[10] Great Britain, 5, *Parliamentary Debates* (Commons), CLIX (1922), 3,229-41.

[11] *DDI*, I, No. 245.   [12] *DDI*, I, No. 247.

the commission, even the French, seemed to grant that Italy's contribution was worthwhile. Mariano D'Amelio, one of the Italian delegates, asked for and received Mussolini's permission to modify the original proposal in accord with British and French sentiments expressed in the commission. A sliding scale clause was thus added, whereby prompt payment by Germany would result in a proportionate reduction of the total reparations bill. This, of course, was calculated to please London. In an effort to offer Paris a counterattraction, the guarantees of payment were more precisely defined, although they remained entirely of a civil nature.[13]

On December 26, with the Paris talks and the fate of the Italian plan still a week away, the Reparations Commission gave Italy another opportunity to mediate. France brought evidence before the commission of German default in deliveries of timber, which were unaffected by the moratorium on reparations in specie. At once the French and Belgian representatives proposed recognition of willful German default under Part VIII, Annex II, paragraph 17 of the Versailles Treaty, which justified the seizure by force of productive pledges: in other words, the military occupation of territory. The British strenuously objected. It was largely through D'Amelio's initiative and calming influence that both sides were brought to accept a compromise. In effect, the commission informed the Allied governments that Germany stood in voluntary default; but, in view of the impending meeting at Paris, the commission recommended only financial sanctions.[14]

But all this was peripheral. The members of the Reparations Commission could humor Italy because the power to make crucial decisions lay not in their hands but in the

[13] *DDI*, I, Nos. 245, 256, 257, 266.

[14] *DDI*, I, No. 270; Reparations Commission, *Report on the Work of the Reparations Commission, 1920-1922* (London, 1923), pp. 248-64.

Quai d'Orsay and Whitehall. Mussolini himself appreciated the situation. Although he affected pleasure at the
tactical successes won in the commission, the report from
London of a British reparations plan in the making convinced him—as the London Conference itself had failed to
do—that his chance for an arbitral coup was for the time
being almost nonexistent. Mussolini, therefore, resolved not
to attend the forthcoming reparations conference in Paris.
Such a decision also satisfied a personal inclination, for his
views on diplomacy by conference had soured. At
Lausanne and London he had expected to be an object
of awe and attention. Apart from one or two embarrassing
moments Lausanne had been tolerable; but in the British
capital the press was unimpressed. Mussolini had fallen
into petty quarrels with the French over the allocation
of hotel suites and the number of delegates to represent each
state at the conference, and had become the object of *bons
mots* retailed behind his back. In general, he had appeared
thoroughly uncomfortable, like "a hunted convict . . . disguised as a man of the world to avoid recognition."[15] Moreover, conference diplomacy smacked of international cooperation, even Wilsonian idealism, all of which was quite alien
to Mussolini who accepted blindly the primacy of national
self-interest. Soon after returning to Rome he announced
that he would not attend the Paris talks, "unless there is
undertaken the necessary work of diplomatic preparation
which alone can render the plenary conference conclusive
and useful."[16] In due course this provided a diplomatic
excuse for abstention. It was the first of Mussolini's many
public acts of aversion to international gatherings.

Mussolini's mood on realizing that his offer to play the
arbitral savior of the Western alliance had been rejected
was one of petulance. If he could not have his own way, he

---

[15] A. De Saint-Aulaire, *Confession d'un vieux diplomate* (Paris, 1953),
pp. 642-44.
[16] *OO*, XIX, 67.

would wash his hands of the entire reparations question. He indicated his disinterest by failing to supply the Italian delegation to Paris with more than the sketchiest instructions. Della Torretta was taken from the embassy in London to lead the delegation; just before the announcement of his nomination he visited Rome, but his discussion there with Mussolini concerned Near Eastern rather than reparations affairs.[17] His written instructions on the latter were simply to press for the adoption of the project submitted by Mussolini to the London Conference with the amendments made in the Reparations Commission, which was a forlorn hope. Therefore, of more importance was the policy to be followed when the Italian plan was rejected and a likely British alternative presented: "If the English project offers an effective and radical solution to the debt question, that is, in a manner corresponding to our interests and to the point of view sustained by us—inasmuch as in this matter it is the British government alone which by virtue of its special position of creditor can speak the decisive word—I [Mussolini] would consider it opportune, to the end of realizing the eventual goodwill of the British government, not to prolong or complicate discussion for the sake of the procedural question."[18] The British plan might or might not contribute to the pacification of Europe, which had been Mussolini's original grandiose ambition, but this was to be of no concern to the Italian delegation. Italy's object was now solely mercenary: debt cancellation could buy Italian support of any British plan. But most significant, Mussolini's obvious disinterest in the reparations question meant that the calculation whether or not a British scheme met the requirements of Mussolini's vague formula was by and large left to Della Torretta and his fellow diplomats in Paris. If Britain offered to cancel most but not

17 *DDI*, I, Nos. 244, 284.
18 *DDI*, I, No. 290.

all of the debt, or if cancellation was hedged with irksome restrictions, the decision to accept or reject would be determined by their interpretation and presentation of events to Rome. While not outright carte blanche, this arrangement offered greater latitude than most twentieth-century diplomats normally can hope to enjoy.

The Palazzo Chigi officials had never shared Mussolini's dream of mediating between Britain and France. Their pessimistic judgment was that Britain and France could not and would not be reconciled, that an open breach between the two was inevitable. When that happened Italy would not be able to avoid taking sides to some extent. And in the minds of the career officials there was one overriding consideration that dictated which way Italy should jump. Italy was habitually dependent for her military potential and industrial health on the importing of coal, which traditionally came mostly from British mines. After World War I the price of British coal rose steeply; Italy was glad to find an alternative in the consignments of free coal from the German Ruhr provided on the reparations account. Those to profit most directly from this arrangement were the north Italian industrialists who had helped Fascism gain power. Mussolini repaid a political debt when he firmly opposed any moratorium on reparations payments in kind. Ambassador Romano Avezzana, who, like most Italian diplomats, came from the same social milieu as the factory owners, expressed the situation plainly to the French: "A great part of our economy is based on the German market. An occupation of the centers of the Ruhr . . . could not be viewed with indifference by our industrial and commercial circles."[19] Italy's freedom of action in the reparations question, then, was severely limited by the need to safeguard her precious supply of Ruhr coal. France was the chief hazard, since Poincaré's government was clearly determined

---

[19] *DDI*, I, No. 246.

to occupy the Ruhr as a pledge of reparations payments. Should Italy join with Britain in opposing the move the Palazzo Chigi was convinced that France would invade the Ruhr alone—except for the not very important support of Belgium. In this case the Ruhr mineheads would fall into the hands of the French, who would be resentful of Italy's desertion; a summary halt in the transport of coal across the Alps could be expected.

On the other hand, about Christmas 1922 there flourished the rumor that the German industrialists, either before or after a Ruhr occupation, "to save themselves and their country from total ruin," would seek an accommodation with France. Supposedly this would take the form of an exclusive Franco-German consortium, which again would give France such influence over the German economy as to deny Italy her reparations coal if Paris so wished. But it proved to be only a rumor, and was probably one of Poincaré's stratagems to frighten the Allies into accepting French policies. In this he had some success, for Romano Avezzana in Paris and many in the Palazzo Chigi gave it credence.[20] Whichever way events went, Italian diplomats foresaw danger in offending France. Italy's only course was to curry French favor, using the rationalization that the more support France received the less precipitously she would act. This was the burden of Contarini's influential advice, while Romano Avezzana put it more explicitly and forcefully than any of his colleagues when he wrote:

I hope I am not mistaken in judging that it is in our best interest to proceed in accord with France with the object of exercising sufficient pressure to force England, America, and Germany to adopt without delay a just but definitive solution. . . . .

[20] *DDI*, I, No. 283; Rosen, *Vierteljahrshefte für Zeitgeschichte*, v (1957), 29-30.

In truth, we need a resoluteness, I would say of so wholehearted a nature as not to weaken even in the face of the application of French sanctions, provided that Italian interests were protected in advance. A firm attitude on our part, while permitting the development of a European program with France, is perhaps the only way to restrain her from proceeding to occupy the Ruhr and to obtain common satisfaction.[21]

Such, indeed, was the mood and outlook of the professional diplomats who were to speak for Italy in the Paris talks.

Until the meeting at Paris opened on January 2, 1923 Italy had been able to keep a middle position between Britain and France only because decisions had been avoided. The London Conference had deferred matters to Paris, and the Reparations Commission was awaiting this last effort to achieve Allied cooperation before turning to the consequences of German default. Thus Paris was the breaking point; either Britain and France would unexpectedly find agreement, or they would go their separate ways. In the latter case Italy would be called on to take a clear stand for one side or the other. Both Poincaré and Bonar Law brought their own reparations schemes to Paris. Poincaré's plan tolerated a two-year moratorium on payments and a reduction of Germany's complete liability below the London schedule, although only to the extent that Britain remitted the war debt. At the heart of the plan, however, were the pledges of payment in the form of taxes on the production of German coal and timber. It took little imagination to see that their realization would probably require a territorial occupation. The British plan featured their most radical solution of the war debt question to date. Britain offered to write off French, Italian, and Belgian debts except for a minor sum which was to be met by the diversion of a small amount of German reparations from the

21 *DDI*, I, No. 177.

Continental Allies to Britain, and by the British appropriation of Allied gold that had been kept in London during the war as token security for the loans. Nevertheless, the plan still amounted to the renunciation of six billion dollars of debt and the virtual end of inter-Allied indebtedness. In return, Britain asked for a four-year moratorium on German payments of specie and a limit on deliveries in kind. Total German reparations were left undefined; there was to be an irreducible minimum not in excess of 50 billion marks; reparations above this figure were to be made flexible and dependent on Germany's economic development, and were to be earmarked for a pool for Allied debt payment to the United States. The guarantees gave little scope for the use of force and consisted of the conventional Allied controls over German finance. Significantly these were to be administered, not by the French-dominated Reparations Commission, but by a new international council.[22] The two plans were far apart; Poincaré and Bonar Law rejected each other's offering emphatically. Neither showed any interest in the revised Italian project which Della Torretta had brought with him.[23] The moment for Italy to choose between France and Britain was reached. For Della Torretta, Romano Avezzana, and the experts from the Reparations Commission who made up the Italian delegation, the decision was automatic.

The affinities between the British plan and what Italy had been proposing all along were obvious: cancellation of the bulk of inter-Allied debt as compensation for the reduction of the fixed amount of reparations to 50 billion marks, use of a sliding scale for other charges, and reliance on civil and economic pledges only. But these were far secondary

[22] The French and British plans, respectively, are in Great Britain, Parliamentary Papers, 1923, Vol. XXIV, *Accounts and Papers,* Cmd. 1812, pp. 101-108, 112-19.
[23] For the Italian plan and Della Torretta's presentation, see *ibid.*, pp. 76, 108-11.

to the need to keep France's friendship; hence Della Torretta reported to Rome: "The first impression of the technical staff of the Italian delegation is that the English project does not conform to our interests." There followed a detailed criticism, much of which applied equally well to the Italian plan. The cancellation of nearly all Allied debt was downgraded; the small sums which London insisted on were held to prejudice Italy's chance of full remission of her American debt; and predictably, the suggestion to curb supplies of reparations in kind was given unflattering prominence. On the contrary, Della Torretta had nothing but praise for the French scheme: "Since Poincaré's declarations at London there has been a considerable evolution of the French proposals in the direction of the Italian project." The controversial productive pledges were dismissed as "some exaggeration with respect to guarantees."[24] Mussolini confirmed his disinterest by returning a brief telegram in which he applauded Della Torretta's denunciation of the British plan, made an unrealistic reference to the Italian plan as a compromise, and in substance confirmed the Italian delegation's freedom to act as it saw fit.[25] On the last day of the Paris meeting, January 4, Della Torretta made a token mention of the Italian plan's merits, then firmly rejected Bonar Law's plan and aligned his delegation with the French and the Belgians.[26]

Although the Paris talks broke up in frustration, Italy's new alignment cleared the way for action in the Reparations Commission. There on January 9 France once more asked that Germany be declared in default of her reparations payments, which would open the door to the seizure of territorial sanctions. German representatives were admitted to state their case; dissent from the French viewpoint was

[24] *DDI*, I, No. 298.

[25] *DDI*, I, No. 300.

[26] Great Britain, Parliamentary Papers, 1923, Vol. XXIV, *Accounts and Papers*, Cmd. 1812, pp. 157-61.

voiced by the British delegate and the American observer. But now the dissenters could muster only one vote—Britain. For Italy's decision, revealed during the Paris talks to protect her interests by collusion with France, compelled her to follow France's lead. It was a foregone conclusion, then, that there would be three votes—the French, the Belgian, and the Italian—and a majority for the French proposal. One spectator commented on the air of inevitability about the session: "It was impossible . . . to escape the impression that this decision had already been made in advance; that the hearing of the Germans and the discussion among the delegates assembled constituted little more than the performance of a ritual."[27] With the vote of January 9 France had legal fiat to move into the Ruhr, and on January 11, 1923 French and Belgian troops crossed the German frontier.

Fascist Italy's role in the events leading to the Ruhr crisis was the target of considerable criticism. It was said that Italy's support had stiffened Poincaré's resolve to seize German territory and that Italy did not recognize a good bargain when it was offered by Bonar Law. These errors were laid expressly at Mussolini's door by the Italian press.[28] However, the accusations missed the point in several respects. First, it may be seriously doubted that Poincaré needed encouragement from anyone to invade the Ruhr. So the Palazzo Chigi surmised; it was this calculation and not the economic merit of respective reparations projects that dictated Italy's course. Italy was too weak to stand alone. "What is to be avoided at all costs," advised Romano Avezzana, "is an attitude which could leave us isolated at

[27] G. Greer, *The Ruhr-Lorraine Industrial Problem* (New York, 1925), pp. 300-301.

[28] On Italian press opinion in January 1923, see *DDI*, I, No. 340; see also Beyens, *Quatre ans à Rome*, p. 153. For standard criticisms by anti-Fascists see F. Nitti, *Rivelazioni* (Naples, 1948), p. 132; Salvemini, *Mussolini diplomatico*, pp. 52-53; and Sforza, *L'Italia dal 1914 al 1944*, pp. 173-75.

such a critical moment."[29] Needing the patronage of at least one of the major Allies, Italy's position in the Paris talks and the Reparations Commission was merely a recognition that the immediate future of her Ruhr coal supplies lay in French, not British, hands. But perhaps the most misunderstood aspect of all was Mussolini's part, for the Duce, albeit for glory, strove to keep Italy in a middle position between Britain and France. The lurch to France's side occurred when Mussolini grew bored and the career diplomats were given free rein. If to back Poincaré was indeed a rash act which abetted a reckless diplomatic and military adventure in the Ruhr, then there is not a little irony in that this was the work of those professionals who had remained in service to keep Fascism on the path of moderation.

Italy's Francophile stand in January 1923 brought its reward. By January 12 Romano Avezzana had Poincaré's word to maintain delivery of Ruhr coal to Italy and to include Italy in any economic negotiations with Germany.[30] On the other hand, the Palazzo Chigi, while making the best it could of the Ruhr invasion, hardly viewed it with equanimity. The damage to the general European economy would be reflected in Italy, and both Britain and Germany were in a position to give economic vent to their resentment at Italian encouragement of France. A portent of unpleasant possibilities was the flight of German capital from Italian banks following the January 9th vote in the Reparations Commission.[31] So, just as soon as Italy had paid the price to protect her supplies of reparations coal by giving sanction to the Ruhr invasion, she began to dissociate herself from the enterprise. Her paradoxical position was epitomized by her part in the occupation itself. Italy sent "technicians" to the Ruhr who were admirably suited to supervise the dispatch of coal to Italy. This participation, it was hoped, would keep France affable. At the same time,

[29] *DDI*, I, No. 308.   [30] *DDI*, I, No. 346.   [31] *DDI*, I, No. 334.

the presence in the Ruhr of Italian civilians only, who were declared not subject to French military authority, emphasized for the benefit of London and Berlin Italy's disengagement from the extremes of French policy. Italy's recent departure from a moderate and independent stand was a temporary tactical maneuver. Now she was trying to recover her original status. As a circular to the main Italian embassies put it: "Concerned at the extent of the French program, the Royal Government has let it be known that it reserves the measure of its solidarity to an examination of circumstances as they arise."[32]

Before Italy could reestablish an independent position, however, Mussolini disconcertingly returned to the center of events. On January 11 the Italian press floated the idea of a Continental economic bloc based on the cooperation of France, Italy, Belgium, and Germany.[33] Mussolini confided his intentions to Ambassador Romano Avezzana. His "western economic syndicate" was to be directed specifically against the British empire. It would resolve the reparations issue solely in the interests of its members. Eventual Russian participation was anticipated, and even American concurrence was not ruled out. Such a comprehensive combination was in the first instance a device to rescue Italy from her immediate awkward position between France and Germany, and from the recurrent fear of a separate Franco-German deal.[34] Mussolini conceived his scheme before Poincaré gave his word to include Italy in any Franco-German negotiations. But there were deeper and more personal motives. The Duce's suggestion was a repetition of his former essay at playing *arbiter mundi*; what was different now was the exclusion of Britain. In Mussolini's eyes this was no more than just desserts for Britain's sabotage of his early

---

[32] *DDI*, I, No. 338.

[33] For the press notices see Di Nolfo, *Mussolini e la politica estera*, p. 74.

[34] *DDI*, I, Nos. 323, 324.

efforts to mediate the reparations dispute. Note, too, that Mussolini's Anglophobia at the time was fed by British opposition to his Near Eastern schemes. Just before the launching of the Continental bloc project France had agreed to join Italy in a Near Eastern consortium, while Britain had refused. Above all, however, the anti-British proposal was an illustration of Mussolini's trait of over-simplification. He loved to view things starkly in black and white; in his melodramatic world one was clearly for or against an issue; one had only close allies and sworn enemies. Applied to the reparations question, his mentality rejected an indeterminate station once the dream of mediation faded and searched instead for a consistent, easily understood line to follow. Mussolini's diplomats appear to have provided the line. Their conduct at the Paris talks and in the Reparations Commission convinced him that France was a friend and Britain an enemy. This distinction clearly fixed, an anti-British bloc was, to Mussolini's mind, a natural outgrowth of recent Italian policy and his advisers' counsel. Even the notion of Russian membership in the Continental bloc recalls the axiom of the old-guard diplomats that Italy should turn periodically to Russia to avoid dependence on Britain. But of course, in his myopia Mussolini missed the subtleties with which the Palazzo Chigi tried to invest Italian diplomacy. To the professionals Mussolini's Continental bloc was not only fantastic, but, because it gratuitously affronted Britain, it was dangerous. Thus Mussolini provoked popular uproar in Britain and consternation within his own foreign ministry.[35]

Doubtless it was because Mussolini was trying in his way to fulfill the logic of Italy's stand on the eve of the Ruhr crisis that he seemed genuinely surprised at the storm which broke about his head. Embarrassed, he hastened to disavow his own brainchild. On January 12 he explained to Romano

[35] *DDI*, I, Nos. 333, 358.

Avezzana: "I believe . . . that we should strive to reach a direct Continental agreement limited for the moment to the questions of a moratorium and reparations. This accord should not be interpreted as in any sense anti-English, even though at the outset England might be officially extraneous to its elaboration."[36] A Council of Ministers communiqué three days later stated bluntly: "As for the project of an anti-English Continental bloc, it does not exist. The Italian government has never made such a proposal and, in any case, could never dream of a Continental union directed against England, both because of the importance that England possesses in the economic life of the Continent and because of the ties which join England and Italy."[37]

At the same time Whitehall was assured that the rumor "arose from absolutely fantastic premises." Credence had been given it only because the British reaction to the Ruhr occupation—withdrawal into an offended isolation—had forced the Continental powers to consider their interests without reference to Britain. Mussolini welcomed Britain's reentry into European politics and suggested joining Italy in "a move conducive to the regulation and equilibrium of opposing tendencies."[38] Here was the hint that the Duce, even before the Continental bloc idea was liquidated, was cogitating what one writer has called "another vast diplomatic action."[39]

This was nothing new, but a fresh variation on the worn arbitral theme. The Continental bloc proposal had caused a storm because of its Anglophobe slant. So Mussolini prepared to amend the project; he would persevere with the mediation inherent in the bloc idea, but now invite Britain to cooperate. He was, in fact, back where he started

[36] *DDI*, I, No. 340.   [37] *OO*, XIX, 101.
[38] *DDI*, I, Nos. 354, 359.
[39] Moscati, *Studi Politici*, II (1953-54), 425.

at the London Conference in December 1922. In view of
what had happened since then, Mussolini could hardly expect British acquiescence. But with or without Britain he
was set on another fling at mediation. His old-guard diplomats were skeptical, but to them a straightforward mediation proposal was quite preferable to the Continental bloc
bombshell.[40] On January 18 the ambassadors to Britain,
the United States, France, and Germany were instructed to
inquire whether those states would accept or associate
themselves with an Italian-sponsored mediation.[41] The
responses were precise—and negative. Britain and America,
having offered nothing more than moral disapproval when
the French entered the Ruhr, were not going further a
mere week later in order to advance Mussolini's prestige.
France would brook no interference at the moment revenge
on Germany was about to be consummated; she complained,
not without justification, that Mussolini's scheme amounted
to "an incitement of the United States to put pressure on
France." Germany, with French troops on her soil, outwardly stood to gain most from mediation, but here again a
firm stand had been taken; negotiations were possible
"only after all political sanctions and pledges have been
definitely renounced," and Mussolini's offer was politely declined.[42] Probably it was this last rebuff that at last persuaded Mussolini of the futility of attempting a Franco-
German reconciliation before the experiment in the Ruhr
had run its course. He expressed this new conviction publicly. Of course Fascist pride prevented any admission that
Mussolini had already tried and failed to mediate. But there
was mortification as well as a resolution not to take the initiative in the future in the Council of Ministers communiqué: "A genuine mediation offer on our part does not exist
and could not be put forward without the prior assurance

[40] *DDI*, I, Nos. 364, 367.   [41] *DDI*, I, Nos. 369, 371, 373.
[42] *DDI*, I, Nos. 375, 377, 379, 391, 405.

that it would be welcomed."[43] With this, Mussolini once more retired from the center of the reparations stage.

The Duce's frustration was evidence that the Ruhr crisis had reached at least a temporary stalemate which, until resolved, imposed a period of diplomatic inactivity on the entire reparations question. The lull provided Italy with the opportunity to resume what had been begun before the interruption of Mussolini's frenetic activity. This was, in defiance of Italy's vote in favor of the Ruhr occupation, the reestablishment of a moderate position on reparations. As long as the possibility of France's enforcement of her demands on Germany remained, Italy, to protect her interests in Germany, could not openly affront the French. But the longer the Ruhr occupation, and the German reply of passive resistance, continued, the less the chance of success for the French policy of wringing reparations out of Germany by force. Germany's obvious economic collapse alone precluded substantial reparations for some time to come. In this situation, given Italy's sensitivity to the European market, Rome naturally reverted to the British line, which put Europe's general economic welfare ahead of the collection of reparations. Mussolini, for his part sought to turn the drift of events to his own advantage. Speaking to Della Torretta at the end of March 1923, Curzon remarked, "for the moment he could not see any way out" of the Ruhr impasse. Unguardedly he inquired whether Mussolini "might not possibly suggest to him some new way."[44] Mussolini seized on the half-query to bring out his mediation project again. This time, inspired by a visit to Rome by the Belgian foreign minister, he postulated an Anglo-Italian-Belgian démarche to compel Germany to make a "reasonable offer" of reparations payments. Mussolini even drew up the outline of what Ger-

[43] *OO*, XIX, 106.
[44] *DDI*, I, No. 654.

many should propose; the outline bore a strong resemblance to the plan he had submitted to the London Conference the previous December. It was assumed that any offer from Berlin could be represented to France as a German surrender; then pressure would be brought to bear on Paris to accept and withdraw from the Ruhr.[45] Like Mussolini's earlier efforts at mediation, this one was fanciful and got nowhere. But this is not to say that Mussolini had learned nothing from his experiences. His new suggestion was made circumspectly, not bruited impetuously in the world's capitals, and he made it clear that Fascist Italy this time would not go it alone: "We cannot consider an Italian action seconded by England. . . . On the contrary, it must be from the start a matter of an Anglo-Italian action."[46]

Although gratified at Italy's return to a moderate reparations policy, the British were reluctant to commit themselves to joint Anglo-Italian action. Before considering any venture, London required consultations to establish as much identity as possible between British and Italian views.[47] To this end, twice in April 1923 a delegation of Italian financial experts led by Alberto Pirelli, who represented pro-Fascist industrialists with a vested interest in a reparations settlement, visited London and conferred with British treasury officials about the technical aspects of reparations. From these exchanges emerged a memorandum which essentially approved the Bonar Law plan rejected by Italy on the eve of the Ruhr invasion. The only concessions to Italy's original objections were a recognition of her special interest in Ruhr coal deliveries and a proviso that the Italian wartime gold deposits in London should be "the object of further amicable consideration."[48] In Italy's view the logical step now seemed to be to transform what after all was a mere bureaucratic recommendation into a gov-

45 *DDI*, I, No. 662.   46 *DDI*, I, No. 727.
47 *DDI*, I, No. 675.   48 *DDI*, I, No. 686.

ernmental agreement. So in July Pirelli and his colleagues went to London a third time, but both they and Ambassador Della Torretta found the British government unwilling to consummate what the experts had prepared. The reason, although never clearly voiced, was simple. Despite Curzon's periodic explosions at Poincaré's stubbornness, the British Foreign Office was greatly concerned about keeping open its line of communication with Paris; it staunchly remained in favor of a negotiated reparations settlement.[49]

Mussolini viewed a formal Anglo-Italian accord on reparations principles as a commitment to his joint mediation project, which would force an Anglo-Italian solution of the Ruhr crisis on France.[50] Whether successful or not, the maneuver would probably wreck the *entente cordiale*. At this price London had no use for the legal compact that Mussolini wanted. The failure to bind the British government to a firm commitment came as a blow to most, if not all, in the Palazzo Chigi.[51] Italy, still involved in the Ruhr occupation, yet with reparations views now akin to those of Britain, could not be counted squarely in either the French or British camp. For this reason she could not rely confidently on either major ally as a guardian of her reparations interests. Independence and the intermediate position were fine catch phrases, but they also meant a kind of dangerous isolation. It was Italian anxiety on this point which, more than anything else, determined Rome's reaction to the process of liquidating the Ruhr crisis which got under way later in 1923.

[49] *DDI*, II, Nos. 139, 153.   [50] *DDI*, II, No. 123.
[51] Romano Avezzana, at the Paris embassy, was one heretic who decried a close Anglo-Italian tie. Britain was not to be trusted, he contended, and everything the Italians said in London was conveyed to Paris. Chiefly he feared the flirtation with Britain would incite Poincaré to attack a variety of vulnerable Italian interests—in Germany, in Tunisia and in the field of Italian emigration to France (*DDI*, I, No. 663; II, Nos. 111, 143).

Germany's Former Allies

In many ways the collection of reparations from Germany's defeated European allies was a facsimile on a smaller scale of the German reparations problem itself. In both cases the legal framework was provided by the peace treaties and jurisdiction vested in the Reparations Commission. Austria, Hungary, and Bulgaria, like Germany, proved unable or unwilling to pay; therefore a choice had to be made between enforcing and revising the peace treaties. However, the victors of World War I were much quicker to take at face value the economic problems of the small Danubian states than they were to recognize German difficulties. By 1922 economic negotiations with Austria, Hungary, and Bulgaria were concentrated as much on reconstruction loans as on reparations. It was hoped that economic rehabilitation would pave the way to the extraction of modest reparations.

Except for temporary support of France at the beginning of the Ruhr invasion, Fascist Italy was a fairly consistent advocate of leniency toward Germany. Yet the sum total Italy might receive under the mildest of suggested German reparations settlements far exceeded anything expected from the Danubian nations. Therefore, there was no apparent economic reason why Italy should not take a charitable attitude toward Germany's recent allies. In the main this did not happen; one reason advanced for Italy's rejection of Bonar Law's proposal on the eve of the Ruhr crisis was that it cancelled the bulk of central and eastern European reparations. Romano Avezzana voiced Italy's motive behind the objection: "The English project . . . would deprive us of any influence in Austria, Hungary, and Bulgaria by taking away all reason for us to participate with authority in the politics of central Europe and the Balkans."[52] If Britain and France claimed the Near East

[52] *DDI*, I, No. 304.

and the Rhineland respectively as their spheres of influence, then the Danube Valley should be an Italian preserve, and reparations constituted a handy wedge. Naturally Italy used the same criterion in judging the proposed reconstruction loans to Austria and Hungary. Italian enthusiasm varied in proportion to Italian hopes of manipulating the loans for exclusive advantage and political ends.

The pattern of events was set in Austria, chiefly because the Austrian economic plight was the most critical. Even before Mussolini reached office, Austria's parlous condition had caused the virtual demise of any hopes of obtaining reparations. On October 4, 1922 the Allies had signed the Geneva Protocols for an Austrian reconstruction loan of $135 million. Security for repayment over the next 20 years was provided by certain Austrian state revenues which, it was generally recognized, were too meager to support reparations charges as well. Moreover the loan was to be floated by a new bank of issue in Vienna, and the use to which it was put supervised by a League of Nations commission. This was a severe setback to the Italian dream of a privileged position in Austria, which, like so many other nationalist ambitions, antedated Mussolini's premiership. However, Italy did not dare renounce even a shared stake in Austria's economy by refusing to participate in the international loan. With marked ill grace Mussolini's predecessors had signed the Geneva Protocols. In view of Fascism's denigration of all schemes of international cooperation it was not surprising that Austria saw fit to inquire shortly after the March on Rome whether Mussolini intended to honor Italy's signature.[53]

The first reply from Rome was indecisive; the new government was taking stock of the situation created by the

[53] *DDI*, I, Nos. 32, 47. On pre-Fascist Italy's acceptance of the protocols see R. Cecil, *A Great Experiment* (London, 1941), p. 137; A. Salandra, *Memorie politiche, 1916-1925* (Milan, 1951), pp. 95-96.

Geneva Protocols.[54] In competition with the array of states backing the international loan, Italy could hardly hope to establish an exclusive position in the Austrian economy; total exclusion would be the probable result. This was the lesson read Mussolini by the new Italian minister to Vienna, Luca Orsini Baroni, and by Antonio Salandra, the well-known conservative and nationalist politician who agreed to represent Fascist Italy at the League of Nations.[55] Italy's obvious, indeed only, recourse was to seek a special position within the framework of the international scheme for Austrian rehabilitation. There was, in fact, support in the Palazzo Chigi for a policy of pressure on Austria to accept an Italian as president of the new Viennese bank that would float the international loan. Accordingly on November 29 Mussolini offered Austria an immediate loan of some $400,000 in return for "a position of pre-eminence in the control of her finances."[56] Prior to the Protocols the Austrian government, desperate for economic aid from any quarter, had dangled before those Italians with transalpine ambitions the prospect of a privileged status. But now Vienna would not endanger the promise of an international loan by a separate deal, no matter how promptly Italian financial help might arrive. The Austrian chancellor, Monsignor Ignaz Seipel, was therefore unaccommodating on the question of the bank presidency.[57]

Rome had another card to play, however, which was to exploit the influence of Maffeo Pantaleoni, the distinguished Italian economist who was chairman of the League of Nations committee in control of Austrian financial reconstruction. But here again Italian expectations proved

[54] *DDI*, I, No. 61.
[55] See, for instance, *DDI*, I, Nos. 32, 207; Salandra, *Memorie politiche*, pp. 96-97.
[56] *DDI*, I, p. 120, n. 2, and No. 218.
[57] *DDI*, I, No. 187.

illusory; Pantaleoni's authority was on the wane. The more
the British, French, and Czechs became reconciled to the rehabilitation of Austria, their former enemy, the more they
took things into their own hands. Pantaleoni could do no
more than advise Mussolini to redirect his attention to the
Austrian government and to raise his price for the bank presidency to an immediate loan of one million dollars, plus,
above all, a clear promise to subscribe to the Geneva Protocols.[58] This was evasive counsel. No bribe Italy could muster was sufficient to tempt Vienna. Moreover, confusion
seemed to reign in the Palazzo Chigi, for an offer in the sense
suggested by Pantaleoni was made several hours after the
news was received in Rome on December 22 that the bank
presidency had already been given to an Austrian. The belated overture included Fascist Italy's unreserved endorsement of the Protocols; Vienna received the endorsement
gratuitously after all. Maybe Italy's attitude had something
to do with Seipel's rejection of a Belgian candidate for the
bank presidency put forward by the Anglo-French-Czech
bloc and his insistence on an Austrian national.[59] But this
was small consolation in Rome. When in May 1923 the post
of foreign counsellor to the Austrian bank of issue became
open, the choice went to an Englishman.[60] On the other
hand, the League of Nations entrusted Italy with the administration of Austria's tobacco monopoly, whose receipts
were to service a small part of the international loan. At
Geneva, Italy was encouraged to associate herself with hy-
droelectric projects in the Austrian Alps. But from neither
of these activities was much political influence expected.
The trend of events was such that Mussolini toyed again
with the idea of retracting Italy's signature on the Protocols, only to reject once more the stratagem as futile.[61]

[58] *DDI*, I, No. 252.   [59] *DDI*, I, Nos. 255, 260.
[60] *DDI*, I, Nos. 643, 701; II, No. 51.   [61] *DDI*, II, Nos. 22, 53.

In theory the matter of an Austro-Italian commercial treaty was extraneous to Italy's vain attempt to thwart or dominate the League of Nations reconstruction program. But when early in 1923 Orsini Baroni broached the subject of a trade pact, Vienna invited the League to include in its consideration of Austria's economic problems her commercial contacts abroad. In other words, Austria's economic weakness drove her to seek trade with Italy but also left her dangerously exposed in any negotiations; so Vienna once more invoked the League as protection against Italian dominance. Bilateral commercial talks between Rome and Vienna did not alarm the League membership at large, but within the Little Entente—and particularly in Czechoslovakia—they revived memories of an Austro-Italian customs union which had been rumored in the days before the Protocols came to Austria's rescue.[62] Therefore Secretary General Contarini embarked on a series of discussions with the Czech minister in Rome. The upshot was an informal agreement for cooperation between Italy and the Little Entente in the Austrian reconstruction question.[63] With Prague thus assured, Italy was now free to get whatever trade bargain she could from Austria. Chancellor Seipel visited Italy at the end of March, where he found himself presented with a variety of demands ranging from improved facilities for Italian rail traffic across the Tyrolean frontier to Italy's assumption of all Austria's traditional minting rights in East Africa. Satisfaction in such matters was presented as a sine qua non of a trade pact. The Italians were adamant in their demands, and negotiations proceeded painfully. Orsini Baroni warned that Vienna was very close to breaking off the talks completely. His words ap-

[62] *DDI*, I, Nos. 306, 318. On the Austrian hints for a customs union in the summer of 1922, see C. Di Nola, "Italia e Austria dall'armistizio all'*Anschluss*," *Nuova Rivista Storica*, XLIV (May 1960), 234-35.

[63] *DDI*, I, Nos. 390, 407; V. Kybal, "My Negotiations with Mussolini, 1922-1924," *Journal of Central European Affairs*, XIII (Jan. 1954), 357.

parently were taken to heart in Rome; after some judicious if minor Italian concessions, a commercial treaty was signed on April 28, 1923.[64]

The terms of the trade pact favored Italy, and Mussolini, of course, extolled its significance. "An event of no little import to the national economy," he described it, and dwelt on the flow of goods now to be directed toward Trieste. He coupled it with the assignment of Austria's tobacco monopoly to Italy, "thereby recognizing implicitly the excellence of our government"[65]—brave and unabashedly propagandistic words to disguise Italy's failure to establish a commanding position within the Austrian economy. The commercial treaty and control of the tobacco monopoly could not offset the reverse to Italian expectations represented by the Geneva Protocols and the League's supervision of the reconstruction loan. The Italian chargé in Vienna put the situation brutally but frankly when he wrote in July: "In allowing Austria to move toward Geneva, despite theoretical recognition of our interests' preeminence, we have in practice lost our preponderance here. Financial help obtained from all the states, while it has decreased Austrian independence vis-à-vis them, has increased it in relation to us. By this and by our temporary renunciation of credits with Austria [reparations payments], our most effective means of pressure on this state have been weakened with consequent disadvantages in all our dealings."[66]

It seems likely that disappointment in Austria stimulated Mussolini's asperity when it came to dealing with Hungary and Bulgaria. Bulgaria's case came to a head first. Like Germany, Bulgaria in 1921 and 1922 had been laggard in making reparations payments. But peculiar to the Bulgarian peace treaty was the proviso that the Reparations Com-

[64] *DDI*, I, Nos. 667, 668, 699, 726.
[65] *OO*, XIX, 237-38, 246.   [66] *DDI*, II, No. 133.

mission might amend both the reparations total and annuities in accordance with Bulgaria's capacity to pay. At the moment Mussolini came to power, a subcommittee in Sofia was engaged in an examination of Bulgaria's economic state. Leniency was in the air; but Fascist Italy countered by proposing that if Bulgaria continued to make no effort to meet her obligations, the Reparations Commission should threaten financial sanctions to be imposed with military help and the Allies should withhold support at the Lausanne Conference for a Bulgarian egress to the Aegean.[67] Although the Reparations Commission seemed well disposed to these forceful suggestions, there was little chance of putting them into effect. The British needed Bulgarian backing at Lausanne too much to antagonize Sofia with quasi-military sanctions. Moreover, the threat to deny an Aegean port was an empty one no matter how much Bulgaria paid in reparations. London could not tolerate Bulgaria's access to the sea at the expense of the Greeks, for Greece continued to be Britain's principal eastern Mediterranean ally. Largely under British pressure, therefore, the Italian initiative petered out in a weak Allied note calling on Bulgaria to cooperate with the Reparations Commission's subcommittee in Sofia.[68]

This left it up to the government in Sofia to propose what it could and would pay. In March 1923 Bulgaria made an offer which the chief Italian delegate to the subcommittee termed "absolutely laughable." At first Britain and France, too, gave it a cold reception.[69] But Sofia quickly went to work to change the Allies' minds. A firm pledge of payment was offered in the form of a lien on customs receipts. French financial circles were won over by a promise to meet private war claims.[70] Sofia could find no specific inducement to offer Italy, and hinted vaguely at the substitution

[67] *DDI*, I, No. 254.
[68] *DDI*, I, Nos. 406, 444.
[69] *DDI*, I, Nos. 575-76.
[70] *DDI*, I, Nos. 577, 596.

of Italian influence in Bulgaria for that of Russia and Austria. Mussolini and the Palazzo Chigi were unimpressed, and continued to regard the Bulgarian offer as unacceptable.[71] Not so the British and French, who proved responsive to Bulgaria's entreaties and assurances. It was at Anglo-French insistence that the Reparations Commission's subcommittee in Sofia and the Bulgarian government on March 21, 1923 reached an agreement which granted much that Bulgaria was asking. In particular, the payment of three quarters of Bulgaria's reparations and the accumulation of interest on it were suspended for 30 years, thereby reducing what Italy could hope to receive during that period to $23 million. In Italian eyes this was insufficient; the entire arrangement was noxious. But the Italian representative on the spot in Sofia considered it "the maximum obtainable today by friendly negotiation."[72] The way was open for Italy to oppose the accord when it came up for approval before the Reparations Commission proper in Paris. But to go on record against a lenient settlement would certainly throw Bulgaria into Anglo-French arms— hardly conducive to the spread of Italy's influence in the Balkans. In other words, there was little choice but to acquiesce, which Rome did, but not very gracefully. The Italian sense of grievance found expression in the demand that Bulgaria provide Italy with retrospective compensation for accepting the lenient reparations settlement; this was to be preferential treatment in reimbursement of Bulgarian occupation costs. The gambit to save face, however, degenerated into a petty wrangle with the British, who accused Italy of bypassing the Reparations Commission.[73] Italy's failure to secure a full pound of Bulgarian flesh also gave rise to recriminations within Italy's diplomatic community.

[71] *DDI*, I, Nos. 599, 608.
[72] *DDI*, I, No. 620. See also Moulton and Pasvolsky, *War Debts*, p. 248.
[73] *DDI*, I, No. 731.

The minister in Sofia was criticized for not presenting Italy's case forcefully enough, and was relieved of his post. But this apparently did not improve things materially, for later Mussolini and Contarini found it necessary to criticize the legation and the Italian delegation to the Allied reparations subcommittee in Sofia for their inability to work together.[74] All in all, the negotiation of a Bulgarian reparations settlement and its ancillary features were an unhappy diplomatic episode for Fascist Italy.

When Italy's attention turned to Hungarian reparations she encountered a case analogous to Austria. Hungary was a new state whose economic viability was doubtful. At the time of Mussolini's coming to power no assessment of Hungarian reparations had been made. An international rehabilitation loan was more likely than the imposition of a reparations burden. Nevertheless, during its first six months the Mussolini government was lukewarm to a loan but insistent on reparations.[75] Then in the spring of 1923 Italy reversed her position in order to accord with the British who, consistent advocates of European recovery at the expense of reparations, were the most important proponents of Hungarian rehabilitation. "I am disposed in principle," Mussolini assured the Hungarian minister in Rome, "to assume the most favorable attitude possible apropos reparations. In fact, I am already in touch with the English government with the object of examining a proposal which would waive reparations payments for twenty years, and would thus free [Hungarian] assets to permit the issue of a loan to which Italy would subscribe, despite the financial difficulty that Hungary's economic reconstruction will certainly entail for her."[76] The conversion was part of the Italians' larger strategy to protect their reparations interests by association with Britain. Rome's grudging acceptance

[74] *DDI*, I, Nos. 581, 639, 646.
[75] *DDI*, I, No. 240.   [76] *DDI*, I, No. 723.

a few weeks earlier of the British version of a Bulgarian settlement had indicated the Anglophile drift of Italy's reparations policy. The nearest Italy came to a definite reparations entente was the meeting in London of a committee of Anglo-Italian economic experts and their issuance of a joint memorandum on April 6; this was the document the Italians vainly hoped to turn into an intergovernmental contract. Its recommendations concerned Germany primarily, but under the heading "Austrian and Hungarian Reparations" it stated: "As soon as possible there should be discussed a project providing for the systemization of the questions referred to above on a liberal basis and taking into due account Austrian and Hungarian conditions, as has recently been done with regard to Bulgaria."[77] Austrian reparations constituted by now an academic question; leniency to Hungary, on the other hand, was considered in Rome a substantive concession to secure British friendship.

Despite this apparent Italian decision, all was not plain sailing. Magyar irredentism was the most virulent of all east European revisionist forces; Hungarian reconstruction in any shape or form hardly suited the Czech, Rumanian, and Yugoslav governments, which had banded together in the Little Entente to preserve the status quo. There developed an inter-Allied split between the Anglo-Italians supporting Hungarian rehabilitation and the Little Entente, backed as usual by France, opposing it. Mussolini professed alarm that "the question thus threatens to take on a political character," for it was suspected in Rome that London was scheming to make Italy play the role of major protagonist against the Little Entente, while Britain quietly established a preferential position in Hungary behind everyone's back.[78] The Italian apprehension that Britain was an unreliable

[77] *DDI*, i, No. 686.
[78] *DDI*, ii, No. 33.

friend was somewhat vindicated when a price had to be found for the Little Entente states' endorsement of a rehabilitation loan. They naturally wanted some assurance that the loan would not be misapplied. Therefore it was suggested that its administration be given to the League of Nations Financial Committee, which included delegates from the Little Entente powers. The original intention had been for the loan to be handled by the Reparations Commission on which the Little Entente had no permanent representation; Italy had counted on her membership and the commission's loose supervision of Hungarian finances to allow her considerable scope to gain an influential position within Hungary. Now the Italian minister in Budapest complained: "I genuinely fear that Hungary will end up with the same committee of vigilance which functions in Austria to the complete detriment of Italian influence."[79] But Italian complaints carried little weight without British backing, and to win the Little Entente's favor London had no compunction about leaving Italy in the lurch. By the fall of 1923 the League's tight control over Hungarian reconstruction was confirmed. Mussolini still hankered after substantive Hungarian reparations in order to save face.[80] But the game was now played out. The Hungarian loan formally launched in March 1924 was accompanied by a reparations arrangement that required no more than nominal payments for the next 20 years.[81] Overall, there was little in the settlement to further Italy's Balkan ambitions or to commend it to Mussolini in any way.

It was always Mussolini's boast that only a Fascist government was capable of standing up to Britain and France

[79] *DDI*, ii, No. 150.
[80] *DDI*, ii, No. 495.
[81] Moulton and Pasvolsky, *War Debts*, pp. 238-39; Royal Institute of International Affairs, *Survey of International Affairs 1924* (London, 1926), pp. 426-27.

and of realizing Italy's postwar claims to the full. But as far as reparations were concerned Mussolini achieved little change in the tenor of Italian policy that had preceded the March on Rome, hence the rapid diminution of his interest in reparations generally in the spring of 1923. By the summer Fascist Italy was forced to rely on British friendship in the unresolved Ruhr crisis, while in matters of Danubian reparations and loans Italy's relationship with Britain at times bordered on the subservient. In the area of reparations, by no stretch of the imagination did Fascist Italy achieve parity with the major Allies. By Fascist standards, if no other, then, Mussolini's reparations policy was a dismal failure.

3. Italian Irredentism on a Leash

The Failure of Rapallo

AMONG THE MANY Italians who held that Italy's victory in World War I had been "mutilated" by the peace settlement, the consensus was that the greatest injustice had been dealt them in the Adriatic. Blame was apportioned between selfish allies and weak Italian statesmen. Criticism of the Italian *rinunciatari* came to center on the work of Carlo Sforza who, during his tenure of the foreign ministry, arranged the Treaty of Rapallo with Yugoslavia on November 12, 1920. By this Italy, in return for a favorable settlement of the frontier between Istria and Yugoslavia, renounced her territorial claims on Dalmatia under the 1915 Treaty of London, except for Zara and some off-shore islands, the most important of which was Lagosta. The heart of the treaty, however, lay elsewhere—in the Fiume settlement. With the breakup of the Habsburg empire Fiume seemed to fall clearly within the confines of the new Yugoslav state. But the commercial center of Fiume was Italian, and majority opinion in Italy reacted quickly to the dangers faced by this "Italian island in a sea of rural Slavs." The ethnic criterion was not readily recognized by Italian nationalists in Dalmatia at large, but in Fiume it was the only card they had to play, as the wartime agreements, not foreseeing the Hapsburg demise, had made no mention of the town.[1] Apart from everything else, Fiume was widely regarded in Italy as the minimum compensation for giving up legal rights to Dalmatia. The Treaty of Rapallo not only renounced Dalmatia, it failed to secure Fiume. Instead, it provided for an autonomous Fiume. Italy was to receive a strip of coast giving direct access to

[1] The most authoritative work on the background of the Fiume dispute is I. J. Lederer, *Yugoslavia at the Paris Peace Conference* (New Haven, 1963).

80

Fiume. By a secret protocol, which remained secret only a few weeks, Sforza promised Yugoslavia sovereignty over the area of the Fiume waterfront known as the Delta and Porto Baros. With difficulty, ratification of Rapallo was achieved in the Italian and Yugoslav parliaments early in 1921, but the treaty could not take effect until machinery for the establishment of the free state of Fiume had been created. Against mounting opposition Mussolini's predecessors at the foreign ministry made laborious progress. Finally on October 23, 1922 success was achieved with the signing of the Santa Margherita Accords. Within a few days the March on Rome began; not surprisingly, in view of the confused political situation, the accords still awaited submission to the Italian parliament when Mussolini took office.[1a]

In large measure Mussolini was swept into power on a tide of resentment at the alleged mutilation of victory in general and suspected injuries in the Adriatic in particular. Before taking office Mussolini at times assumed a reserved and cautious approach in Adriatic matters: for instance, toward D'Annunzio's effort to seize Fiume for Italy and, at first, toward the Treaty of Rapallo itself. But for the most part the Fascists derided Sforza's policy of rapprochement with Yugoslavia. In 1922, especially after the working alliance with the Nationalist party was achieved, Fascist denunciations of Rapallo became strident. And, of course, it was these Fascist policy statements on the eve of power which attracted notice around the world. Italy's diplomats reported the almost unanimous conviction of the European chancelleries that Mussolini's entry into office betokened a fresh crisis in Italo-Yugoslav relations, that the Santa Margherita Accords would never be presented for ratification, and that the Treaty of Rapallo was now a dead letter.[2]

[1a] D. I. Rusinow, *Italy's Austrian Heritage, 1919-1946* (New York, 1969), Chap. 6.
[2] *DDI*, I, Nos. 5, 22, 30, 41, 42.

The clamorous resignation of Sforza himself from the Paris embassy at the start of Mussolini's career in office reenforced the dark forebodings.

On the contrary, however, Mussolini at first exhibited unexpected restraint toward Yugoslavia. Perhaps his early high hopes for startling diplomatic coups in the Near Eastern and German reparations questions were sufficient to engage his ambitious nature for the time being. At any rate, the first telegram to leave the Italian foreign ministry bearing Mussolini's name went to the chargé d'affaires in Fiume, instructing him "to discourage energetically" any pro-Italian demonstration in the town which might be occasioned by Mussolini's appointment to office.[3] More important, if only because of the publicity it received, was his announcement to parliament on November 16 of his intent to honor Italy's signature on the Treaty of Rapallo. "Treaties of peace no matter how good or bad they may be, once they are signed and ratified must be executed. A state that is to be respected can follow no other precept. . . . Like the Treaty of Rapallo, the Accords of Santa Margherita which derive from it will be brought by me before parliament." The total effect was conciliatory, although Mussolini also inserted in his speech the reservation: "If in the course of the execution [of treaties] their absurdity becomes apparent, this can constitute a new situation which opens the possibility of a further examination of respective positions."[4] Fascist Italy would sincerely strive to carry out the terms of the Treaty of Rapallo, but Mussolini himself was pessimistic about its practicability. He elaborated on this position in conversation with the Yugoslav foreign minister, Momčilo Ninčić, a few days later at the Lausanne Conference. Once again Mussolini protested his loyalty to the concept of Rapallo, but he specified certain conditions which he claimed were indispensable to the treaty's successful

3 *DDI*, I, No. 6.   4 *OO*, XIX, 18-19.

implementation. Chief among them was the requirement for "a formal pledge . . . that, while affording the necessary permanent guarantees to Yugoslav economic interests, would assure Fiume's *italianità* which has been the cause of such grievous events and bitter controversy." Whether *italianità*, according to Mussolini's definition, could be safeguarded within the framework of an autonomous Fiume was moot. Ninčić apparently was convinced of Mussolini's sincerity in seeking a mutually agreeable Fiume settlement, but he was adamant against any substantial departure from the letter of Rapallo. While "ready to examine various pending questions . . . where no discrepancy with the Treaty of Rapallo would result," he stated flatly that "no politician [in Yugoslavia] was in a position to accept a revision of the Treaty of Rapallo that might sanction any sort of alienation of territory."[5]

The preliminaries thus disposed of, the next step was to try to apply Rapallo, regardless of Mussolini's skepticism. An effort was made to create the most favorable climate possible. In particular, an agreement was quickly worked out to assure fair treatment of those Italians living in Dalmatia who had chosen to retain their Italian citizenship, and the government in Belgrade undertook a positive campaign to curb the petty annoyances to which such *optanti* were usually subject at the hands of the local Croatian officials.[6] As soon as the Italian parliament met in February, it ratified the Santa Margherita Accords. By this agreement an Italo-Yugoslav commission was to establish the frontier and administrative framework of an autonomous Fiume. The commission was to complete its work within a month and submit insoluble differences to arbitration by the president of Switzerland. After exchange of ratifications of the Santa

[5] *DDI*, I, Nos. 197, 293.
[6] *DDI*, I, Nos. 483-85; C. Umiltà, *Jugoslavia e Albania* (Milan, 1947), pp. 19-21.

Margherita Accords, the commission met for the first time at Abbazia on the Italo-Yugoslav border on March 1, 1923.

A mood of sunny optimism prevailed at the first session, particularly in the Yugoslav camp. Both sides announced the imminent execution of those clauses of the accords due to be fulfilled simultaneously with the meeting of the commission: the Italians, the evacuation of the last of their troops from the so-called third zone of Dalmatia and from the Fiume suburb of Sussak; the Yugoslavs, the resumption of full railroad communication with Fiume interrupted since D'Annunzio's occupation of the city. In addition, the Yugoslav delegation agreed to replace one of their members who was persona non grata to Italy.[7] But in the second session difficulties appeared. Italy refused to withdraw her troops from Porto Baros and the Delta until the free state was created. Nor would Italy countenance Yugoslav possession of these districts; for any part of Fiume to fall under Yugoslavia's sovereignty would be an infringement of the city's *italianità*, the Italians argued.[8] In effect, Mussolini was prepared to abide by the Treaty of Rapallo itself, but not the secret supplement whereby Sforza had promised Porto Baros and the Delta to Yugoslavia. In reply, Ninčić adduced the pressure of the Dalmatian Croats and their influence in the campaigning for the forthcoming elections to explain why the central government in Belgrade had to insist on the payment of all Sforza had promised. Italy was equally inflexible. An Italian note to Vojislav Antonievič, the Yugoslav minister in Rome, deplored Belgrade's "excessive deference to emotional local pressures." While anxious that in commercial matters "Yugoslavia be assured of all desirable guarantees for the use of the *entire* port of Fiume," Italy emphatically rejected any "partition that would damage the vital interests of Fiume."[9]

[7] *DDI*, I, Nos. 569-71.   [8] *DDI*, I, Nos. 574, 578.
[9] *DDI*, I, Nos. 585, 614, 685.

After these statements of position things went rapidly downhill, and many of the minor irritations that customarily afflicted Italo-Yugoslav relations reappeared. Rome soon compiled a string of familiar complaints: about Italophobe remarks in the Yugoslav press, about renewed restrictions on the Fiume railroad, about Yugoslav fleet maneuvers near Fiume which were dubbed "an act of hostility." And, of course, local conditions in Dalmatia served as a barometer of the stormy international scene, as the day-to-day relationship between Serbs and Croats, on one hand, and Italians, on the other, took a decided turn for the worse.[10] In mid-April the Yugoslav government tried to patch things up by proposing to confer certain "high decorations" on Mussolini, Contarini, and other senior Italian officials, a gesture that was rebuffed as "inopportune and embarrassing." "Only a felicitous conquest of present difficulties would furnish a favorable basis for such an action," was Contarini's verdict.[11]

At Abbazia the mixed commission labored on beyond its appointed life of one month and into the summer, completely deadlocked. Whether Mussolini would ever have allowed an independent Fiume to be created is an open question. Certainly it was his refusal to recognize the secret supplement to Rapallo that was the main stumbling block at Abbazia. His calculation that Belgrade would insist on the Delta and Porto Baros had led him to predict an impasse from the start. From anticipating failure it was perhaps only a step to willing it. Yet it was something worth noting that for over six months Mussolini had remained at least outwardly loyal to the principles of Rapallo. It was certainly more than could have been anticipated before the March on Rome.

[10] *DDI*, I, Nos. 678, 679, 692, 702, 730; Umiltà, *Jugoslavia*, pp. 24-25.
[11] *DDI*, I, No. 715.

Malta and Corsica

It was not only at Fiume that Italian nationalist claims could be based on broad ethnic considerations; in and around the Mediterranean, pockets of Italian culture and population offered the chance to promote irredentist campaigns if the government in Rome were so disposed. At first Mussolini seemed eager to exploit certain of these opportunities, perhaps to strike a balance with his initially mild policy in the Adriatic.

On the British island of Malta, Italian culture was only one of many strains. Fascist Italy's interest in fostering an Italian spirit in Malta was anticipated in the island itself. Mussolini's rise to power was greeted in the Maltese parliament by some plain speaking regarding the danger of Fascist propaganda in the island. A Mussolinian display of self-righteous indignation was able to win from the Maltese authorities an expression of regret for such supposedly unjustified Italophobe manifestations.[12] Having thus obtained recognition of the innocence of his intentions, Mussolini proceeded to envisage the cultivation of "an awakening of the Italian national conscience in the Maltese people," and required his diplomatic representative in Malta to keep him "informed of every increase that this movement, now in its indistinct state, will experience in the future."[13]

By the spring of 1923 an Italian Fascist-Nationalist society was established in Malta. The Italian consulate was used as its headquarters. On the other hand, Luigi Mazzone, the Italian consul, warned that the venture was a dubious one in the face of expected strong British opposition and the apparent apathy of the Maltese people in general for the cause of Italian nationalism. Mazzone's fears were confirmed. The early meetings of the newly formed society were

12 *DDI*, I, Nos. 98, 106.   13 *DDI*, I, No. 259.

poorly attended, and the fanaticism of the small nucleus of Maltese Fascists tended to repel rather than attract most of the local population.[14] Mussolini was eventually forced to lower his sights and be content with indirect and cautious propaganda beamed at the Maltese. The matter occasionally threatened to become a formal Anglo-Italian issue, but not during Fascism's early years.[15]

French Corsica was a rough equivalent to British Malta, although here Italy stood on stronger ethnic grounds. The Corsican population was fairly homogeneous; at the very least it was as much Italian as French. The Italian consul at Bastia, Giuliano De Visart, was anxious to exploit Corsica's *italianità*. In December 1922 he reported that the island groaned under French rule, and urged Mussolini's support of a political group called Corsican Action, dedicated to Corsican autonomy. From autonomy to Italian dominion was to be a short step. Mussolini promptly sent the party newspaper money and quantities of propaganda material; De Visart was instructed to establish Italian nationalist associations. All this was accompanied by the injunction to be cautious.[16] Highly incautious, on the other hand, was a Mussolini directive of February 24, 1923 to the Ministries of War and Marine. In the directive the Duce anticipated an imminent Corsican uprising, and ordered that plans be made to furnish the rebels with food and arms.[17] Two months later, the revolt not yet having occurred, Mussolini decided some stimulus was needed, so he suggested to his minister of war, General Diaz, that he might "welcome into the Italian and colonial armed forces senior and junior officers and volunteers from Corsica, forming from them, where it may be most convenient, a small

---

[14] It.D., 425/012568-70, 012572-73, 012575-76.
[15] B.D., C3729/3729/22 (Annual Report, 1926, p. 4); C2925/2925/22 (Annual Report, 1927, pp. 4-5).
[16] *DDI*, I, Nos. 282, 427.
[17] *DDI*, I, No. 548.

corps of foreign legionnaires in order to disguise any irredentist character." At this Diaz himself protested, pleading
administrative difficulties to dissuade Mussolini from this
recklessness. Under pressure from Diaz and probably others,
Mussolini backed down and agreed "to refrain, at least for
the moment, from any measures of this nature."[18] For some
time, Mussolini retreated to a gradualist approach, concen-
trating on the growth of Italian commerce and emigration
to Corsica, lest anything more positive provoke the French
authorities to a stricter surveillance of Corsica's Italian
nationalists.[19]

THE LOWERING of Mussolini's ambitions in Malta and
Corsica was typical of Fascist diplomacy until mid-1923.
During his first nine months as premier, in a variety of questions, the Duce restrained his inclinations in the face of
pressure from his career diplomats, the major Allies, or both
forces acting simultaneously. This happened to his projects
for an Italian colonial mandate, mediation in the Ruhr
crisis, an anti-British commercial bloc, and the manipula-
tion of reparations and loans to gain a special position in
the defeated Danubian states. Retreat on all these fronts,
together with Fascist Italy's unexpected mildness in the
Adriatic, seemed to indicate a pliant and tamed Mussolini,
such as the Palazzo Chigi officials had postulated. But the
moderate stage of Fascist foreign policy came to a sudden
halt. In July 1923 Mussolini embarked on a more unfet-
tered pursuit of his own diplomatic notions, with striking,
if mixed, results.

[18] *DDI*, I, Nos. 705 and note, 742.
[19] *DDI*, III, Nos. 77, 212; IV, Nos. 324, 460.

PHASE TWO
July 1923 to May 1924

4. The League of Nations and Corfu

Italy and Ethiopia's Admission to the League

THE MOST spectacular indication of Mussolini's new, independent course was his altercation with the League of Nations over Corfu. The crisis reached its height in September 1923, but for some weeks beforehand, by way of prelude, Mussolini had been engaged in another League of Nations matter. This concerned the admission of Ethiopia to the League, and it gave an insight into Fascist Italy's general attitude toward the Geneva organization and its role vis-à-vis small nations.

Ethiopia was of particular interest to Italy. It could almost be said that the Italian sense of national grievance, which Mussolini had been put in power to assuage, stemmed from the defeat of Adowa in 1896. It was not so much the rout of an Italian army by Ethiopian forces that had been shattering, as it was that the defeat had compelled Italy to call off her entire colonial venture in Ethiopia, the only time such ignominy was inflicted on a European power in the heyday of imperialism. When Mussolini took office Adowa was still unavenged, a task everyone expected him to try to fulfill. The March on Rome was greeted by the Italian colonialists in Eritrea as the precursor to a march on Ethiopia. However, Mussolini was at first more concerned with other questions; in the meantime Italy's pacific or economic penetration of Ethiopia, which required some cooperation from the Ethiopians themselves, was hardly furthered by creating alarm in Addis Ababa. Thus Fascist Italy in December 1922 felt it politic to assure the Ethiopian government that "the fundamental point of our political action remains firm support of the integrity of

Ethiopia." The message was received with understandable skepticism.[1]

While Mussolini bided his time the question of Ethiopia's admission to the League of Nations came to a head in 1923. Membership in the League would automatically guarantee Ethiopia some protection against imperialist aggression. As the Nationalist Luigi Federzoni, who became Mussolini's first minister of colonies, commented: "What could certainly follow from the admission of Ethiopia into the League of Nations is that we should see ourselves, together with France and England, lose that privileged position vis-à-vis other powers."[2] But the three colonial powers were not united. Britain and Italy were at one in seeking to keep Ethiopia ripe for colonial exploitation; France played a lone role by offering Addis Ababa protection against the Anglo-Italians in return for economic concessions. This was, in fact, to be the pattern of alignments in the Ethiopian question until the momentous year 1935. Thus it was the French who sponsored Ethiopia's request for League membership. On July 4, 1923 France tried to bring the question before the League Council, but in the relative privacy of this small body, controlled by the major powers, it was easy for the Italian delegate Salandra, with at least passive support from his British counterpart, to quash the application. Ostensibly this was done on the grounds that the League Covenant denied membership to states such as Ethiopia, which still tolerated slavery within their frontiers; in reality, it was done "on account of Italian interests in that region."[3]

But this was not the end of the episode. In August Ethiopia made a formal and public application for mem-

[1] *DDI*, I, No. 222.

[2] *DDI*, II, No. 179.

[3] *DDI*, II, No. 165. Ethiopia's application for membership is not even mentioned in the official published record of the League Council's deliberations in July 1923.

bership to the League Assembly, which was due to convene on September 3. This promised to be a different matter from a brief discussion in the League Council. In the assembly Ethiopia would win much sympathy merely by virtue of being a small state, and it would be impossible in the assembly's Wilsonian atmosphere to voice aloud the consideration of Italy's special interests in Ethiopia.[4] Above all, Italy dared not countenance a lengthy, publicized contest lest it irritate the Ethiopian government to the point of restricting Italian concessions in Ethiopia. This was a particular danger, since the conduct of Ethiopian foreign policy had recently passed into the hands of the shrewd and patriotic prince regent, Ras Tafari.

Rome's first reaction was to look for another power to take over leadership of the campaign to keep Ethiopia out of the League. France being out of the question, Della Torretta was instructed to sound out London. But the British government was entirely noncommittal. It saw no more reason than the Italians to jeopardize its position in Ethiopia by antagonizing Tafari.[5] So Fascist Italy fell back on a stratagem first recommended by Salandra, which was to try to profit from adversity by jumping on the bandwagon of Ethiopian admission. Ethiopia was likely to gain entrance to the League no matter what Italy did, so active Italian backing might win the gratitude and concessionary favors of Addis Ababa. Reluctantly, Federzoni recommended that Mussolini follow Salandra's advice.[6] The Duce clung stubbornly to the hope that Britain would oppose Ethiopia's candidacy and thus provide a shield behind which Italy could hide, but ultimately he fell into line: "In the contrary case of an openly favorable attitude on the part of the British delegate, which would certainly be as-

[4] Such was Salandra's calculation at Geneva (*DDI*, II, No. 177).
[5] *DDI*, II, Nos. 161, 169, 172, 181.
[6] *DDI*, II, Nos. 177, 179.

sumed also by the French delegate, we must show ourselves in favor too, and quite possibly try to go further than
the other two delegates in support of the [Ethiopian]
petition."[7] At Geneva the British, in fact, no longer raised
any obstacle to Ethiopia's admission, and the Italian delegation proceeded to execute its instructions with great zeal.
At the September session of the League the Italians there
found themselves under severe criticism because of Mussolini's conduct in the Corfu question. Their avid espousal
of Ethiopia's case was no doubt a sort of answer to charges
of Italian belligerence toward small states, as well as possibly the release of some feelings of guilt. Count Lelio Bonin
Longare, particularly, distinguished himself by persuading
the Political Committee of the League to accept Ethiopian
pledges on the suppression of both slavery and the illegal
arms trade in Ethiopia, which paved the way for a vote in
the assembly on September 28. Ethiopian admission to the
League was unanimously approved.[8]

Italy's belated endorsement of the Ethiopian cause proved
surprisingly effective in some quarters. In his memoirs Lord
Robert Cecil, Britain's chief delegate to the League, who
should have known better, states: "It is doubtful whether
[Ethiopia] would have been admitted but for the earnest
support given to her claims by Italy and, to a lesser extent,
by France."[9] This apparently was the prevailing opinion
at the time in Geneva whence it passed into worldwide
currency. Several reputable historians have accepted the
legend of Fascist Italy's disinterested sponsorship of Ethiopia's candidacy at face value.[10] But in the one place where

[7] *DDI*, II, No. 193.

[8] *LNOJ, Supplement* (1923), No. 13, pp. 124-25; No. 19, pp. 13, 18-
19, 21.

[9] Cecil, *Great Experiment*, p. 153.

[10] For example, R. Albrecht-Carrié, *A Diplomatic History of Europe*
(New York, 1958), p. 485; M. Macartney and P. Cremona, *Italy's For-
eign and Colonial Policy, 1914-1937* (London, 1938), p. 305; F. Walters,
History of the League of Nations (New York, 1952), I, 258.

Italy wanted to create exactly this impression, she met with little or no success. Addis Ababa was not taken in. If the Ethiopian government of its own accord was not skeptical enough of Italian intentions, the French representatives in Addis Ababa eagerly and successfully spread the word that Italy's role at Geneva had been totally hypocritical.[11]

The Janina Murders and Mussolini's Reprisal at Corfu

The Corfu crisis, which involved Fascist Italy in a frontal challenge to the League of Nations and all that it stood for, derived from a long record of poor Italo-Greek relations. These had become particularly strained as a result of the Allied failure to dismember Turkey. Greece's disappointment over renouncing a zone of influence in Asia Minor was compounded by the calculation that, while she received inadequate compensation elsewhere, Italy found some compensation in the Dodecanese. The appearance of a Fascist regime dedicated to the extension of Italian influence throughout the eastern Mediterranean did little to reconcile Greece to Italy's presence in these islands of predominantly Greek population. Not surprisingly, the Dodecanese produced considerable Italo-Greek tension at the Lausanne Conference, where something of a personal duel developed between the formidable ex-premier and archpatriotic representative of Greece, Eleutherios Venizelos, and Giulio Montagna, the Italian minister in Athens, who was head of the Italian delegation and an extreme Helenophobe. Montagna was ready to believe that, sooner than accept Italy's de facto position in the Dodecanese, which was the conference's decision, Greece would resort to unilateral action either by a new invasion of Turkey or a separate Greco-Turkish peace.[12] Despite these fore-

---

[11] *DDI*, II, Nos. 391, 392.
[12] *DDI*, II, Nos. 28, 78, 84.

bodings, Greece, in the event, reluctantly put her signature on the Treaty of Lausanne, although she did so on the clear understanding of further negotiations about the islands. In Athens the Dodecanese remained an issue that rankled.

Relations between the two countries in 1923 were further troubled by the fact that the Greek government was not formally recognized by Italy. In November 1922 the Greek army had ousted the current government and placed its puppet on the throne. As this presaged a right-wing authoritarian regime, it seemed suitable for Italy to show sympathy and support, if only to thwart suspected French designs for a republican regime. Mussolini's first intention was to recognize the new Greek government; then he decided to await evidence of the regime's stability.[13] Within a few days came news of the summary trial and execution of five members of the former cabinet. This so shocked the liberal conscience of western Europe that both Britain and France refused diplomatic recognition of the new Greek king and government. Britain even recalled her minister from Athens. As usual, in his first few months in office, Mussolini followed the Anglo-French lead. Although the Italian minister remained in Athens, formal contact with the Greek government was reduced to a minimum and diplomatic recognition was withheld.[14] In all of this lay a further guarantee of Italo-Greek discord, which might not have been entirely unwelcomed by Mussolini.

During the summer of 1923 there were some fumbling efforts to reach an Italo-Greek détente. These centered on a visit to Rome toward the end of June by the Greek foreign minister, Apostolos Alexandris, on his way home from the Lausanne Conference. Unfortunately the occasion was marred by squabbling. In the first place, both Italy and

[13] *DDI*, I, Nos. 59 and notes, 80.
[14] *DDI*, II, No. 76.

Greece tried to imply that the other had lost face by initiating the visit.[15] Then both governments put out wildly dissimilar accounts of what had been discussed in the conversations that Alexandris had held with Mussolini and Contarini. The Greek version stated that the resumption of full Italo-Greek diplomatic relations was decided on, but that nothing was said about the Dodecanese. Italy's communiqué referred only vaguely to a discussion of "some important economic problems of interest to the two countries." When Mussolini learned of the Greek official statement, he personally drafted a telegram of specific denial for the use of his ambassadors: "I declared precisely that an Italo-Greek question about the Dodecanese did not exist. As for the recognition of the [Greek] regime and the reestablishment of normal diplomatic relations, I limited myself to admitting that I was not opposed, although reserving the right to choose the mode and the time."[16]

Despite the misunderstandings a faction within the Palazzo Chigi hoped to build on Alexandris' visit to achieve an Italo-Greek rapprochement. Secretary General Contarini and Domenico De Facendis, chargé at the Athens legation, were the most outspoken of the group.[17] But anti-Greek voices spoke just as loudly. The Fascist party agent in Paris and, presumably, other superpatriotic Fascists urged Mussolini to maintain his intransigence to Greek overtures.[18] Even among the professional diplomats Montagna opined: "I do not think we have to concern ourselves with the ill-humor of the men who rule Greece today. . . . I believe that we should not proceed to the re-establishment of normal relations if this government has not first given us palpable proof of its goodwill."[19] It was this latter

15 *DDI*, II, Nos. 81, 85, 91.
16 *DDI*, II, Nos. 92, 94, 95.
17 *DDI*, II, No. 99; Legatus, *Vita di Contarini*, p. 90.
18 It.D. (Mussolini's private secretariat), 287/1193/087696-97.
19 *DDI*, II, No. 105.

view that carried the most weight with Mussolini. The Alexandris visit passed without any genuine attempt at Italo-Greek conciliation. In mid-July De Facendis reported that the Greek press, which had adopted a tone of unusual cordiality toward Italy in June, had reverted to its customary Italophobia and "obstructionist resolve."[20]

Against this background of diplomatic tension and newspaper insult Fascist Italy prepared for action. On July 29-30 Admiral Thaon di Revel, the minister of marine, presided over a series of meetings in Rome of high naval officers. Among those present were Admiral Emilio Solari and one of his aides, Commander Antonio Foschini, who has left us an account of the proceedings.[21] Foschini is not the most reliable witness. But 30 years after the event he still approved of Fascist Italy's general belligerence; therefore it may be assumed that he has suppressed little about the bellicose nature of the meeting and that he has given a substantially accurate account. Under discussion was the use of force, which the Fascist government considered a desirable rejoinder to "poisonous diatribes in the [Greek] press accompanied by violent popular demonstrations against Italy, neither hindered nor repressed by responsible quarters." Further Greek "provocations" were expected and even arranged. The idea of a ceremonial proclamation of Italian sovereignty at Rhodes, which the Italian Ministry of Foreign Affairs had averted earlier in July, was revived and calculated to produce "provocatory disturbances in the Hellenic peninsula which the Italian government did not intend to leave unpunished." Alternately—a rare prophecy this—it was hoped that Italo-Greek rivalry within the international commission established to determine Albania's boundaries might produce an incident to justify Italian

---

[20] *DDI*, II, No. 138.
[21] "A trent'anni dall'occupazione di Corfù," *Nuova Antologia*, CDLVIII (Dec. 1953), 401-402.

military action. Whatever the excuse the Greek island of Corfu, strategically located at the entrance to the Adriatic, which the Fascists liked to regard as "mare nostrum," was to be occupied toward the end of August as a pledge of reparations for current and anticipated Greek provocations. The territorial pledge guaranteeing future satisfaction, once taken, might not be so easily relinquished. In fact, this was the stratagem that had enabled Italy to acquire the Dodecanese, a strategy which bore fruit in the Treaty of Lausanne. Given this precedent and the contrived search for a Greek slight to Italy, there is little doubt that Mussolini's object was to seize and hold Corfu permanently. In the Palazzo Chigi Guariglia was convinced that Mussolini nourished this "mad hope." The Fascist leader's conduct throughout the Corfu crisis bore out this conviction.[22]

Mussolini did not have to execute his long-standing threat of an inflammatory show of sovereignty at Rhodes. His other hope for an Italo-Greek incident—in the Albanian frontier question—was realized first. The state of Albania had come into existence in 1913, but the determination of its frontiers was interrupted by World War I. The problem had been inherited by the Conference of Ambassadors in Paris, which was the old Allied Supreme War Council continued under another name. The conference had established an Anglo-French-Italian commission to perform the task of delimitation on the spot, and had appointed as its chairman the Italian general, Enrico Tellini. As Tellini's qualifications for the job derived largely from his part in the Italian wartime effort to infiltrate Albania, his chairmanship was a standing provocation to Italy's rivals in the Albanian area. In particular, a bitter feud developed between Tellini and Colonel Dimitrios Botzaris, head of a

[22] Guariglia, *Ricordi*, p. 29. This conclusion is also reached by E. Anchiere, "L'affare di Corfù alla luce dei documenti diplomatici italiani," *Il Politico*, xx (Dec. 1955), 374-95.

Greek delegation which worked with the international commission when the Greek-Albanian boundary was under discussion.[23] In August 1923 the commission was engaged in a survey of the Greek-Albanian frontier roughly 15 miles from the Greek town of Janina. Early in the morning of the 27th three cars left Janina for the border. In the first was an Albanian delegation, in the second Botzaris and the Greek delegation, and in the third Tellini with three fellow Italians and an Albanian interpreter. There was an interval of 30 minutes between the departure of the Albanians and that of the Greeks; the Italians left Janina a few minutes after the Greeks. En route the Greek car developed engine trouble and was passed by the Italians. After making repairs the Greeks continued. Further on, while still unmistakably in Greek territory, they came upon the Italian car. It had run into an ambush formed by tree branches hastily thrown across the road, and its five occupants had been shot to death.[24] An offense had been committed against Italian nationals, albeit mandatories of an international agency, on Greek soil; Mussolini's anticipated incident had become a reality.

Where to place the blame for the murders has been and very likely will always remain a mystery. A Greek investigation under the supervision of an international body designated by the Conference of Ambassadors established fairly conclusively that the killers came from and returned to Albania. Moreover, a Greek "white book" disclosed that, between August 17 and 27, the Athens government had lodged four protests with the Albanian legation at incursions into Greece by illegal armed bands from Albania.[25] The impli-

[23] *DDI*, I, No. 738; II, No. 210.
[24] For full accounts see J. Barros, *The Corfu Incident of 1923* (Princeton, 1966); and P. Lasturel, *L'affaire gréco-italienne de 1923* (Paris, 1925).
[25] Greece, Ministère des affaires étrangères, *Différend italo-grec, août-septembre, 1923* (Athens, 1923), Nos. 1-4; see also pp. 122-23, 125-26. Referred to hereafter as *Greek White Book*.

cation could be drawn that the Janina crime was simple brigandage. Yet the perplexing fact that it was the second car that was attacked suggests that this was an attack made with fine timing, planning, and possibly a political motive. In particular, the passage of the Albanian car unscathed through the place of ambush seems suspicious. Indeed, if the car's occupants were in league with the brigands lying in wait, the latter would have been told that the next car carried the Greek delegation, whose mechanical breakdown was unknown. In other words, Janina may have been an assassination aimed at the Greeks, which misfired. Certainly the delimitation of the frontier near Janina was a point of continual and substantive disagreement between the Albanian and Greek delegations. Furthermore, a few weeks later an attempt on Botzaris' life appeared to point toward Albanian involvement. It is quite possible that this and Janina were a pair of failures in the same assassination campaign.

Albania was not alone in possessing a political motive. Fascist Italy also had one. The rapidity with which Mussolini moved to exploit the Janina affair bred rumors of his complicity, especially in French anti-Fascist circles.[26] In 1923 it seemed extravagant to suggest that Mussolini had paid Albanian bandits to murder Botzaris in order to provoke Greece, even more so to suggest that he had arranged what actually happened, despite the mix-up in cars—the assassination of an Italian delegation. But now we know that in July the Italian navy had been told to expect an Italo-Greek incident, which would justify the occupation of Corfu in late August. The Janina murders occurred exactly on schedule. Either this was one of the most remarkable coincidences in recent history, or Mussolini had some foreknowledge of the Janina plot.

[26] The anti-Fascist General Sarrail was one source of such a rumor (Lasturel, *L'affaire gréco-italienne*, pp. 58-59).

Of the three powers involved, Greece seemed to have the least plausible motive. But to admit it was far from Italy's purpose. Conveniently, on Tellini's body was discovered a letter to the Conference of Ambassadors which recounted the murdered general's latest quarrel with Botzaris. The crime thus could be represented as planned by local Greek officials acting with or without the connivance of Athens. Undoubtedly the murders took place on Greek soil, and, although a nation's responsibility for crimes committed on its own territory was not generally admitted in international law, the Greek government was to be held accountable in some way. The xenophobic Montagna, now returned to the Athens legation, wrote: "My first impression is that this is a crime with a political background, due in large measure to the systematically hostile attitude toward us of the Hellenic authorities, and to the perfidious anti-Italian propaganda encouraged by the present government."[27] Mussolini needed little encouragement to think in these terms. He was prepared to launch the assault on Corfu at once. A note in Mussolini's own hand, dated the morning of August 28, gave his frame of mind:

1. Political crime, executed by armed bands on Greek soil.
2. Delicacy of the mission that Tellini was engaged on.
3. The present Greek government is not recognized.
4. Therefore, no guarantee that necessary reparations forthcoming.
5. While waiting, the Italian government formulates its demands for guarantees and reparations and as a measure of retaliation Italy occupies by force of arms the island of Corfu.

However, in the margin was added in an unknown hand: "Provisionally suspended by order of His Excellency, the President."[28]

[27] *DDI*, II, No. 184.   [28] *DDI*, II, No. 188.

Apparently Mussolini's Corfu plans took the Palazzo Chigi officials by surprise; they joined the Ministry of Marine in stressing the danger of alienating Britain by a sudden naval action, whereupon Mussolini acceded to diplomatic protocol to the extent of drafting a note to Athens stating Greece's responsibility for Janina and Italy's demands for satisfaction. The demands were: a 50-million-lire indemnity; the participation of Italian officials in an investigation "at the site of the massacre" on Greek soil; and capital punishment of the culprits without recourse to the Greek courts. A 20-hour limit was set for the reply.[29] The note bore a marked resemblance, especially in its demand for an abridgement of Greece's sovereignty in her own territory, to the Austrian ultimatum to Serbia that had brought war in 1914. Like its famous Austrian predecessor, the Italian ultimatum was drawn up to be rejected. Again somewhat in the Austrian tradition of 1914 was Fascist Italy's attempt to secure "blank check" support from third parties. Mussolini turned to Britain and France. The Italian ambassadors in London and Paris were instructed to request that each government, as a member of the Conference of Ambassadors, "give its representative in Athens immediate instructions to associate himself with . . . the steps which will be taken by the Royal [Italian] legation there." Not surprisingly the British and French refused.[30] Therefore, at 8:00 p.m., August 29, the ultimatum was delivered to the Greek foreign ministry in Italy's name only.

The Greek reply the next day was conciliatory in tone, but it emphatically rejected responsibility for the Janina crime, the payment of an indemnity, and "the demands

---

[29] *Greek White Book*, No. 9. See also *DDI*, II, Nos. 189, 195.

[30] *DDI*, II, No. 187. The British Foreign Office at first implied that it might give Mussolini the sort of backing he wanted, but this was a passing phase. France flatly refused, and Poincaré tried to prevent the dispatch of a unilateral Italian ultimatum (*DDI*, II, Nos. 191, 194, 203, 205, 207; J. Laroche, *Au Quai d'Orsay avec Briand et Poincaré* [Paris, 1957], pp. 173-74).

. . . of the Italian note which impugn the honor and sovereignty of the state." Mussolini declared the reply "unacceptable," and the stage was set for the long-cherished occupation of Corfu.[31] The interruption of normal telegraphic communication between Italy and Greece on the 30th had been arranged 48 hours earlier; thus Greek diplomats in Italy were cut off from Athens and Corfu at the crucial moment.[32] An Italian fleet under the command of Admiral Solari waited off Taranto for the signal to sail. The alarmed Palazzo Chigi was able to add to Solari's final orders the injunction, ironic in the light of what was to happen, to avoid incidents involving Corfu's civilian population.[33] The professionals' hand may also be discerned in the last-minute attempt to provide some diplomatic cover for the Corfu action. A circular sent out at dawn on the 31st supplied Italy's representatives abroad with a rationale of the imminent occupation. It cited the Greek "total rejection" of Italy's demands and argued that the Italian step would be "in conformity with the customs and law of nations"; it carried the assurance that Italy had no intention of prejudicing action by the Conference of Ambassadors in the Janina affair and that the Italian occupation of Corfu was to be "of a temporary character."[34] These equivocations reached the world's chancelleries as Solari's ships steamed toward Corfu.

The Corfu action on August 31 was conducted with considerable inefficiency. The naval squadron was supposed to reach the island before noon; instead, it arrived about 3 p.m., leaving only a few hours of daylight to complete the operation. Solari hurriedly sent Commander Foschini ashore with a demand for the surrender of the island, backed by the threat of "any action within the means and

31 *Greek White Book*, No. 10; *OO*, xx, 5.
32 *DDI*, II, No. 190.
33 Guariglia, *Ricordi*, p. 29.
34 *DDI*, II, No. 216.

force at my disposal." Foschini was authorized to promise two hours' grace before resorting to military action, in order to allow foreign nationals time to take shelter. However, Foschini reduced this to 30 minutes.[35] The governor of Corfu was inclined to yield at once, but the military commandant overruled him, insisting that military and national honor required some show of resistance. When Foschini returned with the Greek refusal, the Italians were faced with the choice of launching an amphibious invasion of Corfu or bombarding the island into submission. Recollecting with misgiving Italy's costly efforts to scale Corfu's cliffs during World War I and calculating that a bombardment was the surer way to victory before darkness fell, Solari resolved to open fire. Some warning shots were fired over the town of Corfu, but no white flag appeared. Then shots were directed at the town itself, and specifically at its ancient fortress. After some minutes of shelling a white flag was hoisted over the fort, whereupon Italian troops disembarked and the occupation was completed.

But the incident that was to get the headlines had already occurred. The Corfu fortress in August 1923 was only partly a military establishment; its main function was to house Greek refugees from Turkish Armenia. In the bombardment 16 of the refugees were killed and over 50 wounded. The question asked in the world press was whether this was an act of deliberate or accidental barbarism. The Greeks insisted that when Foschini delivered the ultimatum to the Corfu authorities on the afternoon of August 31, he was told of the refugees' presence in the fort and of the island's ability to offer only token resistance, making an Italian landing credible and bombardment unnecessary.[36]

[35] For the communications Solari was supposed to convey to the authorities and consuls on Corfu, see *DDI*, II, p. 144, n. 1. On the ultimatum actually presented see Foschini, *Nuova Antologia*, CDLVIII (1953) 404.

[36] *Greek White Book*, No. 24.

During the Corfu crisis itself Italy, out of propagandistic necessity, automatically denied the allegations.[37] Foschini's testimony is firm on the point that the Corfu authorities did not state that the island could offer little more than token resistance. On the subject of the refugees he is more evasive. His written report to Solari reads: "The prefect referred vaguely to the fact that Greek refugees were scattered throughout the city, sheltered to some extent in public buildings, etc.; but he never specified that they were in the barracks, the site of the office of military command."[38] Actually what Foschini was or was not told on that afternoon becomes academic in light of a report drawn up a month later in the Italian Ministry of Marine. It reveals that Italian naval reports and information from the Italian legation in Athens indicated clearly Corfu's defenseless state and the presence of civilian refugees in military buildings in the town. Moreover, this information was conveyed to Solari's squadron long before it sailed for Corfu. For this reason the Ministry of Marine report criticized Solari in the frankest terms for the heaviness of the Corfu bombardment and the deliberate disregard of injury to helpless civilians.[39] Thus the widespread popular opinion of 1923 that here was an attack of needless brutality, although at the time based on instinct rather than knowledge of the facts, was indeed justified.

The League of Nations and the Conference of Ambassadors

Immediately and unavoidably the League of Nations was drawn into the Corfu crisis. With a rare if unconcious sense of timing the League Council was scheduled to open its quarterly meeting the very day of the Corfu occupation, and the General Assembly its annual session three days

[37] *LNOJ*, IV (1923), 1,414-15.
[38] *DDI*, II, p. 153, n. 1.
[39] *DDI*, II, No. 414.

later on September 3. Almost as soon as it met, the council was presented with a first-hand account of the Corfu bombardment by Dr. W. A. Kennedy, the British president of the League's Commission for the Protection of Women and Children in the Near East, who had been in charge of the Armenian refugees on August 31. His report called the Italian operation "inhuman . . . revolting, unjustifiable, and not necessary."[40] On September 1 Greece formally asked the council to take cognizance of the Italo-Greek quarrel under Articles XII and XV of the League Covenant, which covered "any dispute between members likely to lead to a rupture" of the peace.[41] For the first time in its history the League was asked to pass judgment on, possibly even curb, the actions of a major power which was a member—and a permanent council member to boot.

In Mussolini's view the League of Nations stood for internationalism and pacifism, the very negation of the virile, self-interested nationalism Fascism claimed to embody. Not surprisingly, Fascist Italy's reaction to the League's possible involvement in the Corfu affair was prompt and negative. Even before Greece made her formal appeal to the League, Antonio Salandra, who headed the Italian delegation, had urged Mussolini to make some communication to Geneva. The suggestion was rebuffed. Salandra was ordered to maintain that, as the Italo-Greek dispute arose from an incident on the Albanian border, it came under the jurisdiction of the Conference of Ambassadors and not into the category of "any hypothesis envisaged in the League Covenant."[42] With these instructions Salandra faced the League Council on the afternoon of September 1. The tenor of the meeting was set at the outset when Lord Robert

---

[40] Kennedy's letter was not printed in the League of Nations *Official Journal*, but the Greeks, of course, were only too glad to include it in their *White Book*, Nos. 20, 23.

[41] *LNOJ*, IV (1923), 1,412-13.

[42] *DDI*, II, Nos. 221, 227.

Cecil, the British representative, dramatically called for Articles XII and XV of the Covenant to be read aloud. The Greek case was presented by Nicolas Politis, a diplomatist of renowned forensic ability. He gave the Greek version of Janina and Corfu, and stressed Greece's moderation throughout. It was apparent that a majority of the council was inclined to accept the argument of Cecil and Politis that here was an affair in which the League could usefully and legally intervene. Salandra found it difficult to contend with this mood. He was able to get the public excluded from the council's meeting, thus reducing somewhat the climate of sympathy for Greece. In addressing the council Salandra contented himself with querying the League's jurisdiction. As for the Corfu incident itself, all the facts were not yet known, he asserted; he asked for a postponement before further discussion. With some reluctance the council agreed to let the matter rest for three days.[43]

During the interim the prospect of a direct clash between Fascist Italy and the League grew alarmingly. The tide of opinion at Geneva and throughout the world was running against Italy, as the murder of Italians at Janina tended to be forgotten in the furor over the killing of Armenian refugees on Corfu. The entire Italo-Greek dispute was frequently pictured in the press outside Italy as an instance of a major power bullying a defenseless minor state, which, of course, was just about correct. In these gloomy circumstances there were signs that some of the non-Fascist Italians who had agreed to serve Mussolini in 1922 in the hope of restraining him from this kind of belligerent adventure, might be ready to desert him. Salandra, a pre-Fascist premier himself, described the situation at Geneva in the most pessimistic terms, and proffered his resignation

[43] *LNOJ*, IV (1923), 1,276-82.

in despair.[44] Secretary General Contarini quietly but pointedly remained at his seaside villa during the tense first week
of September.[45] For unquestioning support of a tough
policy toward both Greece and the League, Mussolini was
forced to rely on his Fascist and Nationalist party cohorts,
along with such xenophobes among his diplomats as
Montagna.

But Mussolini was not perturbed. It has been observed
earlier, in connection with the proposal for an anti-British
Continental bloc, how the Duce's melodramatic nature
led him to pose issues in stark, black and white terms.
Clearly he relished the direct confrontation of Fascist nationalism with the internationalism of Geneva. Indeed, he
went out of his way to emphasize the clash of principles.
He proclaimed the doctrine that the League's jurisdiction
did not extend to matters concerning a state's "national
honor," and followed this suggestion with a threat to withdraw from the organization if it took action in the Corfu
affair.[46] Probably the threat was more than mere bluff; at
least the mode of Italy's exit became an urgent topic of
debate among the Fascist party hierarchs and the legal authorities in the Palazzo Chigi. The stratagem not surprisingly drew further unavailing remonstrances from the old-
guard diplomats.[47] But Mussolini was able to appeal to
their well-developed sense of patriotism, "lest some semblance of hesitation serve to weaken in the present grave
circumstances Italy's international position and prestige."
Salandra, in particular, was enjoined to be firm and to

[44] *DDI*, ii, No. 248. Salandra forbears to mention his resignation offer
in his *Memorie politiche*.
[45] Legatus, *Vita di Contarini*, p. 92. Sforza, *L'Italia dal 1914 al 1944*,
pp. 175-77, contains a good account of the Palazzo Chigi atmosphere
at this point.
[46] *DDI*, ii, Nos. 242, 269; *OO*, xx, 8, 10.
[47] Guariglia, *Ricordi*, pp. 29-30; *DDI*, ii, Nos. 277, 310.

fight a delaying action at Geneva that would allow Italy time to round up diplomatic support.[48]

Mussolini's calculation that diplomatic help was available was correct. France was disposed to lend assistance, if only to recover dwindling Italian support in the Ruhr question. Moreover, Italy's Corfu occupation and France's invasion of the Ruhr were alike, in that they both constituted the seizure of territory in lieu of reparations. Since January 1923 a vocal segment of world opinion had advocated that the League step in and resolve the Franco-German quarrel. This Paris would not entertain, nor did she dare countenance the League's arbitration of the Corfu affair lest a precedent be set for intervention in the analogous Ruhr crisis. By September 3 Poincaré agreed to bail Italy out.[49]

The Franco-Italian strategy was obvious and simple: stall the League long enough for the Conference of Ambassadors, implementing its responsibility for the delimitation of Albania's borders, to take up the Janina assassination.[50] Once embarked on a Janina inquest the conference would find it almost impossible not to take up Mussolini's reprisal at Corfu. With one international agency already engaged, the chance of diverting the League from the entire Italo-Greek dispute would increase appreciably. Furthermore, the conference was certain to follow a totally different pattern of investigation from that of the League. For one thing, it deliberated without the full glare of publicity that was fixed on the League. In this privacy the conference seldom if ever failed to take due account of the national interests of the major victorious powers of World War I,

[48] *DDI*, ii, No. 264.

[49] *DDI*, ii, Nos. 266, 273; F. Charles-Roux, *Une grande ambassade à Rome* (Paris, 1961), pp. 235-46, *passim*; Laroche, *Au Quai d'Orsay*, p. 175.

[50] The strategy was outlined in a conversation between Mussolini and the French chargé in Rome, Charles-Roux, on September 5 (*DDI*, ii, No. 290).

which were its constituent members. Conveniently France and Italy were represented, while Greece was not; Paris and Rome could therefore confidently expect the conference to give a judgment based on political expedience rather than on some principle of abstract justice—a judgment calculated to settle the Janina-Corfu affair with the minimum of fuss.

The first step, however, was to stymie the League Council when it reconvened on September 4. Salandra, still at his post and his earlier resignation offer presumably forgotten, pleaded that he was still without firm instructions, and requested a further delay. In return, he was willing that future council debate should be opened to the public. This piece of horse-trading won for Salandra and Italy an additional 24 hours.[51] The council's meeting on September 5 thus became crucial. Most of the session was taken up by Politis and Salandra, who delivered lengthy interpretations of the events at Janina and Corfu, and, respectively, for and against the League's jurisdiction. Lord Cecil followed by pointedly requiring portions of the Covenant to be read again, then demanded that the council vote on the question of its jurisdiction within the next 24 hours. The turning point of the debate came when the French representative, Gabriel Hanotaux, intervened to head off such a vote, which would in all probability have asserted the League's jurisdiction in the Corfu crisis. Hanotaux urged that a decisive vote should await longer consideration of the statements of Salandra and Politis than Cecil was ready to grant. It was the French representative's insistence that persuaded the council to temporize once more, and to resolve merely that its president should confer privately with Salandra and Politis before reporting back to the council as soon as possible.[52] As it turned out, September 5 was the

[51] *LNOJ*, IV (1923), 1,283-86.
[52] *LNOJ*, IV (1923), 1,287-90.

League's last real opportunity to act. That day the Conference of Ambassadors met and decided to inform the League of its readiness to handle the Italo-Greek dispute.

This escape route from a confrontation with Fascist Italy had been recognized as a possibility at Geneva from the start of the crisis; nonetheless its manifestation in practical terms had an immediate shock effect. When the League Council reconvened on September 6, it was with almost unseemly haste and relief that the Conference of Ambassadors' démarche was greeted.[53] The council's sudden willingness to divest itself of the troublesome Italo-Greek question was somewhat obscured by the facesaving procedure adopted. The Spanish delegate, José Quiñones, proposed that the outline of a tentative solution be sent to the conference for consideration. By this, Greece would assume responsibility for Janina and deposit 50 million lire against an indemnity to be assessed by the Permanent Court of International Justice (World Court), and the League would be invited to participate in and even supervise any investigation at Janina. But this modest proposal, although Quiñones' suggestion avoided all reference to the League's juridical right to intervene, was too much for Salandra. Salandra showed little appreciation of the purport of Quiñones' proposals, grew angry, and engaged in an exchange of invective with Politis. Once more Hanotaux intervened to save his Italian colleague; it was largely through his guidance that the Quiñones proposals were accepted by all the council members, except for Salandra, who abstained. Despite the sound and fury in the council, the Quiñones proposals were no more than recommendations without fiat. In reality, on September 6 the League gave up all hope of exerting any authority and influence. As an interested by-

[53] Informal meetings among the delegates at Geneva—without Salandra and Politis—had prepared the ground before September 6 for acceptance of a dominant Conference role (Barros, *Corfu Incident*, pp. 157-58).

stander, "it would be glad to receive information as to the deliberations of the Conference of Ambassadors," so ran the meek words of the League Council's communication.[54] The Allied ambassadors in Paris were given carte blanche; the League's abdication was complete.

The Conference of Ambassadors had made its first move in the crisis as early as August 31, when it called on Greece to begin an investigation at Janina, while reserving the right to take appropriate measures to obtain satisfaction for the murder of its officials. Fascist Italy had concurred. The Greek reply on September 2 was conciliatory; it invited the conference to go deeper into the affair by persuading Italy to evacuate Corfu.[55] Greece thus sought double protection by appealing simultaneously to the League and the conference. The latter's positive action to resolve the dispute got under way on September 5 in the session which convinced the League that it should step aside. Actually, beyond indicating their readiness to adjudicate, the ambassadors touched only the fringe of the Italo-Greek quarrel at this time. The debate concentrated on the composition of an international commission to supervise Greece's Janina inquiry, and specifically on whether the president of this commission should be an Italian or a "neutral" in the case.[56] An international commission of investigation was welcomed by all, even Mussolini, who, in addition, gave his assent to a non-Italian president.[57] But Mussolini indicated early that he would cooperate with the Conference of Ambassadors only up to a certain point. This emerged from his correspondence with Romano Avezzana

[54] *LNOJ*, IV (1923), 1,294-1,301. Salandra, *Memorie politiche*, pp. 112-14, gives a good account of the meeting.

[55] *Greek White Book*, Nos. 13, 16.

[56] *DDI*, II, No. 287. The *procès-verbal* of the meetings of the Conference of Ambassadors can be found in U.S. State Dept. file 763.72119. However, the accounts in the text following are based on Romano Avezzana's reports which conditioned policy-making in Rome.

[57] *DDI*, II, No. 303.

who represented Italy at the conference. Romano Avezzana was better suited than the excitable and vacillating Salandra at Geneva to uphold the influence of the Palazzo Chigi. Indeed, with the fading of the danger of an imminent clash with the League the old-guard diplomats rallied and sought to reassert themselves. By and large, their objective was to prevent a further Mussolinian adventure and to leave matters entirely in the hands of the ambassadors in Paris.[58] Contarini returned to Rome, expecting, so his biographer assures us, a free hand to ensure this.[59] In Paris Romano Avezzana formed a close relationship with Poincaré in order to work for a settlement through the Conference of Ambassadors. But Mussolini was pursuing his own Corfu policy for reasons not immediately apparent to his diplomats. Although he was content to let the conference block action at Geneva, he was not interested in seeing it dictate a final solution. No matter how accommodating he might be about a conference inquest at Janina, at the same time he took great pains to curb Romano Avezzana's penchant to give that body a completely free hand. This Mussolini did by consistently reminding Romano Avezzana, and all his diplomats, that Italy maintained the right to action and satisfaction above and beyond what the conference might decide.[60] In other words, Fascist Italy was not going to leave Corfu without a struggle, which became obvious after the Conference of Ambassadors' meeting of September 7.

On September 7 the conference, encouraged by the outwardly favorable response to its interest in the case, came

58 Guariglia, *Ricordi*, p. 29, describes his own part thus: "I was put at the head of a small special department, specially created for Corfu, and my principal duty was to prevent Mussolini's ill temper from driving us to leave the League of Nations, and then to persuade him to accept the notable efforts made by Scialoja at Geneva and Romano Avezzana at Paris to settle the dangerous incident."

59 Legatus, *Vita di Contarini*, pp. 92-93.

60 See, for instance, *DDI*, ii, Nos. 281, 290.

up with a comprehensive proposal to resolve the whole dispute. It proposed an international commission, with a Japanese president, to supervise the Janina inquiry. The League, which had requested a part in such an investigation, was totally ignored. In other respects, however, the ambassadors' suggestions were close to the Quiñones proposals. Greek culpability for Janina, despite the dubious legal grounds, was taken for granted, and Athens was expected to deposit 50 million lire with a Swiss bank to cover the anticipated indemnity. This was to be determined on the basis of the Janina inquiry by The World Court—the one gesture to a wider international principle than that represented by the Conference of Ambassadors. Both the League's exclusion and the recognition of Greek responsibility were victories for Fascist Italy. In return Romano Avezzana supplied the assurance that "the Italian government confirms that the occupation of Corfu . . . has no other purpose than that of obtaining fulfillment of the demands which the Italian government has submitted to the Greek government, and that these demands are covered by the above conditions laid down by the conference."[61]

This clear promise to evacuate Corfu should Greece accept the conference's decision was given on Romano Avezzana's own initiative; his lengthy exposition to Mussolini of his own action and of the virtues of the settlement proposed was a measure of his trepidation.[62] The first reaction from Rome came in a telegram from Mussolini on the night of September 8. On the surface the message was affable enough: "The Royal Government takes cognizance of the note that the conference has despatched to Greece and gives to this its approval, reconfirming its intention to evacuate Corfu . . . as soon as Greece will have executed fully and

[61] Text of Conference of Ambassadors' decision of September 7, *Greek White Book*, No. 26.
[62] *DDI*, II, No. 320.

definitively all the reparations demanded."[63] It turned out, however, that this message was intended primarily as Fascist Italy's public face of conciliation for world opinion. It was released almost immediately through the government press agency, the Stefani Agency, in response to the Greek promise to comply with the ambassadors' decision.[64] Romano Avezzana's real instructions, transmitted in another of Mussolini's telegrams a few hours later than the first one, were of an entirely different tenor: "I believe it opportune and urgent to point out to you that the prompt acceptance on the part of Greece of the demands formulated by the Conference of Ambassadors cannot import a simultaneous evacuation of Corfu. Even the deposit of the sum of fifty million [lire] represents a guarantee of execution of one clause only—that of a financial nature—while there remain all the others, among which the most important . . . concerns the search and punishment of the assassins, the definitive fulfillment of which will not only require a suitable period of time, but represents a *conditio sine qua non* of Italy's proceeding to the evacuation of Corfu. I leave to Your Excellency's discretion the choice of an opportune moment to convey the above to the Conference of Ambassadors in order to forestall misunderstandings which would be deplorable."[65]

The capture of the assassins was highly improbable—and Mussolini knew it. He merely wanted an excuse to remain in Corfu.

Romano Avezzana sent Mussolini a long telegram of remonstrance to which he apparently received no reply.[66] Therefore, on September 10 he presented the Duce's response to the conference which, somewhat stunned, adjourned until the 12th to digest the new information.

---

[63] *DDI*, II, No. 323.
[64] *DDI*, II, No. 324; *OO*, xx, 358; *Greek White Book*, No. 27.
[65] *DDI*, II, No. 325.   [66] *DDI*, II, No. 327.

During these two days the crisis changed its complexion radically. Italy's stringent condition for leaving Corfu came hard after reports of the construction of Italian barracks there. Britain and France were thus alerted to Mussolini's intention to stay on the island permanently.[67] With this realization the British, ever mindful of Corfu's strategic importance to a naval power, took the lead in the question.[68] During the struggle to involve or exclude the League Britain had been content to follow France's lead, for despite the enthusiasm of Lord Cecil for the League's intervention, it was well known at Geneva that Cecil quite often spoke more for himself than for his government.[69] The French, for their part, having blocked League intervention, were not interested in prolonging the crisis merely to win Corfu for Mussolini. Now they were only too glad to back a British campaign to get Mussolini out. Significantly it was the British representative to the Conference of Ambassadors, Lord Crewe, who remarked in the session of September 10 that, given Mussolini's prerequisite for a Corfu evacuation, "the occupation might last indefinitely." In Romano Avezzana's words: "The question is changing its character, and the Italo-Greek conflict may give way to an Anglo-Italian contest."[70]

Romano Avezzana's warning had its effect on Mussolini who sent another proposition for submission to the conference: "If, for example, it transpires that the [Janina] investigation does not succeed in naming the guilty parties or that it declares them beyond capture, Italy would be in the inadmissible situation of having received no satisfaction of her just, fundamental demands; and in such case, for the

[67] Barros, *Corfu Incident*, p. 231.

[68] Oddly enough, in London it was the Foreign Office rather than the Admiralty which showed concern for the naval strategic problem (B.D., C14952/742/90).

[69] On Britain's general attitude in the crisis up to this point see Barros, *Corfu Incident*, pp. 107-12, 176-81, 184-87, 214-17.

[70] *DDI*, II, No. 332.

possibility of an evacuation to arise, it would be indispensable to provide some other reparation which could be the full payment of the sum of 50 million lire."[71] In effect, Mussolini was suggesting that Greece might buy back Corfu for 50 million lire. However, when this was presented on the 12th, the British and French delegates were skeptical. Receptive to the substitution of a 50-million-lire indemnity for the capture of the Janina criminals, they seized on the idea that it be justified by the pretense that the Greek investigation would be found unsatisfactory. On the other hand, they discovered in Mussolini's formula no clear guarantee of evacuation. Nor did Romano Avezzana interpret his instructions so as to be able to supply the firm undertaking that was demanded. Hence the matter had to be referred to Rome again. But before the conference adjourned for a further 24 hours to await Mussolini's decision, Lord Crewe posed an unmistakable ultimatum: without Fascist Italy's unreserved promise to evacuate Corfu no later than September 27, Britain would "tomorrow resume complete liberty of action in the whole question."[72]

This was the moment of truth for Mussolini. What the British threatened to do was not clear. A few days earlier the Italian naval attaché in Paris had telegraphed the rumor that Curzon was not averse to putting the Royal Navy at the service of the League of Nations.[73] But it was difficult to imagine France tolerating any role for the League, and direct British naval action at Corfu could not be ruled out. Mussolini himself felt he must face up to some kind of armed conflict with Britain; the prospect, on investigation, was not encouraging. Two reports dated September 13 from the Ministry of Marine appraised Italy's potential in such

[71] DDI, II, No. 338.
[72] DDI, II, Nos. 339, 342.
[73] DDI, II, p. 202, n. 1. L. Salvatorelli, *Fascismo nella politica internazionale* (Rome, 1946), p. 71, conveys best the imprecision of the threat in writing of "an English semiultimatum."

an event. These disclosed that of 17 strategic coastal areas only four were adequately defended, and all four faced east toward Yugoslavia and Greece. To the south and west, where a British or Anglo-French invasion might be expected to land, all defenses were insufficient or nonexistent. Moreover, aerial reconnaissance from Italian North Africa, indispensable for providing information on the route of an invading naval force, was totally lacking. As for an Italian offensive against British positions, Gibraltar was considered impregnable; a land advance on Egypt from Libya and an air strike from Sicily and Sardinia against Malta were considered credible, but required long and expensive preparations. If a lengthy struggle was foreseen, it was necessary that "the supply of food and raw materials across the Alps be assured," a dubious undertaking in light of the economic chaos caused in central Europe by the Ruhr occupation. All in all, it seemed madness to think of fighting Britain for Corfu.[74] There was another consideration which gave Mussolini cause for reflection—world public opinion, an uncharacteristic concern for Mussolini, who had so recently defied it in its forum at Geneva. But as September progressed he began to perceive the opportunity for a coup in the troubled city of Fiume which was disputed by Italy and Yugoslavia. An Italian military governor was dispatched to the city on September 16. If Mussolini's coup was to succeed, it was essential that Yugoslavia be left to fend for herself. To induce this, Italy needed to cultivate a measure of international sympathy as quickly as possible, which, in turn, necessitated a retreat from a belligerent position on Corfu.[75]

[74] *DDI*, II, Nos. 347, 348. Mussolini, of course, did not dare admit his powerlessness, and went out of his way to tell the British ambassador that he had "no fear of the British fleet" (B.D., C2661/2661/22 [Annual Report, 1923], p. 10).

[75] Salandra, *Memorie politiche*, p. 107, mentions that Fiume had to be taken into account in Rome.

Despite diplomatic exigency and gloomy military and naval reports, Mussolini's retreat was grudging. He authorized Romano Avezzana to pledge an evacuation of Corfu by the 27th, but in return demanded that the 50-million-lire indemnity "must be paid to us immediately."[76] In one swoop Mussolini proposed to eliminate both the World Court's determination of just reparations and the Conference of Ambassadors' certification of Greek negligence at Janina to justify payment. In the conference session of September 13 Romano Avezzana, in his own words, "was able to have accepted substantially the proposition which Your Excellency authorized me to make." Romano Avezzana's description of the understanding reached took the form of a declaration which he made to the conference with the other representatives' approval:

> I beg leave to inform the conference that, in its desire to give proof of its attachment to peace, the Italian government, in conformity with its repeated declarations, is resolved to evacuate Corfu and it has decided to do so on September 27, the date fixed by the Conference of Ambassadors for the end of the investigation. But, if on that date, the guilty parties have not been discovered and if it is not established that the Greek government has not been negligent in pursuing and seeking them, the Italian government considers that it would be contrary to morality and justice, as well as to the dignity of Italy, were it to yield, without satisfaction being accorded, those pledges which it had seized in order to obtain satisfaction. It therefore requests that the conference, taking note of the spontaneous decision of the Italian government apropos the evacuation of Corfu on September 27, resolve at this time that, in the eventuality described above, the conference will impose on Greece, in virtue of

[76] *DDI*, II, Nos. 344-45.

penalty, the payment to Italy of the sum of 50 million Italian lire, waiving from that moment any appeal to the Permanent Court of Justice at The Hague.[77]

This, of course, did not provide for the "immediate payment" Mussolini had demanded. Although the World Court was excluded, Romano Avezzana was unable to shake the ambassadors' insistence on the propriety of pronouncing on Greece's Janina investigation before wringing an indemnity from Athens. Romano Avezzana's surrender on this point ran counter to the letter of Mussolini's instructions.

However, Mussolini had made the crucial and substantive concession when he had authorized a firm pledge to evacuate Corfu, and Romano Avezzana calculated that Mussolini would not prove adamant on the procedure whereby Italy received the indemnity. As he assured Mussolini, the Conference of Ambassadors was first and foremost "a political body," and therefore certain to find Greece negligent at Janina, whatever the facts. Moreover, although the Greek inquiry would continue until the 27th, the report of the international commission supervising the Janina investigation was due to be lodged with the Conference of Ambassadors by the 24th; and it was understood that the conference would make a pronouncement on the report at once. But Italy had not contracted to evacuate Corfu until the 27th, and if the report or the conference's gloss on it, by finding no fault with the Greek investigation, thus reneged on the bargain struck, Mussolini would still have time to take stock of the situation and decide to hold on to Corfu if he wished.[78] Romano Avezzana's reliance on these considerations to conciliate Mussolini was well placed.

Mussolini allowed Romano Avezzana's assurance to the

[77] *DDI*, ii, Nos. 352-54. See also Conference of Ambassadors' decision of September 13, *Greek White Book*, No. 28.
[78] *DDI*, ii, No. 362.

conference to stand, although he grumbled privately to his ambassador: "Apropos our diplomatic success in the Conference of Ambassadors which Your Excellency continues to exalt . . . I continue to regard it as a gratuitous and impudent mystification to Italy's detriment."[79] The same discontented frame of mind was revealed in an unpleasant interview granted to the British ambassador on the 16th.[80] Not surprisingly, the Palazzo Chigi lived in a state of alarm lest Mussolini decide to wreck the settlement of September 13. Contarini warned Romano Avezzana: "In such a situation it is absolutely indispensable to obtain immediate payment of the 50 million lire if there is seen to be no possibility of punishment of the guilty parties before the 27th."[81]

Events in the two weeks before Italy's promise to leave Corfu fell due seemed to conspire to foment in Mussolini's mind the suspicion that the British and the French, having won a guarantee of evacuation, now aimed at depriving Italy of the full indemnity. The Italian representative on the international supervisory commission at Janina reported that his British and French colleagues were reluctant to subscribe to a joint report certifying Greek negligence. "A shameful travesty of international justice," wrote Mussolini, and he threatened to withdraw his pledge to evacuate Corfu.[82] Once more Romano Avezzana set about mollifying his chief; Mussolini agreed, grudgingly as always, to await the verdict of the Conference of Ambassadors itself.[83]

The conference convened on the evening of September 25 to discuss the rather ambiguous report which had been sent from Janina. Lord Crewe adopted a moralistic tone in asserting that Greece appeared to have made every effort to

---

[79] *DDI*, II, No. 379. [80] B.D., C16116/15065/62.
[81] *DDI*, II, No. 380.
[82] *DDI*, II, No. 396. On the work of the international commission of investigation at Janina, see Barros, *Corfu Incident*, pp. 258-64.
[83] *DDI*, II, Nos. 398, 399.

capture the Janina criminals; therefore he could not approve the payment of a 50-million-lire indemnity to Italy. The French delegate backed Italy's claim to the full indemnity, while the Japanese was evasive. Romano Avezzana, knowing Mussolini's temper, declared flatly that he could not reaffirm the promise of a Corfu evacuation on the 27th without the entire 50 million lire. The Paris embassy alerted the Ministry of Marine in Rome to the renewed danger of an Anglo-Italian conflict.[84] But before matters reached the boiling point and before Mussolini could use the situation to revive his flickering hopes of remaining in Corfu, the crisis passed. Overnight Crewe received instructions from Curzon in London to yield, and in the morning session on the 26th he gave his sanction to the full indemnity.[85]

The Corfu crisis was now essentially over, but Mussolini found one last trick to play. On the afternoon of September 27 the Italian naval squadron at Corfu, which had completed its withdrawal from Corfu on schedule, was already several hours' sail from the island. Suddenly it was ordered to return to Corfu waters. Mussolini professed to have realized only at that moment that the Greek deposit of 50 million lire in a Swiss bank had been made to the account of the World Court. The money could not be released to Italy without the express authorization of Athens. While this was sought, Italian forces remained off Corfu. If Mussolini hoped that Greece would provide an excuse to reoccupy the island by blocking transfer of the funds, he was disappointed. By the afternoon of September 29 Italy possessed the coveted indemnity in full, and Italian warships left Corfu for good, four weeks and one day after they had arrived.[86]

[84] *DDI*, ii, No. 402 and note.

[85] *DDI*, ii, No. 403; J. Pope Hennessy, *Lord Crewe* (London, 1955), pp. 166-67. See also Conference of Ambassadors' decision of September 26, *Greek White Book*, No. 29.

[86] *DDI*, ii, No. 406 and notes; Foschini, *Nuova Antologia*, CDLVIII (1953), 411.

Neither of the disputants in the Corfu affair was satisfied
with the final settlement. Mussolini had failed in his attempt to annex Corfu, although he was able to hide this
behind a screen of propaganda. Ostensibly Italy had taken
Corfu to secure reparations and had succeeded. Therefore
the propaganda machine of the *Partito nazionale fascista*
seized on this outward appearance of events to project at
home and abroad the image of a vigorous regime jealous of
Italy's honor and interests. In particular, it contended that
the Balkan states viewed Italy with fresh respect after Corfu,
and that this contributed to the acquisition of Fiume from
Yugoslavia in January 1924.[87] Mussolini, always apt to
be convinced by his own propaganda, came to regard Corfu
as "the finest page" of early Fascist diplomacy.[88] Greece, on
the other hand, was made the scapegoat of the affair. Sad-
dled on the flimsiest of pretexts with responsibility for the
Janina murders, she could ill afford the 50-million-lire
penalty. Greece was the victim of major power intrigues behind the scenes at both Geneva and Paris. Although compelled by Anglo-French pressure to swallow the Conference of Ambassadors' decision, Athens understandably included in its note of acceptance a bitter condemnation
of the inequity of the judgment.[89]

The League of Nations, having welcomed the Conference of Ambassadors' intervention in the first place, in due
course bestowed its distant blessing on the *Realpolitik* solution worked out in Paris. Lord Cecil, once in the van of the
advocates of the League's intervention, now provided the
rationalization for inaction—namely, that the League was
a last court of appeal, and not bound to interfere in a dis-

[87] *OO*, xx, 401. See also Foschini, *Nuova Antologia* CDLVIII (1953),
401; Salandra, *Memorie politiche*, p. 120.

[88] Guariglia, *Ricordi*, p. 31.

[89] *Greek White Book*, No. 30. Lord Curzon openly admitted the
injustice of the settlement to his fellow ministers (B.D., Cabinet minutes 47 [23] 1).

pute so long as an alternative avenue of diplomatic negotiation, such as the Conference of Ambassadors, remained
open.[90] The League Council stifled any discussion of Corfu
in the assembly, where Greece enjoyed widespread support
among the smaller states, until September 28, after the
crisis had been resolved. Some harsh words were spoken on
this occasion against both Italy's action at Corfu and the
Conference of Ambassadors' handling of the dispute, but
by this time there was little enthusiasm at Geneva to reopen
the whole troublesome question over a matter of principle.[91] The unresolved problem of what actual legal jurisdiction in international disputes the League enjoyed under
its covenant was effectively removed from the realm
of immediate politics by referring it to a panel of international jurists. Salandra insisted that this be an inquiry of
an academic nature; that is, it would delve into the theoretical limits of the League's competence without reference to the Corfu incident itself. Once this was obtained,
Italy could tolerate, while holding aloof from, what she regarded as a harmless game of words.[92]

Because the Corfu crisis was disposed of quickly and
largely sub rosa at that, it was soon forgotten outside Italy.
Those, and they were numerous and influential, who chose
to regard Mussolini as an anti-Bolshevik bulwark and accepted him as a respected participant in European diplomacy, dismissed the episode as a momentary Fascist aberration. Yet nothing was further from the truth. Corfu dis-

[90] *LNOJ*, IV (1923), 1,305-10. See also Cecil's astonishing statement
in his memoir, *Great Experiment*, p. 151: "On the whole, however, the
League succeeded in carrying out successfully its duties under the
Covenant. A difficult and dangerous dispute was settled rapidly and,
apart from the amount of damages for which it was not responsible,
fairly enough. Corfu was saved and *the jurisdiction of the Council was
confirmed*" (my italics).

[91] *LNOJ, Supplement* (1923), No. 13, pp. 140-41.

[92] *LNOJ*, IV (1923), 1,320-52, *passim*; V (1924), 523-24. See also Salandra, *Memorie politiche*, pp. 115-17.

closed the real nature of Fascism's foreign policy. This fact was recognized, albeit uncertainly and reluctantly, by some of the professionals in the Palazzo Chigi close to Mussolini. After Corfu they were no longer as certain as before of their ability to tame this wild man they had agreed to serve.[93] Corfu was not merely the harbinger of a policy and methods which became apparent in the 1930s in a general way; it constituted a veritable dress rehearsal of Mussolini's quarrel with the League over Ethiopia in 1935. Both times Italy aspired to annex territory. Both times when the League was called on to defend the integrity of one of its smaller members, first France and then Britain sought a solution by undercutting and bypassing the League. In 1923 Britain and France, having decided to take matters into their own hands, were more resolute and Italy less stubborn than in 1935, hence the difference in the outcome of Mussolini's plans. But in both cases the loser was the League of Nations and its status as an agent of collective security. More than any other individual perhaps, Mussolini was responsible for the collapse of the League; Ethiopia was the climax of the erosion begun at Corfu.

[93] Guariglia, *Ricordi*, p. 14; Legatus, *Vita di Contarini*, p. 94; R. Moscati, "La politica estera fascista nel '24-25," *Rivista Storica Italiana*, LXXI (June 1959), 314.

5. The Acquisition of Fiume

The Appointment of General Giardino

THE TREATY of Rapallo predicated an autonomous Fiume state, but by the middle of 1923 the Italo-Yugoslav commission convened at Abbazia to implement an independent Fiume was a dismal failure. Mussolini anticipated this; all along he had in mind an alternative solution to Rapallo, and confidently awaited the day when he could propose it. The stalemate at Abbazia provided the opportunity. As with Corfu, July saw the beginning of a decided shift toward a forcible Fiume policy calculated to please the Italian nationalists. Early in the month Mussolini suggested to Belgrade that the idea of a Fiume free state be dropped. Italy would annex Fiume, except for the Delta and Porto Baros, which would go to Yugoslavia. Yugoslavia would have special commercial privileges in Fiume, and Italy's coastal strip giving direct access to Fiume would be narrowed. It was remarkable, in view of Yugoslavia's earlier attachment to the Treaty of Rapallo, that Belgrade did not reject Mussolini's proposal outright.[1]

But Yugoslavia had little if any room for maneuver. As long as the Yugoslav cabinet sincerely desired a détente with the nationalist regime in Rome, it was precluded from reviving Yugoslavia's own claim to full possession of Fiume. Since the Rapallo compromise appeared unworkable, the question became whether or not to allow Fiume to pass to Italy as the price for an Adriatic rapprochement. The more important members of the Yugoslav cabinet were inclined to make such a bargain. Foreign Minister Nينčić informed the Italian minister in Belgrade confidentially that, "in his opinion, shared also by [Premier Nikola] Pašić, the independence of Fiume is not an immutable principle."[2] How-

[1] *DDI*, II, No. 126.   [2] *DDI*, II, No. 126.

127

ever, the government was to a considerable extent the prisoner of domestic nationalist opinion and felt the need to show more of a territorial quid pro quo for Fiume than merely the Delta and Porto Baros. Specifically Belgrade asked for the Italian outposts in Dalmatia—Zara and Lagosta. This was too much in the tradition of the *rinunciatari* for Fascist Italy to accept. On the other hand, Mussolini was prepared to assist the Belgrade government to save face; so he suggested that Italy be entrusted with the administration of Fiume for one year in return for Yugoslav political sovereignty, although with limited commercial control, over the Delta and Porto Baros. But Yugoslavia would take nothing less than full dominion over the Delta and Porto Baros. The minimum Italian price, it was stated in reply, was administration of Fiume without any time limit, although also without a formal declaration of Italian sovereignty.[3] This was Mussolini's original offer, in substance. Belgrade not only rejected it but proposed submission of the Fiume problem to arbitration, as the Santa Margherita Accords had provided. But international arbitration was totally antithetical to Mussolini's nationalist philosophy; he wrote personally to the president of the Yugoslav Council of Ministers, Pašič, in an attempt to dissuade Belgrade. From Fascist Italy's viewpoint, some sort of vigorous campaign was needed to prevent an appeal to arbitration and to pressure Yugoslavia into accepting a straight exchange of Fiume for the Delta and Porto Baros.[4]

Conditions in Fiume itself supplied the opportunity for some extra persuasion. The town lived on the edge of crisis. The local civil administration was powerless to pursue a consistent policy in view of the town's uncertain future. An Italian military contingent, left from the end of the

[3] For the terms of Italy's proposals and Yugoslavia's counterproposals during the summer of 1923, see the résumé of Fiume negotiations, *DDI*, II, No. 314.

[4] *DDI*, II, No. 326.

First World War, kept a precarious order. Local Fascists and remnants of D'Annunzio's legionnaires daily anticipated word from the nationalist regime in Rome to foment a coup. Mussolini himself claimed to be more embarrassed than helped by their antics.[5] But in this he was disingenuous, for the threat of political turmoil served him well. Fiume, being something of an artificial port, required peace and administrative stability even to approach commercial viability. By the summer of 1923 uncertainty about the town's future and the infighting within Fiume had brought its economy almost to a standstill. Mussolini was able to argue that "the perpetuation of this situation is fatal for Fiume, whose economic, political, and social life is totally disorganized and paralyzed, and for the hinterland which cannot enjoy the services of the port," when on August 8 he sent an ultimatum to the Abbazia commission: "If by August 31 the fate of Fiume will not have been decided by a solution which respects the historic and present *italianità* of the city . . . the Italian government will resolve to follow a different line of conduct." On August 24 he extended the deadline by another two weeks, but obviously it was still intended that September should be the month of decision.[6] In fact, Mussolini had decided to settle scores with two rivals, Greece and Yugoslavia, during September. Although the Corfu crisis, which broke first, tied his hands in the Fiume question somewhat, it did not put a complete stop to his campaign to win the town.

Yugoslavia assumed what the Italian chargé in Belgrade later called a "very correct attitude" in the Corfu crisis.[7] No doubt this stimulated Italian efforts, which were undertaken early in September, to get Pašić and Ninčić to moderate their attitude on Fiume. Pašić on a visit to

---

[5] *DDI*, II, Nos. 106, 109, 115, 116, 124, 137.

[6] *DDI*, II, No. 166; Royal Institute of International Affairs, *Survey 1924*, p. 417.

[7] *DDI*, II, No. 424.

Paris, was approached by Ambassador Romano Avezzana on September 6. A few days later Ninčić, who was attending the League of Nations Council session, of his own accord sought out Count Mauro Tosti di Valminuta, an old friend in the Italian diplomatic service who happened to be in Geneva, too, in order to discuss Fiume. The discussions were completely amicable, especially with Ninčić, who was known to be the most sympathetic in the Yugoslav cabinet to a rapprochement with Italy. But the actual accomplishment of the meetings was only modest. Both Pašić and Ninčić agreed to drop the idea of arbitration for the time being, although probably the reluctance of the Swiss president to take on a thankless arbitral task had a great deal to do with the concession. As for Italian possession of Fiume, both Yugoslavs were noncommittal in the extreme, but expatiated on the difficulty of dealing with Croatian opinion, which, if affronted, could endanger "the existence and cohesion of the trialist kingdom" of the South Slavs.[8]

At the same time the direct talks were producing meager results, efforts were under way to enlist the aid of third parties to persuade Yugoslavia to yield Fiume. French good offices were most likely to prove influential in Belgrade in view of France's special relationship with all the members of the Little Entente. They were also the most readily available to Italy. In the first week of September, France, in order to avoid a precedent for international arbitration in the Ruhr, joined Italy in denying the League of Nations jurisdiction in the Corfu affair. As long as Fiume was an open question, the possibility of arbitration here, too, had to be considered, and Paris could look with no more favor on the precedent of arbitration in Fiume than in Corfu. On these grounds Romano Avezzana requested Poincaré to urge Belgrade to accept Mussolini's formula for a Fiume settlement. Poincaré was caught in an embarrassing position; he supported Italian possession of Fiume as the quickest way out of the imbroglio, yet feared losing Yugoslavia's friendship by appearing to be on the side of her archenemy. Poincaré, therefore, was reticent toward the Italian overture. He was not averse in principle to advising Belgrade to seek a solution within the general framework proposed by Mussolini, so he informed Romano Avezzana, but insisted on keeping to himself the time and method he would use. The French watched the development of the Fiume question closely, and probably exerted some influence on Italy's behalf, but they did so out of sight and with the utmost discretion.[9]

Other Italian appeals for good offices in Belgrade met with less success. The British refused out of hand, which was not surprising, since the Corfu crisis was turning into an Anglo-Italian dispute.[10] Czechoslovakia's response remains unclear. Later, after the Fiume problem was solved, Czech Premier Eduard Beneš claimed to be "the principal author of the rapprochement" between Italy and Yugoslavia. On the other hand, the Czech minister in Rome, admittedly no admirer of Beneš, implies that Beneš jumped on the bandwagon of an Italo-Yugoslav détente at the last minute.[11] Given the personal and ideological animus existing between Beneš and Mussolini, along with Prague's alarm lest Italy detach Yugoslavia from her alignment in the Little Entente, Czech assistance to Italy in the Fiume controversy would have been most unusual.

All of Italy's frenetic diplomacy in the first half of September had not on the surface changed the situation much. At the most, it had prepared the ground for more forceful action. It seemed as if something extra would be required to

[9] *DDI*, II, Nos. 297, 446; Charles-Roux, *Une grande ambassade*, pp. 250-54.
[10] *DDI*, II, No. 336.
[11] *DDI*, II, Nos. 314, 560; Kybal, *Journal of Central European Affairs*, XIII (1953-54), 364; XIV (1954), 68.

nudge Belgrade into conceding the bulk of Fiume to Italy. On September 12 the provisional governor of Fiume, Attilio Depoli, was summoned to Rome and asked to write a letter of resignation. Depoli, who had long urged Italian annexation of Fiume, willingly complied. Together with Michele Castelli, the Italian chargé in Fiume, he drafted a lengthy letter to Mussolini detailing Fiume's current troubles and appealing to Italy to rescue the town from its plight: "I beg to point out that from the day of my retirement from office no other authority will be left, save the command of the Royal Italian troops, and that at the end of the month the city will find itself without the means necessary for its existence."[11a] To no one's surprise, September 15, the day on which Mussolini threatened to resume his "liberty of action," arrived without the Abbazia commission being anywhere near a Fiume settlement. Moreover, 48 hours earlier Mussolini had acceded to the British ultimatum to get out of Corfu, thus to all intents liquidating the crisis and freeing himself of an encumbrance to a forward policy in Fiume. The seizure of Fiume was to be a substitute for the abortive annexation of Corfu. Thus Mussolini took his dramatic step. On September 16 he unilaterally appointed General Gaetano Giardino, a former Italian minister of war, as military governor of Fiume, with instructions to take energetic steps to restore order there. The following day Giardino reached Fiume; within a few hours and without violence the administration of Fiume was taken over by Italy. Mussolini justified his fait accompli to the world on grounds of Fiume's dire straits, and cited Depoli's letter of resignation.[12]

In the abstract, the dispatch of Giardino to Fiume was just as much of a *coup de main* as the Corfu occupation two

[11a] *DDI*, II, No. 258, although here the date of Depoli's letter of resignation is mistakenly given as September 2. Cf. Rusinow, *Italy's Austrian Heritage*, p. 188.
[12] *OO*, xx, 26; *DDI*, II, Nos. 366, 367.

weeks earlier, and Mussolini's enemies in the League of Nations were not slow to make the comparison.[13] But by and large the Fiume action was not equated with that at Corfu, and thus did not arouse the same storm. For one thing, the Italian claim that the municipal life of Fiume could be saved only by strong, even illegal, action was not without validity. Also, there was no bloodshed in Fiume. More important, no major power sprang to Yugoslavia's defense by making an issue of the Fiume takeover. To the British, Fiume did not have Corfu's strategic value; besides, France was Yugoslavia's chief patron. Mussolini, in particular, was concerned about the possible French reaction. (On the eve of Giardino's appointment he went so far as to make an approach to Berlin for a military pact, whereby Germany would neutralize France on the Rhine in the event of a conflict over Fiume.[14]) However, the French response was muted. Only a few days earlier Poincaré had indicated to Romano Avezzana that he could view Italy's possession of Fiume with equanimity. In addition, France was still too deeply involved in the Ruhr occupation to allow involvement in the Adriatic. So France offered only a mild, private remonstrance.[15] To all intents, Belgrade was left to fend for itself. Without French backing Yugoslavia showed no inclination to take steps alone against the Italian military administration of Fiume.

Nowhere was the distinction between Corfu and Fiume clearer than in the Palazzo Chigi. Among the old-guard diplomats there was considerable encouragement for Mussolini's early efforts at a détente with Yugoslavia through fulfillment of the Treaty of Rapallo. On the other hand, it must be remembered that these men still held office because they were at heart nationalists, and they hoped to use Mussolini to achieve certain foreign policy goals. They sub-

---

[13] *DDI*, II, No. 371.   [14] See Chap. 6.
[15] Charles-Roux, *Une grande ambassade*, pp. 255-56.

scribed to the notion of "mutilated victory" and, while advocating Sforza's general policy of rapprochement with Yugoslavia, could still hold that Fiume was Italy's by moral right. When the deadlock at Abbazia appeared to spell doom for Sforza's formula of a free state, they joined in Mussolini's pursuit of an Italian Fiume, hoping against hope that it might prove reconcilable with Italo-Yugoslav friendship in the Adriatic.

Perhaps in Adriatic matters more than in any other, Secretary General Contarini reflected and directed the opinion of the career diplomats. On the evidence of a memorandum by Contarini's private secretary, dated September 7, it would seem that the secretary general agreed with his chief on the Fiume question.[16] The document principally concerned a variety of tactics to secure Fiume under the rubric of "a diplomatic campaign of indirect pressure on Yugoslavia." It may even be that Contarini and the professionals helped to plan the seizure of the town's administration.[16a] Certainly the Palazzo Chigi showed none of the shocked surprise with which it greeted the Corfu exploit. In conversation with the German chargé, Contarini was more alarmed about the lingering impact of the Corfu affair on the Fiume situation than he was about Giardino's appointment.[17] Ignoring inconsistency in their attitude toward the two coups, the professional diplomats after September 16 were anxious only to build by normal diplomacy on Mussolini's success won by unorthodox methods. By this close cooperation with Mussolini, they succeeded in hiding, from the outside world and for the time being, the breach Corfu had opened between Fascism and the Palazzo Chigi.

Whatever the justification, or lack of it, for Italy's action, September 16 was the crucial date in the Fiume question.

[16] *DDI*, II, No. 314.
[16a] See, for example, Rusinow, *Italy's Austrian Heritage*, p. 188.
[17] G.D., 2784H/1385/537505, 537507.

Mussolini might pretend that Giardino's military government was a temporary measure which left the merits of both the Italian and the Yugoslav cases unchanged; but everyone in Rome and Belgrade knew better. Italy was in Fiume to stay, the Abbazia commission ceased to exist, and the Treaty of Rapallo was defunct.

The Pact of Rome

The Yugoslav government took the appointment of General Giardino calmly, even to the extent of curbing the incensed Belgrade press.[18] This was not surprising, as over the summer of 1923 Pašić and Ninčić had accepted Italian possession of Fiume in principle; translation into practice had been thwarted by the difficulties of selling the proposition on the domestic market and extracting sufficient compensation from Italy to assuage public opinion. These problems remained when Ninčić returned home from the League of Nations session to resume negotiations, which now began with the reality of Italy's possession of Fiume, and concentrated therefore on bargaining over the grant of legal title.

In October a variety of stratagems were tried to condition public opinion in both countries and in Fiume to accept an Italo-Yugoslav deal. The Belgrade government, besides seeking to influence the local press, took the precaution of expelling from Yugoslavia the autonomous Fiume party which opposed the town's cession to Italy. The precaution was supplemented by General Giardino's efforts in Fiume to uncover as many of the numerous arms caches as possible in order to forestall the riots anticipated at the announcement of Yugoslav sovereignty over the Delta and Porto Baros.[19] But the major Italian contribution to the relaxation of tensions was the highly publicized recognition of the minority rights of Italy's Slav subjects. The idea

[18] *DDI*, II, No. 377.   [19] *DDI*, II, Nos. 417, 441.

emanated from Belgrade, whence the Italian chargé reported popular concern at the hindrances imposed on Slovene schools and newspapers in Trieste and Udine. Mussolini took the hint and personally charged the prefects of those regions to cease their Italianization activities during "the negotiations pending between Rome and Belgrade from which will emerge a solution of the Fiume question." The gist of Mussolini's directive, if not his motive, was given to the world by the Stefani Agency.[20]

Against this background of gestures of mutual good intent Italy turned once more to diplomacy to garner the fruits of the recent Fiume coup, which meant, in effect, the renewal of earlier attempts to convince official Belgrade to take the Delta and Porto Baros in return for Fiume. But now Italy negotiated from an almost unassailable position. Moreover, this time the campaign of persuasion was not directed solely at Pašić and Ninčić, nor even at the Yugoslav cabinet. For instance, Consalvo Summonte, although holding no more than the status of Italian chargé in Belgrade, enjoyed a wide acquaintance and influence among the permanent officials of the Yugoslav foreign ministry. He exploited the advantage with marked skill as he assembled and directed Yugoslav public servants sympathetic to a Fiume settlement along Mussolinian lines. Three of them were Panta Gavrïlović, Ljubomir Nešić, and Miroslav Spalaïcović, all of whom reputedly had the ear of cabinet members and urged acceptance of Mussolini's Fiume terms.[21]

But of considerably more consequence was the Italian decision to enlist the aid of King Alexander of Yugoslavia. It is not clear where and when this inspired stroke originated. Poincaré had suggested it to Romano Avezzana early in September. But on the other hand, the king was well known as an admirer of strong government in general

---

[20] *DDI*, II, Nos. 424, 448, 451.
[21] *DDI*, II, Nos. 423, 432, 435, 501.

and Fascism in particular, and probably the idea of trading on this ideological empathy had been circulating in the Palazzo Chigi for some time.[22] The role of special emissary to the king was not entrusted to a career diplomat, but to General Alessandro Bodrero. This choice may or may not have reflected Mussolini's contempt for the professionals of the Palazzo Chigi, for Bodrero was something of a lone wolf in Italian official circles and was often outspokenly scornful of diplomats and their ways. Withal, he had many close friends in high places throughout the Balkans, among them King Alexander.[23]

The general arrived in Belgrade before Italy's Fiume coup, and held his first conversation with Alexander on the evening of September 16, the day of Giardino's appointment. To what extent the king was aware of the Italian coup is not clear, but he must have learned something of it, if only from Bodrero. Nonetheless, he was extraordinarily cordial and receptive to the Italian point of view. He was eager to find a quick solution for Fiume outside the Treaty of Rapallo, and at once showed himself substantially in accord with Mussolini on the specifics of a settlement. For reasons not only "of an emotional character but also and above all economic," it was necessary that Yugoslavia receive the Delta and Porto Baros, "without limitation of any kind." "Contemporaneously," the king went on, "Italy would be able to proceed to the annexation of the city and the corridor. Were he [Mussolini], then, to make a proposal in this sense, I pledge myself to have it accepted without reservation."[24] Unlike Pašić and Ninčić, the king was not concerned over the reaction of nationalist Slavs, which may have been calculated or merely illustrative of his authoritarian disregard for public opinion. However,

[22] DDI, II, No. 297; Legatus, Vita di Contarini, p. 103.
[23] Quaroni, Ricordi, pp. 19-25.
[24] DDI, II, No. 372.

whether the king was underestimating the obstacles or not, Italy was pleased with her first approach to Yugoslav royalty.

The impact of Summonte's and Bodrero's efforts was not immediately apparent in practical terms. On October 15 Ninčić again offered to admit Italy's sovereignty in Fiume, but once more at what, to the Italians, was an exorbitant price. This consisted of a 99-year Yugoslav lease on a section of the port of Fiume, Yugoslav ownership of the Lagosta island group, and a rectification in Belgrade's favor of the Italo-Yugoslav frontier in the Giulian Alps, which by the Treaty of Rapallo left Italy in possession of all the strategic mountain passes and almost 500,000 Slavs as well. This was more than Yugoslavia had asked before Italy took over Fiume. Naturally Mussolini refused, although he made an attempt to placate Ninčić with the vague promise, "to examine in a friendly spirit the [Giulian] requests of Yugoslavia but only when a Fiume accord has been reached."[25] To all appearances, the summer deadlock continued. Bodrero and Summonte, however, were not pessimistic. King Alexander, they reported, considered Ninčić's demands "exaggerated," and was endeavoring to persuade his government "to formulate carefully a more modest proposal." Although after four weeks Belgrade had not responded formally to Mussolini's rejection of its last suggestion, Summonte cheerfully calculated that only "demands of little substance" were to be anticipated henceforth.[26] In other words, Ninčić's proposal of October 15 was deemed a last, despairing, even token, effort to win more than the Delta and Porto Baros for Fiume. This confidence was understandable. Short of a resort to force, Yugoslavia had no chance of ejecting Giardino's military government from Fiume, and Rome could afford to sit back and wait until Yugoslavia accepted

---

[25] *DDI*, II, Nos. 466, 467.   [26] *DDI*, II, Nos. 470, 485.

the full import of Italy's Fiume coup, along with the offer of the Delta and Porto Baros as the only realizable trade.

But more than Yugoslav satisfaction in a territorial sense was involved. Throughout 1923 it was understood in Belgrade and Rome that a Fiume settlement should be accompanied by a broad Italo-Yugoslav agreement in the nature of a friendship pact. General Adriatic security was held out to Yugoslavia as an additional reward for letting Fiume go. For Yugoslavia, perhaps even more than for Fascist Italy, an Adriatic rapprochement meant a shift in the whole of recent policy. First, it required Yugoslavia, if she dreamed of expansion anywhere, to look no longer to her northern frontier but to the south—to exchange, in fact, conflict with Italy for a potential rivalry with Greece around Salonika. But more important, rapprochement could involve a radical change in Yugoslavia's position within the Little Entente. Such was the enmity between this group and its patron, France, on the one hand, and Fascist Italy, on the other, that any general Italo-Yugoslav détente might well be construed as a Yugoslav denial of existing ties with France, Czechoslovakia, and Rumania. This had been readily admitted on one occasion or another by Ninčić and King Alexander. Both were critical of what they considered Yugoslavia's excessive dependence on France and on the Little Entente, which they held to be dominated by Czechoslovakia. A friendship pact with Italy, then, appealed to them as an avenue of escape from a servile attachment to the Little Entente.[27] Although a complete reversal of alliances was hardly contemplated, Yugoslavia faced a decision that could not be taken lightly.

Belgrade was understandably slow to make up its mind, and it was not until the evening of January 5, 1924 that it gave the signal for an Italo-Yugoslav détente by agreeing to Mussolini's terms for Fiume. At last Fiume proper went

[27] *DDI*, II, Nos. 337, 499.

to Italy; in compensation Yugoslavia received the Delta and Porto Baros and the adjoining Fiumara canal, a variety of commercial privileges in Fiume, including a 50-year lease on one of the port's three basins, and the contraction of Italy's stretch of the Adriatic coast linking Fiume with Italian Istria. Given the heat so recently generated by Fiume, Yugoslavia's surrender of the town could not but appear startling. There was something of a scramble to claim credit for the spectacular decision. Within the Belgrade foreign ministry, for instance, Spalaïcović asserted that his own persuasion had been needed "to overcome the objections and final hesitation of Pašić." Summonte, who was probably as objective as any other participant, reserved the palm of "principal artisan of the accord" for King Alexander.[28]

The Fiume accord made possible an Italo-Yugoslav friendship pact, the terms of which had still to be worked out. By January 7 Bodrero was en route to Rome with the Yugoslav text of a proposal. Of the four articles in it, three were mild, and were readily accepted in Rome. They reaffirmed Italo-Yugoslav allegiance to the postwar Danubian settlement, stipulated mutual consultation in the case of "international complications," and fixed the treaty's duration at five years. The teeth, if any, were in the remaining article, Article II, whereby each party agreed to observe a benevolent neutrality to the other, "if attacked without any provocation." In itself this was not unconventional or unacceptable, but an addendum to the article was unusual. The Yugoslav text provided that in the event of "subversive movements or violent incursions against one of the two parties, the other party undertakes to lend political and diplomatic support to remove the cause of disturbance."[29] What this meant was not clear. Beneath the surface Yugoslavia seemed to be offering not to foment dis-

28 *DDI*, II, No. 536.   29 *DDI*, II, Nos. 537, 538.

satisfaction among the Slavs under Italian rule, in exchange for Mussolini's promise to keep out of Croatian intrigues for an autonomous state. Despite the bitter antipathy between Croats and Italians manifested in the struggle for Fiume, Yugoslav popular opinion axiomatically suspected that all Croatian subversion aimed at dismantling the young South Slav state had Italy's backing.[30]

In December 1923 the Croatian leader in exile, Stjepan Radić, requested aid from the Rome government via the Italian embassy in Paris. The prospect of using Croatian nationalism to weaken Yugoslavia was not dismissed out of hand, even by some of the old-guard diplomats, who were better known for their advocacy of an Adriatic détente. It was only that the moment was not propitious. Ambassador Romano Avezzana wrote: "A meeting with Radić could be interesting, above all if negotiations for Fiume do not arrive at any result and no real understanding with Yugoslavia appears possible."[31] Of course, with Yugoslavia on the verge of ceding Fiume, Italy was not going to alienate Belgrade, and refused to enter into any relationship with Radić. "I shall remain with the Serbs," Mussolini is reported to have said.[32]

But if the Yugoslav government hoped to remove the threat of Italo-Croatian collaboration by its terminology for mutual aid under a pact of friendship, Italy refused to go along. Piously decrying any clause that might be construed as unwarranted Italian interference in Yugoslavia's "in-

[30] See, for instance, *DDI*, I, Nos. 175, 741.

[31] *DDI*, II, No. 499.

[32] A. Tamaro, *Vent'anni di storia* (Rome, 1953), p. 378. See also *DDI*, II, No. 516. Tamaro, who was the Fascist party agent in Vienna, was approached in January 1924 by Radić who had got wind of the Yugoslav proposal to Italy for mutual aid against internal subversion. This encouraged Radić and the Croats to give fresh life to the rumor in existence long before Mussolini's accession to power, that Italy would assist Yugoslavia to put down any Croatian uprising and be paid for this service with part of Dalmatia (*DDI*, II, p. 334, n. 2; see also *DDI*, II, No. 651).

ternal order," Rome insisted on a more innocuous pledge.[33] As in any treaty negotiation, a common denominator could only be found at the lowest level of obligation acceptable to any one of the participants, and in this case Belgrade had to respect Rome's limit. The text of Article II ultimately agreed on referred explicitly to attacks from beyond Yugoslav and Italian territory, which alone now supplied grounds for invoking the aid of the other party. (The Macedonian bands that threatened Yugoslavia's southern border, not the Croats inside Yugoslavia, were thus made the prototype of the danger anticipated.) The watered-down pledge read: "In the event of the safety and interests of one of the High Contracting Parties being threatened as a result of forcible incursions from without, the other Party undertakes to afford political and diplomatic support in the form of friendly cooperation for the purpose of assisting in the removal of the external cause of such a threat."[34]

The exchanges over Article II indicated that Yugoslavia put more store by the friendship pact than did Fascist Italy; it was Belgrade, too, which sought to confer luster and importance on the pact by promoting a ceremonial meeting of the two heads of government, Mussolini and Pašić, to sign the accord. Mussolini, never one to avoid a display, went along with the idea. It was agreed that the meeting should take place toward the end of January, and that in the meantime its purpose should be announced as the signing of the Fiume settlement alone. The pact of friendship was to remain secret until the moment of signing.[35]

But on January 11, at a gathering of foreign ministers of the Little Entente, Ninčić found himself under pressure to begin negotiations for a pact with France similar to the Franco-Czech military alliance about to be concluded.

[33] *DDI*, II, No. 549.
[34] Royal Institute of International Affairs, *Survey 1924*, p. 506.
[35] *DDI*, II, Nos. 436, 456, 550, 551.

Not for the first time, Ninčić showed resentment at the importunity of the French and Czechs, and countered by disclosing the essence of the impending Italo-Yugoslav treaty of friendship, which in spirit, if nothing else, was difficult to reconcile with the creation of fresh ties between Belgrade and Paris.[36] In reality, neither France nor Czechoslovakia was completely taken by surprise. Both had been aware for several months that something more than a mere Fiume settlement was brewing. Nonetheless, they set about to mitigate the effect of what they considered Yugoslavia's act of desertion. In turn, France and Czechoslovakia offered to adhere to the Italo-Yugoslav treaty and make it into a pact *à trois*. Indeed, Contarini for some time had held out such a prospect to the French and Czech representatives in Rome, and in early 1924 the secretary general still advocated extension of the pact.[37] But this did not suit Mussolini; the pact's exclusiveness was its attraction because it liberated Yugoslavia "from French tutelage."[38] The Belgrade government also felt this way. It signally failed to take up the cause of a tripartite agreement. Moreover, when France invited Pašić, for the sake of appearances, to go on to Paris after his meeting with Mussolini, the Yugoslav premier, not without some Italian prompting, declined.[39] So the pact signed in Rome on January 27, 1924 (it became henceforth the Pact of Rome) remained strictly an Italo-Yugoslav arrangement with a distinct anti-French and anti-Little Entente flavor.

With the Pact of Rome Fascist Italy achieved what had seemed only a year earlier virtually impossible—possession of Fiume and a simultaneous détente with Yugoslavia. This was, moreover, complete satisfaction of the ambivalent

[36] *DDI*, II, Nos. 552-53.
[37] Charles-Roux, *Une grande ambassade*, pp. 256-63; Kybal, *Journal of Central European Affairs*, XIV (1954), 69-71.
[38] *DDI*, II, Nos. 554, 562.
[39] *DDI*, II, Nos. 431, 434.

aims of the Palazzo Chigi officials, who were nationalist enough to thirst after Fiume, while at the same time desirous of Sforza's policy of Adriatic peace. Whether Mussolini and the career diplomats would continue to see eye to eye was another matter. By and large, the professionals regarded the acquisition of Fiume as at least temporary satisfaction of Italian dignity in the Adriatic; they were prepared now to concentrate on cultivating Yugoslav friendship within the framework of the Rome pact.[40] Indeed, this was only realistic, if Fiume was to bring any tangible profit to Italy. As a port it had begun as an artificial creation of the Habsburgs to appease Slavic sentiment within their empire. Fiume could not survive unless trade from its Slavic hinterland was deliberately funneled through it, a service lying clearly within the province of Yugoslavia, whose goodwill therefore had to be not only won but kept.

Yet Mussolini's appreciation of Yugoslav friendship, either as a prerequisite of Fiume's viability or of Adriatic peace at large, had to be accounted dubious. It was only to be expected that he would remain responsive to that current of nationalist discontent in Italy which had helped him into power, and which clamored for further Adriatic victories at Yugoslavia's expense. Certainly in the first months of 1924 Fascist Italy showed more inclination to exalt the Fiume victory than to breathe life into the generalities of the Pact of Rome. Mussolini was decorated with the Collar of the Annunziata expressly for his Fiume triumph. And he lost no time in ordering the full integration of Fiume into the Italian state, particularly by the imposition of an Italian customs regime. The whole process was to be topped off with a ceremonial proclamation of sovereignty on the spot by King Victor Emmanuel.[41] In his zeal, however, Mussolini was riding roughshod over

[40] Legatus, *Vita di Contarini*, pp. 106-108.
[41] *DDI*, II, Nos. 598, 610; *OO*, xx, 182, 231-32.

the sentiments and commercial interests of the Fiumians themselves, who found a champion in General Giardino. The general suggested July 1925 as a practicable date for the final absorption of Fiume into Italy's bureaucratic system. But Mussolini conceded only a fraction; the application of Italian tariffs and proclamation of sovereignty were postponed for some four weeks. This was insufficient for Giardino, who promptly tendered his resignation as governor.[42]

From all this, it was plain that Mussolini considered Fiume a genuine prize. By comparison, the Pact of Rome roused his enthusiasm hardly at all. In this sense, the new Italo-Yugoslav rapprochement from the start possessed some insecure foundations.

[42] *DDI*, II, No. 659; III, Nos. 30, 32, 40.

6. Mussolini and German Nationalism

The Dawes Plan

ONE MIGHT expect to find that Italo-German relations, like most other features of European diplomacy in the early 1920s, were conditioned by the reparations problem. Yet this did not occur. Although German public opinion was opposed to Fascist Italy's contribution to the Ruhr occupation, the German government anticipated Italian policy in the crisis of January 1923, and took it, not as voluntary action, but the product of unavoidable circumstances. On January 20 a relieved Italian ambassador in Berlin reported: "In these [official] circles it is generally understood that Italy could not have acted very differently from the way she did, in view of her multiple and complex relations with France and also in view of her clear and material need to provide for the distribution of as much coal as it is possible to obtain in the present circumstances from the areas occupied by Franco-Belgian troops. In all my conversations with persons in authority I have heard in this regard only reasonable and even benevolent understanding and consideration."[1] The Germans thus determined, correctly, that Italy could be solicited to espouse again a lenient reparations settlement.

Italy had no quarrel with Germany so long as coal as payment of reparations crossed the Alps. The Germans, despite Italy's role in the Ruhr invasion and regardless of passive resistance, voluntarily maintained consignments of reparations coal to Italy as long as possible.[2] This was a considerable boon once the French found themselves un-

---

[1] *DDI*, I, No. 533.

[2] *DDI*, I, p. 246, n. 1; G.D., 824L/5115/241118; 2784H/1385/537437-38, 537441.

able to wrest more than a modicum of coal from the occupied Ruhr. But inevitably, in the long run, the fantastic inflation of the mark and Germany's general economic misery took their toll. On August 11, 1923 Berlin announced that it was impossible to guarantee further reparations payments in kind to Italy or any other country.[3] Mussolini tried to avert the stoppage by cajolery and threat. He offered to pay the transportation costs, and suggested a separate Italo-German agreement that would circumvent the Reparations Commission. He was also willing to take the lead in another mediation campaign and to present Germany's case in Paris.[4] When none of this had any effect, Mussolini warned that Germany's stand was driving Italy into France's arms—still to no avail. After mid-November the German government disavowed any responsibility for further deliveries of coal.[5]

Yet Italy's coal supplies at the time depended less on the German government than on the Ruhr industrialists and mine owners. By the fall of 1923, in order to keep their plants and mines in operation, they were ready for almost any agreement with the occupying authorities, including the promise to make reparations payments in kind out of their own pockets. For some time Mussolini had been trying to achieve some rapport with the Ruhr coal and steel barons—the formidable Hugo Stinnes had been received in Rome amid much fanfare in March 1923—but with little success.[6] So Stinnes and his colleagues negotiated almost exclusively with the French and Belgians in the Ruhr, while Italy looked on sourly, fearing an arrangement harmful to Italian interests. Her fears were groundless, however, for an agreement reached on November 23 provided for Italy's full percentage of reparations payments, although they

3 Royal Institute of International Affairs, *Survey 1924*, p. 286.
4 G.D., 824L/5115/241592; 2784H/1385/537458-59, 537468.
5 G.D., 2784H/1385/537512-13, 537514-15, 537518.
6 G.D., 2784H/1385/537536.

were to be resumed on a reduced scale. A month later the German government formally underwrote its assurance to Italy.[7] Within a few weeks the Italians, through no fault of their own, had seen their supply of coal vanishing in the collapse of the German economy; then, without any effort on their part, they found a good part of it restored. Obviously Italy was in no position to take the initiative in the reparations question. She could only react to the play of forces over which she had no control. It was doubtless resentment of this humble fate that accounted for Italy's prickly attitude when serious negotiations to resolve the Ruhr crisis got under way.

In September 1923 the chaotic condition of the German economy forced Berlin to change its policy. A new government headed by Gustav Stresemann took office and at once called off passive resistance. Shortly thereafter, a more conciliatory attitude emerged in Paris. Since the end of the war France had counted on large reparations. Germany's near bankruptcy shattered this prospect, a shock that was expressed in a crisis of confidence in French financial circles. Poincaré's rigid policy was discredited; France now seemed ready to match Germany's new, more flexible position. Milder attitudes on both sides stimulated fresh efforts by third parties for a compromise settlement. Specifically, pressure was exerted on France, chiefly by Britain, to heed an American suggestion which in fact antedated the Ruhr occupation. An international commission of experts, with United States participation, would explore Germany's capacity to pay, and devise a plan to enable her to pay whatever was decided on. Among other attractions, the proposal hinted at American investment in Europe and lenient war debt settlements. Ultimately Germany and France, both somewhat chastened, accepted an international investigation, and on November 30, 1923 two committees were

[7] Royal Institute of International Affairs, *Survey 1924*, pp. 288-90.

148

appointed. Their recommendations were to become the basis of the Dawes Plan, named after General Charles Dawes, the American banker who was chairman of the first committee.[8]

Despite Mussolini's frequent assertions of the link between German reparations and American war debt, Italy did not join actively in the campaign to bring the United States into the reparations picture. Before agreeing to participate in the international investigation of Germany's economy, Italy hedged and called, albeit in vain, for an Allied understanding beforehand.[9] What Italy feared was plain enough: America's entry and British reentry onto the scene would diminish what little influence Italy enjoyed, and thereby would increase the chance of an undesirable reparations settlement to Italy.[10] For Mussolini there was another and more personal reason for disliking the turn of events. His persistent ambition in the Ruhr crisis had been to win esteem for Fascist Italy by forcing his own mediation services on the protagonists. He had tried at first alone and then in conjunction with Britain. Now the establishment of the Dawes committees was mediation imposed by the Anglo-Americans, with America playing the part Mussolini coveted. But he blamed the British for this; they had spurned him in favor of the United States. The Duce awaited an opportunity to give vent to his wounded feelings. When London proposed Anglo-Italian collaboration to prevent the automatic reelection of a Frenchman as president of the Reparations Commission, he contemptuously rejected the overture as a typical British trick to embroil Italy with France.[11]

The accession of Ramsay MacDonald's Labour government to office shortly afterward did nothing to dispel Mussolini's umbrage. One of MacDonald's first acts was to send a

8 *Ibid.*, pp. 240-44.
9 *DDI*, II, No. 458; *USFR, 1923*, II, 87, 100.
10 *DDI*, II, Nos. 498, 604.   11 *DDI*, II, Nos. 526, 528.

personal letter to Poincaré; Mussolini felt slighted, and compulsively suspected a deal giving Paris a free hand to bring about "a direct economic and political agreement between France and Germany and the consequent creation of a gigantic industrial and financial bloc in the Rhineland and the Ruhr dominated by France."[12] Assurance was forthcoming, that MacDonald's letter was no more than a "polite gesture" deemed necessary because of Anglo-French discord over reparations, which did not exist between Rome and London.[13] But Italy's preoccupation with exclusion from Anglo-French counsels was not to be allayed by mere words. Italian misgivings in the spring of 1924 would only recede if Britain took steps to guarantee Italy's reparations coal supply, either by converting into a governmental obligation the Anglo-Italian experts' accord of the previous summer or by backing Italy's plea for an Allied agreement before considering the Dawes report. The British gave no hint of doing either, and Rome continued to suspect their good faith.[14]

When the Dawes report appeared in March 1924 the Italian tendency to expect the worst virtually forced them to find some fault with it. Although there was no discrimination against Italian interests, the report was criticized because it said nothing about the cancellation of the Allied debt owed to Britain.[15] On April 12 General Dawes visited Rome. Mussolini seemed to be flattered by the attention, and treated Dawes' visit as important. The American was impressed, saying: "After leaving him I felt as if I had seen Julius Caesar."[16] The meeting also quieted Mussolini's doubts about the Dawes report; Italy, at any rate, could not afford to oppose the report alone. So on April 17, via a cir-

[12] *DDI*, II, Nos. 608, 655.
[13] *DDI*, III, Nos. 36, 42.
[14] *DDI*, III, Nos. 21, 24, 126, 164.
[15] *DDI*, III, Nos. 90, 146.
[16] Dawes, *A Journal of Reparations* (London, 1939), pp. 224-27.

cular to the major Italian embassies, Italy declared herself "disposed to approve wholeheartedly the work of the experts and the principles underlying it."[17] Mussolini was heartened by another visit, this time by the Belgian premier and foreign minister, on May 18-19. In fact, he was encouraged to make a final attempt to revive Italy's waning influence in the reparations question. With arrangements under way for an international conference to discuss the recommendations of the Dawes committees, he suggested that Italy, with Belgium, mediate the remaining Anglo-French differences on the sanctions to which Germany was to be subject under the Dawes Plan. He also proposed that the forthcoming conference be held in Italy.[18] These overtures were futile, and Rome lapsed into an inert pessimism about the fate of Italy's interests and of the reparations conference, scheduled to open in July. The German ambassador in Rome remarked: "The Italians, because of their scant influence at the London Conference, would not be sorry to see it end without result."[19]

The fact of the matter was that while steps were being taken toward the Dawes Plan, Mussolini was preoccupied with the Mediterranean and Adriatic. Since his first efforts at mediation and his anti-British bloc idea had exploded in his face early in 1923, he had shown only a passing interest in the German reparations problem. Not surprisingly, then, Italy's reparations policy lacked direction and vitality.

The career diplomats filled any vacuum left by Mussolini. But during the winter of 1923-24, they tended to join him in doubting British intentions and sounding the alarm for Italian interests. The ambassador in Paris, Romano Avezzana, was perhaps the most certain that Italy was about to be sold out. His counterpart in London, Della Torretta,

17 *DDI*, III, No. 150; cf. *OO*, xx, 250.
18 *DDI*, III, No. 207.
19 G.D., 2784H/1385/537742-43.

veered from week to week between assurances of British integrity and half-formulated suspicions. In Rome Secretary General Contarini, the most reliable weather vane of Palazzo Chigi opinion, commented to the German ambassador on the events leading to the Dawes Plan in tones of gloom and misgiving. Italy's churlish and unenlightened reception of the Dawes Plan, then, can be ascribed neither to Fascist nor old-guard influence; it was the humor of combined Italian officialdom.

Stresemann and the German Revisionists

Italy's fading from the picture in the German reparations question left the way open for the elaboration of another factor in the relations between Italy and Germany, a factor destined to transcend all others. This was Mussolini's approach toward German political and military revival. Fascism had come to power because it expressed best Italian dissatisfaction with the peace treaties of 1919-20. It was a moot question whether Mussolini would be able or willing to deny this revisionist heritage. The professionals in the foreign ministry were pledged to keep Italy loyal to her wartime allies, but the extent of their influence was unknown. Of all the forces seeking to revise the postwar settlement, Germany was potentially the strongest, hence the most likely to attack it. It was natural that other discontented elements in Europe would rally to the cause of German nationalism either out of sympathy or self-interest. Germany, then, would provide a criterion of Mussolini's revisionism and radical diplomacy, and also of the Palazzo Chigi's capacity to control its Fascist chief.

During a brief visit to Germany six months before attaining power, Mussolini got the impression that underneath Weimar Germany's democratic and pacific front pre-1914 German militarism and nationalism thrived, awaiting only an opportunity and a leader. This impression was reflected in Fascist support of the French case for a punitive German reparations policy during the months before the March on Rome. Although once in office Mussolini found it inexpedient to follow a harsh reparations policy toward Germany, his appraisal of the potential strength and danger of German nationalism was unchanged. This was evident in a preface Mussolini wrote for *La Germania repubblicana* by Roberto Suster, Berlin correspondent of Mussolini's *Popolo d'Italia*, which was published in September 1923. The Duce referred to his past warnings of German nationalism in *Popolo d'Italia*:

> The fall of the Empire has left a void in the German mind. The Republic has not filled it. Berlin is an imperial city. Its decor is too ostentatious for a republic of the *petite bourgeoisie*. Berlin yearns secretly to return to the sparkling stage of an empire. . . . Despite the republic, and perhaps in consequence of the republic, the whole of Germany is moving uniformly and progressively toward the right. . . .
>
> The pacifism of Germany is forced. . . . Germany is pacific because she is *incapable* of waging war. But what is important to seek out and know is whether machine guns still remain hidden in factory basements and forest caves: it is important to seek out and know what is the state of mind of the new generation of Germans.

Mussolini went on to alert his countrymen to their responsibilities:

> The important position that we have acquired in the world imposes on us new duties and new preparation. The Germany that, in consequence of war and defeat, represents the axis around which gyrates and on which depends practically everything, cannot be ignored or known only superficially.[20]

20 *OO*, xx, 29-31.

Mussolini, as befitted a good nationalist, exhorted Italy rather than Europe to take note of the German phenomenon. He intended to judge German nationalism solely by Italian criteria and, regardless of the implied threat to the European status quo, to foster and exploit it if Italy's interests might better be served. Significantly, as Mussolini's comments appeared in print, he was planning to enlist the aid of German nationalism.

By September 1923 the hope of establishing a Fiume free state, as prescribed in the Italo-Yugoslav Treaty of Rapallo of 1920, was dead. This provided Mussolini with the opportunity to pressure Yugoslavia and win the city for Italy. To this end he planned a mild coup; indeed, in mid-September General Giardino was sent to restore order in Fiume. Coming while the Fascist occupation of Corfu was still an unresolved question, this further unilateral action was likely to produce serious international repercussions. Rome particularly feared France's reaction, since she was the self-appointed guardian of Yugoslavia. Early in September, during a conversation in Rome with Count Alessandro De Bosdari, the Italian ambassador in Berlin, Mussolini surprised the diplomat with the question whether Germany, in the event of an Italo-Yugoslav conflict, "would be in a position . . . to immobilize part of the French army on the Rhine." De Bosdari promised to reply to "such a sudden and unexpected question" after he had made inquiries in Berlin.[21] The reaction of Stresemann, who had been German chancellor and foreign minister for a month, on hearing of the notion of Italo-German military cooperation was astonishment, also. Having only recently renounced passive resistance in the Ruhr to mollify France and world opinion, his government was not likely to compromise its position by reckless association with Mussolini in order to enhance

[21] Extract from De Bosdari's unpublished "Memorie," in *DDI*, ii, p. 238, n. 3.

154

the Italian position in the Adriatic.[22] Stresemann's definite answer was given the day after the dispatch of an Italian governor to Fiume, by which time it was clear that France, involved in the Ruhr, was prepared on this occasion to leave Yugoslavia in the lurch. It was the only conceivable reply. In De Bosdari's words: "He [Stresemann] had pondered deeply on developments . . . in the event of an Italo-Yugoslav conflict. The result of his reflections was that Germany, being compelled to devote herself to her economic reestablishment and to the solution of the reparations problem, could not see her way to taking sides in such a conflict."[23]

This rebuff apparently disturbed the Germanophile De Bosdari. In estimating the German situation for Mussolini, he commented scornfully on the weakness of the Stresemann regime: "With this government completely in the hands of the Social Democrats, there is nothing to be anticipated save shameful capitulation." Yet De Bosdari refused to regard Germany as an irreparably broken reed. He thought the physical requirements for a reconstitution of German power already existed or could be produced in the near future. But if Mussolini thought of deriving profit from association with Germany in the future, he should make contact with those elements responsible for such "signs of revival and recovery, however sporadic, timid, and uncertain" as Weimar Germany had hitherto evinced.[24] Putting his opinion into practice, De Bosdari soon approached Karl Helfferich, head of the German National People's party. Not surprisingly, Helfferich castigated Stresemann's fulfillment policy, advocated a foreign policy based on a breach with France, and expressed the hope that, "in

[22] *DDI*, ii, No. 351. See also G.D. (Stresemann papers), 716H/3104/154066-67; in this report from Vienna, references to press speculations on an Austro-German-Italian bloc and the international repercussions of such an alignment to Germany's detriment in the Ruhr question are underlined.

[23] *DDI*, ii, No. 373. [24] *DDI*, ii, No. 389.

view of possible radical changes in international politics, Germany and Italy will not delay in coming to an understanding." The report of these views and preparation for an exchange of views with a hypothetical German nationalist government were congenial to Mussolini. According to De Bosdari the Duce granted that "for the moment it was not convenient to initiate any action. However, he considered it desirable that I [De Bosdari] should remain with due caution in opportune contact in order to be able effectively to take such action in future should the occasion arise."[25]

Activity, then, continued in Berlin. During October and November 1923 attention was focused on German nationalism in a military guise. The creation of a parliamentary nationalist society under General Paul von Lettow-Vorbeck was observed closely, and "the tendencies and objects of this association and the possibility of agreement with Italy" noted. The actual approaches to the German generals were made not by De Bosdari but by the Marquis Salvatore Denti di Piraino, the naval attaché in Berlin. Two military men interviewed by Denti were Generals Hans von Seeckt and Paul Hasse. Both spoke of a war of revenge against France and, to facilitate this, requested Italy's diplomatic aid in ridding Germany of the Allied Military Control Commission, as well as assistance in German rearmament. Both were enthusiastic about an Italo-German alliance; Seeckt offered to send a personal emissary to Italy to lay the foundation of an agreement, and undertook "to speak to Stresemann of the eventuality of a possible accord." The indication that Stresemann might not after all be opposed to closer political ties with Italy was corroborated in another conversation between Denti and Baron Ago von Maltzan, secretary of state for political affairs in the German foreign ministry. While deprecating Stresemann's parliamentary compromises and dissimulation, Maltzan regarded the foreign minister as de-

25 *DDI*, II, No. 405; De Bosdari, "Memorie," *DDI*, II, p. 265, n. 1.

voted to the restoration of German power and prestige, and convinced of the necessity of removing the control commission and challenging France. Assertedly, Stresemann was cognizant of the value of Italian support in the event of Franco-German hostilities: "If to the discreet overture of the Italian ambassador with regard to the special case of an attack by France and Yugoslavia on Italy, he had been forced to reply with an unfeigned declaration of neutrality, this is not to say that, if a more definite and comprehensive overture reached him from Italy, he would not be receptive to a convention of a military nature."[26]

At the end of December 1923 Stresemann himself took the initiative, thus seeming to substantiate the hints and appraisals of Seeckt and Maltzan. The German ambassador in Rome, Baron Konstantin von Neurath, was informed that Stresemann had been considering for some time past a meeting with Mussolini, but had been deterred by the likely repercussions in Britain and France. Now as an alternative, the foreign minister suggested that during his forthcoming vacation at Lugano he meet privately for an exchange of views with "an authoritative figure" from Italy who conveniently might also be visiting the Swiss watering place. Neurath was given latitude to broach the proposal confidentially in Rome.[27] What lay behind Stresemann's move is not entirely clear. Possibly he wished merely to discuss Italy's stand on the reparations question[28]—although this was not likely. Stresemann's insistence that his rendezvous with an Italian "spokesman" be of a clandestine nature augured something momentous and conspiratorial. In view of Fascist Italy's overture for military cooperation

[26] *DDI*, II, No. 489; De Bosdari's "Memorie," *DDI*, II, p. 329, n. 2.
[27] G.D., 2784H/1385/537566.
[28] H. Bretton, *Stresemann and the Revision of Versailles* (Stanford, 1953), p. 74, suggests that toward the end of 1923 Stresemann tried to frighten Britain into a conciliatory reparations policy by rumors of an Italo-German agreement.

only three months earlier, Stresemann must have realized
that his own démarche was a clear invitation to reopen the
subject of an Italo-German pact if Mussolini so wished.[29]
But Mussolini's response was unexpected. He suggested
that Stresemann, following his stay at Lugano, continue his
trip to Capri where Mussolini himself would be on vacation.[30] But to do so would risk the publicity and international speculation Germany sought to avoid, and Neurath
was scolded for allowing Mussolini to twist Stresemann's
overture so as to place Germany in an embarrassing position. After some soul-searching to discover whether a visit
by Stresemann to Italy could not be rationalized somehow,
Berlin decided that the risk of upsetting Britain and France
and forfeiting a lenient reparations settlement and evacuation of the Ruhr presaged by the formation of the Dawes
committees was too great to run. Therefore, Mussolini's
invitation was declined.[31]

The rejection of Stresemann's plea for secrecy in an Italo-
German exchange of views ran counter to Mussolini's earlier caution in encouraging German nationalism. Plainly
he wished to use a visit by Stresemann as a propaganda coup,
involving nothing substantive which could not bear the
full glare of publicity, rather than as a confidential negotiation that might lead to a military understanding. It
may even be that Mussolini anticipated rejection of his
offer of a publicized visit to Italy. At all events, it seems certain that Mussolini at this moment had lost interest in a
military alliance with Germany. This is corroborated by
De Bosdari, who at the beginning of 1924 was called to
Rome to report on his contacts with the German national-

[29] It is worth noting the exuberant hope expressed by Stresemann
at this time, that "within the foreseeable future we shall regain our
strength and once more become 'bündnisfähig' to our friends and
dangerous to our enemies" (G.D. [Stresemann papers], 7120H/3099/
146310).

[30] G.D., 2784H/1385/537568.

[31] G.D., 2784H/1385/537570, 537571-74, 537577.

ists. To his astonishment, Mussolini brushed aside the ambassador's communication. While in Rome, De Bosdari learned of the conclusion of a Fiume settlement and an Italo-Yugoslav friendship pact. "I understood that there had disappeared at least for the moment," he wrote, "the presupposition of a conflict with our neighbor which, six months earlier, had caused Mussolini to think of our coming to a military accord with Germany."[32]

Whereas the relaxation of Adriatic tension had prompted Stresemann to explore the possibility of an Italian connection, in Mussolini's eyes it removed the rationale of immediate Italo-German military cooperation. On the other hand, Mussolini's disenchantment was not so much with German nationalism per se as with the current Stresemann-dominated regime in Germany. Despite the testimony in Berlin to Stresemann's nationalism, De Bosdari continued to regard him as a tool of France and the German Socialists, and too pusillanimous for a German military revival or military collaboration with Italy. Stresemann's overture for a confidential exchange of views notwithstanding, Mussolini concurred. The Duce's candid opinion of Stresemann was expressed on the latter's death in 1929, which was, Mussolini told his Council of Ministers, "an advantage to us. Stresemann hated Italy and hated Fascism."[33] But as early as 1923 Mussolini was prepared to regard Stresemann and the Weimar Republic as temporary phenomena. After them might come the day of true German nationalism, and it seemed necessary to provide insurance against this contingency. While rebuffing Stresemann, Mussolini resolved to nurture his contacts with the right-wing German factions that claimed to sponsor and embody a national revival. Moreover, he was willing to pro-

---

[32] De Bosdari's "Memorie," *DDI*, p. 329, n. 2.
[33] It.D. (Ministry of Interior, Italian Social Republic), 329/1295/112729.

vide tangible proof of Fascist Italy's sympathy for German nationalism.

During the winter of 1923-24 the Duce took the opportunity to show his favor in numerous small ways and in a variety of questions bearing on German prestige and thus close to the heart of the German nationalists. In November 1923 he threw Italy's support behind the German right wing's request that the crown prince be allowed to return to Germany.[34] In early 1924 Mussolini canceled an investigatory trip by De Bosdari to the Palatinate, lest the journey seem to contradict the German thesis that rumors of separatist agitation there were merely French propaganda.[35] However, it will be remembered that the *Reichswehr* chiefs, when first approached by Mussolini, made it clear that there was one issue of paramount importance in which Italian aid was solicited: rebuilding German military strength. To facilitate this it was desirable to minimize the scope of the Allied Military Control Commission in Germany. From the end of 1923 on, Italy was profuse with assurances that she was working within the Allied camp toward this goal.[36] Italy's position within the still extant wartime alliance, however, was a secondary one; Mussolini's very liaison with the German nationalists was both a reaction and testimony to this. As Contarini admitted, Italy could not set the pace in the control commission question; she could only follow the lead of Britain, the senior ally well disposed toward Germany.[37]

This inability to realize promises of diplomatic aid inevitably put a premium on Mussolini's direct participation in German rearmament behind the back of the control commission. As might be expected those involved have left

34 G.D., 4530H/2284/138765.

35 G.D., 2784H/1385/537592, 537602.

36 G.D., 4530H/2284/138812, 138802, 138613-15; 2784H/1385/537557, 537696, 537788-90; 2784H/1386/537923-24.

37 G.D., 4530H/2284/138744-45.

behind them little evidence of such flagrant contravention of the Versailles Treaty. But there exists enough information to establish that Mussolini went the whole route in courting the German nationalists, and sent secret consignments of arms to Germany. In December 1923 the Austrian customs authorities at Innsbruck, for unexplained reasons, stopped and examined 11 railroad cars coming from Italy. The contents, listed as food supplied for Latvia, were heavy machine guns, antiaircraft weapons, and the appropriate accessories to mount and service them. Their destination was not clear, but, after inquiries had been made of Bavarian customs officials and the German defense ministry's representative at Munich, it was decided that the arms were intended for the *Reichswehr*. As these were in the category of weapons forbidden Germany by the Versailles Treaty, the Innsbruck Social Democrats were extremely interested in this apparent treaty breach, and the affair reached the columns of the local and Viennese press. However, the Austrian authorities, under pressure from the Italian consul at Innsbruck, quickly hushed up the matter. The railroad cars were hurriedly sent on their way, now with a police escort, presumably to their secret destination in Germany.[38]

A few weeks later, there was an incident that provides another indication of Italy's involvement in secret German rearmament. In Berlin, De Bosdari talked with Seeckt. Seeckt revealed to the ambassador, to De Bosdari's surprise, that he had been approached recently by an Italian senator named Riccardo Bianchi. The senator's commission was to explore the possibility of establishing an Italian subsidiary of a German concern for the production of poison gas.[39] In

[38] G.D., 2784H/1385/537560, 537562.
[39] *DDI*, III, No. 43. Unfortunately there is no reference to these dealings in Seeckt's own papers captured by the Allies at the end of World War II. In this connection H. Gatzke's observation (*Stresemann and the Rearmament of Germany* [Baltimore, 1954], p. 120) is worth

corroboration of these hints, General August von Cramon in the summer of 1925 informed the German press that he was ready to supply details of Mussolini's support of Germany's military rehabilitation. Neurath reported that "public discussion of this matter was distasteful to Italy's highest circles," and suggested that Berlin dissuade Cramon from his threatened indiscretion.[40] Thereupon Cramon, called to the German foreign ministry, promised in an interview with the head of the press bureau, Walther Zechlin, to keep silent. The account of the conversation, which was sent to Neurath, makes interesting reading. Cramon told Zechlin that negotiations for the delivery of a variety of Italian arms to Germany began as early as 1922. As representatives of the *Reichswehr* in these talks, Cramon named, besides himself, General Erich Ludendorff and Marshal August von Mackensen; on the Italian side he identified the war hero, General Luigi Capello, and his aide, Lieutenant Henrici. Although Cramon was invited several times to visit Mussolini in Rome, he never made the trip, and, he insisted, the negotiations fell through.[41] Despite this outcome there remains little doubt that Italy, through many contacts with Germany's militarists, contributed in a material way to the secret rearmament of Germany.

It has already been noted that Mussolini's courting of German nationalism led to a departure from orthodox diplomatic channels. With the denigration of Stresemann's patriotism, the bypassing of the German foreign minister and direct approaches to the German nationalist parties and *Reichswehr* generals became standard Italian procedure. From their Fascist contacts the German nationalist politicians learned something of the Italian overture to Berlin at

---

recalling: "There was a constant fear on the part of everyone involved that news of the *Reichswehr's* operations might leak out. And as Severing once put it: 'If one writes it down, it is as good as betrayed.'"

40 G.D., 2784H/1386/537967.

41 G.D., 6001H/2810/442375-76.

the height of the Fiume crisis, and Stresemann found himself accused by the German right of rejecting a military alliance with Italy. Not surprisingly, Stresemann vainly expostulated over the confidence and support bestowed on his political opponents by Mussolini.[42] Soon after making this protest, presumably in an attempt to reestablish lost communication with Mussolini, Stresemann revived his plan to visit Italy. Although Italy made no objection, Stresemann's advisers once more raised the possibility of alienating Britain and France when delicate negotiations for the evacuation of the Ruhr were pending, and the idea was dropped.[43]

It was not only Stresemann, however, who came to be excluded from Mussolini's intrigues; the Italian diplomatic service did not enjoy the Duce's confidence either. From the beginning of 1924 the Germans began to perceive that certain Italian representatives were unaware of Mussolini's professed desire to meet German nationalist wishes with regard to the Allied Military Control Commission. General Riccardo Calcagno, the Italian representative, seemed disposed to resist any reduction in the commission's power. The same stand was taken in the Allied Conference of Ambassadors by Romano Avezzana who told the German ambassador in Paris that he received few instructions from Mussolini on German matters.[44] Moreover, there is De Bosdari's assurance that in Rome Secretary General Contarini seemed completely ignorant of the nature and extent of Mussolini's association with the German nationalist right.[45]

But the most striking testimony to Mussolini's preference for irregular channels of communication was his sidestepping of the Italian embassy in Berlin. We have seen that,

[42] G.D., 2784H/1385/537677; *DDI*, III, No. 85.
[43] G.D., 4530H/2582/325915-16, 325902-3, 325899-900; 2784H/1385/537688.
[44] G.D., 4530H/2284/139110, 139329-30; 4530H/2285/140055-56.
[45] De Bosdari, "Memorie," *DDI*, II, p. 329, n. 2.

at the very moment Mussolini was feigning disinterest in German nationalism before De Bosdari, another Italian was negotiating with Seeckt about poison gas. It also seems that De Bosdari was kept in the dark about the possibility of a Stresemann visit to Italy.[46] The exclusion of the ambassador from the heart of Italo-German matters was hastened by General Capello's arrival in Berlin in February 1924. The general's task was "to hold confidential conversations with certain military and nationalist elements which had exhibited the desire to keep in contact with the Italian government with a view to the future development of policy in the two countries." De Bosdari was required to assist the general in establishing appropriate connections and especially to introduce him to Seeckt. In return, De Bosdari argued that, as Capello was not an official representative of the Italian government, it was not part of his role as ambassador to make introductions, "without first knowing in principle what were Mussolini's ideas." Mussolini seized on his ambassador's reluctance. Commending De Bosdari's caution, he absolved him from the task of putting Capello in touch with his German informants. In De Bosdari's words: "I was to remain extraneous to all [Capello's] actions, limiting myself to the requirement that I be kept *au courant*, so that he might give ear to such counsel and information as I judged convenient to give him." Capello thus proceeded alone in conducting negotiations with the German nationalists. He reported some of his findings to De Bosdari who joined in summarizing the conclusions for Mussolini.[47] Eventually Capello himself lost Mussolini's favor; in November 1925, on the grounds of his links with Franco-Italian freemasonry, he was arrested in connection with the trumped-up Zaniboni plot to assassinate Mussolini. The Fascist police took the precaution of confiscating all of the general's papers.

[46] *DDI*, III, No. 142.
[47] De Bosdari, "Memorie," *DDI*, III, p. 30, n. 1; see also *DDI*, III, Nos. 39, 43.

During his trial, held in camera in April 1927, Capello referred obliquely to his mission in Germany, "when there arose the occasion, although not a Fascist, I offered to render a delicate and dangerous service to my country." But he refused to elaborate further. Nonetheless, he was sentenced to 30 years in prison.[48]

Meanwhile De Bosdari became aware that Capello was not Mussolini's only personal agent in Germany, and was thus in no doubt that he was on the periphery of affairs. He implored his foreign minister to consider "whether the dispatch of unofficial agents to Germany . . . is advisable or, on the contrary, ought not . . . to be regarded as rather imprudent and calculated to diminish the confidence that the present [German] government has always placed in the official representative of His Majesty, who, I believe, is in a better position than anyone else to speak . . . on any issue of the most reserved and confidential nature." He further observed that on the German side, not only Stresemann, but Seeckt was far from happy about Mussolini's use of unorthodox agents.[49] To no avail; De Bosdari, who had originally encouraged Mussolini to avoid Stresemann and deal directly with the German nationalists, now found the Germans unwilling to deal with Italy through the Berlin embassy.[50] Ultimately he turned to Stresemann and confessed his failure to handle or understand the German nationalists.[51] De Bosdari held a precarious tenure at the Berlin embassy; his resignation was rumored for over a year before it took place in 1926.[52]

It was perhaps inevitable that a gulf would develop between Mussolini and his foreign policy advisers—sym-

[48] It.D. (Mussolini's private secretariat), 172/683/051199. See also *OO*, XXI, 543-46, and C. Delzell, *Mussolini's Enemies* (Princeton, 1961), pp. 33-34.
[49] *DDI*, III, No. 85.
[50] *DDI*, III, No. 186.
[51] G.D. (Stresemann papers), 7129H/3113/147917-22.
[52] G.D., 2784H/1385/537849, 537853.

bolized by De Bosdari's unhappy situation—on the issue of German nationalism. To be sure, the Italian foreign ministry officials had agreed to serve Mussolini partly in the hope of exploiting to Italy's advantage the international alarm occasioned by Fascism's reputation. But this was to be accomplished by negotiation with Britain and France on North African and Mediterranean subjects, not by the creation of a dangerous revisionist force in central Europe. Rather, Mussolini's secret espousal of German nationalism was the sort of novel and adventurous foreign policy they had remained in office to prevent. It constituted a notable failure of the Palazzo Chigi officials during Fascism's early years in Italy.

The Bavarian Right

Mussolini's association with the nationalists in southern Germany merits attention for several reasons. First, there was Bavaria's proximity to Italy's northeastern frontier. Moreover, Bavarian nationalism was a more virulent type than that found anywhere else in Germany, to the extent of Bavaria's seeking to secede from a pacific Weimar Republic, possibly to form an Austro-Bavarian union under a restored monarchy. And it was in 1923 in Munich that the Nazis made their first serious bid for power.

Because of an ideological similarity between Italian Fascism and south German conservatism, the March on Rome spurred the Bavarian right into imitative agitation, which culminated in the forced resignation of the moderate Bavarian minister president. Soon rumors of Italian support for a Bavarian separatist coup appeared in the press.[53] Mussolini was stirred by Bavarian developments. Only five days after taking office he urgently requested the Italian consul in Munich to send information "on the pos-

[53] Rosen, *Vierteljahrshefte für Zeitgeschichte*, v (1957), 20, 22.

sibility of action by elements of the extreme right."[54] But the Italian foreign ministry was accustomed to receive its news of south German events less from the Munich consulate than from Adolfo Tedaldi, an Italian attached to the Allied Rhineland Commission at Bad Ems, a source of information Mussolini inherited.

In mid-November 1922 Tedaldi prepared for Mussolini a comprehensive report on Bavarian right-wing politics.[55] According to the report the Bavarian right was counting on Fascist Italy. The separatists, in particular, hoped for Italian economic, and possibly military, aid in the early days of the hoped-for Bavarian independence. The possibility was held out to Rome of an increase of south German exports through Trieste and other Italian ports on the Adriatic. It was suggested that the creation of a common Italo-Bavarian frontier would promote this. On the other hand, Tedaldi warned Mussolini of the dangers of encouraging Bavarian nationalism because nearly all the groups involved were totally unreconciled to Italy's possession of the Alto Adige, obtained from Austria in 1919 by the Treaty of St. Germain. This region, with its German-speaking population of about 250 thousand, was the key to relations between Italy and all German nationalists. When in September 1923 Mussolini began to establish ties with the nationalists in Berlin, De Bosdari strongly warned him against "too violent an Italianization policy in the Alto Adige."[56]

Yet the possibility of Italian support of some form of Bavarian nationalism, in return for recognition of Italy's position in the Alto Adige, was clearly present. Tedaldi thought a Bavarian coup, "a probability that, given certain premises, could be a reality within a few weeks." In view of "the dangers that would accrue to Italy were Bavarian secession to take place, not under our control,

[54] *DDI*, I, No. 65. [55] *DDI*, I, No. 131.
[56] De Bosdari, "Memorie," *DDI*, II, p. 265, n. 1.

but under that of another power," he urged Mussolini to consider sending food and coal, and the extension of financial credit to any emergent Bavarian state. The Bavarian right's opportunity arose soon after Mussolini came to power with the embarrassment to the central German government caused by the occupation of the Ruhr. Although the feared south German disturbances failed to materialize immediately, an agent of Mussolini was in Munich to "sound out certain plans in connection with the Ruhr invasion."[57] But as long as Bavaria did not explode in insurrection, Mussolini was able to avoid showing his hand openly.

Yet there existed one Bavarian nationalist faction which, if not disposed to take advantage of the Ruhr crisis at once, was prepared in its own good time to exploit German confusion in 1923. This, of course, was the Nazi party, which flattered Mussolini by calling itself Fascist. Moreover, Tedaldi had singled out the Nazis as the only Bavarian right-wing group ready to write off the Alto Adige in payment for Italian support, a stand made perfectly plain in the Nazi press.[58] Even before Mussolini had gained power, Hitler began to lay the foundation for a bargain on these terms.[59] In September 1922 Kurt Ludecke was sent to Rome, where, using General Ludendorff's name to effect an introduction, he met Mussolini at the office of the *Popolo d'Italia*. The two men found themselves in fundamental agreement on political philosophy, and Mussolini seized the opportunity to insist that the Alto Adige remain Italian for strategic reasons. Told of this interchange, Hitler

[57] G.D., 5272H/2582/325762.

[58] C. Latour, *Südtirol und die Achse Berlin-Rom* (Stuttgart, 1962), pp. 15-18; W. Pese, "Hitler und Italien, 1920-1926," *Vierteljahrshefte für Zeitgeschichte*, III (April 1955), 123-24.

[59] De Felice, *Mussolini: Il fascista*, I, p. 234, holds that Mussolini's first contacts with the Nazis were during his trip to Germany in March 1922.

expressed himself ready to pay the price for Italian support.[60]

Having prepared the ground, Hitler sought to reap the harvest as he planned the putsch that took place in November 1923. In September Ludecke was again sent to Italy, charged with getting out of Mussolini whatever he could, but particularly money. Mussolini proved much less accessible this time, and Ludecke was passed on to his *chef de cabinet*, Barone Russo, who, as a representative of non-Fascist Italian officialdom, was unlikely to go along with a subversive German group. Ludecke received "no help or special commitment."[61] Ludecke's account is probably truthful, if only because there would seem to be no motive for not telling the truth. The German embassy in Rome, estimating Mussolini as "too clever to compromise himself," also acquitted Fascism of complicity in the Munich putsch.[62] Further, the only official Italian document on the events of November 8-9 in Munich that we possess—a factual report to Mussolini by the Italian consul, Count Ercole Durini di Monza—ends with a scornful disparagement of the plotters and the comment: "In this respect, permit me to recall the 'monosyllabic' definition which Your Excellency bestowed on these worthies on the occasion of my recent visit to Rome: 'clowns' [*buffoni*], a definition with which I agree, as then, but even more fully than ever today."[63] Unless Mussolini was dissembling before the consul, which seems unlikely, his label for Hitler and Hitler's associates hardly betokens a Fascist involvement in the beer-hall putsch.

On the other hand, politicians have been known to conspire with those they despised, either to exploit them or to prepare for the day when such "clowns" gained power. There are ample indications that Italy was not so innocent

[60] K. Ludecke, *I Knew Hitler* (New York, 1937), pp. 65-73, 76-78.
[61] *Ibid.*, pp. 134-35, 140-43.
[62] G.D., 529K/4154/151953; 5272H/2582a/326512-13.
[63] *DDI*, II, No. 474.

as appearances suggest. Apparently some Nazis counted on help from Mussolini, for in January 1925 the Italian legation in Bern reported rumors of a Nazi plot against him because he had not delivered assistance in November 1923 as expected.[64] Undoubtedly this concerned a Nazi group acting unofficially, for the Nazi hierarchy was consistently friendly to Mussolini. But it does suggest that Mussolini might have engaged in the beer-hall putsch in a way Ludecke was unaware of. Ludecke himself testifies that a faction within the Nazi party worked against him, presumably to exclude him from Hitler's inner council. It seems fairly clear that Ludecke was not the only, nor perhaps the most important, Nazi envoy to Mussolini before the Munich putsch. Certainly his enemies succeeded in getting him a prison sentence in March 1923; at precisely this time Neurath reported an overture to Mussolini by an unspecified Nazi agent in Rome.[65] Filippo Anfuso, who was to be Mussolini's last ambassador in Berlin, writes in his memoirs of "emissaries bearing verbal messages" between Hitler and Mussolini in 1923, and cites a list of names besides that of Ludecke.[66]

On the subject of clandestine agents, the most interesting information comes from a public airing of the matter six years after the putsch. In 1929 Hitler successfully prosecuted a libel suit against some south German leftist journals which had accused him of accepting Italian Fascist money in 1923 in return for soft-pedaling the Alto Adige issue. The verdict was appealed on the grounds that fresh evidence had been uncovered. This was the testimony of a journalist, Werner Abel, who claimed to have introduced Hitler in 1923 to a Captain Migliorati attached to the Ital-

[64] De Felice, *Mussolini: Il fascista*, I, p. 234.

[65] Ludecke, *I Knew Hitler*, pp. 105-106, 111-19; G.D., 529K/4154/151953.

[66] Anfuso, *Da Palazzo Venezia al Lago di Garda* (Rocca San Casciano, 1957) p. 34.

ian embassy in Berlin. Abel contended that Migliorati had admitted to him conveying Fascist money for the putsch. On the deposition of this information, the libel appeal suit was suspended while Migliorati was sought. At the same time Hitler lodged an indictment for perjury against Abel.[67] Migliorati was unearthed in New York, where, in a legal office serving as an adjunct to the German consulate and in Abel's presence, he admitted his earlier acquaintance with Abel but denied carrying Italian funds to Hitler. This denial he agreed to repeat under oath in a German court.[68] But when the Abel case came before the Munich courts again in June 1932, Migliorati did not appear, although his New York deposition denying Abel's charge was read out. The earlier judgment of libel was upheld, and on the count of perjury Abel received three years' hard labor.[69]

Of more importance than the verdict itself were the circumstances and conduct of the trial, which indicate that justice was not served. When the defense called Kurt Ludecke to the stand, the wrong Ludecke was produced. The real Ludecke, who was in the United States during the trial, learned only later from Alfred Rosenberg that his name had been mentioned. His version of Rosenberg's statement is calculated to raise further suspicion about Abel's trial: " 'Another ramification of that old story about Hitler's being in foreign pay. A very delicate affair. You know, of course,'—this in a voice of veiled irony, accompanied by a suggestive smile—'that Hitler has declared in court that he never received foreign pay from any source and never even asked for it.' "[70] Another peculiarity of the Abel trial was the fact that Hitler refused to submit to direct interrogation by a Jewish defense lawyer, a refusal that was

[67] *Berliner Tageblatt*, May 7, 8, 14, 1929; Feb. 4, 5, 6, 1930.
[68] *New York Times*, Dec. 17, 1930.
[69] *Berliner Tageblatt*, June 7, 8, 9, 14, 1932.
[70] Ludecke, *I Knew Hitler*, p. 401.

upheld by the court.[71] The harsh punishment meted out
to Abel was a political, not a legal, act. In Salvemini's
words: "A political sentence involving a man of Hitler's
stamp, in a country as frenzied as Germany in 1932, is of
scant value."[72] In this connection, Hitler's own words, "I
am ready to commit perjury half-a-dozen times a day!"
have been quoted to good effect.[73] Mussolini kept a discreet
silence throughout the case, although the Italian press, by
now a captive of the Fascist government, axiomatically assumed the falsity of all tales of Hitler-Mussolini collaboration.[74] Nothing more was forthcoming from Abel, for the
Nazis came into power before his prison term was over, and
he met a predictably tragic end at Dachau in 1935. The most
that can be said is that if Abel's story was not proved neither
was it satisfactorily disproved.

One further item of evidence linking Mussolini to the
beer-hall putsch exists. This consists of the revelation by the
Bavarian state commissioner, Gustav von Kahr, at the trial
for his part in the events of November 8-9, 1923, that at
the height of the attempted coup he was congratulated on his
enterprise by Durini, the Italian consul in Munich. From
another source it was established at the trial that Kahr and
the Italian consul had indeed talked together at midnight
on November 8, at which time Kahr criticized Hitler's usur-
pation of the plot and expressed his doubts about its success. But when pressed on the point, Kahr himself experienced a sudden—and for Fascist Italy, convenient—loss of
memory. He could not be certain that he had talked to the
Italian consul at all on November 8, and positively could
not remember being congratulated by the Italian even if

[71] (London) *Times*, June 10, 1932.
[72] Salvemini, *Mussolini diplomatico*, p. 60.
[73] K. Hiller, *Köpfe und Tröpfe* (Hamburg, 1950), p. 327.
[74] See *Messaggero* (Rome), May 8, 1929; and *Corriere della Sera* (Milan), June 10, 1932.

they *had* talked together.[75] In his report to Mussolini on the Munich putsch, found in the Italian foreign ministry files, Durini did not mention a meeting with Kahr. Now he formally denied Kahr's allegation, while De Bosdari assured Stresemann that the story was "absolutely inconceivable."[76] (Coincidentally, Durini was transferred from the spotlight of his Munich post to the Budapest legation.) Italy's protestations of innocence might carry more weight, however, were it not for the fact that at the time they were made Mussolini's party agents, in the wake of the putsch, were, as we shall see, in touch with Kahr, among other south German nationalists, with a view to future collaboration. Moreover, amid all these half-hints and contradictions one is left wondering what possible motive could have prompted Kahr to his indiscretion about the Italian consul's attitude if the tale was not true. If it was true, one may be justly curious about what lay behind the Italian diplomat's unprofessional conduct.

But if Italian Fascism was in fact implicated in Hitler's first bid for power, the tracks were thoroughly covered. It cannot be denied that the circumstantial evidence of Mussolini's complicity falls short of convicting him in any court of history, where innocence is presumed until the contrary is proved conclusively. The absence of an outright case, conjoined with a strong and not irrational suspicion of guilt, would perhaps be best met by the Scottish legal decision of "not proven," a verdict that acquits but not without opprobrium.

No matter what Mussolini's role in the Munich putsch was, the event seems to have kindled, or perhaps rekindled, his faith in the energy and stature of the Bavarian

[75] "Gericht München," "World War II Collection of Seized Enemy Records," Microcopy T-84, National Archives, Washington, D.C., serial 1, roll 2, frames 1647-49, 1654-56.
[76] De Bosdari, "Memorie," *DDI*, III, p. 57, n. 2.

right. This may be assumed from the campaign launched
in early 1924 to reach an accommodation with certain Bavarian rightist circles. De Bosdari's complaints about Mussolini's bypassing the Italian embassy referred not only to
intrigues in Berlin but also to the dispatch of irregular
agents to south Germany. In March 1924 the ambassador
wrote: "There is positive information of frequent re-
unions of secret military and national associations to prepare for future developments. The most important of these
was that of February 5 at Munich in Bavaria, which was
called by Cramon and in which there participated Kahr,
Losta, Erard, an agent of . . . [code not deciphered] etc.,
in order to announce the possibility of Italian support for
a government of the right. From inquiries made by me, it
would appear that such a presumption was based on declarations made in Munich, Bavaria, by Italians visiting
there in recent months and bearing authority as Fascist
party representatives."[77]

As befitted the most forward of the Bavarian right-wing
groups, and the only one to renounce the Alto Adige, the
Nazi party received preferential treatment. After the
Munich putsch, Göring and other prominent Nazis were
granted comfortable asylum in Italy. On his release from
prison, Hitler, in gratitude for these and perhaps other unspecified services rendered, immediately sought an interview with Mussolini. Although the interview was not
granted, there is no doubt that at this point Nazi-Fascist relations were most cordial.[78] In sum, regardless of Mussolini's possible involvement in the Munich putsch of 1923,
the first steps on the road to the Rome-Berlin Axis of the
1930s were taken within a few years of the March on Rome,
and long before the Nazi achievement of power.

[77] *DDI*, III, No. 39.
[78] Anfuso, *Da Palazzo Venezia*, p. 34.

7. Eastern Europe

Fascist Italy and the Little Entente

THE LITTLE ENTENTE, consisting of Czechoslovakia, Rumania, and Yugoslavia, was formed in 1921 to combat revisionism. Had the full extent of Mussolini's collusion with the German nationalists been known, an angry clamor would undoubtedly have risen from Prague, Bucharest, and Belgrade. On the other hand, the Little Entente was directed primarily at any revisionism in the Danube Valley and the Balkans. The vital determinant of Italy's relations with the Little Entente was Mussolini's attitude toward the defeated and irredentist nations, Hungary and Bulgaria. Conceivably Italian discontent with the postwar settlement, subsumed in the Fascist movement, might spill over into alignment with disaffected Hungary and Bulgaria. Such was anticipated gloomily in some Little Entente circles and optimistically in Budapest and Sofia.

Only two weeks after Mussolini came to power Count Stephen Bethlen, the Hungarian premier, made a bid to trade on Italy's latent revisionism. His proposition was for Italian participation in "the financial reconstruction of Hungary and at a later date perhaps even her military reconstruction."[1] However, Hungary's economic position at the time was conditioned by the still open question of reparations. Mussolini made it clear that any Italian favors to Hungary depended on a satisfactory reparations settlement.[2] On the Austrian pattern, no precise reparations bill was ever presented to Hungary. Instead, an international rehabilitation loan was arranged with Mussolini's reluctant acquiescence. Then, over Italian objections administration of the loan was entrusted to the League of Nations. Such dis-

[1] *DDI*, I, No. 115.   [2] *DDI*, I, No. 240.

appointments, although not entirely Hungary's fault, did nothing to commend her to Mussolini during his first year in power. Much the same was true of Bulgaria. Italy at first hoped and tried to exact the maximum of reparations, but was forced to accept much less from the majority on the Reparations Commission, a sequence of events which cast a pall over relations between Rome and Sofia.[3]

But the reparations issue would eventually fade from prominence. A more persistent, and from the viewpoint of Balkan politics more vital, problem was the territorial claims of Hungary and Bulgaria against their neighbors. Here, too, Mussolini started out by giving little comfort to Hungary and Bulgaria. When the French occupied the Ruhr in January 1923, it was feared that the occupation might be followed by other border incursions in imitation of France's action. One of the contemporary alarms had it that Magyar bands were marching on Rumanian Transylvania. Mussolini, who was prone to believe such melodramatic rumors, leaped into action. In short order, he offered Italian troops to patrol the Hungarian-Rumanian frontier, Italian mediation between the antagonists, and his own cautionary advice to Budapest.[4] Nothing came of it, but, significant in the artificial crisis, Italy showed no sympathy for Hungary's claim to her lost Transylvanian lands. Nor did Bulgarian irredentism initially fare better at Mussolini's hands. Bulgaria's territorial ambitions lay in the direction of the Macedonian region of Yugoslavia. Skirmishes on the frontier were constantly reported. Whenever they seemed to approach a flash point, Italy sided with Yugoslavia, laying the blame for the trouble at the door of the government in Sofia, which Mussolini would urge to exercise restraint.[5]

[3] *DDI*, II, No. 114.
[4] *DDI*, I, Nos. 337, 338, and p. 260, n. 1; II, No. 176.
[5] *DDI*, I, Nos. 393, 394; II, Nos. 49, 50, 68, 71, 72.

At one point there was a rumor that Mussolini would become involved in Balkan domestic politics. In June 1923 the Bulgarian peasant leader and premier, Alexander Stambuliski, was overthrown and mysteriously killed. In his diplomacy Stambuliski had shown a preference for Belgrade over Rome; such had been Mussolini's antagonism that Italy was accused of having aided the coup in Sofia. Admittedly the Duce was jubilant over Stambuliski's fall, and was much more at ease with his conservative successors.[6] But there is no evidence that he conspired against the Bulgarian premier; in fact, he seemed to go out of his way to avoid entanglement in Balkan intrigues. For instance, both Bulgaria and Hungary bred their own, indigenous Fascist parties, which understandably looked for aid and comfort to the Italian legations in Sofia and Budapest. But the legations, on instructions from Rome, maintained a formal and aloof position.[7] All in all, Fascist Italy's initial attitude toward Hungary and Bulgaria was nearly all the Little Entente could ask for.

The situation naturally encouraged prospects for serious diplomatic cooperation between Italy and the Little Entente states. Such a rapprochement had been the dream bequeathed by Carlo Sforza, Italy's foreign minister in 1920-21, to Secretary General Contarini and other Palazzo Chigi officials. Their contention was that Italy, like Czechoslovakia, Rumania, and Yugoslavia, was successor to territory of the Habsburg empire and that all successor states had a joint vested interest in preventing the rise of Danubian and Balkan revisionism.

The linchpin of the Little Entente by virtue of economic and military superiority was Czechoslovakia. Therefore an Italian rapprochement with Czechoslovakia was a prerequisite to one with the Little Entente as a whole. (By con-

---

[6] *DDI*, II, Nos. 83, 87; G.D., 2784H/1385/537425.
[7] *DDI*, I, No. 580; II, No. 302; III, Nos. 183, 219.

177

trast, an Italo-Yugoslav reconciliation, which came about when the Fiume problem was resolved, was no guarantee of friendly relations between Rome and the other Little Entente members.) So it was to Prague that the Contarini faction looked to fulfill Sforza's goal of a league of succession states. They were seconded in their efforts by Vladimir Kybal, the Czech minister in Rome and a strong proponent of Italo-Czech agreements.

But if Contarini and Kybal were of one persuasion, the diplomatic strongmen in Rome and Prague were of another. Mussolini and Beneš, the Czech premier, developed a hearty dislike of each other, derived largely from their respective ideological positions. Mussolini in the 1920s was an exemplar of nationalism in foreign policy and domestic authoritarianism, while Beneš was an admirer of Wilsonian internationalism and the main representative of parliamentary democracy in central Europe. Neither man was reticent in claiming to be a universal spokesman for his particular creed. Such personal and symbolic differences obstructed from the beginning any attempt to achieve an Italo-Czech rapprochement.

An effort to bring together the Prague government and the Fascist regime in Rome got under way in the summer of 1923. Beneš visited the Italian capital to discuss central European matters. Unfortunately this took place only three days before Italian warships bombarded Corfu and Mussolini began his defiant campaign to exclude the League of Nations from the Italo-Greek dispute. Such conduct did not sit well with Beneš, who was a prominent figure at Geneva. Nor could he be expected two weeks later to condone Italy's sudden dispatch of General Giardino to Fiume, which put pressure on his Yugoslav partner in the Little Entente to cede the town. In the first instance, then, Mussolini's Adriatic policy divided Italy and Czechoslovakia.[8]

[8] Kybal, *Journal of Central European Affairs*, XIII (1953-54), 364-65.

178

Eventually, however, Italy's success in Fiume prompted the Czechs to abandon their aloof hostility. The conjunction of the Pact of Rome with the Fiume settlement was a clear indication that Yugoslavia, at least for the moment, put a premium on Italian friendship and discounted her position in the Little Entente. To preserve the solidarity of the Little Entente, therefore, Czechoslovakia had to find some way to counter the Pact of Rome. Prague first tried to join the pact in order to neutralize its effect. When this was refused, Czechoslovakia was forced into the alternative course of demonstrating that the pact was not a stark shift in Yugoslav policy because relations between Italy and the Little Entente were cordial, and friendship with both was compatible. This was not true at the time of the Pact of Rome, but it could become so if an Italo-Czech accommodation were speedily reached. In the early months of 1924 the Contarini-Kybal faction came to the fore and set to work again.

The formal initiative came from the Czech side when Beneš proposed another visit to Rome.[9] Mussolini remained somewhat passive, waiting to see how much Czechoslovakia would be willing to pay for an accord. On the other hand, the Duce was not averse to lending some encouragement, although he preferred to see an economic agreement precede a political pact. Czech financial obligations to Italy on account of liberation costs had been a point of discord between the two states since the end of World War I. Although inflexibly set against their cancellation, as Prague desired, Rome was now willing to consider a flexible payment schedule.[10] Also, an Italo-Czech commercial treaty, pending for some time, was finally settled in March and signed in May.[11]

[9] *DDI*, III, No. 31.
[10] *DDI*, III, No. 5.
[11] Kybal, *Journal of Central European Affairs*, XIV (1954), 71.

These economic achievements had only a modest influence on the forthcoming political negotiations. The fundamental problem of the nature of the proposed Italo-Czech pact was still unresolved. Beneš purportedly wanted a precise, firm agreement, "un accordo distinto," in the words of Count Bonifacio Pignatti, the Italian minister in Prague. But it was difficult to say what it would consist of. The natural meeting ground for Italy and Czechoslovakia was opposition to Habsburg and Hohenzollern restoration and imperialism, but these were remote, formless dangers in 1924. Not surprisingly, many Italians suspected that Beneš was still plotting to transform the Pact of Rome into an accord *à trois*. Pignatti advised Mussolini, therefore, "to greet overtures by Beneš with great reserve."[12] Contarini, still avid for an understanding with Czechoslovakia, tried to prevent or delay the Duce's perusal of such warnings from Prague.[13] But Mussolini was skeptical without prompting. Expectations diminished further when, a week before Beneš was due in Rome, it was made known that Kybal, one of the architects of the putative Italo-Czech détente, was soon to be transferred from the Rome legation despite his indignant protests.[14]

It was an unpropitious atmosphere for Beneš who reached Rome on May 10 and talked with Contarini and Mussolini. We do not know exactly what took place, although Kybal has supplied a general account.[15] Apparently the negotiations turned on the Italian demand to learn the contents of any treaty to which Czechoslovakia was a party. In January 1924, partly in response to the Pact of Rome, Czechoslovakia had signed a military alliance with France. Although the treaty was obviously directed first against Germany, rumors arose, chiefly from the Hungarians, that it contained secret clauses intended to check "any foolish am-

---

[12] *DDI*, III, No. 178.   [13] *DDI*, III, No. 182.
[14] Kybal, *Journal of Central European Affairs*, XIV (1954), 73.
[15] *Ibid.*, pp. 73-76.

180

bition of Italy toward the Serb-Croat-Slovene state."[16] Almost certainly these suspicions were ill-founded; nonetheless, they lay behind Italy's demand. When Beneš refused to give the information, all chance of a concrete Italo-Czech accord vanished. A "pact of cordial collaboration" did, in fact, emerge from the exchanges, and was signed on July 5, but it was, in Kybal's phrase, a "rather anemic" document that did no more than reaffirm the parties' attachment to the postwar settlement in central Europe and to joint consultation in the future. To all intents, then, the attempt to overcome personal and ideological divisions failed.

The member of the Little Entente intrinsically best disposed to Italy was Rumania. Unlike Czechoslovakia, postwar Rumania lived under a monarchy and fairly autocratic form of government. On ideological grounds ruling circles in Bucharest admired rather than deplored Italy's Fascist experiment. Unlike Yugoslavia, Rumania was geographically distant enough from Italy so that territorial and expansionist ambitions did not overlap. In addition, there existed something of a cultural tie between Italy and Rumania in that both were generic Latin societies. In this sense, Ionel Bratianu, the Rumanian premier, held that his country "should be for Italy a bridge with the Little Entente and Slavic world."[17]

But there was a more immediate reason for Rumania to cultivate Italian friendship. Rumania was concerned about holding on to those lands acquired at the close of World War I; the backing of Mussolini's regime was important but uncertain. First, Bucharest feared that Fascism would be drawn into the Hungarian revisionist campaign to recover that part of Transylvania presently in Rumanian hands. Second, although Rumania had acquired de facto possession of Bessarabia from Russia at the end of the war, international recognition of the transfer of territory was

16 *DDI*, ii, No. 545.   17 *DDI*, i, No. 423.

slow in coming. By a protocol of October 1920, Britain, France, Italy, and Japan had accorded recognition, but the agreement was not valid until ratified by three of the four signatories. Britain ratified in 1922 and France in 1924; Japan did not want to affront Russia with ratification for the sake of picking up European friends that were of no use in the Far East. Therefore Italy's ratification was crucial, and was still pending at the time of the March on Rome.

With Transylvania and Bessarabia clearly in mind, Rumanian Foreign Minister Ion Duca hastened to Rome only a few weeks after Mussolini took office to confer with him and Contarini. Immediately after his return to Bucharest at the end of January 1923, he proposed an Italo-Rumanian "political accord."[18] In Rome there was no sign of an inclination to line up firmly against Hungary and Russia, which a political accord would essentially entail. At least, if Italy was to give up freedom of action, she was not going to do so for nothing. Mussolini's formula, that a political agreement should be preceded by economic cooperation, both postponed a treaty and defined its price. Specifically Italy asked for a prominent role in the exploitation of the newly opened oil fields in Rumania. Then, for good measure, Mussolini added a demand for preferential treatment for Italian holders of certain Rumanian treasury bonds recently consolidated. Again the Duce was trying to repay Italy's financial community for the support it gave his regime.[19]

At first Bucharest did not look favorably on these prerequisites for a political treaty; it was even suggested darkly that Italy aspired to an "economic protectorate."[20] But eventually Rumania adopted a more politic tactic of holding out the hope of meeting Italy's economic demands some day. While Vintila Bratianu, the prime minister's brother

[18] *DDI*, I, No. 419.   [19] *DDI*, I, No. 422; II, No. 9.
[20] *DDI*, I, No. 429.

and also minister of finance, maintained a role of tough and uncompromising negotiator, Premier Bratianu himself expatiated amiably, if in general terms, to Baron Pompeo Aloisi, the Italian minister in Bucharest, on the vast opportunities awaiting Italian capital in Rumania.[21]

This elaborate charade was all very well so long as the vague promises to satisfy Italy were not taken too seriously in Rome. However, this is precisely what seems to have happened in March 1924. From hints dropped by the Rumanian premier and the foreign minister and by the Rumanian minister in Rome, Italian officials got the impression that Bucharest was ready "to clear the terrain of pending financial questions"—in particular, to compensate the Italian holders of Rumanian bonds.[22] Whether or not this was a justifiable assumption is impossible to say. On this basis a Rumanian royal visit to Italy was planned, obviously to set the stage for more accords. When it was learned that what the Rumanian government had in mind was nothing more than informal compensation of some individual bondholders by Prince Stirbei, Mussolini called into question the propriety of the royal visit. Rumania's King Ferdinand then canceled his visit while letting it be known that monarchs did not expect their movements to depend on vulgar political considerations.[23] Mutual recriminations abounded, and Mussolini, as usual in affairs involving personal or national good faith, grew blustery.[24] After the storm blew over, the stalemate remained as before; the Rumanians sought political and the Italians economic assurances, with both sides reluctant to equate one set of desiderata with the other.

Up to mid-1924, Fascist Italy's relationship with the Little Entente was ambivalent. On one hand Mussolini had not

21 *DDI*, I, No. 573; II, Nos. 9, 26.
22 *DDI*, III, No. 89.
23 *DDI*, III, Nos. 45, 54-56, 120-21, 139.
24 *DDI*, III, No. 127.

encouraged Danubian and Balkan revisionism. On the other, Italy had not achieved a concrete agreement on outstanding issues with Rumania, the friendliest of the Little Entente members to Rome. Pacts of friendship and collaboration had been signed with Yugoslavia and Czechoslovakia. But there remained some doubt about Mussolini's dedication to a long-term rapprochement with either country. There was particular skepticism about the Italo-Czech pact; it was Prague which tended to set the tone for all of the Little Entente. Thus, although outwardly relations were cordial, between Fascist Italy and the Little Entente there persisted an unmistakable strain.

Recognition of the Soviets

Between 1919 and 1922 Mussolini was accepted by the Italian establishment (and ultimately by Europe at large) as a shield against bolshevism. In those postwar years conservative Western governments tended to display an anti-socialist animus by opposing every Soviet diplomatic maneuver and by endeavoring to keep the regime in Moscow diplomatically isolated. Mussolini might reasonably have been expected to follow this path. But in fact he did not. In the first instance, this can probably be attributed to the influence of his professional diplomats. Contarini, for one, recalled that Italy before 1914 had offset dependence on Britain in the Mediterranean by cultivating Russia's friendship. And Italian diplomacy between 1918 and 1922 had indicated that the change in Moscow from Czar to commissar had not wholly invalidated the principle in the eyes of the foreign ministry. After World War I Italy had refrained from subscribing to Allied support of the White armies in Russia. Nor had Italy joined with Britain and France in signing the treaty recognizing the transfer of Bessarabia from Russia to Rumania. Italy had been among the first European nations to establish trade connections with Soviet Russia, one result of which had been a Russo-Italian exchange of commercial missions in 1921. At Mussolini's accession to power these missions were serving as substitutes for regular diplomatic representation. Within the Italian foreign ministry the sensible view was widely held that Russia was bound to return to the European concert someday and that a prompt and peaceable return by invitation was preferable to a belated reentry by force.[25]

The Lausanne Conference, set for the end of 1922 to arrange a peace settlement with Turkey, offered Fascist Italy an early chance to show goodwill toward the Soviets. Mussolini appeared eager to seize it. So Vatzlav Vorovsky, Soviet Russia's representative in Rome, assured the Soviet commissar for foreign affairs, Giorgi Chicherin, in a telegram that was mysteriously intercepted in Switzerland and then fell into the hands of the Italian delegation at Lausanne.[26] Vorovsky quoted Mussolini as saying: "There is no doubt that at this conference, as at so many others, France and England will come to some agreement between themselves and once more divide the major portion of the booty. Italy cannot tolerate such a situation. Russia is considered a natural ally and, above all, Russian mediation is counted on in separate *pourparlers* between Italy and the Turks." This, of course, was typical Mussolinian hyperbole. To be sure, Italy supported Russia's full participation in the Lausanne Conference, and Mussolini publicly advocated it.[27] On strategic grounds Rome favored the Russian position on the Straits, which would have left them under Turkish control. But to break the united front with Britain and France would have been a daring, even rash, act; as we have seen,

[25] The subtitle of *Vita diplomatica di Contarini* by Legatus is *Italia fra Inghilterra e Russia*; see esp. pp. 94-101. See also Sforza, *L'Italia dal 1914 al 1944*, pp. 119-20.

[26] The Lausanne delegation relayed the telegram to Contarini, perhaps to put the Palazzo Chigi on its guard against possible recklessness by Mussolini (*DDI*, I, No. 321).

[27] *OO*, XIX, 31.

the Palazzo Chigi at the beginning of Mussolini's tenure of office was influential enough to veto it. In the clutch, Italy accepted the exclusion of Russia from the conference, except for discussions restricted to the Straits question, and also accepted the internationalization of the Straits demanded by Britain. The Russo-Italian harmony at Lausanne was confined to nonsubstantive matters and personal relationships. Contarini instructed Guariglia to avoid any step that might upset Britain, but privately to keep in close touch with Vorovsky who was leading the Russian delegation.[28] When Vorovsky was assassinated in May 1923, the Italian delegation proposed an Allied expression of sympathy. When this was turned down by Britain and France, Italy alone conveyed condolences.[29]

The Soviets were not insensitive to Fascist Italy's token gestures of cordiality. Moscow's automatic response to the March on Rome was negative; after all, in the Marxist-Leninist dialectic, Fascism was only an attribute of monopolistic capitalism. Immediately after Mussolini's accession to power Italian commerce in the Black Sea began to feel the weight of this ideological disapproval in the form of petty harassment, in defiance of the trade pact of 1921.[30] However, practical considerations intervened. *Pravda* was often frank in admitting the Soviets' need for Western capital, machinery, and technical knowledge. From this, the head of the Italian trade mission in Moscow, Giovanni Amadori, surmised that were Mussolini to offer himself as a bridge with the West, Moscow would be glad to deal with him, his reputation as an enemy of the proletariat notwithstanding.[31] Furthermore, the Bolsheviks very likely calculated that it was easier to negotiate with an autocratic regime like Mussolini's than with a genuinely democratic one answerable to volatile public opinion. As Vorovsky observed

---

[28] Guariglia, *Ricordi*, p. 25.   [29] *DDI*, II, No. 35.
[30] *DDI*, I, No. 148.   [31] *DDI*, I, Nos. 151, 163.

to Chicherin in the telegram that fell into Italian hands: "Obviously it is simpler for a revolutionary government like that of Mussolini, a government dependent on no one, to come to terms with the Soviet government."[32]

That Soviet Russia and Fascist Italy soon found each other tolerable, even compatible, was evidenced by their efforts in early 1923 to reach a more comprehensive commercial accord than that of 1921. Despite the groundwork laid by Contarini and Vorovsky before his death, however, for a time progress was slow toward a trade pact and a general understanding. At first this seemed attributable to a series of small irritants. Moscow complained that the Soviet economic delegation in Rome was given insufficient protection against attacks by zealous *fascisti*. Mussolini countered with charges of subversion in Italy by Moscow's agency of world revolution, the Comintern, to which the Soviet government replied with its customary disclaimer of responsibility.[33] Then on the resumption of the Lausanne Conference, Moscow chose Mussolini as intermediary to deliver a note of protest at the conditions laid down for Russian admission. But the Italian foreign ministry failed, most likely inadvertently, to deliver the message to the secretary general of the conference; so the Soviet delegation arrived at Lausanne unannounced, and the Swiss refused the Russian courier a diplomatic passport.[34] This was followed by an Italian security leak in which a telegram from Amadori in Moscow, suggesting that Italy break off the Russo-Italian trade negotiations in order to embarrass the Bolshevik regime and further its "liquidation," found its way into the *Manchester Guardian*. The anti-Communist Amadori was hurriedly dismissed, but the episode was an unpleasant reminder of latent ideological differences.[35]

On the other hand, such contretemps hardly constituted

[32] *DDI*, I, No. 321.
[34] *DDI*, II, Nos. 1, 8.
[33] *DDI*, I, Nos. 514, 557.
[35] *DDI*, I, No. 721; II, No. 60.

a permanent obstacle to a Russo-Italian rapprochement. The absolute precondition for this, as Mussolini discovered, was simple: Italian de jure recognition of the Soviet government. Soon after Mussolini's coming to power, Amadori reported that the Soviets gave priority to "the further evolution of political relations." By mid-1923 his successor in Moscow was told plainly that "the Russian government sees neither the necessity nor possibility of reaching a definitive commercial treaty if 'de jure' recognition of the present Russian government by the [Italian] Royal Government has not first been accorded."[36] In effect, Mussolini was asked to lead the way in breaking the West's diplomatic ostracism of Bolshevik Russia. The Soviets had received formal German recognition in 1922, but then, Germany was another outcast. Recognition by Italy, one of the Allies, would be a genuine opening of the door to the West, to a kind of peaceful coexistence, and possibly to Western cooperation in the industrialization of Russia.

This was the sort of opportunity Mussolini was always loath to pass up. To exploit Italy's median position between the Allies and the Soviets in order to reintroduce Russia to Europe would be to attain that dazzling goal of arbitrating among the great powers. On achieving a Russo-Italian rapprochement in 1924, he was to explain:

The Royal Government . . . has been guided above all by the conviction that every move aimed at settling Russia's present international situation and at easing the return of the Russian state and economy to the sphere of world politico-economic activity is, in fact, conducive to general peace and prosperity. . . .

By effectively overcoming considerable difficulties in the way of an accord between two such different economic systems, Italy deserves credit for having been the first

[36] *DDI*, I, No. 185; II, No. 104.

to undertake the study and solution of a difficult question to the benefit of all.[37]

There were other motives. It was calculated in Rome that recognition of Soviet Russia might dispose Moscow to give Italy a free hand in Asia Minor.[37a] Moreover, Mussolini subscribed to the common illusion that the Ukraine would serve as Italy's granary and the Soviets at large as a market for Italian industrial exports.[38] In addition, it has been speculated that, by a rapprochement with the Soviets, Mussolini hoped to rid himself of any internal threat from the Italian Communist party.[39]

In late 1923 Mussolini took the initiative in several diplomatic areas. But in the case of Soviet recognition, he seems in the last resort to have been pushed into action by circumstances. In September Fascist Italy was forced out of Corfu by Britain, acting with tacit French agreement. In contrast, as Mussolini told the Italian parliament, "the only European press sympathetic to Italy in the month of Corfu was the Moscow press." The Corfu affair, then, can scarcely have induced Mussolini to keep up the Allies' united anti-Soviet front merely to please London and Paris. More important, however, in November emerged the prospect that the pending British general election might produce a Labour government; and Labour's program included de jure recognition of the Soviets. Faced with the danger that his arbitral position would be preempted, Mussolini responded promptly on November 30 by announcing in the Chamber of Deputies: "As for the so-called de jure recognition of Russia, there is no difficulty on the part of the Fascist government."[40] Moscow was delighted over the

[37] *DDI*, ii, No. 645.
[37a] G. Carocci, *La politica estera dell'Italia fascista (1925-1928)* (Bari, 1969), p. 62.
[38] *OO*, xx, 198-200.
[39] De Felice, *Mussolini: Il fascista*, i, p. 563.
[40] *OO*, xx, 121-23.

declaration; trade talks, the barometer of Russo-Italian relations, picked up immediately.

The Italian Fascist party agent in Vienna was approached by a Comintern representative and asked to convey to Rome the suggestion that the détente be extended to a secret alliance of Russia, Italy, and Germany.[41] Apparently the overture came not from the Soviet government, but from a Trotskyite faction within it, and nothing developed. Italy, nevertheless, paid deference to the hypothesis of a Russo-Italo-German triangle. Gaetano Paternò, the Italian commercial representative in Moscow, kept the influential German ambassador, Count Brockdorff-Rantzau, closely informed of the impending Russo-Italian rapprochement and even requested Germany's good offices to offset suspected French moves against it.[42] But Germany was cool to the idea, and Mussolini was forced to turn to the British Labour government for support against France.

Both London and Rome required Soviet assurances about trade before proceeding to actual recognition. Both saw that to compete for Russia's favor, especially by promising to be the first to grant recognition, would be to give Moscow a strong bargaining advantage. Therefore on January 27, 1924 Italy agreed to an understanding with the new British Labour government to act *pari passu* in the recognition question. By this Mussolini was obligated not only to match the timing of Italy's recognition to that of Britain, but also to send no more than a chargé d'affaires to Moscow, although earlier Mussolini had led the Soviets to expect a full ambassador. The insistence on a chargé was patently a device by Labour to mollify the British conservative establishment. Whitehall's rationalization to Della Torretta was that an ambassadorial appointment should be held in reserve as a prize which Russia might at-

[41] *DDI*, II, No. 517.
[42] G.D., 2784H/1385/537563, 537584-85, 537603.

tain by future good behavior, namely, by relaxing Comintern activity. Whatever Mussolini might have thought about British ratiocination, he valued London's cooperation highly enough in this case to accede to its conditions for a common policy toward the Soviets.[43]

Having protected himself by alignment with Britain, Mussolini could reasonably look forward to smooth sailing for his Russian rapprochement. But suddenly, on February 1, Britain's Labour Prime Minister MacDonald, apparently under pressure from his party's left wing, announced his government's recognition of the Soviets without waiting for the conclusion of a trade pact and without consulting Italy.

This was exactly the insensitive disregard for Italian interests and feelings which Italian nationalists claimed was characteristic of Allied diplomacy since 1918 and which Mussolini was pledged to stop. At once he informed London that he was resuming liberty "to act in further Russo-Italian relations in the way in which I shall judge most useful to Italian interests."[44] Then he set about convincing the world in general and Moscow in particular that Italy had in fact recognized the Soviets before Britain. This had been accomplished, he asserted, by his own remarks on January 31 to the final plenary session of the Russo-Italian commission which was negotiating a trade pact.[45] Such a claim was an obvious ploy to save face, but it was also a reply to the Soviet deputy commissar for foreign affairs, Maxim Litvinov, who on at least one occasion had threatened to hold up a commercial treaty if Italian recognition did not precede that of Britain.[46] Almost certainly, however, Russia was more impressed by Mussolini's return to his original in-

---

[43] *DDI*, II, Nos. 597, 605.
[44] *DDI*, II, No. 612.
[45] *DDI*, II, No. 618. In this telegram the date of the last meeting of the joint commission is mistakenly given as January 3.
[46] *DDI*, II, p. 429, n. 2.

tention for an exchange of diplomatic representatives of ambassadorial rank.

The British sought belatedly to dissuade Italy. Ambassador Graham in Rome and Sir Eyre Crowe, undersecretary at the Foreign Office in London, both apologized for MacDonald's hasty and gauche act of recognition. But Mussolini, now intent on striking his own bargain with Russia, was unmoved.[47] His strategy succeeded, and on February 7 a Russo-Italian commercial accord of the most-favored-nation variety was signed. To the Soviet request for a formal note of recognition, Mussolini gladly complied; he took care to stress that Italy's recognition antedated Britain's by 24 hours. To drive home the point, the Italian note was sent directly to Moscow and not, as originally planned, handed to the Russian delegation at the signing of the trade treaty on February 7, lest it seem that this was the actual date of recognition.[48] The Soviets humored Mussolini; Soviet historians even today contend that Italy was the first among the Allies to offer recognition.[49] To this extent, Mussolini saved face.

The confusion attendant on Italy's recognition of the Soviets was an ominous portent for the future of a Russo-Italian entente. Almost from the start, Mussolini's expectations were disappointed. In company with other states of the West, Italy discovered that the promise of post-recognition trade, especially in grain, was illusory. The commercial agreement of February 7, 1924 required amendment within a few weeks. In discussing it in March before the Council of Ministers, Mussolini was obliged to dwell on its limitations in the investment field. In March 1925 he admitted to parliament that the treaty had not brought

[47] *DDI*, II, Nos. 623, 626.

[48] *DDI*, II, Nos. 630, 631.

[49] V. Potemkin, ed., *Geschichte der Diplomatie* (Moscow, 1945-47), III, 352, the official Soviet view, carefully records that Italy was the first state to announce an intention to recognize.

"startling results."[50] Mussolini fared no better in seeking the other objective of recognition of the Soviets: his dream of mediation between bolshevism and the West. Admittedly Italian and British recognitions of Soviet Russia were followed by a score of others over the next three years, but it was hard to pretend that they were in imitation of Italy and not Britain. No government requested Italian good offices in Moscow.

With these disappointments there was a renewed awareness of the ideological divide between Fascism and bolshevism. Although officials in Rome and Moscow were willing to keep the differences hidden, they were never far below the surface. Quite a few in the Palazzo Chigi, including Contarini, had grown profoundly uncomfortable with Mussolini's Russian policy. Moscow complained that some Italian diplomats, clinging fast to their anti-Bolshevik principles, still held aloof from Soviet representatives. The Vatican, of course, indirectly conveyed its displeasure at the flirtation with bolshevism, and King Victor Emmanuel was perplexed by the whole thing.[51] Mussolini himself, for that matter, evinced considerable alarm over the news that Italian sailors from ships docked in Russian ports were exposed to Communist propaganda.[52] The Russo-Italian rapprochement, then, began to peter out almost as soon as it was achieved. It constituted a rough parallel to the Italo-Czech pact. In neither case did it prove possible to overcome ideological differences and deep-rooted mutual distrust.

[50] *DDI*, III, Nos. 13, 19; *OO*, XX, 198-99; XXI, 319, 337-40.
[51] *DDI*, III, Nos. 17, 104; N. D'Aroma, *Vent'anni insieme: Vittorio Emanuele e Mussolini* (Bologna, 1957), p. 162.
[52] *DDI*, III, No. 432 and note.

8. Fascism Outside Italy:
The United States and France

IT WAS NOT only in relations with Soviet Russia that ideology played a part in early Fascist Italian diplomacy. On more than one occasion Mussolini confessed his true métier to be that of a journalist, which was his main career before gaining office. His undeniable successes in political propaganda before and after 1922 were due to his peculiar journalistic talent. Journalism to him was not a means to report and inform dispassionately, but to persuade by sensationalism and by the reduction of issues to simplistic black-and-white terms. Most of his speeches read like a succession of newspaper headlines, full of dogmatic assertions and easy catch-all answers. In other words, he exhibited the rigidity and simplicity of a fanatic ideologue; he was one of the "terrible simplifiers" of recent times. Mussolini's ideology might be intellectually formless, and certainly it changed radically more than once during his career, yet his taste for ideologies as such was undeniable. In 1922 it was an open question whether he would be content to entrench Fascism in Italy alone or whether, using his propagandistic talent, he would attempt to spread Fascist ideas throughout the world.

On coming to power Mussolini stressed publicly that Fascism was "a typically Italian phenomenon," and that "every country has its own problems and its own methods of solving them."[1] But this was dissimulation to conciliate foreign governments. From the start, he ostentatiously pitted Fascism against Marxian socialism—although this was muted during the Italo-Soviet détente of 1923-24—and also against social democracy and the liberal state. His challenge to these movements carried a strong implication of Fascism's relevance beyond Italy.[2]

[1] *OO*, xx, 80, 113.
[2] See, for example, his speeches during the week before the March on Rome (*OO*, xviii, 433-40, 453-59).

In private Mussolini revealed his plans to export Fascist doctrine. The journalist Roberto Cantalupo describes in his memoir, *Racconti politici dell'altra pace*, under the date November 1922, an interview with Mussolini that he obtained through Barone Russo's influence.[3] Asked about his attitude toward Italian emigrants living abroad, Mussolini responded that his plans for them included three phases. First, a general campaign would be undertaken to stimulate a sense of "national sentiment in all the emigrant masses . . . and a strengthening of their ties with the mother country"; but this would be done while "avoiding conflicts with foreign governments and peoples." Stage two would see a shift to emphasis on the "new generations" of emigrants. In the third phase there would be a further concentration on a minority of young emigrants to achieve "the spiritual and cultural penetration of other countries . . . to found, that is, a policy of prestige, and to entrust it to new organisms to be created, suitable for diffusing Italian culture and civilization, commensurate with our increased influence in the world." Vague enough words and ambitions, to be sure, but certain aspects stood out. Mussolini had no intention of permitting Italians abroad to be assimilated into an alien nation. Instead, they were to be agents in a definite program to disseminate Fascism, for by "Italian culture and civilization" the Duce always meant his own Fascist style and mores. He was not deterred by anticipated resistance from the host countries. Cantalupo is not the most reliable witness and may well have embroidered his account of the interview, but at the least, Mussolini's actions were to correspond closely to the program described by Cantalupo.

One instrument by which Mussolini hoped to inculcate Fascism abroad was the network of Fascist clubs outside Italy (*fasci*) established after the March on Rome. To co-

[3] Cantalupo, *Racconti politici dell'altra pace* (Milan, 1940), pp. 302-306.

ordinate their impact a *Segreteria dei fasci all'estero* was instituted in Rome and first entrusted to Giuseppe Bastianini. Almost immediately Bastianini was impatient to embark on an international ideological crusade, arguing that "the *fasci* of Europe are mature enough to pass from their organizational to their political stage."[4]

But in Europe generally, although there was considerable sympathy for Italian Fascism, there was in the 1920s little disposition to adopt its formulas. Rather, North America offered more fertile soil for Fascist propaganda. While Mussolini spoke to other European nations as an Italian and a foreigner, he was able to address himself to fellow Italians in the United States. For there resided a sizable, newly arrived Italian population that was still emotionally attached to the home country. Mussolini's pledge to rejuvenate Italy made a strong appeal in these circles, as illustrated by the foundation of Fascist clubs and transformation of some older Italo-American societies into *fasci* in the months after Mussolini reached power. The situation offered positive encouragement to propagate Fascist ideas. At home Mussolini's strength lay in his ability to fuse nationalist and Fascist principles; in the United States an appeal to *italianità* would amount to a call for Fascism. Thus the United States was given prime attention, or so we may assume from a file in Mussolini's propaganda ministry (*Ministero della cultura popolare*) which fell into Allied hands at the end of World War II. Entitled "Miscellaneous Documents Taken from Files on the United States 1920-27," it deals almost exclusively with the dissemination of Fascist doctrine through the American *fasci*. In addition, it reveals the reaction of Italy's diplomats to Mussolini's ideological foreign policy.

From the start the *fasci* were a bone of contention between Mussolini and the Italian embassy in Washing-

[4] It.D. (Mussolini's private secretariat), 286/1200/087176.

ton. The ambassador, Gelasio Caetani, in the fashion of the pre-Fascist diplomats who served Mussolini, sought to impose his own caution on his foreign minister. Early in 1923 he observed that the *fasci* were being depicted in the Hearst press as haunts of criminal and subversive elements, and their unsavory reputation used to justify American discrimination against Italian immigrants. Inasmuch as the *fasci* were regarded as the Mussolini government's responsibility, criticism of their activities could only hurt Italy in the pending question of funding her American war debt. Caetani, then, warned emphatically against a campaign to spread "national Fascist doctrine" among Italo-Americans by "Fascist officials in Italy or any highly placed personage unaware of the delicacy of the situation here, and ignorant of the American psychology which is profoundly hostile to any foreign pressure." If Rome had to tamper in the situation at all, Caetano recommended, it should be to impose restraint and transform the *fasci* from political into cultural societies.[5] Opposing these prudent counsels and painting a rosier picture of Fascist prospects in the United States were the party enthusiasts on both sides of the Atlantic. Their reports to the Italian foreign ministry and the *Segreteria dei fasci all'estero* listed nearly 40 North American *fasci* in mid-1923, and a year later claimed that "Fascism in America is at its most favorable juncture." The chief difficulty, according to these party "questori in missione," lay in "the more or less open hostility" to the American *fasci* of the Italian diplomats in general and the "inexplicably poor attitude" of the ambassador in Washington in particular.[6]

Although undoubtedly this latter view predominated in Rome, for the time being lip service was paid to Caetani's

[5] It.D. (Ministry of Popular Culture), 31/429/014592-96, 014630, 014606-11.

[6] It.D. (Ministry of Popular Culture), 31/429/014665-70, 014713-19, 014735-36.

concern. Twice in 1923 the Fascist Grand Council commanded the *fasci all'estero* to forswear politics in favor of "activity of a spiritual and moral nature," and to respect the authority of Italy's diplomatic representatives. Furthermore, the council denied any connection between the *fasci* and either the Mussolini government or the *Partito nazionale fascista*.[7] But this moderation was only the public face of Fascism. On the heels of the Grand Council pronouncements came a confidential circular from the *Segreteria dei fasci all'estero* reasserting its own strict control over the American Fascist clubs—recently proclaimed policy to the contrary—and carrying a clear intent to use them as a propaganda weapon. Ambassador Caetani characterized this as "an act of duplicity to the hospitable United States nation," and foresaw dire diplomatic complications if the directive should fall into American hands.[8] In the imprecise circumstances created by conflicting instructions, the Italian diplomats in the United States tried to stay aloof from the *fasci*.[9] But frequently an Italian consul would deem the activities of the local *fascio* unduly provocative, and impose a restraining hand. Not surprisingly, the smoldering hostility between a cautious bureaucratic class and exuberant party zealots burst into the open in a dozen places in the United States.[10] So for most of two years the Fascist propaganda campaign in North America proceeded in disorganized and spasmodic fashion.

In the meantime the Duce's concept of Fascism's role outside Italy threatened to make an issue of the Italian anti-Fascists who fled abroad, chiefly to France. It was only nat-

---

[7] *OO*, XIX, 141-42, 337-38.

[8] It.D. (Ministry of Popular Culture), 31/429/014696-700.

[9] *DDI*, IV, No. 204.

[10] It.D. (Ministry of Popular Culture), 31/429/014728-32. An unusually bitter dispute developed between the consul and *fascio* in Boston (It.D. [Ministry of Popular Culture], 014773-80, 014785-87, 014790-93).

ural for those who escaped or were expelled from Mussolini's Italy to head for Paris. The cultural affinity of France
and Italy meant that they could live and work in the French
capital with a minimum change in social habits. Moreover,
the Italian exiles, who were mostly to the left politically,
were especially warmly received by the French socialists and
radicals who, out of their French Revolutionary tradition,
tended to assume the moral leadership of all European
campaigns against right-wing forces such as Italian Fascism. So Paris, long the haven of Europe's political refugees, became the rendezvous of Mussolini's enemies.

At first, Mussolini pretended to be unmoved by the exiles'
criticism and activity; he referred to them derisively as
fuorusciti—outsiders; the emigrés, most of whom were proud
to be "outside," thereupon adopted the name. Actually, as
early as 1923 Mussolini was agitated enough to warn the
French government against allowing them license. "To
strive to defame the Fascist party movement means, today,
to seek to defame the Italian state and nation," he wrote
portentously in January, and later in the year: "Every offense against Fascism comes by definition to constitute an
offense against the Fascist nation state."[11]

Mussolini went even further; he dispatched agents to
France to keep an eye on the *fuorusciti*, a move that was
fraught with trouble for Franco-Italian relations. This was
illustrated in March 1924 when Nicola Bonservizi, the
chief Fascist agent in France, was murdered on the terrace
of a Paris café by an anarchist *fuoruscito*. Bonservizi had
been a confidant of Mussolini who was understandably disturbed. But Poincaré refused to be drawn into a quarrel
about French police methods of treating the *fuorusciti*.
The assassin was caught and tried in a French court, where
he received an eight-year sentence.[12] By the time of the

---

[11] *DDI*, I, No. 310; II, No. 68.
[12] *DDI*, III, No. 152; Delzell, *Mussolini's Enemies*, p. 46.

trial, however, Fascist Italy was convulsed by another political crime, this time involving the disappearance of the Socialist deputy, Giacomo Matteotti.[13] Largely because it was overshadowed by the Matteotti affair, the Bonservizi murder case did not develop into a cause célèbre; nevertheless, the portents were ominous. Mussolini's concern to promote and protect Fascist groups and ideas abroad was hardly orthodox diplomatic activity. In the long run, it could hardly fail to embroil Fascist Italy in international controversy.

[13] See Chap. 11.

9. The Western Mediterranean, France, and Spain

Tunisia and Tangier

FASCIST ideology and the *fuorusciti* were potential hazards in Franco-Italian relations. Of more immediate concern during the second stage of early Fascist diplomacy were questions related to the Mediterranean Sea. As Mussolini started to formulate his own foreign policy in late 1923 and early 1924 his prime attention was clearly directed—via the Adriatic—to the Mediterranean; Corfu and Fiume pointed the way. Predictably rivalry with other Mediterranean powers began to increase. When Mussolini turned to the western end of the Mediterranean, in particular, he found himself opposing France on a number of points.

One contentious matter long antedated the March on Rome—the Italians living in Tunisia. Tunisia, by soil and climate a virtual extension of southern Italy across the Mediterranean, was a natural outlet for Italy's surplus population. Emigration had been unchanged by France's seizure of Tunisia under Italy's nose in 1881; at the end of the First World War there were more Italians than French in Tunisia, about 110,000.[1] Their status was regulated by three conventions, dated 1896, which guaranteed the right to maintain Italian nationality and operate Italian schools, hospitals, clubs, and so on. But in September 1918 France arbitrarily abrogated two of the conventions, then proceeded to renew them at three-month intervals. The precariousness of Italian rights was increased in 1921 when a series of French nationality decrees proclaimed that any child born of residents in a French colony was ipso facto a

[1] French and Italian estimates of the Italian population in Tunisia varied; see Salvemini, *Mussolini diplomatico*, p. 117.

citizen of France. These would automatically apply to Italians in Tunisia if ever Paris let the 1896 conventions lapse at the end of a three-month period. For good measure France launched a campaign of discrimination, largely economic, against non-French residents of Tunisia. It was not as severe as the Italian community pretended; nonetheless it was onerous enough. Any attack on the concept of *italianità* could provoke only one response from Mussolini; the Italians of Tunisia were exhorted by all the organs of Fascist propaganda to preserve their national heritage.

The argument could be reduced to simple terms. Italy contended that the special status of her nationals in Tunisia was due by virtue of the 1896 conventions until they were disavowed or renegotiated by both parties. This the French denied, holding that Rome would have to buy privileges for its expatriates by concessions in other fields. The divergence of interpretations was always present in the twenties to wreck a succession of efforts to find a permanent accommodation. On occasion either Rome or Paris, finding itself in some diplomatic embarrassment, was constrained to move some way toward accepting the other's position. But invariably, sooner or later, either Italy or France would overcome the temporary diplomatic weakness and revert to an obdurate stand on Tunisian rights.

Mussolini came to power with Italy in a superficially favorable position. France's attitude toward German reparations, which soon culminated in the gamble of the Ruhr invasion, promised unforeseen complications and some degree of diplomatic isolation. In the words of Ambassador Romano Avezzana in Paris: "If then the [Ruhr] conflict . . . is to be protracted, I think we might profit from this by seeking to settle with France some of our more important issues . . . like Tunisia and equality of treatment in the colonial field." On the other hand, although some concession in Tunisia might be wrung from France, the price would surely be exacted in the German question. Romano Avezzana wrote: "There is no doubt that to the word Tunisia, Poincaré would reply with the word Ruhr."[2] But this was the one area where Italy was not disposed to compensate France. After initial support in January 1923 to ensure supplies of Ruhr coal, Italy drifted steadily away from the French position on reparations. Therefore Romano Avezzana recommended caution, and for a few months his advice was heeded in Rome.

However, Mussolini's more intemperate spirit prevailed when he began to assert himself in foreign affairs in the summer of 1923. He was incited to action in July on learning that London had obtained a separate settlement for British nationals resident in French colonies, while Paris was simultaneously proposing to fortify France's recent nationality decrees by enacting them into parliamentary legislation. At once the Duce directed Romano Avezzana to approach Poincaré without circumlocution: "If the French government reciprocates, as I should like to believe, my active desire that the continuation of good relations between the two countries should not be seriously compromised, it is necessary to act in such a way as to give proof at once that such a [nationality] law is not directed against Italy. It seems to me that the only efficacious way is to proceed immediately to a renewal of the convention[s] of 1896 for a period of not less than ten years. In any case we must maintain a constant reserve against the French right to legislate in this matter."[3]

Romano Avezzana found the French premier in an affable mood. Poincaré promised at least to delay new nationality legislation, and, more important, "not to denounce the existing accord, considering it better counsel to leave things as they are and await the propitious mo-

[2] *DDI*, I, No. 417; II, No. 117.
[3] *DDI*, II, No. 130.

ment to find a solution satisfactory to both countries." Rome responded to this gratifying statement by offering to settle by way of a temporary modus operandi for a 5-year rather than a 10-year renewal of the 1896 conventions. But it was also plain that Poincaré's fair words were meant to put Italy off until France had stabilized the Ruhr situation. So Romano Avezzana was instructed "to reach without delay a definitive solution of the delicate problem."[4] But when Poincaré refused categorically to entertain any thought of renewing the 1896 conventions longer than three months, Romano Avezzana suggested a brand new approach. Paris would exempt the present and next generations of Italians in Tunisia from French nationality laws, and Rome would recognize that third-generation Italians 40 or 50 years hence should be automatically French. This principle of delayed nationality was to run through future negotiations on Tunisia until it became the basis of a solution more than 10 years later. In the summer of 1923 Poincaré did not reject the notion out of hand, but asked for time to ponder it.[5] On the other hand, it is not entirely clear to what extent Romano Avezzana's proposal had Mussolini's backing, and how much the ambassador acted on his own initiative or that of the old guard at the Palazzo Chigi. The Duce did not formally disavow Romano Avezzana, but he did ask him to come to Rome for consultation.[6]

During the ambassador's return to Rome the Corfu crisis broke. Romano Avezzana hurried back to Paris where all his energies for the next few weeks were engaged by the crisis. More important, France helped Italy circumvent the League of Nations in the Corfu crisis; after it was over, she expected to be repaid for her "clear and loyal" support. Romano Avezzana discovered this when he took up the subject of Tunisia again with Poincaré in late 1923.

[4] *DDI*, II, Nos. 134, 135.   [5] *DDI*, II, No. 173.
[6] *DDI*, II, No. 175.

Poincaré, "in his worst humor," declared that "he was not disposed to adopt an attitude of surrender." He went on to threaten an abrogation of the 1896 conventions if a new and definitive settlement was not reached within six months. On further inquiry in Paris, Romano Avezzana found other French officials more congenial than Poincaré. They let it be known that the French government and even Poincaré was prepared to consider a Tunisian settlement based on delayed nationality, in return for "some manifestation of a political character guaranteeing to France a benevolent attitude on Italy's part in case of a European conflict."[7]

On the face of it, this was a restatement of the Ruhr-Tunisian bargain Romano Avezzana had warned against. But by early 1924 the Ruhr crisis had lost its intensity; probably of as much immediate concern to Poincaré was the Pact of Rome, which threatened to take Yugoslavia out of the French orbit. To get rid of this danger France hoped to be admitted to the pact; this was likely to be a prominent item in Poincaré's bill for what he regarded as a Tunisian concession. Romano Avezzana found much to commend in Poincaré's suggestion. There was no longer much danger of an unwise specific Italian commitment in the Ruhr, and a general agreement between Italy and France would encourage the latter "to fulfill her function of barrier to Germanism in its drive toward the Mediterranean."[8] In the matter of the Balkans, Romano Avezzana, like most of the Palazzo Chigi officials who followed Sforza's example, saw a Franco-Italian rapprochement as complementary to an accord between Italy and Yugoslavia. Hence there could be no objection to French adherence to the Pact of Rome. But the drift of Mussolini's foreign policy was in the opposite direction. His method of warding off German nationalism was to soothe it and turn it against France, while

7 *DDI*, II, Nos. 507-509, 603.   8 *DDI*, II, No. 604.

the Pact of Rome was for him an exclusive agreement deliberately aimed at injuring France in the Balkans. The result was something of a compromise. Romano Avezzana was to inform Paris that the mere postponement of the application of French nationality laws to Italians in Tunisia did not warrant payment in the form of a comprehensive agreement. Italy would be glad to oblige France "in minor continental questions," and a general accord might follow a Tunisian settlement in due course. But the sine qua non of any progress was France's renewal of the 1896 conventions for a certain number of years ("un periodo più o meno lungo").[9]

Of course, this left Poincaré free to execute his threat to abrogate the conventions. Yet in the event, although repeating his refusal to renew them, even for three years, he withdrew his threat of arbitrary cancellation. In fact, this danger was not as great as it might seem at first sight. Early in 1924 it became apparent that Poincaré's government, faced with the failure of its Ruhr policy, was on its way out, and was likely to be replaced by a cabinet less nationalistic and responsive to the French colonial lobby. Certainly in Rome, the impending fall of Poincaré was regarded as creating "a particularly favorable political moment" in which to press for negotiations on Tunisia.[10] Up to a point this calculation was correct. French elections in May 1924 put in office a left-wing coalition, the *Cartel des gauches*. But before Rome could try to take advantage of the change, Italy entered upon a new diplomatic phase amid circumstances that made it difficult or even impossible to seize any initiative. The Tunisian stalemate was to plague Franco-Italian relations for many years.

[9] This account of Italy's attitude is drawn from a directive to Romano Avezzana found in the Palazzo Chigi files, which apparently was never sent (*DDI*, III, p. 39, n. 1). Nonetheless, Romano Avezzana acted along the lines indicated.

[10] *DDI*, III, No. 110.

Tangier was another source of discord between Paris and Rome; in many ways it complemented the quarrel over Tunisia. In both Tangier and Tunisia the French strenuously resisted Italian claims, giving rise to mortification and indignation on the part of nationalists and Fascists in Rome.

Due primarily to its strategic position at the entrance to the Mediterranean, Tangier traditionally was regarded as a problem distinct from its Moroccan hinterland. The city's special status had been recognized in the international Act of Algeciras of 1906. In 1912 the proclamation of Moroccan protectorates by France and Spain appeared to threaten Tangier's independence. Largely at Britain's insistence, a conference was called to draft a new international statute for Tangier, but it made little progress before World War I came. After the war the powers had more pressing concerns than Tangier, until 1923 when plans for a new conference were devised.

Although all the signatories of the Act of Algeciras had a legal claim to be consulted on Tangier, in 1912 the conference, by tacit general consent, was confined to Britain, France, and Spain. But the attempt to re-create a similarly limited conference 11 years later inevitably drew Fascist Italy's fire. Italy had undeniable interests in the area. Six hundred Italians living in Tangier, and 100,000 in Morocco at large, provided some justification for participation on the grounds of "proletarian imperialism."[11] In strategic and commercial terms Tangier was as sensitive a spot to Italy as it was to Britain. But in the last resort Mussolini did not anticipate that Italy's material interests would be damaged by a restricted conference. Italy's exclusion was intolerable

[11] The phrase "proletarian imperialism" was popularized before 1914 by the nationalist Corradini (S. Saladino, "Italy," in *The European Right*, ed. H. Rogger and E. Weber [Berkeley, 1965]), pp. 234ff. It is used with particular respect to Italian workers abroad by M. Boveri, *Mediterranean Cross-Currents*, tr. L. Sieveking (New York, 1938), p. 191.

primarily because of the prestige factor. "Inasmuch as this constitutes a Mediterranean question," ran one instruction to Romano Avezzana, "we cannot in principle admit that Italy, a great power and predominantly Mediterranean, should be excluded."[12] The Fascist regime lived on prestige, which had to be upheld at all costs.

The Tangier conference was scheduled for October 1923 in Paris. Rome expected that Britain and Spain would not object to Italy's admission. The main stumbling block was thought to be France, but even here there were grounds for optimism, as the French embassy in Rome expressed sympathy for Italy's claim.[13] Actual negotiations were conducted in Paris between Romano Avezzana and Poincaré, and they quickly revealed no common ground whatsoever. The argument proceeded on two levels. On the legal level France insisted that by the colonial agreements of 1902 and 1912, in return for a free hand in Libya, Italy had pledged disinterest in Morocco, including Tangier. In reply, Italy contended that Tangier had always been extraneous to Moroccan settlements and that the French had recognized this in the past, particularly in 1904, 1906, and 1912, when Morocco was the subject of international agreements. But more important than the legal gloss was the political dispute. Having no substantive demands to make in the Tangier question, Italy could promise "to find points of contact with French interests" in return for participation in the conference. France, on the other hand, would offer only the exact opposite; a guarantee of Italy's material interests in Tangier if Mussolini would drop the conference issue. It was solely to placate Britain that France had agreed to negotiate on Tangier in the first place, and Paris saw no reason to bring in superfluous outsiders. To admit Italy, it was argued, was to set a precedent for the entry of undesirable aspirants to a conference seat—such as the United

12 *DDI*, ii, No. 419.
13 *DDI*, ii, Nos. 433, 438; Guariglia, *Ricordi*, p. 33.

States, whose open-door trade policy in colonial areas was not welcome.[14] France, then, would not retract, so the conference met without Italy, and on December 18, 1923 produced a new international statute for Tangier.

But the matter was far from closed. Although France, Spain, and Britain might draft a Tangier statute, there was no disguising the fact that the finished product required endorsement by all the Algeciras signatories. Apart from the legal aspect, no statute stood a chance of implementation without cooperation from all of the powers' representatives in Tangier. Early on, Mussolini had threatened this sort of noncooperation if Italy was not represented at the statute's drafting. And the French and the British seemed to go out of their way to ensure that he carried out his threat. When Mussolini protested Italy's exclusion from the Paris conference France and Britain replied that Italy had not applied formally for admission in time. In view of Mussolini's strident demands for participation for weeks before the conference, this was an outrageous quibble. Mussolini reacted predictably by proclaiming his complete liberty of action in the Tangier question.[15]

There matters rested. Britain, France, and Spain set about making practical arrangements to implement the statute. Obviously they hoped that by the time it was put into effect Mussolini would be more amenable. For his part, Mussolini had to wait until the three powers attempted to make the statute work before he could execute his threat to wreck it. When the third phase of early Fascist diplomacy opened in mid-1924, the Tangier statute was as live an issue as that of the Italians in Tunisia.

Partnership with Spain

French obduracy over Tunisia and Tangier considerably influenced Mussolini's approach to Spain. The idea of countering French supremacy in the western Mediter-

[14] *DDI*, II, Nos. 419, 420, 438.   [15] *DDI*, II, Nos. 521, 583.

ranean by enlisting the support of Spain did not originate with him, however. At the outset of his regime he set little store by Spanish friendship. Rather, the strategy was urged by his ambassador in Madrid, the Marquis Raniero Paulucci de' Calboli who as Barone Russo's father-in-law presumably had Mussolini's ear. According to Paulucci, in June 1923, anti-French feeling was increasing in Spain, "where by a natural reaction the sympathy of this country has been turning of late toward Italy."[16] But the prospect of a substantial Italo-Spanish rapprochement was bedeviled by a squabble over tariffs. Under an existing most-favored-nation trade agreement Spain shared in a reduction of duties on imports into Italy provided for in recent Italian commercial treaties with France and Switzerland. Understandably Rome asked for commensurate privileges in the Spanish market. At first Spain offered much less than Mussolini required, but by June 1923 capitulated to the extent of offering to negotiate a definitive commercial treaty and implement a long-deferred visit of King Alfonso XIII to Rome. Mussolini, while gratified, remained guarded, awaiting a concrete economic move before considering a political entente.[17]

In the fall of 1923, however, several factors combined to change Mussolini's coolness. First, he was in an assertive diplomatic mood; Corfu and Fiume demonstrated this, while the decision to recognize the Soviets testified to Fascist Italy's new spirit of adventure. A rapprochement with Spain could be regarded as a western counterpart to the one planned with Soviet Russia. Second, it was at this juncture that Poincaré was proving uncompromising in the Tunisian and Tangier questions; consequently Spanish friendship took on added value in Rome. The third, and perhaps most important, item of encouragement to Mussolini was

16 *DDI*, II, No. 77.
17 *DDI*, I, Nos. 683, 703, 735; II, Nos. 74, 97.

the entry into office in September of a new government in Madrid, the Directorate, headed by General Miguel Primo de Rivera. Like Mussolini, Primo de Rivera achieved power partly by threat of force and a program, like that of the *Partito nazionale fascista*, which consisted of a generic nationalist authoritarianism. In a telegram to Paulucci, Mussolini commented jubilantly on the affinity. As if to gauge how far it might be exploited, he demanded that a commercial treaty be concluded before King Alfonso's visit to Italy. Primo de Rivera assented; although some difficult negotiations were still to come, Italy succeeded in holding him to his promise.[18] On November 15 a commercial convention was signed, and four days later King Alfonso arrived in Rome.

On the surface the Spanish royal visit was an unqualified success. By paying his respects at the Vatican and the Quirinal, as well as to Mussolini, Alfonso contributed inestimably to the impression of Fascism's alliance with respectable and traditional authority. But more important was the fact that Primo de Rivera accompanied the king. A few days earlier, at a dinner given by Ambassador Paulucci where the wine flowed freely, the new Spanish premier was expansive about his country's future in collaboration with Italy; he even foresaw an Anglo-Italian-Spanish-Portuguese bloc to frustrate French hegemony in Europe.[19] Primo de Rivera and Mussolini held several private conversations during the visit. From them emerged a draft treaty that was to be the basis for further negotiation. Its contents have never been disclosed, but from later correspondence between Mussolini and Paulucci, we know that it had six points and covered benevolent neutrality, commercial collaboration in South America, cooperation (possibly naval) in the Mediterranean, and the localization of colonial wars, pre-

[18] *DDI*, II, Nos. 378, 453, 459, 478.   [19] *DDI*, II, No. 476.

sumably in North Africa.[20] Mussolini regarded the draft treaty as a triumph, for as usual his enthusiasm was running to excess. After his earlier skepticism he had become an ardent convert to the stratagem of using Spain against France. But Spain was not caught yet, and Primo de Rivera's pledges in Rome held reservations as Mussolini was compelled to admit: "We discussed the most suitable means for putting into practice such a desire for an understanding. To this end, we succeeded in drafting the outline of an accord which both participants recognized as generally in harmony with the goals which the two contracting parties proposed to reach, but even as a draft plan it was not decided upon because General De Rivera for his part considered it his duty to consult and sound further his colleagues of the Directorate before adopting the outline of the plan."[21]

Spanish reservations, in fact, were serious. The new year 1924 came and went before Primo de Rivera could be brought to speak again of an Italo-Spanish accord. In mid-January he began to denigrate what had been conjectured in Rome. He particularly found fault with the proposal for a joint commercial offensive in South America which, Primo de Rivera now argued, would threaten the Latin American republics. Mussolini replied by outlining the benefits to Spain of an accord with Italy; more practically, he offered to consider all and any modifications to the draft treaty which Primo de Rivera cared to propose. But Primo de Rivera was not to be persuaded. When Paulucci, on Mussolini's instructions, grew insistent, the Spanish leader countered with criticisms of the Mediterranean and colonial points of the tentative agreement reached in Rome, and went on to stress Spain's unworthiness as a partner. When a jingoist general had recourse to national self-deprecation, the hope of an Italo-Spanish pact was indeed dead.[22]

<hr>

20 See especially *DDI*, II, No. 590.   21 *DDI*, II, No. 510.
22 *DDI*, II, Nos. 582, 590.

Primo de Rivera's objections to the details of the draft treaty were obviously camouflage. The real reason for his about-face was simply that France would not countenance an Italo-Spanish pact which, given Mussolini's Francophobia, would inevitably be turned against France. All along, the handwriting had been on the wall. During the visit of King Alfonso and Primo de Rivera to Rome, the diplomatic world had scented an Italo-Spanish accord in the offing; rumor had it that Rome and Madrid planned a naval agreement to which Britain was to be invited to adhere. At once new rumors emanated from Paris concerning a French démarche in London for a naval arrangement to counter any Italo-Spanish agreement. Whether France seriously made such an overture must be doubted. More likely it was her way of warning against any Italo-Spanish alignment in the western Mediterranean. At the same time, Poincaré berated Ambassador Romano Avezzana for Italy's ingratitude in trying to turn Spain against France after France's aid to Italy in the Corfu crisis.[23] Certainly Primo de Rivera took French displeasure to heart. Paulucci reported that the Spanish premier was preoccupied with Morocco and Tangier, matters of importance to Madrid, in which France called the tune. So "he no longer employed toward France the cold and critical language of several weeks ago," and "he did not hide his lively concern at the bellicose and aggressive attitude of France."[24]

Spain's diplomatic vassalage to France, which derived from economic, strategic, and colonial considerations, was an established fact of European politics. As such, it was accepted, with the notable exception of Paulucci, by most of the Palazzo Chigi officials who argued that the road to Spain lay through a rapprochement with France, not through the construction of an anti-French bloc.[25] By

23 *DDI*, II, Nos. 491, 492, 496, 507-509. 24 *DDI*, II, Nos. 566, 590.
25 Guariglia, *Ricordi*, p. 34.

ignoring this and trusting to ideological empathy to override political realities, Mussolini, and briefly Primo de Rivera too, disclosed not so much inexperience as the gulf fixed between the diplomatic concepts of the new men and those of the traditional diplomats. The collapse of the design for an Italo-Spanish pact was the more notable because it paralleled Mussolini's experience with Curzon at the Lausanne Conference. In both cases personal interviews promised much and delivered nothing. Admittedly, whereas Mussolini deluded himself at Lausanne, Primo de Rivera made promises in Rome which he failed to keep. Nonetheless, in little more than 12 months Mussolini's two main essays in personal diplomacy had ended in abject failure.

As far as Spain was concerned, Mussolini was not about to be burned again. After Primo de Rivera's rebuff in January 1924, he made no attempt to revive the Italo-Spanish project. Indeed, perhaps out of spite, he seemed to go out of his way to avoid collaboration and even contact with the Spanish government. When King Victor Emmanuel visited Madrid in June, Mussolini resolved not to emulate Primo de Rivera's trip of six months earlier with its political overtones, and stayed in Rome.[26] The ideological tie remained, and Mussolini in his capacity as senior dictator could not resist the temptation to offer advice to the neophyte, Primo de Rivera. When the Spanish government prepared to deport Miguel de Unamuno, the Duce was ready with advice on how to cope with independent and troublesome writers; over a period of years he sent a series of private letters to Primo de Rivera on similar subjects.[27] It was this sort of association which more than anything else restored Italo-Spanish relations to a condition of general cordiality.

But the truth remained that whatever mutual good feeling existed between Rome and Madrid rarely extended be-

[26] *DDI*, III, No. 229; *OO*, xx, 384.
[27] *DDI*, III, Nos. 52, 59; Guariglia, *Ricordi*, p. 33.

yond the superficial to matters of political substance. Those who approached Mussolini with schemes for a Latin bloc composed of Italy, Spain, and France made little headway.[28] On the contrary, Italy's precondition for any close Italo-Spanish association—that Madrid desert the French for the Italian orbit—remained. And there was never a hint of this in the twenties. Mussolini's frustration in dealing with Primo de Rivera probably contributed to the avidity with which he seized the opportunity to supplant French influence in Madrid offered by the Spanish civil war a decade later.

[28] See, for example, the vain attempts of Ezio Maria Gray described in R. MacGregor Hastie, *The Day of the Lion* (London, 1963), pp. 154, 193, 200-201, 207.

10. Colonial Aspirations

Bargaining with Great Britain:
Curzon and MacDonald

FRENCH PREDOMINANCE in the western Mediterranean, thwarting all of Italy's designs there, persuaded Mussolini to look eastward. In February 1924 a Council of Ministers communiqué carried the Duce's significant observation: "Now Italy can only move to the east. In the west there are old-established nation states. . . . The direction of pacific penetration for Italy therefore lies toward the east."[1] This naturally put added emphasis on the Dodecanese, whose de facto possession by Italy was confirmed in the Treaty of Lausanne in July 1923. The treaty also left the final and de jure disposition of the islands to future negotiations between Italy and other interested parties, particularly Great Britain. In the summer of 1923 Mussolini was anxious to open talks at once, but, under pressure from his professional advisers, he left the timing of an approach to London up to the Italian ambassador there, Della Torretta. Given Italy's de facto hold on the Dodecanese, the legal sovereignty of the islands was perhaps an academic question. Nevertheless, the matter was something to be cleared up before Italy pursued other objectives in the eastern Mediterranean.

Della Torretta, apparently on his own initiative, raised the issue again in London in October 1923.[2] Since this was only a few weeks after Mussolini's abortive attempt to annex Corfu, it scarcely seemed a propitious moment to secure British recognition of Italy's legal title to strategic islands in the Mediterranean. But the Italian ambassador sensed a drift in British party politics favorable to Italy.

[1] *OO*, xx, 181. Cf. *DBFP*, II, No. 289.　　　　[2] *DDI*, II, No. 429.

The days of the Conservative government were numbered; on November 13 Prime Minister Baldwin announced the dissolution of parliament. The December elections resulted in Conservative losses, which made probable the entry into office of Britain's first Labour government when parliament reassembled in January 1924. The prospect appalled Lord Curzon. He confided to Della Torretta his "grave concern at the difficulty which might arise between Italy and England upon the advent of a Labour foreign secretary." Consequently he was determined "to profit from the short period of power left to the Conservatives to resolve those questions still pending."[3]

What Curzon had in mind was not just a resolution of Dodecanese sovereignty. Fearing that the socialists were about to betray Britain's colonial interests, he wanted a package deal that would also dispose of Italian claims to British territory in Africa. The conjunction of the Dodecanese with African problems was neither unreasonable nor novel, but it did militate against the sort of quick settlement Curzon wanted.

Part of Italy's price in 1915 for intervention in the war on the Entente side had been African territory. Article XIII of the Treaty of London promised Italy "equitable compensation" to match Anglo-French colonial gains. After the war it had fallen in the main to Britain, as principal legatee of Germany's possessions in Africa, to redeem the promise.[4] At the start of negotiations the British had made two territorial offers: a rectification of the frontier between Egypt and Libya about the oases of Jarabub; and, more important, the cession of Jubaland, a region of East Africa

3 DDI, II, No. 504.
4 Great Britain, Parliamentary Papers, 1920, Vol. LI (Accounts and Papers, Vol. xxv), Cmd. 671, "Agreement between France, Russia, Great Britain, and Italy, April 26, 1915," p. 6. In September 1919 the French contributed a little to meeting Italy's African claims by a slight change on the frontier between Libya and French Equatorial Africa.

bordered by Italian Somaliland, British Kenya, and the southern frontier of Ethiopia. After some demurring Rome had agreed to take what London offered as fulfillment of Article XIII, and in 1920 an accord had been worked out by Lord Milner and Vittorio Scialoja to serve as a basis for the delimitation of the frontier.

Apart from minor details, the Milner-Scialoja Accord settled the substance of the Jarabub cession, although transfer was delayed by the British grant of legal independence to Egypt in 1922. But in the case of Jubaland, the accord was soon to be called into question, for it referred to Jubaland as part of the entire postwar colonial settlement, which included the Near East. As soon as Italian expectations in the Near East were shattered by the demise of the Treaty of Sèvres, Rome demanded compensation in the form of a larger Jubaland than agreed on in 1920. But London stood firm on the Milner-Scialoja Accord. The only hint that Italy's request might be granted came from the British manner of linking Jubaland with the Near Eastern situation; this was to propose a joint settlement of Jubaland and the Dodecanese. More bluntly, Italy could buy a larger Jubaland by ceding the Dodecanese, a proposition any Italian statesman would have found difficult to entertain seriously. By the time Mussolini came to power, the Jubaland question had reached an impasse.

Now at the end of 1923 Curzon proposed in effect to revive the formerly unacceptable bargain. He suggested, with Della Torretta's encouragement, that the Dodecanese be split. The more important islands, including Rhodes, would go to Italy, but the rest were to be ceded to Greece at some future date. In return, Curzon hinted at concessions on Jubaland.[5] Mussolini's response was unclear. On the one hand, he was emphatic that "no substantive connection

[5] B.D., C2661/2661/22 (Annual Report, 1923, p. 7); DDI, II, Nos. 513, 514.

could or can exist between the cession of Jubaland and the Dodecanese." But on the other, he directed Della Torretta to explore what Curzon proposed as recompense for Italy's "incontrovertible rights."[6]

The Italian ambassador somehow managed to fulfill these contradictory instructions: "Without my ever having admitted the principle, the conversations have been conducted on the plane of attempts for a contemporaneous solution of both questions in the brief period that is left before Curzon's departure from the Foreign Office."[7] But he could not report that London held out much inducement to a bargain. Curzon offered watering privileges within Kenya for the Somali tribes of Jubaland, but he would not consider—or, as he averred, the Colonial Office would not consider—any territorial grant beyond the Milner-Scialoja line. Instead, Curzon now held out the vague promise of Italian participation in British railway concessions in Anatolia. When pressed by Della Torretta to suggest a Greek quid pro quo for Italy's relinquishment of some of the Dodecanese, the British foreign secretary airily observed that this "would have to consist only in the political benefits resulting from friendlier Italo-Greek relations."[8]

Della Torretta shared Curzon's pessimism about the prospects for negotiation between Fascist Italy and a British Labour government. The ambassador forecast "a delicate and difficult situation" if his current talks with Curzon should come to nothing; therefore he urged Mussolini to consider negotiating on the basis proposed by Curzon.[9] After all, the fulfillment of a pledge to negotiate with Greece over some of the islands could be delayed indefinitely; this would be typical Palazzo Chigi pragmatism. But Mussolini had not denied Turkey the islet of Castellorizzo in order to promise, however halfheartedly, a good number

[6] *DDI*, ii, No. 518. [7] *DDI*, ii, No. 532.
[8] *DDI*, ii, Nos. 520, 533. [9] *DDI*, ii, No. 520.

of the Dodecanese to Greece. Moreover, Fascism's veneration of *force majeure* dictated that Italy's "effective possession of such islands since the Libyan War" should preclude any surrender. Mussolini accordingly dismissed the British proposal out of hand: "From the negotiations of Della Torretta with Lord Curzon it appears: (1) That Italy must surrender some unspecified islands of the Dodecanese. (2) That this surrender is in no way to be compensated for, neither in Anatolia nor in Africa, neither by Greece nor by England. (3) That on this basis agreement is impossible."[10]

Curzon was perhaps the last person to whom Mussolini was inclined to make a concession, even a token one, for it was Curzon who at Lausanne had allowed Italian hopes for a mandate among other Near Eastern desiderata to rise only to dash them shortly thereafter. Now, just over a year later, Curzon again stood guilty of insincerity in Mussolini's eyes. To make plain his grievance to the world, Mussolini threatened a public statement of Italy's case in the Dodecanese, a move that might include revelations about the recent Curzon-Della Torretta talks. So Curzon assumed, for he retaliated by expressing preparedness to protect his reputation by compiling a documentary publication from the British Foreign Office archives. Although Della Torretta considered a formal declaration "indispensable," calmer counsels from other quarters prevailed and the threats did not materialize."[11]

Mussolini's instructions to his ambassador, then, were "to conclude the conversations with an official declaration

10 *DDI*, II, No. 523, and p. 371, n. 1.
11 *DDI*, II, Nos. 542, 556-58. An example of the Palazzo Chigi's diversion of Mussolini's indignation in the direction of minimum harm was a memorandum by Guariglia (*DDI*, II, No. 547), which suggested that, in the light of the impasse in the Della Torretta-Curzon talks, Italy ignore the understanding that inter-Allied consultation would precede ratification of the Lausanne Treaty. Immediate Italian ratification would be no more than a procedural violation of the Allied front and a token insult to Britain; and it might raise Italy's stock in Ankara.

which would confirm our thesis in the most precise fashion but calculated to leave behind an amicable situation"; to achieve the latter result it was deemed "suitable to avoid a written declaration."[12] In a final and "always friendly" conversation with Curzon, Della Torretta recapitulated Mussolini's view that Italy had fulfilled her promise to consult London over the final disposition of the Dodecanese, and that "now there was no longer any bar to her full and complete sovereignty." As for Jubaland, Mussolini would be content with "the execution of the cession of Jubaland within the limits established by the Milner-Scialoja Accord, but with the satisfactory ruling of the question of tribes and wells promised by Curzon"—now, however, without any Aegean quid pro quo. Curzon, in reply, made it plain that Whitehall rejected the Italian pretense that the question of Dodecanese sovereignty was closed, and insisted to the last on the necessity for a tandem settlement of Jubaland and the Dodecanese.[13] A considerable gulf between London and Rome remained when Labour took office on January 23, 1924.

In retrospect, it is hard to believe that there was more than a slim chance of a Jubaland-Dodecanese deal being concluded as long as Curzon remained at the Foreign Office. Given the vast difference in economic and strategic worth of Jubaland and the Dodecanese, Italy was hardly likely to yield anything material in the Aegean for a stretch of East African desert and swamp. What such Italians as Della Torretta, who was the most eager to come to terms with Curzon, had in mind was a vague promise of Dodecanese concessions in the future. But this would be merely a facesaving device for Britain, certainly not enough to satisfy Curzon. Now everything was in the hands of Ramsay MacDonald's Labour government, which was not expected to go out of its way to provide cheap diplomatic

[12] *DDI*, ii, No. 580.   [13] *DDI*, ii, Nos. 580, 584.

victories for a Fascist regime. Mussolini assumed that an ideological antipathy would automatically infuse Anglo-Italian relations. Still, British Labour, like most European socialist parties which before the war had subscribed to the international brotherhood of the masses, responded readily to President Wilson's crusade for peace among the nations. It was an open question whether MacDonald's attachment to international reconciliation would override his socialist distaste for Fascism, or vice versa.

The first indications were that MacDonald, who became both prime minister and foreign secretary, was relying heavily on the Foreign Office, which hewed closely to the Curzon line. Curzon seemed to be speaking through the mouth of Labour's parliamentary undersecretary when the undersecretary told the House of Commons that Jubaland and the Dodecanese would have to be resolved in a joint accord. MacDonald himself made it plain that he expected further discussion of the Dodecanese, and he even touched on the forbidden topic of the islands' ethnic character.[14] Early in March 1924 Della Torretta, summarizing the situation for Mussolini, emphasized that "no British government will ever disinterest itself in the definitive fate of the Dodecanese." Once more he suggested offering a promise of future negotiations with Greece over "some Dodecanese islands of no interest to Italy."[15] This was the sort of vague agreement Della Torretta had tried to work out with Curzon, only to be thwarted by Mussolini. Now the Duce apparently perceived that his ambassador was seeking a formula to save Britain's face rather than yield anything substantial. So he allowed the proposal to be submitted in London as part of a memorandum of the recent Curzon-Della Torretta talks. But he remained suspicious, and

14 *DDI*, ii, No. 660; iii, Nos. 27, 143.
15 *DDI*, iii, Nos. 34-35.

warned his ambassador that "it is not possible for me to change my fundamental point of view."[16]

In the event, the ambassador's advice was sound. As the Labour government began to show signs of freedom from Foreign Office restraint, it revealed more taste for the Wilsonian brand of international goodwill than ideological anti-Fascism. As a first gesture Labour ceased to demand joint negotiations on the Dodecanese and Jubaland; MacDonald announced publicly his intention to reexamine the Dodecanese question "from the beginning."[17] Although this soon turned out to be phraseology designed to spare Mussolini's susceptibilities more than any substantive change, the intent to gratify Italy was clear enough.

On April 1 MacDonald sent a personal letter to Mussolini; commenting on the Dodecanese-Jubaland link he explained that, "without making the settlement of one depend on the other, we should come to an understanding on both concurrently." Although MacDonald went on to assure Mussolini: "I am anxious immediately to execute the promises which we have made you in regard to Jubaland," it was clear that he meant immediately after agreement on the Dodecanese was reached. As for a Dodecanese solution MacDonald left the initiative squarely in the Duce's hands: "If you on your part would inform me of your intentions regarding the Dodecanese, I should be willing to study them with a sincere desire to settle the whole matter."[18] In reality, the contents of the letter were less important than the fact that it was dispatched in the first place. On assuming office MacDonald had sent a personal communication to Poincaré, the news of which had roused Mussolini's indignation at this supposed discrimination against himself. Now

---

16 *DDI*, III, No. 41. 17 *DDI*, III, Nos. 73, 111.
18 *DDI*, III, No. 122.

the Fascist leader's ego was to be placated by equal treatment.[19]

Although MacDonald's unusual and conciliatory letter was, then, a patent effort to break the deadlock, Italy continued to be reserved and skeptical. More than a month passed before Mussolini, on May 2, responded with a letter to the British prime minister. In it Mussolini treated MacDonald to a rather querulous restatement of Italy's rights in the Dodecanese, and went on to argue that the cession of any of the islands to Greece would be an incitement to Turkey and a disturbance of the eastern Mediterranean balance of power. This, at any rate, served as an excuse to avoid all but token satisfaction of Anglo-Greek wishes. "Only for some islands of minor interest to Italy could I contemplate the possibility of a different settlement, but this dispensation could only be justified in terms of an effective contribution to a peaceful and definitive order in the Middle East and it would, therefore, require adequate guarantees and compensation." Put more plainly, as apparently it was in a conversation between Mussolini and Ambassador Graham, Italy would negotiate directly with Greece at an indeterminate time in the future regarding some unspecified islands in the Dodecanese group.[20] Essentially this was what Della Torretta, and probably other Palazzo Chigi officials who were no more inclined than Mussolini to sell Italian interests short, had been urging for the past six months. Only a British government as dedicated to international conciliation in all circumstances as MacDonald's was could have found such a proposition satisfactory and imposed it on Athens. So general and hedged with conditions was Italy's undertaking that all of the parties had to have grave doubts of its execution. Nevertheless, London

[19] *DDI*, II, Nos. 607, 608. The idea of a personal letter to Mussolini may have come from Graham, the British ambassador in Rome, an inveterate flatterer of the Duce (*DDI*, III, No. 143).
[20] *DDI*, III, Nos. 165, 206.

224

accepted the Italian proposal with alacrity, and at once the Jubaland issue was unraveled. Within three weeks identical British and Italian communiqués announced a Jubaland settlement on the basis of the Milner-Scialoja Accord, with provision for tribal access to wells in neighboring British territory. On July 15 the final transfer was signed.[21] On August 6 Britain ratified the Treaty of Lausanne. This was implicit acceptance of Italy's sovereignty over the Dodecanese and was, for all practical purposes, a guarantee of uniform international recognition of Italy's legal title. The Dodecanese issue was at last truly closed.[22]

In little more than a year after taking office Mussolini had brought off both a Dodecanese and a Jubaland settlement. But these were not unalloyed Fascist triumphs, especially in Jubaland where Mussolini retracted the territorial claims levied by his Liberal predecessors. Who were the *rinunciatari* here? In any case, Mussolini's role was largely one of holding a watchful and cautionary brief. They were not the sort of novel, spectacular successes Fascism craved. There was little opportunity in the situation for a display of Fascist vigor or boasting. On the other hand, the territorial gains could be regarded as steppingstones to further advances in the eastern Mediterranean and East Africa. Mussolini seemed intent on putting the Dodecanese to this use without delay. In the early stages of the Lausanne Conference he had shown that his Near Eastern ambitions went beyond mere acquisition of the islands. Even as Mussolini

[21] *DDI*, III, Nos. 210, 388. Guariglia negotiated the final details with Harold Nicolson in London (Guariglia, *Ricordi*, pp. 35-36).

[22] The promised Italo-Greek discussions never materialized. A report, dated February 1925, that the Greek government still hoped for Dodecanese negotiations with Italy bears Mussolini's annotation—a laconic but expressive exclamation point (*DDI*, III, No. 708). Cf. Mussolini's remark in May 1926 that "every island and every rock in the Dodecanese" must be "Italian for all time" (quoted in B.D., C3729/3729/22 [Annual Report, 1926, p. 20]).

negotiated with MacDonald in the spring of 1924, his plans to leap from the Dodecanese into Asia Minor were maturing.

Turkish Apprehension

At the Lausanne Conference the Italian delegation had tried to play a double role. While preserving the united Allied front on substantive matters, it had aspired to play a mediatory role between Britain and Turkey. The latter aspiration became pronounced toward the end of the conference when all the major items, including the Dodecanese, had been set aside. Behind the strategy lay the hope of establishing a special relationship with Turkey. On leaving Lausanne Montagna wrote: "As for our relations with Turkey, it may be asserted that not only have these emerged from the conference improved, but perhaps Italy among all the states represented here stands to derive most advantage. Now we have to exploit and realize these advantages in other fields."[23] Whether this optimism was well-founded or not, Mussolini had other ideas.

The Duce looked at the eastern Mediterranean in a Social Darwinian fashion. The extension of Italian influence in the direction of Asia Minor was to be accomplished not by cultivating Turkish goodwill but by contest. Optimistically Mussolini envisioned a confrontation of a virile Fascist Italy and a decadent Turkey cast in a pre-Kemalist mold. The Turks themselves, in making Castellorizzo an issue at the Lausanne Conference, showed that they had not mistaken Mussolini's belligerence. Turkish alarm did not abate, and came to be expressed vehemently in both press and government circles during the first half of 1924. Apprehension was voiced about a variety of Italian actions. A Council of Ministers communiqué hinted at Italian emigration to the Near East, which the Turks viewed as a sinis-

[23] *DDI*, II, No. 140.

ter imperialist design. Another suspect instrument of Italian colonial ambition, which was denounced as such, was the Franco-Italian accord for Near Eastern economic cooperation signed a year earlier but about to go into effect early in 1924.[24] By May the Turkish press was full of a more specific and immediate hazard; reports of Italian troop concentrations on the islands of Sicily and Rhodes fueled an invasion scare.[25] Mussolini expressed concern at all this derogation of Italy's reputation, and made appropriate disclaimers of militant intent.[26]

Yet Mussolini's concern may not have been genuine. After all, the specter of a fire-eating, expansionist Italy portrayed in the Turkish press amounted to a success for Fascist propaganda, which sought to produce abroad an attitude of respect based on fear. Although deploring the Italo-Turkish feud for form's sake, some of Mussolini's actions seemed calculated to keep it alive and in the public eye. When he learned early in June that Italophobia in Turkey was on the wane, rather than leave well alone, he issued a communiqué restating Italy's side of the argument. To add fuel to the fire he soon contrived another issue to perpetuate ill will by accusing the Turkish government of aiding the Libyan rebels against Italian colonial rule in North Africa.[27] Such behavior could have been mere contentiousness; more probably it had an ulterior motive.

It was a characteristic of Mussolini to regard a war of words waged via national presses as a prelude and pretext for armed conflict. In 1923 an exchange of public insults between Athens and Rome had set the stage for Mussolini's descent on Corfu. Similarly by June 1924 Mussolini believed that several months of bitter Italophobia reflected by all shades of Turkish opinion had provided him with an excuse

[24] *OO*, xx, 181; *DDI*, iii, Nos. 190, 193, 194, 218.
[25] *DDI*, iii, Nos. 211, 227, 234.
[26] *DDI*, iii, Nos. 216, 235; *OO*, xx, 255.
[27] *DDI*, iii, Nos. 245, 390.

227

to attack Turkey; and clearly he at least considered seizing
the opportunity. This is plainly revealed by an instruction
to his war minister, "to study the modality of an eventual
war against Turkey and to estimate the means for conducting it."[28] In June 1924 there was no likelihood of the
Turks attacking Italy, so Mussolini must have been planning for the opposite. In this vein of military preparedness
was a consular report from Smyrna on the state of Turkish coastal defenses, while the consolidation of Italian power in the Dodecanese outpost and springboard was hurried forward.[29] It was all very reminiscent of Corfu.

Mussolini may well have calculated, also, that the international situation was propitious. In Corfu Italy was
pitted against Greece and Britain. Nine months later, he
could rationalize that these two eastern Mediterranean
powers would not obstruct a Fascist blow at Turkey. The
Italo-Greek reconciliation after Corfu was the more unexpected. It was not based on public sentiment. Although press
diatribes across the Adriatic came to be muted under official pressure, popular animosity was never far below the
surface.[30] It was governmental calculation in Rome and
Athens that dictated a détente. A prerequisite, of course,
was formal Italian recognition of the current Greek regime.
Before Corfu Mussolini had indicated he was willing to
follow Britain and France in the matter. Corfu itself gained
for the Greek regime considerable sympathy throughout
the world; the governments in London and Paris reflected
this when they announced early in 1924 their intention to
resume full diplomatic relations. Mussolini resolved to follow suit.[31] Italian recognition automatically drew attention to the character of Italy's diplomatic representative
in Athens, Montagna. The minister was remembered for
his Hellenophobe stand during the Corfu crisis. Tactfully

[28] *DDI*, III, No. 604.   [29] *DDI*, III, Nos. 258, 437, 440-43.
[30] *DDI*, III, No. 221.   [31] *DDI*, II, No. 570; III, No. 154.

he remained absent from Athens for most of the winter, and at the end of February 1924 was moved from the Athens post altogether. Recognition and the change of representatives produced a noticeable shift in the tenor of Italo-Greek relations. This was evident in May when Greece accepted the settlement of Dodecanese sovereignty worked out by MacDonald and Mussolini. Like most rapprochements, the one between Italy and Greece thrived on common hostility to third parties. Turkey was an ideal mutual enemy. Given the centuries-old Greek hostility to the Turks, Athens would likely join a Mussolinian attack on Asia Minor.

As for Britain, in June 1924 Mussolini was not faced with the British administration that had threatened him with naval action at Corfu. It could be assumed that MacDonald, so recently cooperative about the Dodecanese and Jubaland, would be reluctant to engage in gunboat diplomacy in the eastern Mediterranean, in the manner of a traditional Conservative foreign secretary. Furthermore, while London and Ankara had come to terms at Lausanne, there remained one outstanding issue to put a strain on Anglo-Turkish relations—the undefined Turkish frontier at Mosul, whose oil wells the British wanted to include in their mandated territory of Iraq. In view of the Mosul dispute Britain's readiness to save Turkey from Italy could be called into question.

There was yet another power with a vital interest in the Turkish situation. This was Turkey's neighbor to the north, Soviet Russia. However, it could be calculated that Fascist Italy's de jure recognition of the Soviets early in 1924 and the brief Russo-Italian rapprochement which followed might neutralize to some extent Moscow's potential opposition to Mussolini's designs in Asia Minor.

Against this background Mussolini was clearly edging toward war with Turkey in June 1924. Why did he draw back? Hardly because the Turkish press adopted a milder tone toward Italy. Mussolini had the wit to keep the verbal quarrel boiling if need be. Rather, the explanation lay in the domestic political upheaval that overtook Italy on June 10, 1924—the Matteotti affair. Almost overnight the Duce's attention dramatically swung away from international affairs.

THE ABRUPT end of the Italo-Turkish crisis was symptomatic of a larger change in Italian foreign policy. Since the summer of 1923 Mussolini had injected himself forcefully into many diplomatic questions. Sometimes he had supplemented the efforts of the Palazzo Chigi; sometimes he had ignored his advisers' counsel. For most of a year Italian foreign policy had betrayed the distinctive Fascist characteristic of aggressive restlessness. Now the metamorphosis was halted (temporarily) by the Matteotti crisis. June 10 constituted the terminal date of the second stage of early Fascist diplomacy, a stage that began with the Corfu affair and ended with its near repetition in Asia Minor.

PHASE THREE
June 1924 to April 1925

11. The Matteotti Affair

Diplomatic Apathy

GIACOMO MATTEOTTI was a leading member of the Italian Socialist party and an outspoken critic of Fascism. His denunciations reached their zenith following the elections of April 1924, in which systematic violence was used to gain a substantial majority for Mussolini's list of candidates. Matteotti's criticism brought several threats on his life, once openly by Mussolini in the Chamber of Deputies.

On June 10 Matteotti was attacked by five men on the sidewalk outside his home. They bundled him into a car which sped off. Through the windows a melee of flying arms was seen by at least two witnesses who alertly took the car's license number. The police quickly found the car, which had a bloodstained interior, and arrested five members of the Fascist party. The ringleader was Amerigo Dumini who had recently been put in charge of a special strong-arm squad with an office in Mussolini's Ministry of the Interior. Its express task was to terrorize anti-Fascist spokesmen into silence; on orders from the top, Matteotti became a prime target. None of this was known publicly at the time, and it was not until August that Matteotti's body with knife wounds was discovered in a shallow grave in the country north of Rome. But long before this all of Italy was sure Matteotti had been killed by Fascists, and had assumed that Mussolini was implicated.[1]

Matteotti was not the first to die at the hands of the Fascists, although he was the most prominent. Coming on top of the recent election violence, and two years after Mussolini became premier, it made a mockery of the contention

---

[1] On the Matteotti affair see M. Del Giudice, *Cronistoria del processo Matteotti* (Palermo, 1954); and A. Schiavi, *La vita e l'opera di Giacomo Matteotti* (Rome, 1957). Briefer accounts are De Felice, *Mussolini: Il fascista*, I, Chap. 7; and Kirkpatrick, *Mussolini*, Chap. 9.

that Fascism would grow milder with the responsibilities of office. Public revulsion swept Italy, giving rise to the possibility of a united anti-Fascist front. In many moments of crisis throughout his career, Mussolini showed a marked reluctance to take decisive action, so in the summer of 1924, faced with the first real threat to his regime, he lapsed into a strange inertia. He set much store by the deserted Palazzo Venezia, which he had made the seat of his administration, as the timeservers stayed away awaiting developments. Occasional visitors found him alone in his office, often unshaven and red-eyed, in fear of a popular uprising.[2] There was no attempt to use foreign adventures to distract attention from troubles at home, although the Fascist press did not cease to call for action abroad.[3] Mussolini's paralysis included diplomacy as well as domestic administration.

The headstrong foreign policy of the past year was replaced by worried concern for Fascist Italy's reputation and support. According to the selections published in *I documenti diplomatici italiani*, Mussolini's sole preoccupation in the weeks following Matteotti's disappearance was the impact of the crime abroad.[4] Perforce he gave up any protest he might have been contemplating at French handling of the Bonservizi murder case. For the duration of the Matteotti affair Italy's ambassadors were treated to a series of instructions, many drafted by Mussolini himself, requesting reports of any change in foreign opinion of Fascist Italy and requiring that steps be taken to counter unfavorable

[2] L. Fermi, *Mussolini* (Chicago, 1961), pp. 237-38; Kirkpatrick, *Mussolini*, pp. 225-26.

[3] G. Rumi, " 'Revisionismo' fascista ed espansione coloniale," *Il Movimento di Liberazione in Italia*, No. 80 (July 1965), 48.

[4] This is the subject of every published document between June 18 and 24 (*DDI*, III, Nos. 270-304). For the next week, June 25 to July 2, 45 of the 59 pieces published concern Matteotti directly or indirectly (*DDI*, III, Nos. 305-63).

publicity.[5] Most were couched in general terms; others, more specific, ranged from the imposition of "maximum discipline" on Fascists in Switzerland to a request to Della Toretta in London for precautionary "information on English scandals concerning the violation and slaughter of children . . . and in general other atrocities and political crimes, especially in Ireland."[6]

Italy's relative inactivity in international affairs during the last half of 1924 reflected Mussolini's concern; caution and conciliation were uppermost. The German reparations problem was a case in point. The London Conference to examine the Dawes report convened on July 16. Leading the Italian delegation was Mussolini's minister of finance, Alberto De Stefani, whose instructions, in granting him substantial freedom of action, recalled those Mussolini had sent to the last Italian mission to a reparations conference on the eve of the Ruhr invasion.[7] Like its predecessor, which had committed Italy to approval of France's seizure of a territorial pledge, De Stefani's delegation showed signs of establishing a special rapport with the French. In particular, De Stefani was inclined to take up the proposal of the French premier and foreign minister, Edouard Herriot, for confidential talks on the status of the Ruhr occupation under the Dawes Plan and joint Franco-Italian action to wring concessions from Britain in the war debts question.[8] But here the parallel ceased as Mussolini intervened to curb De Stefani's initiative: "I can only confirm to you the absolute necessity of proceeding in this question with the utmost caution and prudence, above all avoiding that any pretext be given to insinuate later in some way that our conduct served to hinder the work of the conference and

---

[5] See esp. *DDI*, III, Nos. 264, 270, 292, 318, 321, 498, 542, 644, 652.

[6] *DDI*, III, Nos. 289, 318. Five years later Rome was still sedulously gathering information on Britain's Irish atrocities (It.D. [Ministry of Popular Culture], 30/428/014498).

[7] *DDI*, III, No. 392.   [8] *DDI*, III, Nos. 399, 406, 423.

prejudice its outcome."[9] Actually, sometime earlier, Mussolini had written off the reparations question as an area for diplomatic maneuver and prestige-hunting. The Matteotti affair therefore confirmed a tendency. The London Conference completed its work with Italy largely a passive spectator. The conference ended on August 16 and the Dawes Plan went into effect on September 1, 1924. Its terms were not unlike what Italy had advocated during most of the Ruhr crisis. The plan provided for a speedy evacuation of the Ruhr. Although there was no overt reduction of Germany's total liability nor cancellation of war debt, they could be inferred. The plan arranged for a sliding scale of reparations annuities and reliance on civil guarantees of payments, both of which had figured in Italy's own proposals before the occupation of the Ruhr. Moreover, Italy's share of reparations was intact and her supply of reparations coal uninterrupted.[10] Yet this affinity for Italian policy and interests notwithstanding, it remains broadly true that the Dawes Plan came into being with very little help from Fascist Italy.[11]

Another question that came to the fore again at this time was Tangier. France, Spain, and Britain were ready to ratify the new international statute, and once more requested Italy's adherence. The shaken Fascist regime, desperate for friends abroad as well as at home, was plainly apprehensive about maintaining an adamant stand against the Tangier statute. Moreover, the murder of Matteotti was likely to bring out the latent anti-Fascism of the new left-of-center government in Paris, the *Cartel des gauches,* which had taken office in May. So Rome deemed it politic to try to use Britain's good offices. After all, the new British

[9] *DDI*, III, No. 426.
[10] Moulton and Pasvolsky, *War Debts*, Chap. 9, *passim*; Royal Institute of International Affairs, *Survey 1924*, pp. 351-55.
[11] Mussolini later reacted sharply to this charge, which would seem to lend it extra validity (*DDI*, III, No. 577).

Labour government might be expected to wield special influence with the *Cartel des gauches*. The compromise Italy now proposed to London was to overlook exclusion from the conference of 1923, if a protocol were added to the statute guaranteeing a number of posts in Tangier's international administration to Italian nationals.[12] The contents of the proposed protocol were not an excessive demand in a concrete sense; they were intended purely to save Italy's face by providing a show of participation. The British response was slow in coming, chiefly because MacDonald needed time to acquaint himself with the Tangier question. His request for a written statement of Italy's terms for adherence to the Tangier statute was refused by Mussolini. Later Ambassador Della Torretta on his own initiative supplied a confidential memorandum of Italy's demands for the British premier to study, but to no avail. MacDonald clung to the opinion of the Foreign Office, which was that Britain had long ago promised that admission to the Tangier negotiations would be up to the French. That was the price for getting France to the conference table. To grant Italy's request would be to go back on that promise and risk wrecking the whole effort to maintain Tangier's international status. In late September Mussolini was informed flatly that London could not take Italy's part.[13]

After this setback Italy cast about for other means of bypassing France. Rome would have liked an association with the United States on Tangier. However, the one conceivable ally in sight was the Soviet Union, the only power besides Italy not to have ratified the new Tangier statute. The Italian diplomatic agent in Tangier did indeed advocate exploiting this common ground between Italy and the Soviets, and toward the end of 1924 the Italian ambassador in Moscow began to sound out the deputy commissar

[12] *DDI*, III, Nos. 396-97.
[13] *DDI*, III, Nos. 403, 410, 433, 445, 501, 516.

for foreign affairs, Maxim Litvinov, about a common front.[14] Whether this was a serious overture—indeed whether Mussolini himself authorized it—is doubtful. Italy's position in late 1924 was to remain quietly rather than stridently opposed to the Tangier statute.

Somewhat unexpectedly, late in the year France embarked on last-minute overtures to win Italian endorsement of the statute which was due to go into effect on January 31, 1925. Aristide Briand, chief French delegate at the December session of the League of Nations Council, spoke generally of satisfying Italy in Tangier. Also Barrère, about to leave the Rome embassy, held out the prospect that France might "accord Italy some satisfaction in her capacity as a great Mediterranean power—apart from the other powers signatory to the Act of Algeciras."[15] As a result, Mussolini authorized Ambassador Romano Avezzana to open negotiations in Paris on both the Tangier and Tunisian questions. The ambassador found that it was in fact now French official policy "to recognize Italy's position as a great Mediterranean power and the need to admit her participation in the administration of the [Tangier] zone in a manner definitely distinct and privileged beyond other nations."[15a]

A natural bargain seemed about to be struck: a French concession on Tangier for a quid pro quo on Tunisia. Romano Avezzana suggested that while he handled the Tunisian problem in Paris, a formula to amend the Tangier statute might be devised in Rome through the agency of the new French ambassador, René Besnard. Rome thus became the center of Tangier negotiations for a time. At the end of March 1925 Besnard gave a token of French goodwill by approving steps to elevate the status and role of

[14] *DDI*, III, Nos. 219, 409, 461, 554.

[15] *DDI*, III, Nos. 635, 641; G. Suarez, *Briand, sa vie, son oeuvre avec son journal* (Paris, 1938-52), VI, 127.

[15a] *DDI*, III, No. 692.

Italy's diplomatic representation in Tangier. The agreement was verbal only pending a complete Franco-Italian accord on Tangier and Tunisia.[16] Yet for the moment the restraint forced on Italy by the Matteotti affair, and Italy's admission of weakness in the hint of a Tunisian concession, had apparently won more than all Mussolini's earlier bluster.

During the Matteotti affair Mussolini tried to avoid any suspicion of revisionism. His encouragement of the German right languished. It has been observed, for instance, that Hitler was denied an interview by Mussolini. In the Balkans, too, the revisionists were kept at arm's length. Hungary launched a campaign in September 1924 to exclude the watchful states of the Little Entente from the military control commission, and asked for Italian support. The proposal involved a definite change in the postwar settlements, which Mussolini took a firm stand against: "Italy, having made the observance and maintenance of the peace treaties a cardinal tenet of her own policy, cannot tolerate the principle of the revision of the Treaty of Trianon." His only concession was the not very substantive one that the manner of military control should be "as little burdensome as possible."[17]

In the Balkans Mussolini was more concerned about cultivating the friendship of a Little Entente member— Rumania. In August 1924 Rumania provided a settlement of the treasury bond issue acceptable in Italian financial circles. There is no evidence that this was bought by Italian promises in the Bessarabian question, although it is possible. Certainly the Rumanians immediately raised the issue of Bessarabia, and Mussolini's first reaction was to agree to discuss the subject. In fact, he was so anxious to hasten a détente with Rumania that he alarmed the cautious elements in the Palazzo Chigi. Unsure of what the Duce in-

[16] *DDI*, III, No. 775.　　　　[17] *DDI*, III, Nos. 486, 490, 502.

tended, Contarini managed to impose on Mussolini a "corrected" version of the latter's original instructions to the Bucharest legation. Thus Italian minister Baron Aloisi was ordered "not [to] speak too freely but conduct himself with the greatest tact and prudence."[18] For his part, Aloisi indicated that it would be better if ratification of the Bessarabian protocol of 1920 and a full-fledged political accord awaited further economic tokens of Rumanian goodwill, including a commercial treaty. Aloisi also came to the aid of Palazzo Chigi officials who were seeking to contain Mussolini's ebullience with the suggestion that Mussolini try to mediate the Bessarabian dispute.[19] This appealed to the vanity of Mussolini the self-styled Olympian arbiter. Even if he failed to reconcile Rumania and Russia, he at least might persuade Moscow to tolerate Italy's ratification of the Bessarabian protocol. But of most importance to the old-guard diplomats, the tactic blocked any immediate Italian action on Bessarabia. With the promise of good offices behind the scenes, then, Bucharest had to be content for the time being.

There is no record of how Mussolini undertook his task of mediation. It may even be that he bowed to the exigencies of domestic politics and made no effort at all. All that can be said with certainty is that he failed utterly. Moreover, in October Stefani, the official Italian press agency, published a communiqué categorically denying any intention of recognizing Rumania's claim to Bessarabia. Presumably it was necessary to convince the Soviet Union that Mussolini's desire to talk about Bessarabia did not portend any quick action by Italy; or, as Aloisi explained in Bucharest, it served to disguise what Italy was really after. But the Rumanian press understandably took the communiqué at face value, and Foreign Minister Duca expressed his

18 *DDI*, III, Nos. 437, 438.
19 *DDI*, III, Nos. 428-29.

"growing anxiety" about the situation.[20] The attitude of Rumanian officials gradually changed to downright skepticism as the winter of 1924 passed without a sign that Mussolini had budged the Soviets an inch.

Together, the Duce's attitude to the Dawes Plan, to Tangier-Tunisia, and to Danubian politics illustrate how far Fascist Italy retreated from an energetic foreign policy. But the clearest test occurred on the eastern shore of the Adriatic. There the outbreak of civil war in Albania, which coincided with the beginning of the Matteotti affair, put an immediate strain on the Italo-Yugoslav Pact of Rome. The choice before Mussolini was clear. On one side, Italian nationalist sentiment, which he claimed to personify, demanded intervention in Albania and a challenge to Yugoslavia. On the other, the Sforza and Contarini policy of rapprochement with Belgrade dictated restraint. In a memorandum apparently well-known in the Italian foreign ministry, Contarini as early as 1923 had forecast a scramble for privileges in Albania, but had concluded that an independent and stable Albania was in Italy's best interests.[21] In 1924 the internal condition of Fascist Italy constrained Mussolini to favor the moderate approach of the Palazzo Chigi.

Civil War in Albania

Italian designs on Albania antedated Mussolini's accession to power. Postwar disappointments there contributed to the famous picture of Italy's "mutilated victory," and the weakness of the pre-Fascist parliamentary regime was held to be manifest in the forced withdrawal of Italian troops from Valona in 1920. Yet this was not a case of Italian nationalism against the world. Italy's special interest in Albania had a sort of international sanction. As a legally recognized state Albania had not come into existence until

[20] *DDI*, III, Nos. 538, 540, 560.   [21] *DDI*, III, No. 609.

1913, and her boundaries were still undetermined when World War I broke out. After the war the Conference of Ambassadors addressed itself to the task of frontier delimitation and appointed an international commission to operate on the spot. (It was the murder of the Italian delegation to the commission that sparked the Corfu crisis of 1923.) At the time the Conference of Ambassadors established the Albanian frontier commission on November 9, 1921, it also issued a declaration confiding the integrity of the infant state to the care of the League of Nations. In this the conference went out of its way to enunciate Italy's special position vis-à-vis Albania by "recognizing that the violation . . . of the independence of Albania might constitute a danger for the strategic safety of Italy." Therefore, the statement continued,

> If Albania should at any time find it impossible to maintain intact her territorial integrity, she shall be free to address a request to the Council of the League of Nations for foreign assistance.
>
> The Governments of the British Empire, France, Italy, and Japan decide that, in the above-mentioned event, they will instruct their representatives on the Council of the League of Nations to recommend that the restoration of the territorial frontiers of Albania should be entrusted to Italy.[22]

Such was the cloak of international approval behind which Italy might try to establish some form of protectorate across the Adriatic.

The Pact of Rome, at least to the Albanians, appeared a device whereby Italy, in return for Fiume, might have agreed to share her special position in Albania with Yugo-

---

[22] Quoted in J. Swire, *Albania, Rise of a Kingdom* (New York, 1930), p. 369. Also on Italo-Albanian relations in the aftermath of World War I, see P. Pastorelli, *Italia e Albania, 1924-1927: Origini diplomatiche del Trattato di Tirana del 22 novembre 1927* (Florence, 1967), pp. 11-18.

slavia. In particular, Tirana expressed alarm lest Italy back Yugoslav designs on Scutari.[23] Certainly at first, Rome and Belgrade saw eye to eye on Albania. In June 1924 the civil war in Albania began between the partisans of the Orthodox bishop, Fan Noli, and the incumbent government representing the political faction led by Ahmed Zogu. At once both appealed to Mussolini for help.[24] The advice of the Marquis Carlo Durazzo, the Italian minister in the town of Durazzo that served as Albania's diplomatic capital, was to show as much favor as possible to Noli; not only was he likely to win but Zogu was thought to be Yugoslavia's protégé.[25] On the other hand, Mussolini was told that Zogu could be bought and that an Italian naval base in Albania could be had in return for arms to help Zogu recover power. This was the message brought by Alessandro Lessona, a Fascist deputy in parliament associated with Italian oil interests in Albania and a friend of Zogu himself.[25a]

But Mussolini, under the cloud of the murder of Matteotti, bent over backward to avoid taking sides and becoming involved. He turned Zogu's offer aside with the request that it be put in writing; but it was unrealistic, Lessona explains in his *Memorie*, to expect "a written document on so explosive a subject." Lessona's recollection in places is not trustworthy, but here it is clear that Mussolini put off Zogu.[26] With Noli he was equally circumspect. As long as Noli was in the position of an insurgent, Italy's neutrality in the Albanian civil war operated in his favor; but as soon as the Noli faction seized the government in Tirana, which it did by the end of June, it sought diplomatic recognition from Italy. Although Durazzo urged him to curry

[23] *DDI*, III, Nos. 28, 61, 78.   [24] *DDI*, III, Nos. 222, 230.
[25] *DDI*, III, Nos. 243, 246.
[25a] Carocci, *Politica estera dell'Italia fascista*, pp. 33-34.
[26] A. Lessona, *Memorie* (Florence, 1958), pp. 81-85. On Lessona's reliability, see Di Nolfo, *Mussolini e la politica estera*, p. 176.

favor with the new regime by granting recognition at once, Mussolini refused to do so ahead of the other powers.[27] In response to direct communications from Noli, he promised friendship and support but in the blandest terms. When Tirana tried to interpret a friendly exchange between the Duce and the Albanian chargé in Rome as a firm offer of assistance, Mussolini insisted this had been only a "generic conversation." Nor would he receive Noli and his finance minister en route to the League of Nations, lest it "be erroneously interpreted at Geneva by the foreign representatives gathered there, and give them the impression that the Albanian ministers had wanted to get special directives from Italy before presenting themselves to the League."[28] All this caution provided Yugoslavia's opportunity. In the words of the Italian chargé at Durazzo: "No Albanian government . . . can rule without effective support from outside"; therefore if Italy did not back Noli forcefully, "Albania is on the road to becoming the sphere of influence of another state (of Yugoslavia, if Ahmed Zogu and his followers were to prevail)."[29] But while he was overwhelmed by Italy's internal problems, Mussolini preferred to put his trust in the Pact of Rome to prevent Belgrade from stealing a march in Albania; up to a point, the strategy worked.

When open warfare broke out in Albania, Yugoslav Foreign Minister Ninčić, doubtless fearing Italian intervention, indicated his willingess to let matters work themselves out without external interference. Rome seized on this and, to hold Ninčić to his promise, suggested that a joint Italo-Yugoslav declaration of nonintervention be issued publicly. This was quickly accomplished and created the anticipated favorable impression. Italy and Yugoslavia agreed further to proceed *pari passu* on recognizing Noli's regime.[30]

[27] *DDI*, III, Nos. 366-67, 374.
[28] *DDI*, III, Nos. 306, 431, 434, 460.
[29] *DDI*, III, No. 462.
[30] *DDI*, III, Nos. 236, 240, 242, 247, 317.

Thus during the summer of 1924 it seemed as if Yugoslavia was effectively neutralized; the very success of the reputedly anti-Yugoslav Noli bore this out.

Yet before the summer was over the pattern changed. Tension grew between Tirana and Belgrade, and King Alexander of Yugoslavia complained to Mussolini of Albanian forays across the frontier. Mussolini dutifully remonstrated with Noli.[31] The story from Tirana, of course, was the reverse. The trouble on the Albanian-Yugoslav border arose from Zogu, now in Belgrade and the recipient of Yugoslav aid in his efforts to regain power. Noli appealed for Italian help frequently and through a variety of channels, even via D'Annunzio in semi-retirement.[32] Mussolini, however, steadfastly refused, and clung to the promise of Yugoslav nonintervention in Albania, which Ninčić obligingly reiterated early in December.[33]

But without help from Italy, Noli was unable to hold power. On December 13, 1924 Zogu, with the connivance of the Yugoslav military, led his troops across the frontier and by Christmas Eve was back in Tirana. The reversal was a setback for Italian ambitions. The danger, of which the Durazzo legation had long warned Rome, that Albania might become a "Yugoslav province," appeared for the first time a reality. Italy's response, typical of Mussolini's preoccupation with prestige, was first to tackle the problem of how defeat would look. Ninčić was asked for public assurance, which "it was indispensable to offer to Italian public opinion," to the effect that "recent events in Yugoslavia and Albania were not directed against Italy's political position in Albania." Belgrade, not surprisingly, raised no objection to reaffirming the purity of its intentions, so Mussolini got his declaration for public consumption.[34] On the other

31 *DDI*, III, Nos. 420, 421, 425.
32 *DDI*, III, Nos. 500, 519, 521, 579-80, 622.
33 *DDI*, III, Nos. 524, 625; *Corriere della Sera*, Dec. 14, 1924.
34 *DDI*, III, Nos. 634, 638, 639.

hand, there were signs that Rome's concern would not stop
short at putting a favorable gloss on Albanian events and
that faith in the Pact of Rome as a restraint on Yugoslavia
was wearing thin. As early as December 10 the Marquis
Durazzo had been alerted that "it is opportune that . . .
our situation with regard to Albania be providentially and
carefully re-examined."[35] But no real change in Italian diplomacy was to be expected until Mussolini disposed of the
Matteotti affair and recovered his political nerve. In early
1925 Mussolini did reassert Fascist authority in Italy. But
he remained preoccupied with domestic affairs for some
months. Thus Italian diplomacy in Albania took on an
ambivalent character. On one hand, Mussolini apparently
felt free to consider intervention in Albanian politics, as
the Italian nationalists wanted. On the other, for a time
he still proceeded cautiously. At any rate, he had no work-
able plan for reversing the setback to Italian imperialism
in Albania—until a startling change of form on Zogu's
part gave him an opening. By all accounts Zogu was Belgrade's man, but once before he had offered to bargain with
Mussolini. Actually, as it was soon to become plain, Zogu
held the Yugoslav threat to Albanian integrity higher than
the Italian, an appraisal which apparently was strengthened by Belgrade's readiness to intervene in the Albanian
civil war in order to bring Zogu back to power. Moreover, such irredentist designs as Zogu now cherished were
at Yugoslavia's expense. Both for defense and offense, then,
Albania needed to use Italy against Yugoslavia. Zogu had
no sooner returned to Tirana than he began to make overtures to Mussolini via Durazzo, the Italian minister, and
the Fascist deputy, Lessona.[36] Rome's official reaction was
understandably skeptical. Italian recognition of Zogu's
government was delayed and pointed reference made to the

[35] *DDI*, III, No. 609.
[36] *DDI*, III, No. 654; Lessona, *Memorie*, pp. 85-87.

rumor that the Albanian police force was to be reorganized by Yugoslav and British advisers. On the other hand, there was no objection to Durazzo inquiring what Zogu had in mind. As for Lessona, by his own account, without consulting Mussolini, he rushed off excitedly to Tirana to interview Zogu.[37]

Zogu was affable to all Italian emissaries. First, the Italian minister was informed that the scheme of foreign advisers for the Albanian police had been withdrawn. Durazzo also won Zogu's promise, "to recognize our [Italian] predominant economic interest in Albania and to promote it."[38] If Lessona is to be believed, Zogu was even more outgoing with him. Zogu proved receptive, not only to the idea of Italian economic concessions in Albania, but to the possibility of a political agreement. Reports of these exchanges had their effect in Rome; Lessona implies that as early as February 1925 Mussolini instructed the Palazzo Chigi, with Lessona's help, to draft a treaty.[39] Be that as it may, Rome made it clear that "prompt and tangible evidence" of Zogu's goodwill was the prerequisite of any serious negotiation.[40] It was a favorite Mussolinian device, when he was unsure whether to go on to a political accord, to demand economic favors as a token of good faith. So now an increase in Italy's economic stake in Albania was deemed the first step.

The first portent was not encouraging. Zogu announced the grant of a valuable concession to the Anglo-Persian Oil Company. When Italy complained, Zogu pleaded his weakness in the face of British pressure and suggested that Mussolini seek an understanding with Britain on Albanian oil.[41] So an approach was made to London. The exchanges were punctuated by mutual recriminations, as Mussolini

---

[37] *DDI*, III, Nos. 660, 665, 670; Lessona, *Memorie*, pp. 86-87.
[38] *DDI*, III, No. 674.   [39] Lessona, *Memorie*, pp. 87-96.
[40] *DDI*, III, No. 686.   [41] *DDI*, III, Nos. 701, 705, 710-11.

accused Britain of bad faith in forcing a quick ratification of the Anglo-Persian oil deal. But ruffled feathers were quickly smoothed; Italy was accorded another, if lesser, oil concession, and Anglo-Italian cooperation was established to check the advances of American oil interests in Albania.[42] While this Anglo-Italian agreement was pending, Zogu offered to make amends to Italy for the Anglo-Persian oil concession. He proposed to establish an Albanian national bank with capital supplied almost exclusively from Italy, an idea which Rome seized on. Lessona was sent back to Albania, where this time he collaborated with the Italian legation. By mid-March 1925 Albania was granted an immediate loan of one million gold francs, "so as to assure Ahmed Zogu of that independence necessary for him to arrange calmly the systemization of affairs in his country"; and a convention was signed with a group of Italian financiers to underwrite Albania's national bank. Henceforth economic negotiations, conducted on the Italian side by Ugo Sola, the new Italian minister to Albania, and Mario Alberti of the Credito Italiano, proceeded swiftly and smoothly.[43] The way was cleared for a political and military treaty—at just the moment that Mussolini was prepared to embark anew on an adventurous and forward type of foreign policy.

Backing for The Duce from Respectable Europe

Mussolini's regime survived the Matteotti shock mainly because the opposition lacked strong leadership. This in turn was due to the refusal of either the monarchy or the Vatican to lead a united anti-Fascist front. In short, the majority of the Italian power structure, which had countenanced Mussolini's accession to office in 1922, were

[42] *DDI*, III, Nos. 720, 722, 727-31, 737, 739, 752-53.

[43] *DDI*, III, Nos. 732, 735, 763; Lessona, *Memorie*, pp. 97-100. Both Sola and Alberti were proponents of the open door in Albania, but were importuned by Mussolini into implementing a policy of Italian economic penetration (Carocci, *Politica estera dell'Italia fascista*, pp. 36-38).

loath to desert him. And of course, the conservative, aristocratic Palazzo Chigi officials were a solid pillar of that power structure. In 1924 they remained uniformly loyal to their class and to Mussolini. By so doing the old guard at the foreign ministry also contrived to imply approval of Mussolini's foreign policy over the previous two years, Corfu notwithstanding.

What happened within Italy was matched by world reaction to the Matteotti murder. Predictably a cry of rage came from Europe's anti-Fascist left. In addition, one or two governments evinced positive disapproval of Fascist violence. Czechoslovakia, despite the recent friendship pact with Italy, adopted the most censorious attitude. Beneš found an excuse not to come to Rome for the actual signing of the treaty of friendship on July 5, and a visit to Italy planned by Thomas Masaryk, the Czech president, was also canceled.[44] Furthermore, the Soviets took an anti-Italian line. Not only did the Matteotti affair compel a clear ideological choice between right and left, but the consequent turmoil in Italian politics reawakened the Comintern's interest in Italy as a potential area for revolution. The Fascist deputies in parliament and Mussolini's paper, *Popolo d'Italia*, illustrated the hardening of ideological attitudes on the Italian side by stepping up their anti-Bolshevik tirades.[45] Thus Italy's rapprochements with Czechoslovakia and Soviet Russia, both so laboriously constructed during the first half of 1924, suffered badly from the Matteotti affair.

Against this, however, could be set the fact that some governments, of which anti-Fascist animus might have been predicted, remained cordial to Mussolini. For example, the governing Labour party in London and the *Cartel des gauches* in Paris appeared embarrassed by the anti-Fascist

[44] *DDI*, III, Nos. 282, 285, 344, 464.

[45] *DDI*, III, Nos. 342, 350, 408, 747, 852. See also Tamaro, *Vent'anni*, pp. 435-36.

outcry from some of their supporters.[46] Indeed, in over-whelming numbers, politicians and publicists of various shades of opinion continued to find Mussolini's regime tolerable. The "benevola aspettativa" of the middle of the road majority in 1922 had crystallized into a complaisance not to be shaken even by assassination. Mussolini's fear of international ostracism turned out to be groundless.

That Mussolini still enjoyed the backing of the international power structure, so to speak, was signified by the League of Nations. In the wake of their clash over Corfu, Italy and the League contrived a rapid improvement in their relationship—akin to the post-Corfu détente between Italy and Greece. The initiative seems to have come from Geneva, and particularly from the League's secretary general, Sir Eric Drummond. At the end of the Corfu affair Drummond was cognizant and critical of the blow dealt the League of Nations by Mussolini, but he was prepared to forget the past in the hope that Italy might become reconciled to the League. (Later, between 1933 and 1939, as the Earl of Perth and British ambassador to Rome, he was to show even more positive signs of sympathy toward the Fascist regime.[47]) Only a few weeks after Corfu, Drummond visited Rome, where he enjoyed several conversations with Mussolini, who described the exchanges as "highly satisfactory."[48] Mussolini's response to this attention was to reverse completely the tendency to drift away and even leave the League. Instead, he began to complain that the League was an Anglo-French preserve and to demand more posts for Italians in its secretariat. He expressed this to the Senate on November 16, 1923 in the words: "The problem may be stated in these terms: should we withdraw from the League?

[46] B.D., Cabinet minutes, 38 (24)16; *DDI*, III, Nos. 280, 304, 320, 324, 362.
[47] F. Gilbert, "Ciano and His Ambassadors," in *The Diplomats*, pp. 544-48.
[48] *DDI*, III, No. 471.

Speaking generally, I prefer to join rather than leave."[49] Drummond took the hint, and the following year Salandra was made a League of Nations vice-president.

Furthermore, before the end of 1923 Italy had gone a step further in hinting that the League Council might like to hold one of its quarterly sessions in Rome. This notion germinated until the League's fall session of 1924, when the Italian delegate, Salandra, proposed that the next council meeting set for December take place in Rome. The project aroused some opposition, chiefly from the Swedish delegate, Hjalmar Branting, who had been one of the most vocal critics of Italy during the Corfu crisis. But it had the vigorous backing of Drummond, who prevailed on the British to accept it. With only Branting abstaining, the council then voted to accept Italy's invitation—only a few weeks after the discovery of Matteotti's body.[50] There was, of course, the danger of a clash between the League and Fascist hotheads in Rome. But in December 1924 the black-shirts were still chastened after the furor caused by the murder of Matteotti. Branting, who had announced his intention of laying a wreath at Matteotti's grave, was conveniently indisposed and unable to visit Rome. The council's session took place without incident.[51] Of course the presence in Rome of many luminaries of international diplomacy added cubits to Mussolini's stature at a climactic moment of the Matteotti affair.

The League, meeting in Rome, served Mussolini well by bringing him into personal contact for the first time with Sir Austen Chamberlain. The new British foreign secretary epitomized his country's aristocratic elite; he took Mussolini's claim to have saved Italy from bolshevism at face value and sympathized with Mussolini throughout the Matteotti

[49] *OO*, xx, 108-109.
[50] *LNOJ*, iv (1923), 1,320-52, *passim*; v (1924), 523-24. See also *DDI*, iii, Nos. 492, 528.
[51] Salandra, *Memorie politiche*, pp. 123-24.

uproar. This pro-Fascist line was set at the very top of the British social structure. King George V had been well disposed toward the Fascist regime since his visit to Rome in May 1923. On July 5, 1924, a few weeks after Matteotti's disappearance, the king expressed his pleasure that Mussolini had been able to surmount Italy's internal crisis.[52] The congratulations were premature, as it turned out, but presumably welcome in Rome just the same. The overwhelmingly conservative British press—with the London *Times* and *Morning Post*, both voices of the British establishment, in the van—invariably put the most favorable construction on Mussolini's actions throughout the Matteotti affair.[53] Yet British conservatism was denied full opportunity to show its support for Mussolini in his travail so long as a Labour government held office. But in November, after an election victory, the Conservatives returned to office. At once Chamberlain broke the strained silence that had characterized Labour's attitude. On November 10 he addressed a letter to Ambassador Graham in Rome, although it was also intended for Mussolini's eyes. In it the foreign secretary wrote:

> I wish I had had the good fortune to meet Mussolini, but he assumed office after I had left the government. I have spent many happy holidays in Italy, and have great sympathy for the Italian nation. I hope that with Signor Mussolini or with any Government which represents Italy, it may be my good fortune to continue and strengthen the historic friendship of our two countries.
>
> I think that my predecessor on assuming office sent a greeting to Poincaré, and that the singling out of France from the other Allies caused some heartburnings in Italy. We have decided on this occasion to revert to the

[52] *DDI*, iii, No. 373.

[53] *DDI*, iii, Nos. 311, 353, 401, 402, 646, 657-59. See also Fasano Guarini, *Rivista Storica del Socialismo* (May-Dec. 1965), pp. 176-77.

old practices, and no such messages will be sent to anyone. It seems unnecessary to assure our late Allies of our desire to continue the most friendly co-operation with them.[54]

Because of the use of the ambassador as intermediary, this could not be classed a private communication, yet it came close to "singling out" Mussolini and Italy for special attention on Chamberlain's part.

In December Chamberlain attended the League of Nations meeting in Rome. There he went out of his way to meet Mussolini more than once, perhaps in a deliberate attempt to lend him prestige. The signed photograph of Mussolini which Chamberlain procured as a memento for his family indicated the exchanges were unusually cordial. Apparently the two foreign ministers came to no political agreement of a precise nature.[55] But there was one question of immediate concern on which they found themselves on common ground, albeit any understanding may have been unspoken.

In 1924 the international movement to add teeth to the League of Nations Covenant reached its zenith. Sponsored by the leftist premiers of Britain and France, MacDonald and Herriot, the Geneva Protocol proposed that League members obligate themselves to submit to a measure of compulsory arbitration either by the World Court or the League itself, and to join in League sanctions against any state refusing arbitration, on the grounds that such a refusal would ipso facto constitute aggression. Once in effect, this would have represented an enormous increase in the League's power beyond the ill-defined right to take cognizance of "disputes likely to lead to a rupture," which obtained at the time of the Corfu crisis. Although in no way

[54] *DDI*, III, p. 334, n. 1.
[55] B.D., C3343/3343/22 (Annual Report, 1924, p. 7); and Chamberlain papers, Vol. 256, Dec. 14, 1925, and Jan. 10, 1926; *DDI*, III, No. 616.

a response to Corfu, the Geneva Protocol was a clear and potent expression of Woodrow Wilson's dream of international arbitrament which Mussolini had struggled to gainsay by word and deed throughout that affair. Italy's reconciliation with the League notwithstanding, Mussolini was implacably hostile to the Geneva Protocol. He referred scornfully to "homage to the League" in September when the protocol was launched at Geneva.[56] But by the next session of the League Council, Mussolini found a powerful ally in resisting extension of the League's power. The British Conservatives, now back in office, had consistently opposed the protocol. When Mussolini and Chamberlain met in Rome in December 1924, they saw eye to eye on the subject.[57] Mussolini felt bold enough on December 11, while Chamberlain and the League Council were still in Rome, to deride the entire project before the Senate: "The atmosphere of Geneva in September, one might say, was a rather lyrical atmosphere with a leaning to the mystical. . . . It is a question of knowing whether we are creating at Geneva the Superstate, with a general staff and chief of general staff at its disposal."[58] In diplomatic circles he let it be known that, although Italy might sign the protocol after the other major states had done so, she would still insist on a reservation that "the most serious questions, of a non-juridical nature, relative to the fundamental elements of a nation's life . . . be excluded from the agreement."[59] Mussolini's reservation remained a hypothetical threat, for at the League Council's session of March 1925 Britain openly torpedoed the protocol and swung to the support of a regional pact outside the League. Mussolini greeted the protocol's demise with unabashed joy; even though the substi-

[56] *DDI*, III, Nos. 475, 488.
[57] B.D., C3343/3343/22 (Annual Report, 1924, p. 12).
[58] *OO*, XXI, 227.
[59] *DDI*, III, No. 640. See also *DDB*, II, No. 1.

tute, which was to become the Locarno Pacts, never commanded his active enthusiasm, at least it was preferable to the strengthening of the hated institution at Geneva.

BROADLY speaking it was the British, and especially Sir Eric Drummond and Sir Austen Chamberlain, who set the tone for the mild international response to the assassination of Matteotti. Because of this, neither Fascist Italy's repute nor her material interests suffered much in the latter half of 1924. And Mussolini's lack of diplomatic energy cost Italy little. As for the consequences of this complaisance toward Italy, one can only conjecture how far the moral support Mussolini received from Chamberlain, and inferentially from the League of Nations, in December 1924 encouraged him to resolve the impasse in Italian politics by resort to outright dictatorship a few weeks later.[60]

[60] There is no doubt that the main reason why Mussolini embarked on dictatorship was to allay discontent among the activists of the Fascist party (A. Lyttleton, "Fascism in Italy: The Second Wave," *Journal of Contemporary History*, 1 [Jan. 1966], 75-100).

PHASE FOUR
May 1925 to February 1927

12. Grandi and Contarini

ON JANUARY 3, 1925 Mussolini spoke before the Chamber of Deputies, from which the anti-Fascist opposition had withdrawn as a gesture of protest. For the first time he accepted the onus for Matteotti's death: "I declare before all Italy that I assume full responsibility for what has happened." He did not hide the fact that this presaged a dictatorship: "Italy wants peace and quiet, and calm in which to work. This we shall give her, by love if possible, by force if need be."[1]

The apparatus of a dictatorial regime was established quickly, in little more than a year. When the parliamentary secessionists tried to return to the Chamber of Deputies they were barred at the door by armed blackshirts. Anti-Fascist parties were proscribed; parliament, reduced to the proverbial rubber stamp, gave Premier Mussolini virtually limitless power to rule by decree. Local elections ceased. The prefect and a new official named the *podestà*, both appointed in Rome, took over from elected mayors and councils. Independent trade unions, Socialist and Catholic, were outlawed. Perhaps most important, however, was suppression of the free press. Independent newspapers, rather than a malleable parliament, had been the true forum of Italian public opinion. Not only was censorship imposed, but Fascist stooges were put in charge of such famous liberal papers as Milan's *Corriere della Sera* and Turin's *La Stampa*.[2]

Naturally the suppression of dissent left Mussolini free to pursue his own idiosyncratic policies abroad as well as at home.[3] Yet obviously, priority had to go to the solidifica-

---

[1] *OO*, XXI, 238, 240.

[2] For a reliable factual account of these measures see L. Salvatorelli and G. Mira, *Storia d'Italia nel periodo fascista*, 5th ed. (Turin, 1964), Chaps. 6 and 7; R. De Felice, *Mussolini: Il fascista*, II (Turin, 1968), Chaps. 1-3.

[3] On the interplay of the domestic dictatorship and foreign policy see C. Seton-Watson, *Italy from Liberalism to Fascism* (London, 1967), pp. 693-94.

tion of Fascist power at home. As we have seen in the instance of Albania's civil troubles, it was only gradually during the spring of 1925 that Mussolini edged toward his preferred nationalistic foreign policy. This makes it difficult to assign an exact date to the opening of the fourth phase of early Fascist diplomacy. Probably the most convenient starting point is May 15, 1925, which saw a significant change within the Palazzo Chigi—namely, the appointment of Dino Grandi as undersecretary for foreign affairs.

Grandi was one of the earliest Fascist hierarchs, known for his violence as a leader of the *squadristi* in Bologna, prominent in the March on Rome, and a member of the Grand Council of Fascism. He was just the man to be Mussolini's henchman in bringing the Palazzo Chigi to heel. The post of undersecretary of foreign affairs, now entrusted to Grandi, was not traditionally regarded as an important one. Mussolini's first appointment to the office had been Ernesto Vassallo, a staunch ally of Contarini and a member of the Catholic Popular party. In the former capacity he did nothing to challenge the ascendancy of the secretary general; in the latter, he resigned in March 1923 when his party broke its formal tie with Mussolini's coalition government. After this, the position was left vacant until 1925.[4] Its occupancy by so important a figure as Grandi promised to raise the stature of the post immeasurably, and commensurately to decrease the formidable power of the secretary generalship under Contarini.

Under circumstances to be described below, Contarini in fact resigned within less than a year of Grandi's appointment. On the surface, then, it would appear that the Palazzo Chigi was the scene of a struggle for power between the new undersecretary and the secretary general. Yet this smacks of

[4] L. Ferraris, *L'amministrazione centrale del Ministero degli esteri* (Florence, 1955), p. 62; Moscati, *Studi Politici*, II (1953-54), 403.

ex post facto reasoning, for the appointment of Grandi was Contarini's own suggestion. Mussolini having indicated that some *fascistizzazione* of the foreign ministry was imminent, Contarini looked about for a Fascist who would be least dangerous to the old-line officials. On occasion Grandi had shown independence of, and even insubordination to, the Duce. Contarini shrewdly judged him "malleable and understanding, to the extent of being able to conform to those prevailing tendencies in foreign policy followed hitherto by the Palazzo Chigi."[5]

The appointment of Grandi signified Mussolini's intent clearly enough: to brook no opposition from Italy's foreign ministry in the pursuit of whatever foreign policy he chose. But the career diplomats' strategy was not to oppose Mussolini openly. Rather, as evidenced by Contarini's tolerance of Grandi, their inclination was to rely on cooperation and friendly persuasion. Perhaps they reasoned that after the shock of the Matteotti murder Mussolini might be especially amenable to advice. At any rate, there was no dramatic confrontation between Fascism and the Palazzo Chigi, nor a sudden elimination of the influence of the old guard. As long as Contarini remained secretary general, a balance was maintained between Mussolini's temerity and the Palazzo Chigi's caution. For the remainder of 1925, Grandi's presence in the foreign ministry constituted no more than a hint of the troubles in store for the permanent officials there.[6]

[5] Guariglia, *Ricordi*, p. 47.
[6] Grandi's ambivalent role within the Palazzo Chigi is discussed in Carocci, *Politica estera dell'Italia fascista*, pp. 23-25.

13. Settlement of War Debts

THE ISSUE OF funding Italy's war debt came to a head in the second half of 1925. Technical economic questions, as the reparations problem had demonstrated, did not lend themselves readily to Mussolini's assertive style of diplomacy. On the other hand, war-debt negotiations provided a rough test of international feeling toward Fascist Italy now that Mussolini's regime had become an outright dictatorship.

When discussing reparations in the past, Italy had persistently mentioned her debts to the United States and Britain in order to justify the collection of reparations from the defeated nations. Although these invocations were specious negotiating maneuvers, the sums involved were not negligible: at Mussolini's accession to power over two billion dollars in principal and interest owed the United States and 2.5 billion owed Britain. The American debt, while smaller, loomed larger, because by 1923 Britain was ready to write off most of the Allied debt in return for a congenial German reparations settlement. At the time, Italy rejected this; but the knowledge of Britain's disposition to consider cancellation provided comfort for the future. By contrast, the Congressional act of February 9, 1922, which created the United States Debt Funding Commission, categorically forbade cancellation. In the first funding agreement reached by the commission—with Britain in February 1923—the British undertook to repay their debt in its entirety. On the surface, the outlook for American leniency to the other Allies, including Italy, looked bleak.

There were two courses open to Italy. One was to follow the pre-Fascist policy of letting others, France in particular, act first. Because of her wartime sacrifices France was peculiarly suited to win a lenient funding settlement and establish a precedent from which Italy might profit. But since she had denounced the American debt funding act at its inception, there was no immediate prospect of a Franco-American settlement of any sort for Italy to follow. An alternative policy was to seize the initiative and seek a funding agreement ahead of most other European debtors. This line of action was favored by the Italian embassy in Washington, which was under pressure from the State Department to open debt negotiations.

Ambassador Gelasio Caetani observed that Fascism promised an Italian economic revival within a few years and with it an increase in Italy's capacity to pay. If Rome was intent on lenient terms, argued the ambassador, a settlement "based on Italy's present financial condition and economic capacity will be less than if she has reestablished a balance of payments and reconstituted her economy." Perhaps more persuasive, though, was the argument that an Italian overture would produce "the best moral effect" in America.[1] This was desirable because Italy aspired to a giant concession from the United States. The meager immigration quota assigned Italy in 1921 hit overpopulated Italy hard. It also affronted the sensitive nationalism of the Fascists. Mussolini on taking office set out to right the wrong at once. He suggested that Washington increase Italy's quota to 100,000 a year and offered to screen emigrants for their suitability to American conditions.[2] With considerable fanfare he introduced measures designed to curb malpractices at the Italian end of the emigration process. He even sponsored an international conference on emigration and persuaded an American delegation to attend.[3] The power to grant what Mussolini wanted lay with Congress, or American opinion acting through Congress; in the last resort, the standing in the 1920s of any European state in Congressional and popular opinion was determined

[1] *DDI*, I, Nos. 540-41.　　[2] *OO*, XIX, 11.　　[3] *OO*, XX, 271-73.

by its demeanor in the debt question. The trade of a quick debt-funding agreement for immigration favors undoubtedly entered the speculations of Italian officialdom.

A positive overture for debt funding was closer to the Fascist style of action than the patient waiting on France reminiscent of pre-Fascist foreign ministers. During the first half of 1923 Mussolini edged toward such an overture. The Washington embassy's financial counsellor was authorized to approach American officials, first to assure them of Italy's intention to pay and later to explore "in a confidential manner the possibility and limits of an eventual accord."[4] A precise plan of campaign for a debt settlement was to be worked out during Caetani's next visit to Rome.

But during the summer and fall Mussolini backed away. Caetani, who still urged that Italy "enjoy to the full the credit accruing from a spontaneous move," now received the discouraging instructions to await an official step by the United States government before proceeding further in the debt question.[5] Such caution may have reflected no more than the ascendant influence in Rome of the Italian Ministry of Finance, which consistently opposed early funding negotiations. But Italy's enthusiasm was also dampened by America's adamant stand against any change in immigration quotas which were reduced further by legislation in 1924. Thus there seemed nothing tangible in "the credit accruing from a spontaneous move," and Italy reverted by default to the policy of following France's example.[6]

The French gave no indication of funding their debt until 1925 when the American involvement in Europe's economy by the Dawes Plan was an accomplished fact. This commitment to European recovery, it was expected, would dispose the Debt Funding Commission in Washington to leniency. Italy prepared to imitate France, but not

4 *DDI*, I, No. 712; II, No. 64.   5 *DDI*, II, Nos. 452, 460.
6 *USFR, 1925*, I, 162.

wholly voluntarily. For several months the international value of the lira had been declining, a reflection of suspected Italian instability after the Matteotti affair, as well as of world economic conditions. One conceivable means of restoring Italian credit was to inject a liberal amount of American capital into Italy. Mussolini was always eager for American investment; when the post of United States ambassador to Italy became vacant he had suggested that it be filled by "an important financier, an important industrialist or an eminent political figure well versed in the American economy."[7] In the spring of 1925 the Italian government approached J. P. Morgan and Company for a short-term loan of $50 million. The House of Morgan and other Wall Street bankers were receptive to Italian overtures. But American capital was not invested abroad without Washington's approval; in this case the State Department "could not withhold objection . . . unless in the meantime the Italian government had taken suitable steps looking toward the settlement or refunding of its own indebtedness."[8] Italy tried to turn this rebuff to advantage by requesting a promise of American governmental backing of a loan once a funding agreement was reached. Although Washington was understandably noncommittal, nothing was done to discourage Italian expectations.[9] So Italy was constrained to open funding negotiations, not only by the French example, but also for her own immediate needs.

In June Mussolini informed the United States of his readiness to begin negotiations. In public he called for leniency equal to that which might be accorded France and a settlement based on Italy's capacity to pay.[10] Through the confidential channel of the Italian embassy in Washington he spelled out what he considered to be

[7] *DDI*, II, No. 616.
[8] State Dept. files, 800.51 W 89 Italy/29A. See also *DDI*, IV, No. 72.
[9] State Dept. files, 800.51 W 89 Italy/41.
[10] *OO*, XXI, 320-21, 369.

an acceptable formula. This would have wiped out all past and most future interest and spread the repayment of the principal over 90 years, beginning with annuities of only one-half percent of the total after a moratorium of 10 years.[11] This one-sided proposition was rejected at once by the Debt Funding Commission, which awaited the dispatch of an Italian delegation to negotiate from scratch in Washington. In Rome American Ambassador Henry Fletcher urged the sending of a delegation of high caliber, and tried to moderate Mussolini's optimistic notions of a feasible settlement.[12]

An Italian negotiating commission left for the United States in October. The American embassy in Rome observed that Italy's bankers and industrialists, being those who most coveted American loans, were the most ardent for a debt settlement; it remarked with pleasure that the delegation was headed by the new minister of finance, Count Giuseppe Volpi, and included other spokesmen for Italian finance, Alberto Pirelli and Mario Alberti. Although Franco-American debt negotiations had collapsed, thereby making it likely that an Italian settlement would precede a French one, the Rome embassy also learned that the Volpi mission was under instructions to reach an agreement come what may. "Remain, if necessary a year, but do not return until negotiations concluded," Mussolini was reported to have telegraphed Volpi.[13]

The task of the Volpi mission was not overly difficult. Although the United States refused to be stampeded into leniency, official Washington was willing to be charitable. According to the State Department, "Italy's debt to foreign governments appears to be considerably heavier relatively than that of France"; Italy therefore should be burdened

11 *DDI*, IV, No. 34.
12 State Dept. files, 800.51 W 89 Italy/36A, 51, and 57.
13 State Dept. files, 800.51 W 89 Italy/71, 79, and 85.

with only modest debt annuities, at least to begin with.[14] The Italian delegation found other factors working in its interests—the sympathy of Wall Street, the backing of American Catholics, the concern of politicians for the Italo-American vote, and the support behind the scenes of such influential figures as Dwight Morrow, Archbishop Hanna of San Francisco, and even President Coolidge. Indeed, there was considerable admiration in the United States for the Fascist experiment and for Mussolini himself. In short, the Italians compared favorably in American eyes with the obdurate French.[15]

With American goodwill and Italian determination to find a settlement, a funding agreement was quickly reached and signed on November 14, 1925. It provided for debt payments totaling just under $2.5 billion to be paid at an increasing annual rate over a period of 62 years. The most startling feature was the overall compound interest rate of 0.4 percent. Since war debts were contracted originally at 5 percent, which by the terms of the Congressional act of 1922 was supposed to be reduced after funding no lower than 4.25 percent, this virtual extinction of interest released Italy from almost 80 percent of her legal debt.[16] This remained the most lenient treatment accorded any debtor nation. Italy was not relieved of all problems, however; the Italian economy would find it difficult to meet the starting annuities of $5 million, and the United States adamantly refused to discuss the basic problem of the transfer of payments. But withal, Mussolini could claim the debt settlement as a striking success for his government.

The agreement faced criticism in the U.S. Senate; to ensure its ratification, it was only prudent to avoid publicizing the extent of the concessions given Italy.[17] Mussolini's

[14] State Dept. files, 800.51 W 89 Italy/35.
[15] DDI, IV, p. 126, n. 2.
[16] Moulton and Pasvolsky, *War Debts*, pp. 87, 444-45.
[17] DDI, IV, Nos. 173, 204.

public boasting, then, was for him somewhat restrained, and he concentrated on acclaim of the Volpi mission in such terms as: "The Americans, when faced with representatives of the new Italy, showed immediate sympathy."[18] Senate critics had their fling. Senator Blease complained that the Volpi debt mission had violated the prohibition laws by bringing its own wine. This and other criticisms bearing more directly on the debt settlement itself bruised Italian feelings sufficiently to provoke a formal protest by the Italian embassy in Washington.[19] But ratification was accomplished by the end of March 1926. Even before ratification the real goal of Italian debt policy was obtained—opening of the American money market to Italy. On November 30, 1925 a loan of $90 million was issued to the Italian government by a banking syndicate headed by J. P. Morgan and Company.[20]

Unfortunately for Italy and contrary to Rome's fond hopes, there was no rush by American investors to subscribe to Italian loans.[21] Moreover, world economic factors continued to depress the value of the lira, which discouraged Wall Street further. But such faith had been put in an American debt settlement and American investment as a cure for Italian economic ills that Fascist Italy found it hard to approach the lira crisis rationally. It was general talk in Rome that there was a worldwide anti-Fascist conspiracy against the lira.[22] This explanation appealed to Mussolini's melodramatic tastes; regarding the lira's fall as artificially contrived, he believed it could be raised by the artificial or "psychological" move of revaluation and pegging at a high level.[23] This doubtful economic doctrine

18 *OO*, XXII, 26.

19 Grew, *Turbulent Era*, I, 661-63; State Dept. files, 800.51 W 89 Italy/144.

20 McGuire, *Italy's Economic Position*, pp. 392-94.

21 *DDI*, IV, Nos. 288, 309.

22 See, for example, Volpi's opinion (*DDI*, IV, No. 310).

23 *DDI*, IV, No. 387.

was challenged by the experts in Rome, but Mussolini's insistence that the lira's value be kept up at all costs prevailed.[24] Yet the lira continued to fall sporadically. Mussolini had to content himself with vehement instructions to his ambassadors to counteract the widespread notions abroad that the currency decline betokened instability at home, political as well as economic.[25]

The Italo-American debt-funding agreement naturally turned the spotlight on the unresolved question of Italy's British war debt. Hitherto, Anglo-Italian talks had foundered on Rome's insistence that Britain write off the bulk of debt as promised at the Paris reparations conference in January 1923. But the British understandably declined to be bound by an undertaking intended as part of a reparations settlement which never materialized. Instead, London required reasonable repayment so that the British could meet their extensive obligations to the United States.[26] In the face of this attitude, Italy had customarily taken refuge in the tactic once employed in the Italo-American negotiations—to await a French debt-funding agreement, in this case with Britain, in the hope of being able to follow a lenient precedent.[27] The successful conclusion of the American negotiations, however, emboldened her to go it alone once more. As soon as the Volpi mission returned from the United States, Mussolini prepared to send substantially the same delegation to London almost at once.[28] There was some popular resentment in Britain that Italy's debt settlement with the United States should be so much lighter than its Anglo-American counterpart. Nevertheless, the British government at the start of the talks was inclined to cancel if not all Italy's debt at least a considerable portion of it. The British embassy in Rome advocated a substantial con-

[24] *DDI*, IV, p. 300, n. 1, and No. 472.
[25] *DDI*, IV, Nos. 480, 483.   [26] *DBFP*, I, No. 179, n. 1.
[27] *DDI*, III, Nos. 403, 423.   [28] *OO*, XXII, 58.

cession in the war debt question in order to win Italy's favor in the colonial field, a point also emphasized in British cabinet discussions.[29] In the closing days of 1925, on the eve of the Volpi delegation's departure for London, Foreign Secretary Sir Austen Chamberlain and his family, on vacation in the Mediterranean, met Mussolini and Barone Russo at Rapallo. Almost certainly Chamberlain assured them of British goodwill in the forthcoming debt talks.[30] Other evidence of Britain's official opinion was given by the chancellor of the exchequer, Winston Churchill, in a conversation with Ambassador Della Torretta. Churchill congratulated Italy on her American debt settlement; although Italy was not to expect any arrangement more lenient than that obtained from the United States, Britain judged Italy's capacity to pay as being one-third that of France.[31] Italy's prospects in the London negotiations were bright.

An Anglo-Italian debt agreement was signed January 27, 1926. Of the $2.5 billion worth of debt outstanding at the moment of funding, Italy contracted to pay about half, and interest over the 62-year payment period was canceled. In addition, Italy was allowed under certain conditions to postpone payment of annual installments for some two years, and Italian gold deposited in London during the war was to be returned. Italy's initial annuities were twice her first annual payments to the United States but, this advantage to Britain aside, the Anglo-Italian agreement could be regarded as even more favorable to Italy than her American debt settlement.[32]

As in the case of the Italo-American debt-funding agreement, there was some criticism within the creditor country that the Anglo-Italian settlement was too lenient. The *Manchester Guardian* and the *Spectator* used the occasion

29 *DBFP*, I, No. 179 and n. 6; B.D., Cabinet minutes, 1 (26)4.
30 For the official communiqué of the meeting see *OO*, XXII, 476-77.
31 *DDI*, IV, No. 194.
32 Moulton and Pasvolsky, *War Debts*, pp. 116-17, 456.

270

for criticism of Mussolini's Fascist dictatorship. But the dissenting voices were in a minority, and the Foreign Office took care to instruct the British press on the advantages of the Italian debt settlement.[33]

Mussolini was delighted. More paeans of praise, therefore, were heaped on Volpi and his colleagues.[34] Mussolini was so grateful that he wished to confer on the British chancellor of the exchequer the distinguished Order of Saints Maurice and Lazarus, to which London replied that "Churchill was most sensible of the honor which it was desired to confer on him, but that it was impossible for one of his Britannic Majesty's ministers to accept foreign decorations."[35]

The concessions granted Italy by Washington and London were in line with most other war-debt settlements made in the mid-1920s and with the current spirit of international conciliation. On the other hand, they could also justifiably be taken as representative of the fund of international goodwill on which Fascist Italy—Matteotti's murder and Mussolini's dictatorship notwithstanding—might still draw. Of course, in the debt-funding negotiations the United States and Britain did not deal directly with Mussolini. Like his approach to the German reparations problem, the Duce's interest in the complex and technical matter of Italy's war debt was spasmodic. It came to life only when a quick profit or startling development seemed in the offing. Most of the time, Italian war-debt policy was in the hands of the professionals of the ministries of finance and foreign affairs. Consequently the war-debt settlements did nothing to reveal the growing difficulties and dwindling influence of Mussolini's professional advisers.

[33] *DBFP*, I, No. 209 and n. 2.
[34] *OO*, XXII, 67-68.
[35] *DDI*, IV, No. 254.

14. Locarno and the Alto Adige

The Anschluss *Danger*

THE INDETERMINATE status of the Palazzo Chigi officials in 1925-26 was sharply illustrated in the matter of the guarantees of western European frontiers, which were proposed as a substitute for the defunct Geneva Protocol. Suggestions for regional security appealed to Italy's career diplomats who hoped to educate Mussolini in the ways of international cooperation. Also, because London was a prominent sponsor of these regional arrangements, it was believed that Italy's adhesion would bring Mussolini closely into line with British policy—another Palazzo Chigi ambition. Italy's participation in the security pacts of 1925, then, would represent a considerable victory for the career diplomats.

On the other hand, any discussion of Europe's frontiers was almost certain to raise the issue of the postwar Austro-Italian border set at the Brenner Pass and of the Alto Adige with over 200,000 German-speaking people consigned to harsh Italian rule. On this subject Mussolini was the prototype of Italian chauvinists, belligerent, intolerant, and impervious to the Palazzo Chigi's moderating counsels. Emphasis on the Alto Adige could only work to the detriment of the old guard at the foreign ministry.

Mussolini's liaison with the German nationalists dictated that the divisive problem of the Alto Adige be put on ice. Yet Fascist Italy's policy in the province itself did not make this easy. During 1923 a program of Italianization was put into effect with much energy and some brutality by Senator Ettore Tolomei, member of a Tyrolean family long associated with Italian Alpine irredentism. Particularly noxious to the German minority in the Alto Adige was the compulsory use of Italian in all elementary schools.[1] With Berlin's

[1] Tolomei, *Memorie di vita* (Rome, 1948), Chap. 43. See also P. Herre, *Die Südtiroler Frage* (Munich, 1927), Chap. 11; Rusinow,

attention diverted by the Ruhr crisis, the immediate response of German nationalism came from Austria. The *Landtag* of the Austrian Tyrol unanimously asked the federal government in Vienna to bring the plight of the Alto Adige Germans before the League of Nations. But postwar Austria, dependent on international economic aid for existence, was in no position to lead a German peoples' crusade. Both privately and publicly Chancellor Seipel reproved the Tyroleans for their excessive nationalism, while in confidence he begged the Fascist government to moderate its Italianization policy in the Alto Adige. Unfortunately, in speaking to the Italian minister in Vienna, Seipel referred to opposition within Italy to the denationalization of German groups, an opposition voiced mainly by the leftists, archfoes of Fascism.[2] As a result, Mussolini was little disposed to sympathize with Seipel in his delicate position. After toying with the idea that the Italian frontier be closed to *Landtag* members and officials of the Austrian Tyrol, Mussolini contented himself with a tart reminder to Vienna that "educational policy in the Alto Adige . . . represents the exclusive concern of Italy," that "the anti-Italian agitation making its headquarters in Innsbruck" was the responsibility of the central Austrian government, and that this agitation, unless checked, "might reach the point of compromising good relations between the two countries."[3] To make perfectly clear his reaction to the outburst of German nationalism across the Brenner, Mussolini openly raised before his fellow countrymen the specter of an Austro-German union, or *Anschluss*, which was the worst threat pan-Germanism could offer Italy's hold on the Alto Adige.[4]

Italy's Austrian Heritage, pp. 170-79; and M. Toscano, *Storia diplomatica della questione dell'Alto Adige*, rev. ed. (Bari, 1968), pp. 98-101.

[2] *DDI*, II, Nos. 479-80, 483, 486.

[3] *DDI*, II, Nos. 480 and note, 500.

[4] *OO*, XX, 110.

The affair of the Tyrolean *Landtag*'s motion was only a harbinger. As the sagacious Contarini observed in June 1925, it was merely a matter of time before weak Austria was relieved of the duty of protecting German minority rights in the Alto Adige by potentially powerful Germany.[5] During 1925 this gradually became apparent. The implementation of the Dawes report offered the beginnings of a solution to the reparations tangle, and released Germany from the hypnosis of the Ruhr occupation. Striking testimony of this came in February with Stresemann's offer of a security pact to the Allies. It was not to be expected that Mussolini would welcome any security arrangement which had at its core a Franco-German rapprochement; that would thwart his idea, conceived in the Fiume crisis of 1923, of using Germany to neutralize France. A more serious consequence would be to divert German nationalist attention from the Rhine to the Alps. This is just what happened in the spring of 1925 at the very moment that the election of Field Marshal Paul von Hindenburg as president of the Weimar Republic indicated the reviving influence of the imperial nationalist tradition. Rome, indeed, anticipated a Hohenzollern restoration.[6] Shortly afterward, the German National People's party, presuming on its special relationship with Italian Fascism, went out of its way to reassure the Italian ambassador of its hope for a revival of the pre-World War I Italo-German alliance, but added as "indispensable conditions . . . Italy's renunciation of her absolute veto over the reunion of Austria to the *Reich* and also of her denationalization policy in the Alto Adige."[7]

It was not in Germany alone that the notion of an *Anschluss* gained currency. From Paris, Romano Avezzana warned that in certain international circles an *Anschluss* was considered a tolerable revision of the postwar peace

[5] G.D. (Stresemann papers), 7314H/3143/159131.
[6] *DDI*, III, No. 825.   [7] *DDI*, IV, No. 66.

treaties, and a convenient quid pro quo to offer Germany in return for the fulfillment of the western territorial clauses of the Versailles Treaty within the framework of an international security pact.[8] In March the pro-German British ambassador in Berlin, Viscount d'Abernon, made a pointed if perhaps naïve inquiry about Italy's attitude toward such a contingency.[9] Not surprisingly Mussolini was adamantly opposed to an *Anschluss* under any circumstances, and lukewarm to the whole idea of a security pact.[10]

The *Anschluss* question came to a head in May. The German chancellor, Stresemann, intimated to Ambassador De Bosdari in Berlin that not all the powers were as opposed as Italy to an *Anschluss*; and he regretted Mussolini's uncompromising stand against this panacea for Austria's troubles.[11] Warned by Neurath of the consternation caused in Rome by De Bosdari's highly charged report, Stresemann hastened to deny any intention of raising the *Anschluss* issue, and ascribed the misunderstanding to De Bosdari's exaggeration of a casual reference.[12] However, the German hint decided Mussolini on a counteroffensive. Speaking before the Senate on May 20 he reiterated Italy's opposition to an *Anschluss*, and went on to raise the matter of an international guarantee of the existing Austro-Italian frontier at the Brenner: "Not only must the Rhine frontiers be guaranteed but those of the Brenner also."[13] Stresemann renewed his disavowals of *Anschluss* plans, but, in return, asked for an assurance that Italy had no intention of bring-

[8] *DDI*, III, Nos. 682, 699.

[9] *DDI*, III, No. 772. Cf. *DDB*, II, No. 54.

[10] *DDB*, II, No. 52; *DDI*, III, Nos. 761, 781; G.D., 2784H/1385/537890.

[11] *DDI*, III, No. 846; G.D., 2784H/1385/537929-30. The Italian and German accounts of the interview differ markedly in conveying how directly Stresemann threatened to raise the *Anschluss* issue.

[12] G.D., 2784H/1385/537933-34, 537935-36.

[13] Salvemini, *Mussolini diplomatico*, p. 97, records Mussolini's actual words. The official version which appears in his collected works has been doctored; see below, note 15.

ing up the Brenner for international discussion.[14] This the
German embassy in Rome was able to obtain with surprisingly little difficulty. The official text of Mussolini's Senate
speech was changed to read fairly innocuously: "There is
no need to guarantee the Rhine frontier alone by making
less firm the sureties for the Brenner."[15]

In substance, what had emerged from the exchange was
a stalemate. Germany feared to broach the subject of an
Austro-German union lest Mussolini demand and possibly win international confirmation of Italy's Brenner
frontier and possession of the Alto Adige, while Italy dared
not seek this desired assurance lest it bring nearer an internationally sanctioned *Anschluss* as compensation. In Berlin at least, the situation was viewed in these terms. An
unsigned article in the *Hamburger Fremdenblatt* some
time later described precisely the Italo-German standoff
over an *Anschluss* and Brenner guarantee. Unsigned articles
in this journal was one of Stresemann's favorite means of
disseminating his ideas, and a copy of this article, underscored and annotated, is in Stresemann's papers.[16]

Although Mussolini dropped his public references to a
Brenner guarantee, he continued to refer to it in diplomatic
circles. He cited it in a circular to his ambassadors to justify his persistent negative stand on the proposed security
pact: "If the conclusion of the pact were to give rise . . . to
an exclusive, specific superguarantee limited absolutely to
the frontiers in the west, implicitly there would be established two different categories of obligations with respect
to the terms of the [peace] treaties. In consequence, Italy
would have no particular interest in participating in this
pact."[17]

[14] G.D., 2784H/1386/537938, 537944-49.
[15] *OO*, XXI, 319. For the Palazzo Chigi's version of the exchanges see
DDI, IV, No. 13.
[16] G.D. (Stresemann papers), 7318H/3168/159901.
[17] *DDI*, IV, No. 21.

It became apparent in June that France was anxious enough to obtain Italy's adherence to a security pact to buy it with a provision of some sort of guarantee for Mussolini's northern frontier. The French themselves knew that this could not be an international pledge, because, apart from the problem of forcing Germany into a recognition of the status quo to the south, the British had made it clear all along that they were no more disposed to involve themselves on the Brenner than on the Vistula.[18] Therefore, all France could offer was a separate Franco-Italian pact "for reciprocal security of respective frontiers." French Foreign Minister Aristide Briand went out of his way to secure Britain's blessing on such an agreement before approaching Italy.[19]

Nonetheless, the proposal had serious drawbacks, from Mussolini's point of view. First, even a Brenner guarantee which was less than international in scope might raise again the threat of an *Anschluss* as part of the anticipated security pact. But more important, it was one thing for Mussolini himself to stand firm against pan-Germanism on the Brenner; it was quite another to form an exclusive alliance with France against it. That would have been to fly directly in the face of Mussolini's private foreign policy, which was to find an accommodation with the German nationalists at France's expense. Faced with a choice between German and French nationalism, Mussolini preferred to remain attached to the former. This drove him to the peculiar contention that German nationalism on the Brenner and an *Anschluss* in particular, while "a danger in itself, is much less serious for Italy than for France." But at least, it afforded a pretext to brush aside Briand's overture as a trick to subordinate Italy to France's anti-German policy.[20]

With an international Brenner guarantee out of the question and Briand's substitute unacceptable, Fascist Italy saw

---

[18] *DDI*, III, Nos. 751, 756, 787. [19] *DDI*, IV, Nos. 27, 37.
[20] *DDI*, IV, No. 120.

little value, in terms of narrow national self-interest, in a Rhine security pact. In the late summer of 1925 Mussolini remained extraneous to the negotiations, deliberately holding in abeyance his decision whether to join in such an agreement.[21] The Palazzo Chigi officials, with Secretary General Contarini and Ambassador Romano Avezzana in Paris in the van, were not backward at this time in giving Mussolini their advice. They were nonplused by Mussolini's rejection of Briand's offer, but with or without a Brenner guarantee they strongly advocated adherence to a security pact which promised to obtain the signatures of nearly all the European states.[22]

In reality, despite his outward disinterest, Mussolini shared their view. As early as August he was resolved to swallow the dislike of international conferences which he had conceived after his experiences at Lausanne and London, and to attend any meeting of Stresemann, Briand, and Chamberlain. In addition, he assigned Grandi, recently appointed undersecretary at the foreign ministry, to the fruitless task of trying to arrange a foreign ministers' meeting to sign a security pact on Italian soil.[23] But he still gave no firm undertaking to participate in a meeting outside Italy, although he assured Sir Austen Chamberlain, who was foremost among foreign statesmen in urging the Duce to attend, that he would "do his utmost to be present at the conference."[24]

Indeed, he did appear at the Swiss resort of Locarno on October 16 to sign the Rhine pacts. He came at the last moment; for public consumption his attendance was announced as an 11th-hour decision. But despite his the-

21 *OO*, XXI, 369; G.D., 2784H/1386/538034-35, 538041-43.

22 *DDI*, IV, Nos. 116, 126, 129, and p. 90, n. 1. See also Legatus, *Vita di Contarini*, pp. 119-20; R. De Dampierre, "Dix années de politique française à Rome," *Revue des Deux-Mondes* (Nov. 1, 1953), pp. 16-17.

23 *DDI*, IV, Nos. 102, 118-19.   24 *DDI*, IV, No. 137.

atrical entrance, he was as uncomfortable as ever at international gatherings; he found himself boycotted because of the Matteotti murder by the local inhabitants, most of the press, and even some delegates.[25] He tried to put a brave face on events. Not to be present would have been "an inexcusable discourtesy," he announced in explanation of his sudden arrival. Actually the head of the Italian government could not afford, for reasons of prestige, to be absent from so important a meeting as the Locarno Conference. Also, in the interests of national pride he took the occasion to deny blatantly that Italy had ever sought a Brenner guarantee.[26] But Mussolini's chagrin at Locarno without provision for the Brenner was ill-disguised; soon after the conference his feelings were reflected in sarcastic comments to foreign diplomats in Rome on the new distinction between "first and second-class frontiers."[27]

If Mussolini believed Italy had gained nothing from Locarno, he calculated that Germany had made concrete profit. As De Bosdari interpreted his Fascist chief's estimate to Stresemann, Germany was now secure enough in the west to attempt a new policy in the south threatening Italy's position in the Alto Adige.[28] Consequently it was in the Alto Adige that the repercussions of Mussolini's appraisal were felt. At the beginning of 1925 German Ambassador Neurath had warned his government that Fascism's recovered hegemony over Italian political life after the Matteotti affair would be paralleled by an affirmation of Fascist policy in the Alto Adige in the form of sterner Italianization measures.[29] This, indeed, occurred as 1925 progressed, but it was Mussolini's almost pathological fear in the new situation created by Locarno of German machi-

25 Kirkpatrick, *Mussolini*, pp. 249-50.
26 *OO*, XXI, 411-12.
27 G.D., 4530H/2285/139995-98; 2784H/1386/538059.
28 G.D., 2784H/1386/538073, 538093.
29 G.D., 529K/4154/152059-60.

nations on Italy's northern frontier that provided the final
and most positive spur to an intensely nationalist program. The maximum Italianization of the Alto Adige was
to serve, like Mussolini's call for a Brenner guarantee,
as a deterrent to German revisionism and a frenetic assev-
eration of the permanence of Italy's ownership of the region.

Mussolini's post-Locarno insistence on the creation of
italianità in the Alto Adige roused the opposition not
merely of the Austrian pan-Germans—as had been more
or less the case in the early days of Tolomei's Italianization
program two years earlier—but also of the Bavarian nationalists and the German patriots in the Reichstag, who
during 1925 increasingly had taken to speaking on behalf
of German minority rights in the Alto Adige. Mussolini
was quick to reaffirm publicly and forcefully that the Alto
Adige was Italy's domestic concern.[30] This placed Stresemann in an embarrassing position. He shared with the German embassy in Rome the view that German foreign policy
was not furthered, at least in 1925, by a display of pan-Germanism on the Brenner. Indeed, he did his utmost, admittedly with limited success, to curb the south German
irredentists.[31] But meanwhile German nationalist circles
continued to exert pressure on Stresemann to take up the
cause of the Alto Adige Germans.[32]

As 1926 began Stresemann implored Mussolini to make
some gesture of conciliation to German feeling to supplement Stresemann's endeavors to restrain the German nationalists.[33] When nothing was forthcoming from Rome,
Stresemann on February 3 felt constrained to associate himself and the German government with the German popula-

[30] *OO*, XXI, 423; XXII, 10-11. See also Toscano, *Storia diplomatica
dell'Alto Adige*, pp. 106, 113.

[31] G.D., 442K/4011/126620-23, 126647-50, 126624-26, 126818-22, 126658-
59, 126728; 2784H/1386/538082-83, 538096-98.

[32] See, for instance, evidence of the lobbying activities by the *Verein
für das Deutschtum im Ausland* in G.D., 442K/4012/126914-18, 126919.

[33] G.D., 2784H/1386/538084-86, 538114-15, 538124-25.

tion in the Alto Adige in its struggle to preserve minimum national rights.[34] Mussolini replied promptly and astringently; Stresemann responded; then Mussolini—all of these exchanges being made publicly within a week. The arguments used on both sides varied in quality. On the one hand, there was maintained at least the pretense of distinguishing between a minority's political privileges, legally at the mercy of Italy in the Alto Adige, and cultural identity, commonly regarded as a minority's inalienable moral right; on the other hand, there were mutual threats of trade and tourist boycotts. At one point Mussolini threatened "to carry the Italian standard across the Brenner." On the topic of the Brenner, Stresemann pointed to Mussolini's essays and failure to secure a guarantee of his northern frontier at Locarno, and Mussolini once more indignantly denied the attempt.[35]

Of the two protagonists Mussolini was the more vituperative, perhaps because of his extreme personal dislike of Stresemann. Mussolini had conceived a contempt for the German foreign minister as an unlikely figure to sponsor either a German national revival or an alliance with Italy. Now, ironically, Mussolini faced a Stresemann championing German rights in the Alto Adige, but his loathing seems to have remained unchanged. Mussolini began his acrimonious exchange with Stresemann suddenly; only a few days earlier he had cordially promised to withhold his Fascists from anti-German demonstrations.[36] Significantly the Anglo-Italian war-debt settlement was signed on January 27. Mussolini presumably wanted to secure the concessions embodied in that agreement before provoking a crisis over the Alto Adige that would be distasteful to London. But, once given the opportunity of a public dispute

[34] G. Stresemann, *Vermachtnis*, ed. G. Bernhard (Berlin, 1932-33), II, 486-89.
[35] *OO*, XXII, 68-73, 74-78; Stresemann, *Vermachtnis*, II, 490-99.
[36] *ADAP*, III, No. 43. Cf. *ADAP*, III, No. 22.

with Germany, the Duce used it as a transitory contrivance to set the seal on what he had started out to accomplish. This was to publicize before European opinion the dangers of pan-Germanism on the Brenner, even if it meant deliberately provoking the German nationalists into extreme pronouncements. At the same time, he sought to emphasize in the most dramatic way possible Italy's resolution to cling to the Alto Adige, even if it meant indulging in an internationally unpopular display of Fascist braggadocio. These ends could be regarded as achieved with the public spectacle of the Mussolini-Stresemann exchange of invective. Consequently, Mussolini was now in a mood to relax Fascist severity in the Alto Adige and allow the artificial Italo-German crisis to subside. By the end of February the storm subsided as swiftly as it had arisen.[37]

In the Alto Adige was to be found the key to all of Mussolini's German policy. German national consciousness was to be encouraged to express itself on the Rhine, not in the Alps. To this end, Italy's moral and material support went to the *Reichswehr* generals and right-wing politicians in Berlin. In the same vein, Mussolini rejected Briand's offer of a French Brenner guarantee, clearly anticipating that Germany's quarrel with France would continue. In the words of an inspired article in the *Corriere della Sera:* "Franco-German dissensions were fundamental and rooted deep in history. They could not be eliminated in a day."[38] Obviously, if Germany assumed the function assigned by Mussolini, and became embroiled in the Rhineland, Italy stood to profit both by France's embarrassment and by Germany's distraction from the Alto Adige. The Bavarian right, on the other hand, could not be expected to concern itself with France to the exclusion of affairs across the Bren-

---

[37] *DBFP*, I, Nos. 271, 292; Herre, *Die Südtiroler Frage*, pp. 382ff; Toscano, *Storia diplomatica dell'Alto Adige*, pp. 118-20.
[38] *Corriere della Sera*, Sept. 24, 1926.

ner. But Hitler's departure from the Bavarian norm was tailor-made to fit Fascist Italy's strategy. Hence it was the Nazi chief who came to enjoy an exalted position in Mussolini's graces. From him the Duce had a specific promise of what he could only hope to receive in gratitude from other German nationalists in Berlin and Munich—a free hand in the Alto Adige. It was a promise Hitler kept until Mussolini's overthrow in 1943.

To find a coherent pattern in Mussolini's German policy is not to account that policy wise. By encouraging German nationalist circles in the hope of obtaining security in the Alto Adige as a reward, Mussolini played the role of the first interwar appeaser. The late 1930s revealed German nationalism as a force too big for Mussolini to manipulate or even strike an equal bargain with. The ugly fate of Mussolini himself, his regime, and his country in World War II was an apt commentary on the enormity of his miscalculation.

Contarini's Resignation

Mussolini's belligerent insistence on Italy's hold over the Alto Adige had a momentous side result within the Palazzo Chigi. The permanent officials were shocked by his public argument with Stresemann. Their perturbation was the greater because Mussolini's outburst came so soon after Italy's adhesion to the Locarno Pacts, which the staff of Italy's foreign ministry regarded as a triumph for their own principles.[39] The Duce's image as a good European, fostered by his attendance at Locarno, was shattered almost as soon as it was made.

Mussolini not only embarked on his noisy dispute with Stresemann with great suddenness, but he gave his diplomats no inkling of what he was up to. In Berlin Stresemann

[39] The British ambassador commented on the Palazzo Chigi's loyalty to Mussolini on the morrow of Locarno (B.D., Chamberlain papers, Vol. 258, Nov. 6, 1925).

found De Bosdari woefully uninstructed by his foreign minister on the Alto Adige situation. And Contarini and other Italian officials in Rome showed a much more conciliatory attitude than their chief.[40] De Bosdari's resignation had been rumored for some time; thus it came as no surprise when he left his Berlin post in the wake of the Mussolini-Stresemann quarrel. Ambassador Neurath tartly anticipated a replacement "who will be heeded by the Fascist government more than was the case with Bosdari."[41] What did constitute a veritable bombshell was Secretary General Contarini's exact same reaction. In March 1926 he too tendered his resignation.[42]

Due to Contarini's own reticence the exact circumstances of his resignation are unclear. Plainly tension between the secretary general and the Duce had been building up throughout 1925, particularly over Mussolini's increasingly cavalier attitude toward the Italo-Yugoslav rapprochement and the Pact of Rome.[43] It is beyond question, however, that the immediate cause of Contarini's departure was Mussolini's threat, made publicly on February 6, 1926, to march across the Brenner. Speaking a few days later to Graham, the British ambassador in Rome, in whom he sometimes confided, Contarini revealed his concern over the influence on Mussolini of such extremists as Luigi Federzoni and Alberto Rocco.[44] After his resignation became known, Contarini again talked with Graham, and described his position as "untenable owing to various currents that surround" Mussolini. Despite Contarini's circumspection the

[40] G.D., 2784H/1386/538074-75, 538095, 538117, 538129.
[41] G.D., 2784H/1386/538269.
[42] Mussolini accepted Contarini's resignation on March 19, although probably the secretary general had intimated his intent to resign earlier (Carocci, *Politica estera dell'Italia fascista*, p. 56).
[43] See Chap. 16.
[44] *DBFP*, I, No. 262.

British ambassador was left in no doubt that his alarm arose from Mussolini's German and central European policies.[45]

Nevertheless, one cannot avoid the suspicion that Contarini's quarrel was less with the merits of Mussolini's foreign policy than with the method whereby it was formulated. Mussolini's conduct in the Alto Adige question was familiar Fascist bluster, and the affair blew over quickly without materially changing Italo-German or Italo-Austrian relations. On the other hand, there were signs that Contarini was frequently being excluded from the diplomatic decision-making process. The appointment of Dino Grandi as undersecretary in May 1925, no matter how pliable Grandi himself might be, symbolized Mussolini's denigration of the secretary general and his office. In Albania, from early 1925 Mussolini was inclined to bypass the career diplomats and use the Fascist deputy, Alessandro Lessona. No doubt Contarini was also aware, from De Bosdari's reports, of Mussolini's private messengers to the German nationalists. Mussolini's verbal attack on Stresemann, without prior notification to Contarini, was patently the last straw. Contarini was not known for his humility. The continual slights that Mussolini visited on him, inadvertently or otherwise, must have been a grievous affront to his sense of self-importance, thus forcing his decision to retire.

Despite his disparagement of Contarini, Mussolini was aware of his value. The secretary general commanded respect, not only within Italy's diplomatic corps, but in chancelleries abroad as well. His mere presence in the Palazzo Chigi could be used for propaganda purposes in refutation of the charges of recklessness and aggressiveness raised against Fascist Italy. Mussolini therefore tried to keep Con-

[45] *DBFP*, I, No. 368, n. 1. Legatus, *Vita di Contarini*, pp. 121-24, gives Mussolini's Brenner speech of February 6 as the immediate cause of Contarini's resignation.

tarini within the fold by offering him alternative diplomatic employment; the London embassy or leadership of Italy's delegation to the League of Nations were mentioned. Although Contarini refused to serve Fascism any longer, he was prepared to hide his breach with Mussolini as much as possible. His resignation was not made known generally until March 27. And when he left the Palazzo Chigi on April 16, he did so with a minimum of publicity.[46] On occasion during the next two years there was speculation in diplomatic circles that Contarini might return to the Palazzo Chigi, but this seems never to have been a real possibility.[47]

Predictably, Contarini's retirement was regretted outside Italy, although not as an absolute catastrophe.[48] Considerable store was put in Italy's signature on the Locarno Pacts as a surety of future good behavior. But the real import of Contarini's resignation was not readily perceived at the time. The consequences were most severe within the fastness of the Italian foreign ministry. Contarini's strong personality had enabled him not only to stand up to Mussolini with some success, but also to dominate utterly his professional colleagues. Over six years Italy's career diplomats had grown accustomed to taking their cue from the arbitrary secretary general; his control had sapped their individual initiative. Without Contarini's leadership it was doubtful how much resistance to the Duce and his Fascist advisers the Palazzo Chigi would be able to muster. Contarini's successor as secretary general, Antonio Chiaramonte Bordonaro, came to the post from the Vienna legation. Described by a British diplomat as "a capable and reasonable man, possessed of great charm of manner [and] quiet

---

[46] B.D., C3943/77/22; *DBFP*, I, No. 368; Ferraris, *L'amministrazione del Ministero degli esteri*, p. 66; Legatus, *Vita di Contarini*, pp. 123-25; *Times* (London), March 27, 1926.

[47] Carocci, *Politica estera dell'Italia fascista*, p. 22.

[48] See, for instance, Whitehall's reaction (*DBFP*, I, No. 422).

refinement," there was nothing in Chiaramonte Bordonaro's record or character to suggest that he would be able to meet the foreign ministry's need for a strong-willed mentor and spokesman.[49] The situation was an open invitation to Mussolini to assert himself in diplomatic affairs.

[49] B.D., C4240/77/22.

15. The Anglo-Italian Colonial Entente

The Foundations: Jarabub and Ethiopia

ONE OF THE fixed tenets of Italian foreign policy, according to the Contarini school of thought, was the absolute necessity of a close relationship with Great Britain. Guariglia recognized Italy's geopolitical situation with the quaint statement that Italy was "historically constrained for intrinsic and obvious reasons . . . to take refuge on rainy days . . . under the ample and capacious mantle of England."[1] A quasi-island in the middle of the Mediterranean, Italy was highly dependent on sea imports, especially of coal and grain; Britain's Mediterranean fleet almost at will could invade Italy's long coastline or cut off her supplies at Gibraltar and Suez. Mussolini had discovered this for himself in 1923 when the mere threat of British naval action was sufficient to frustrate his attempt to annex Corfu. "Italy must dominate or be the prisoner of the Mediterranean," went one aphorism of the interwar years.[2] Of course, the Mediterranean was Italy's lifeline to Africa, and any Italian statesman who dreamed of an African empire thus had to take London into account.

Sir Austen Chamberlain had demonstrated as soon as he became foreign secretary at the end of 1924 that he was eager for an accommodation with Italy. Under his aegis an Anglo-Italian entente burgeoned during 1925. Chamberlain put a considerable value on Mussolini's signature on the Locarno Pacts as a token gesture of Fascist Italy's willingness to fall into line with British thinking. He indulged in the fond illusion that it was at Britain's urging that Italy joined the pacts, and was warmly appreciative of Musso-

---

[1] Guariglia, *Ricordi*, p. 146.
[2] Macartney and Cremona, *Italy's Foreign and Colonial Policy*, p. 3.

lini's attendance at Locarno.[3] The lenient Anglo-Italian debt settlement in the new year 1926 was in the nature of a reward for Mussolini's good conduct at the conference. But in the last resort, it was in the colonial field that British and Italian interests touched most frequently. Not surprisingly, the Anglo-Italian entente which Chamberlain and the Palazzo Chigi officials wished to create took the form of a colonial understanding, and the principal focus of agreement was Africa.[4]

The first substantial African matter to be taken up by Chamberlain and Mussolini concerned the area on the Egyptian-Libyan border known as Jarabub. This area, along with Jubaland, comprised the colonial territory Britain had agreed to cede to Italy in conformity with Article XIII of the Treaty of London of 1915. The delimitation of Jubaland and Jarabub had been accomplished by the Milner-Scialoja Accord of 1920. With the execution of the Jubaland cession by MacDonald in 1924, Mussolini understandably expected Jarabub to be forthcoming next.

Strictly speaking, since the British recognition of Egypt's independence in 1922, Jarabub had been an Italo-Egyptian question. Egyptian nationalists had welcomed Mussolini's arrival in power because they thought Fascist Italy might become an ally against Britain. On the other hand, they did not want to yield Egyptian territory to Italian colonialists, although they stopped short of openly denouncing the Milner-Scialoja provisions for Jarabub. For two years the Egyptians had made no move to arrange the cession. Once the Jubaland question was out of the way, Mussolini tried to inject a note of urgency into the Jarabub proceedings. A revolt of the Senussi tribes in Cyrenaica, the eastern part

---

[3] *DBFP*, I, No. 5.

[4] On December 14, 1924, only a few weeks after Chamberlain's coming to the Foreign Office, the governors of the British Sudan and Italian Eritrea concluded a minor local agreement concerning the River Gash. It was a portent of future Anglo-Italian African accords (*DDI*, III, Nos. 632, 688).

of Italian Libya, had been smoldering for two years. In July 1924 Italy began to charge that Jarabub on the Cyrenaican-Egyptian border was the route by which the rebels received outside aid. Accompanying the charge was a rumor, perhaps deliberately planted by Rome, that Italy would seize Jarabub by force of arms on grounds of colonial security. Mussolini was willing to disclaim any intention of using force, although the promise was "subordinate to exigencies that might arise and especially to the condition that Jarabub . . . does not become a base of concentration and supply for the Libyan rebels and agitators."[5] It was a fairly obvious device to force the Egyptians' hand.

In September Egyptian Premier Zaghlul Pasha visited France and Britain; Ambassador Romano Avezzana and Gabriele Preziosi, the Italian chargé in London, were instructed to sound him on Jarabub. They found Zaghlul difficult to pin down. He made vague promises to open the final Jarabub negotiations on his return to Cairo. Romano Avezzana, suspecting that the promises would prove empty and thus drive Mussolini to the use of force, tried to dissuade Mussolini from "seizing a territory over which [Italy's] title is not yet perfect." Preziosi was more straightforward: "My conversation with Zaghlul Pasha has left me with the impression that he is determined to resist us as long as possible in the Jarabub question."[6] Cairo then tried to read into Italian denials of an imminent descent on Jarabub a positive pledge to maintain the status quo, which provoked Rome into a fresh threat to resume liberty of action.[7] All in all, Fascist threats fell on deaf ears, which was perhaps only to be expected considering that they were made at the height of the Matteotti affair. Fascism's enemies, including the Senussi rebels and Egyptian nationalists, took heart from what they expected to be the begin-

[5] *DDI*, iii, No. 418; *Corriere della Sera*, Nov. 9, 1924.
[6] *DDI*, iii, Nos. 437, 509, 522.
[7] *DDI*, iii, No. 525.

ning of the end of Mussolini's regime. And given Mussolini's parlous situation, he was not in a position to embark on Corfu-like adventures abroad. As Romano Avezzana reported, Zaghlul was confident Italy at this time would not dare defy the British veto on the unilateral occupation of Jarabub.[8]

But Egyptian intransigence was, in the last resort, marginally important. Egyptian independence in foreign affairs was, in the words of Guariglia whose department in the Palazzo Chigi handled the Jarabub question, "more formal than substantial." The last word still rested with London.[9] Naturally then, at the same time direct approaches were made to Zaghlul, an appeal went out to London. Sir William Tyrrell, deputy undersecretary at the Foreign Office, gave explicit assurances that Britain would honor the Milner-Scialoja Accord, while MacDonald, too, was sympathetic.[10] But there was no sign that British pressure was about to bring Egypt to the conference table—that is, until Chamberlain took over the Foreign Office. No sooner had he done so than the British governor-general of the Sudan was murdered in Cairo. Chamberlain, in conversation with Della Torretta, stressed the necessity of the occidental nations standing together against the rising tide of anti-colonialism. In reply Della Torretta hinted that it might then be appropriate for Britain to prevent Egyptian aid being given to the Senussi revolt.[11] Events moved forward when Chamberlain, visiting Rome for the League of Nations session in December 1924, held several friendly conversations with Mussolini. An anonymous memorandum drawn up in the Palazzo Chigi ahead of time listed those "questions which might form the subject of the forthcoming talks with Chamberlain"—and put at the head the

8 *DDI*, III, No. 509; see also No. 357.
9 Guariglia, *Ricordi*, p. 37.
10 *DDI*, III, Nos. 505, 508, 518.
11 *DDI*, III, No. 578.

need to resolve the Jarabub issue within the context of suppressing the Senussi revolt.[12] Italian representations were not without effect. Two weeks later Egypt offered to negotiate the last details of the Jarabub cession; appropriately, Mussolini promised to keep Chamberlain informed.[13]

Chamberlain's backing meant certain Italian possession of Jarabub in the foreseeable future. Nonetheless, Egypt managed to spin out the final rites for most of 1925. Chamberlain set out to serve as mediator between Rome and Cairo, once writing personally to Mussolini urging patience. The gist of his message was that Italy should appreciate the subtleties of Egypt's internal situation. Thus Italy should await the Egyptian elections before opening talks; Italy should also spare the Egyptian government embarrassment by not insisting on a public renunciation of Jarabub and by allowing the pretense that Egypt was not bound by the Milner-Scialoja Accord, even while reaching a settlement on that basis. Mussolini deferred to this advice, "as a proof of my friendly disposition toward the British government and also toward the person of Signor Chamberlain."[14] Apparently Mussolini was so well-disposed toward the British foreign secretary at this point that he even considered yielding Cyrenaican territory on the Mediterranean to Britain in exchange for the Jarabub oases, but was dissuaded by the Italian army chiefs of staff.[15] In keeping with this subdued approach, Italy sought a rapprochement with the rebel Senussi chiefs who had been encouraging Egypt not to give up Jarabub.[16] But as 1925 wore on, Italian irritation with Egyptian delays returned and Britain veered more to the Italian side. In July, London, working always behind the scenes, arranged that the Italian and Egyptian negotiators immediately get in touch with each

[12] *DDI*, III, No. 605.   [13] *DDI*, III, Nos. 633, 661.
[14] *DDI*, III, Nos. 725, 740, 834.   [15] Guariglia, *Ricordi*, p. 37.
[16] *DDI*, III, Nos. 600, 687; IV, Nos. 79, 128.

other, although they would not formally meet until October.[17] Mussolini reported to King Victor Emmanuel: "The old question of Jarabub is moving to a solution, albeit with Levantine slowness."[18]

The meeting of Italian and Egyptian experts began in October and lasted for some two months. The settlement that emerged contained only one surprise, and that a victory for Italy. Italian possession of the Jarabub oases could take place without waiting for the Egyptian parliament's ratification of all of the treaty. Mussolini quickly fixed February 1, 1926, as the *"improrogabile"* date, and set about to impress Italian public opinion with what was, according to Guariglia, only a "small political success."[19]

Here was the core of the matter, indeed. For Jubaland and Jarabub, whatever fuss might be made over their acquisition, merely added to Italy's "collection of deserts"— poor recompense for Article XIII of the Treaty of London. By Guariglia's account, this was tolerated in Rome only because it was deemed a necessary price for British friendship and ultimately, richer prizes. Italy's specific objective was Ethiopia. Ethiopia (or Abyssinia) was not a noticeably rich portion of Africa, no matter what some Italians thought of its suitability for Italy's surplus population. But in view of Italy's humiliating defeat there at the end of the nineteenth century, Ethiopia had a tremendous psychological fascination and value for Italian nationalists.

In 1906, a decade after the Adowa defeat, Italy, Britain, and France, whose possessions surrounded Ethiopia, had entered into an agreement delineating respective spheres of influence in Ethiopia. In effect, this was a self-denying instrument, whereby each party was obligated to consult the other two before pushing too far ahead in its own zone. But Italy's ambition for Ethiopia, if shackled, was not dead.

---

[17] *DDI*, III, Nos. 800, 813; IV, No. 62.   [18] *DDI*, IV, No. 60.
[19] *DDI*, IV, No. 221; Guariglia, *Ricordi*, pp. 40-42.

Eritrea on the Red Sea remained an Italian colony, providing a gateway to Ethiopia. During World War I and at the
Paris Peace Conference the Italians had sought to increase
their stake in the area by acquiring from France the port
of Djibuti, only to be consistently repulsed. But any proposal for penetration into Ethiopia proper as satisfaction
of Italian claims under Article XIII of the Treaty of London had to be taken up with Britain; for the headwaters
of the Nile were in Ethiopia, and Egyptian considerations
came into play. What the Italians wanted was carte blanche
to exploit their Ethiopian zone designated by the 1906
accord and to build a railroad from Eritrea to the Ethiopian capital, Addis Ababa. In 1919 and 1922, when the matter had been broached with the British, the reply had been
negative.[20] Moreover, in 1923 Italy had been forced to acquiesce in Ethiopia's admission to the League of Nations,
thus creating an additional barrier to the colonization of
Ethiopia.

That Ethiopia gained entry to the League was due
largely to the skill and energy of her prince regent, Ras
Tafari, later to become the Emperor Haile Selassie. But
this was only the start of Tafari's efforts to raise the international status of his country. In the summer of 1924 he
visited Britain, France, and Italy, where each government
went to great pains to flatter him with ceremonial recep-
tions and to emphasize a constant desire to be of service in
Ethiopia's economic development.[21] But Tafari's ambition
was just the reverse: less, not more, foreign influence in Ethiopia. His main purpose in Europe was to reopen the question of an Ethiopian outlet to the sea, which
would have to run through British, French, or Italian colonial territory. This was a long-standing ambition of Addis

[20] Guariglia, *Ricordi*, pp. 42-44, 763-66.
[21] *DDI*, III, Nos. 196, 422.

Ababa, which the Italian minister there attributed to "the rather simplistic conviction that once the outlet to the sea is obtained, Abyssinia will completely escape from any control whatsoever on the part of the three [limitrophe] powers and will be able to receive freely whatever quantity of arms she desires."[22] Although there was no desire in Rome to enhance Ethiopia's freedom of action, Italy dared not reject Tafari's overture out of hand lest it drive him into France's arms. Indeed, the Ethiopian outlet most frequently mentioned terminated in the French port of Djibuti. So Italy humored Tafari while he was in Rome to the extent of actually drafting the outline of an agreement for a corridor through Italian Eritrea. But the French got wind of this, and held out some sort of counteroffer regarding Djibuti. This attracted Tafari enough to cause him to put aside negotiations with Italy, which probably did not displease Rome. Guariglia wrote: "It would indeed have been strange and painful had a Fascist government been induced to yield a slice of our territory, and particularly one carved from territory where our colonial history had its beginning."[23] In the event, neither Italy, France, nor Britain was prepared at this time to make Ethiopia an outright grant of territory, which was what Tafari wanted, so in this respect his trip to Europe was a failure.

But there were other Tafari initiatives to increase Ethiopia's independence, which aroused Italian alarm and opposition. Soon after his return from Europe he proposed to buy up the British, French, and Italian-owned shares in the Bank of Abyssinia, which had been established as an international house by the accord of 1906. Italy was not in the least inclined to relinquish a foothold in Ethiopia, and

[22] *DDI*, III, No. 466.

[23] Guariglia, *Ricordi*, pp. 766-67. See also *DDI*, III, Nos. 558, 590, 598, 614.

Italian shareholders were forbidden to sell. For good measure, Italy, on not much evidence, ascribed Tafari's scheme to French intrigues.[24]

In 1925 Tafari returned to the question of Ethiopia's access to defensive weapons. By the 1906 accord, and as a condition of admission to the League of Nations, importation of arms into Ethiopia was supposed to be stringently controlled, and Britain, France, and Italy on Ethiopia's frontiers were in a geographical position to enforce the condition. It was partly to evade this blockade that the Ethiopian government was so anxious for a sea outlet. But with the dwindling of this prospect, Tafari approached the League to lift some of the legal restrictions on Ethiopia's right to import arms. Italy was adamantly opposed. After all, the guns might someday be fired at Italian soldiers— another Adowa perhaps. However, Ethiopia still had the sympathy of the smaller powers at Geneva and, despite big-power disapproval, in July won some relaxation of arms controls.[25] This was a token victory, for arms would still have to come through British, French, and Italian territory. Ethiopia would continue under blockade as long as the three colonial powers cooperated.

All the time, Tafari was trying to play off Britain, France, and Italy against each other. In doing so, he ran the risk that his ambitious diplomacy would drive all three, or at least two, of Ethiopia's colonial neighbors into a common front, which is what happened. Tafari's vigorous efforts to free his country from European dominance, coupled with French willingness to aid him up to a point, produced an Anglo-Italian counterstroke in the guise of an understanding on Ethiopia. There had been premonitions of this for some time. As early as November 1923 London was resolved to neutralize Italy's opposition to the build-

24 *DDI*, III, No. 457.
25 *DDI*, IV, Nos. 9, 16, 38.

ing of a British dam on Lake Tsana in northern Ethiopia.[26] In the summer of 1924 the British minister to Addis Ababa observed that he "had often suggested to his government a special accord with Italy regarding Abyssinia, joint action by Italy and England at Addis Ababa being the only way to counterbalance French influence that has been growing ever more obtrusive."[27] Soon thereafter, Della Torretta reported from London that the British government had failed to come to terms on economic concessions with Tafari during his stay in London. Then the flight of British capital from Ethiopia, as a result of Tafari's efforts to gain control of the Bank of Abyssinia, caused the Foreign Office to mutter about the "new friends" the government in Addis Ababa was turning to.[28]

All this must have been encouragement to the Palazzo Chigi to aspire to a special arrangement with London. Certainly, when in December 1924 the Italian foreign ministry drew up a hypothetical agenda for the Mussolini-Chamberlain talks in Rome, "Ethiopian questions" figured prominently. Specifically posed was "the reconfirmation or, if necessary, revision of the 1906 accord about zones of influence in Ethiopia, an accord about which England has manifested doubt inasmuch as it has been weakened by Ethiopia's entry into the League of Nations."[29] It seems unlikely, however, that Chamberlain at this time responded to any Italian hint. So we may surmise from Guariglia's statement that when Britain indeed made a concrete proposal six months later, "it fell like a thunderbolt out of a clear sky."[30] Yet the timing was comprehensible. By the summer of 1925 Britain and Italy had just been challenged by Tafari in the arms control question. Simultaneously the way was cleared for an Anglo-Italian ac-

26 B.D., C2661/2661/22 (Annual Report, 1923, p. 14).
27 *DDI*, III, No. 196. 28 *DDI*, III, Nos. 391, 413.
29 *DDI*, III, No. 605. 30 Guariglia, *Ricordi*, p. 44.

cord by Chamberlain's persuasion of Egypt to negotiate on Jarabub, thus resolving the last African problem between London and Rome left from Article XIII of the Treaty of London. Furthermore, Chamberlain had been in office long enough to become established before beginning to construct the Anglo-Italian entente he undoubtedly had in mind all along.

What Britain suggested was an agreement for mutual assistance in obtaining concessions in the respective British and Italian zones of Ethiopia delineated in the 1906 accord. This was essentially what Italy had sought in the immediate postwar years; so the British démarche was a godsend in the opinion of most Italian officials. On the other hand, the Italian colonial ministry officials, and in particular the governor of Italian Eritrea, Iacopo Gasparini, were congenitally as suspicious of Britain as of France in East Africa and therefore skeptical of any deal with Britain. Apropos of their demands, the British ambassador in Rome remarked: "In such matters the Italians are apt to open their mouths to an extent with which no crocodile would compete." But the Italian colonial ministry was speedily brought to heel, not least by Contarini.[31] Because the Ethiopian arrangement projected was a simple one, little Anglo-Italian negotiation was needed. Thus an accord was worked out during the summer of 1925, but due to "bureaucratic punctilio" (Guariglia's phrase), it was not formalized until December 14. One may suspect that, in addition, Mussolini's signature on the Locarno Pacts in October was required to bring the Ethiopian agreement to fruition. In substance, it comprised an exchange of notes between British Ambassador Graham and Mussolini.[32] On

[31] B.D., Chamberlain papers, Vol. 258, May 1, 1925 and July 30, 1925. On the clash between Italy's cautious career diplomats and the colonial activists backed by Fascist zealots, see G. W. Baer, *The Coming of the Italian-Ethiopian War* (Cambridge, Mass., 1967), pp. 18-21.
[32] Guariglia, *Ricordi*, pp. 44-46.

December 29 the seal was set when Chamberlain, again visiting Italy, met Mussolini at Rapallo. This encounter was as much social as political, but as the official communiqué said: "The examination of recent major events in international politics emphasized the possibility and utility of keeping in vigor the collaboration presently established between the two countries."[33]

The Mussolini-Graham notes amounted to the sort of accord that says little but connotes much. Britain was promised Italian help in gaining concessions in the region of Lake Tsana in northern Ethiopia. In fact, the British white paper on the agreement was called "Notes Exchanged between the United Kingdom and Italy respecting Lake Tsana."[34] In return, "Italy's exclusive economic influence in western Abyssinia," as the Italian gloss on the accord put it, was reconfirmed, and Rome could count on British support in seeking to build a railroad between Eritrea and Italian Somaliland which passed through Addis Ababa. Italy undertook not to divert the Nile headwaters insofar as they were within the Italian concessionary zone.[35] The understanding was to remain secret, at least at first, although early in 1926 the British, overriding Italian objections, insisted on publishing its contents.[35a]

The terms of the Anglo-Italian understanding did not, in reality, go beyond the 1906 accord, which gave rise to the inevitable questions: Why was it necessary to renew the 20-year-old accord? More to the point, why was it done without one of the original signatories, France? Because, so London and Rome claimed, the French and Tafari by their actions had called the 1906 accord into question. But as the Italian minister in Addis Ababa observed, the likeli-

---

[33] *OO*, XXII, 476. Cf. *DBFP*, I, No. 166, n. 2.

[34] Great Britain, Parliamentary Papers, 1926, Vol. XXX (*Accounts and Papers*, Vol. XV), Cmd. 2680.

[35] *DDI*, IV, No. 208.

[35a] Carocci, *Politica estera dell'Italia fascista*, pp. 228-29.

hood of the Anglo-Italian entente facilitating concessions envisioned in 1906 was a small one.[36] Was the new agreement, then, intended to go further than the old one? As far as we know, there were no secret clauses to the accord, only its innocuous surface.

The Mussolini-Graham notes were more symbolic than substantive. Essentially they announced to the world that in colonial matters London and Rome had entered on a special relationship, yet the vagueness of the colonial entente left it to both parties to interpret it at will. The scope for misunderstanding was boundless.

The Entente in Action: East Africa and Asia Minor

Naturally enough, an excellent test of the new special relationship was provided by the Ethiopian question in the aftermath of the Anglo-Italian exchange of notes. A preparatory step had certainly been taken on the long road to Fascist Italy's attack on Ethiopia in 1935. In May 1935 Mussolini told the Chamber of Deputies. "This [Ethiopian] problem does not date from today nor from January 1935, but as proved by documents which may be published in due course, it goes back to 1925. It was in that year that I began to examine the problem."[37] Despite the usual Mussolinian rhetoric, there was more than a germ of truth in this. In the new year 1926, Mussolini was enthusiastic about taking the initiative in Ethiopia. Rumors of an imminent attack from Italian colonial territory began to circulate; Addis Ababa grew anxious.[38]

Although Ras Tafari expressed himself personally satisfied with Anglo-Italian assurances regarding the Mussolini-

[36] *DDI*, iv, No. 211.

[37] *OO*, xxvii, 79.

[38] See, for instance, *DDI*, iv, No. 257. In Rome strategy for an Italo-Ethiopian war was, in fact, under review in 1926 (Carocci, *Politica estera dell'Italia fascista*, p. 230).

Graham notes, the Italian minister to Addis Ababa, Count Colli di Fellizano, warned that "over the long period of time in which I have held this legation, our position in Abyssinia has never been as . . . complicated as it is today."[39] In fact, while dissembling toward Italy, Tafari on June 19 lodged a protest at the Anglo-Italian accord with the secretary of the League of Nations. This was the Englishman, Sir Eric Drummond, who soon let Mussolini know what Tafari was up to. The Duce was angered by what he considered Ethiopian duplicity, and promptly canceled the ceremonial visit to Addis Ababa which the Duke of Abruzzi was about to make. Colli's advice was not to undertake any "direct action" at Geneva to counter Tafari's move, for it "would certainly be interpreted as fear on our part to submit ourselves to the verdict of the League of Nations." Mussolini was, of course, the last person to allow the League to sit in judgment on Italy, but Colli's advice prevailed to the extent that Rome was content to work diplomatically behind the scenes at Geneva. After all, the League, dominated by the major powers in the council, could be relied on not to let the matter get out of hand. In the first week of August, both London and Rome sent letters to the League in which they denied any aggressive intentions toward Ethiopia. Tafari managed to have his written protest and the Anglo-Italian letters laid before the League Council at its September session, but there the matter ended. The League did not take up the question whether the Mussolini-Graham notes indeed represented a threat to Ethiopia. Tafari had to be content with publicizing the Anglo-Italian disclaimers.[40]

[39] *DDI*, IV, No. 354. The uneasy Italo-Ethiopian situation in early 1926 was the subject of considerable correspondence between Rome and the Italian legation in Addis Ababa (*DDI*, IV, Nos. 259, 267, 328, 338, 350, 354, 364, 374).
[40] *DDI*, IV, Nos. 382, 391, 418; *LNOJ*, VII (1926), 1,517-25. Cf. Baer, *Coming of the Italian-Ethiopian War*, pp. 17-18.

Ethiopia's reaction to the Mussolini-Graham notes was predictable, although in the last resort it was unlikely to deter Mussolini. Of equal importance to Rome was the reaction of other colonial powers, especially France. The French resented their exclusion from the reaffirmation of the 1906 accord, to which they had originally been a signatory. Paris wanted to be invited to join the Anglo-Italian agreement, and expected that Italy, in return for recognition of her special position in Ethiopia, would now bow to French demands in Tunisia and Tangier.[41] But Mussolini repulsed France on both counts. It was clearly within his power to prohibit French participation in the Anglo-Italian agreement, so he laid down a series of stiff but vague preconditions: "Precise assurances that the French government, not only will prevent its officials continuing both in Ethiopia and Europe the present campaign of incitement to our detriment, but also in the League of Nations will support neither directly nor indirectly future unjustified complaints by Abyssinia."[42] This virtually quashed any chance of a French adherence. In short, Mussolini succeeded in keeping the Ethiopian agreement an Anglo-Italian affair.

Undoubtedly Mussolini hoped to use the Anglo-Italian entente against France, not only in Ethiopia, but in a wide range of colonial questions. This ran directly counter to British objectives. Although in London it might be deemed necessary to isolate France in Ethiopia, this was an ad hoc policy which stopped at Ethiopia's borders. London had not patched up the quarrel over reparations only to provoke a new crisis with Paris by fighting Italy's quarrels with France over the entire colonial field. On the contrary, Chamberlain aspired to be the patron of a Franco-Italian

---

[41] On France's general attitude toward the Mussolini-Graham notes see *DBFP*, I, No. 223 and n. 6.

[42] *DDI*, IV, No. 368.

rapprochement.[43] Britain did not regard the Anglo-Italian colonial entente as the forceful arrangement Mussolini wanted it to be. What London intended by the Mussolini-Graham notes was simply to gain a measure of insurance. In 1925 London came to the conclusion that it was necessary to enlist Italian support in the forthcoming diplomatic campaigns to wrest Mosul from Turkey and to preserve the British position at Suez; the nebulous understanding on Ethiopia was a part of the bribe.[44]

In Ethiopia, however, Britain showed little inclination to encourage actual Italian penetration. In the months immediately following the Anglo-Italian exchange of notes, the British representative in Addis Ababa, over Italian objections, was busy, in concert with the French minister, arranging to supply Tafari with a modest consignment of arms. "Ambiguous and not entirely loyal" was Colli's judgment on the British legation.[45] At the heart of the matter was the fact that Britain and Italy were as much colonial rivals as partners. By insisting on the publication of the precise terms of the Mussolini-Graham notes, the British intended to disclose the limits of their commitment to Fascist Italy. The clash of interests in East Africa was perfectly apparent to the colonial ministries in Rome and London. During 1926 each was greatly concerned over the other's growing influence in the Red Sea and Arabian

[43] B.D., C3729/3729/22 (Annual Report, 1926, pp. 8-9); *DBFP*, I, Nos. 300, 329; II, Nos. 282, n. 4, 288, and p. 927; *DDI*, IV, Nos. 319, 320, 432, 494, 510.

[44] See Della Torretta's analysis of the motives behind British goodwill toward Fascist Italy (*DDI*, IV, Nos. 320, 344). For what it may be worth, a Foreign Office memorandum of April 1926 listing "British Commitments in relative Order of Importance" placed the Ethiopian agreement of 1906 in seventh place out of 13 (*DBFP*, I, Appendix, p. 880).

[45] *DDI*, IV, No. 413; also on the arms question, see Nos. 318, 348, 524. A lengthy report in the files of the Ministry of Italian Africa is entitled "English Activity on the Ethiopian Frontier" and covers the years 1924-1926 (It.D., 5/409/003103-85).

peninsula.[46] For example, a treaty of commerce and friendship which Italy signed with the King of Yemen on September 2, 1926, was construed in both London and Rome as a setback to British ambitions in Arabia.[47] Nevertheless, Mussolini, ever the wishful thinker, strove to keep his faith in the special relationship with Britain alive. Thus he attributed Anglo-Italian colonial difficulties to the "excessive zeal of local British agents." Moreover, he set great store by an arrangement worked out by British and Italian experts in the aftermath of the Italo-Yemeni treaty and concluded in January 1927 for cooperation in the exploitation of Arabia.[48]

Yet even the Duce had to attune his policy to the realities of the Anglo-Italian entente. This was made clear as early as 1926 by his acceptance of an overture from Ras Tafari for an Italo-Ethiopian nonaggression pact. As Ethiopia's suspicions of the Anglo-Italian exchange of notes had been visited overwhelmingly on Italy and not Britain—thanks to Fascism's lack of subtlety—the Italian quest for economic concessions in Ethiopia did not go well in 1926. Thus some humoring of Addis Ababa was in order.[49] A friendship pact was not likely to protect Ethiopia from Italy in the long run, as Tafari must have known, but its violation could mobilize world opinion on Ethiopia's side. More important, Mussolini's willingness to obligate himself by a nonaggression pact was a token sign that he had been forced to adopt a more patient attitude toward his intended Ethiopian prey. This, in turn, was certainly due to

[46] DDI, IV, Nos. 245, 414. See also Lessona's Memorie, Chap. 9, passim; Lessona, after his Albanian experience, was appointed undersecretary at the Italian colonial ministry in 1927.

[47] DBFP, II, No. 445; DDI, IV, Nos. 397, 462, 466; Royal Institute of International Affairs, Survey of International Affairs 1928 (London, 1929), pp. 312-314.

[48] DDI, IV, Nos. 557, 591. For the details of the Anglo-Italian talks on Arabia, see DBFP, II, Nos. 459-65, 468, 469.

[49] DDI, IV, No. 568.

the failure of the Anglo-Italian entente to live up to Mussolini's expectations.[50]

Much the same pattern of events unfolded in Asia Minor. The consolidation of the Anglo-Italian entente rekindled Mussolini's imperialist dreams, which had been temporarily laid aside on the outbreak of the Matteotti affair. But in the long run, British support turned out to be ephemeral.

London at this time had a precise goal in the Near East —the incorporation of oil-rich Mosul into the British mandate of Iraq. Technically a definition of the frontier between Turkey and Iraq rested with a neutral League of Nations commission. But Britain and Turkey concentrated on cultivating the moral support of other powers. Chamberlain plainly resolved to enlist Italy in Britain's cause. At their initial meeting in Rome in December 1924, Chamberlain and Mussolini discussed Asia Minor and agreed not to thwart each other's interests there.[51]

Mussolini was eager and willing to help Iraq gain Mosul. This was expressed in a set of instructions to the Italian embassy in Constantinople: "The policy of cordiality toward Great Britain which the national government has seen fit to follow and which has assured for Italy complete English support in international questions of notable interest to Italy, especially in the colonial and Mediterranean fields, could not permit us to assume an attitude of open hostility to Great Britain in the [Mosul] question."[52] In practical terms Mussolini's support of Britain amounted to an attitude of unremitting hostility toward Turkey. It meant an extension of Fascist Italy's détente with Greece, a

---

[50] Although Mussolini acceded to the principle of a nonaggression pact in 1926, a treaty of friendship was not signed until August 2, 1928. The negotiations were so protracted because they became involved with another attempt to work out provisions for Ethiopia's access to the sea (Guariglia, *Ricordi*, pp. 54-59, 767). Cf. G. Vedovato, *Gli accordi italo-etiopici dell'Agosto 1928* (Florence, 1956).

[51] *DDI*, III, No. 605.   [52] *DDI*, IV, No. 184.

British auxiliary and a Turkish archenemy. The Duce discovered an ideological bond with the new authoritarian regime headed by General Pangalos. And he showed his goodwill by facilitating the Greek purchase of arms from Italy.[53]

The Anglo-Greek-Italian alignment was a formidable combination. The French, who after the Lausanne Conference had resumed their traditional role of British colonial rival in the Near East, made at least one unsuccessful bid to detach Mussolini.[54] The Turks, directly threatened, tried to reach an accommodation with Italy on several occasions. The first proposal, made in August 1925 as Europe eagerly anticipated the series of agreements which were to materialize in October at Locarno, was for "some political understanding in the nature of those pacts which are now in fashion." Whatever the Turks intended, Mussolini dismissed the suggestion as "mere words." His negative attitude was shared by Montagna, now ambassador to Constantinople. Forgetting his plea on the morrow of the Lausanne Conference for Italo-Turkish cooperation, he now chauvinistically held that all problems stemmed simply from Turkish wickedness.[55]

The tone of reports from Constantinople changed when Montagna was replaced by Orsini Baroni, a more typical, circumspect career diplomat. In February 1926, when Turkey, more beleaguered than ever in the Mosul question, once more suggested an accord, Orsini Baroni urged the idea on a reluctant Mussolini. Grudgingly Mussolini allowed Orsini Baroni to explore the possibility.[56] On February 23 the Turks responded by proposing talks on questions of mutual interest in the Balkans and the Mediterranean, technical agreements for Italian economic invest-

---

[53] *DDI*, III, No. 606 and note; *DBFP*, I, No. 129.
[54] *DDI*, IV, No. 156.
[55] *DDI*, IV, No. 90 and note.
[56] *DDI*, IV, Nos. 235, 236, 238, 247.

ment in Asia Minor, and—most important in view of Turkey's fear of an Anglo-Italian-Greek combination—a "treaty of complete political neutrality against every third power." It was left to Mussolini "to choose an opportune moment to examine in detailed fashion and to conclude this treaty."[57]

Faced with a concrete overture Mussolini soon showed that he had no intention of coming to terms with Turkey. In the second week of April 1926 he made a ceremonial visit to the Italian North African colony of Libya. In the course of this "theatrical journey," in Guariglia's phrase,[58] he gave several fiery speeches about achieving "a suitable colonial outlet for the Italian population."[59] Grandi, who was visiting London in April, indicated that Italy had Asia Minor in mind.[60] Mussolini's bluster was a frank demand for parity within the Anglo-Italian entente. If British-mandated Iraq got Mosul, Italy required an equivalent gain at Turkey's expense. Relying on the opinion of Ambassador Graham in Rome, Whitehall recognized the possibility of an Italian descent on Asia Minor, but tended to discount it as an immediate danger.[61]

Italy's career diplomats, on the other hand, seemed genuinely apprehensive of a Mussolinian coup. Contarini was known to favor some Italian designs in Asia Minor, but without doubt Mussolini's belligerence went beyond his prescription.[66a] Of course, Contarini had submitted his resignation only a few weeks before the Duce's trip to Libya; it seemed as if the absence of the secretary general's restraining hand was being quickly felt. Thus, it was left to the remaining foreign ministry officials to dissuade Mus-

---

[57] *DDI*, IV, No. 255.

[58] Guariglia, *Ricordi*, p. 51.

[59] This was the phrase used by one Italian diplomat to summarize the gist of Mussolini's Libyan speeches (*DDI*, IV, No. 317). For the actual texts, see *OO*, XXII, 111-15, 423-24.

[60] *DBFP*, I, No. 449.

[61] *DBFP*, I, Nos. 488, 582.

[61a] Carocci, *Politica estera dell'Italia fascista*, p. 22.

solini from precipitate action. They had recourse to an argument unusual in the Palazzo Chigi, known for its advocacy of a close tie with Britain: Italy was playing Britain's game in too servile a fashion. Mussolini's ambassadors in Constantinople, London, Paris, and Moscow all issued warnings: Mussolini's belligerence forced Turkey closer to Soviet Russia and, while making Ankara needlessly and dangerously hostile to Italian economic interests in Asia Minor, helped Britain to secure control of Mosul's oil wells.[62] A "gratuitous service" to Britain born of Mussolini's "many illusions," Guariglia wrote scornfully in his *Ricordi*.[63]

In the wake of Mussolini's Libyan trip the Turkish press was alive with rumors of an imminent Italian or Italo-Greek attack.[64] Although Mussolini's speechmaking served ample notice that an Italo-Turk pact was a vain hope, the government in Ankara apparently was desperate enough to make one more attempt. This time a tripartite neutrality pact between Italy, Greece, and Turkey was the project. Mussolini's answer was as usual evasive and in reality negative; the "delicate international situation" dictated delay in starting negotiations.[65] Soon Mussolini learned that the Turks had apprised Paris of their scheme for a neutrality pact and possibly intended to invite the French to join. This afforded him an excellent opportunity to impute a breach of confidence on Ankara's part and to affirm his reluctance to enter into any positive understanding.[66]

Then on June 5, 1926 Turkey succumbed to Britain and signed a treaty consigning Mosul to the mandated territory of Iraq. The Turks' immediate concern to detach Mussolini from his British association thus vanished. Turkish

[62] *DDI*, IV, Nos. 296, 300-301, 326, 372, 492.
[63] Guariglia, *Ricordi*, p. 51.
[64] *OO*, XXII, 112-18; *DDI*, IV, Nos. 298, 475.
[65] *DDI*, IV, Nos. 307, 311.
[66] *DDI*, IV, Nos. 314, 316, 330.

interest in an Italian accord at once became lukewarm; in clarifying talks with Orsini Baroni at the end of the month the Turkish foreign minister spoke cautiously of the "eventual neutrality pact" and a "possible Mediterranean accord," the same type of equivocal language used by Mussolini.[67] With both Rome and Ankara now officially unenthusiastic, the project for an agreement quickly ceased to be mentioned at all.

The Turkish calculation that Fascist Italy would not attack without British support was borne out. If Mussolini did indeed dream of finding in the Anglo-Turkish quarrel an opportunity to invade Asia Minor, he was thwarted by the Mosul settlement which he himself had helped to bring about.[68] Even more, he was checked by a semiofficial conversation with Chamberlain, which took place on September 30 off Leghorn while the British foreign secretary was on a vacation cruise. During the encounter Chamberlain to all intents placed his veto on an Italian attack on Turkey, and Mussolini acquiesced. The two foreign ministers took refuge in the fiction that Turkey was on the verge of internal collapse; not until this came about, it was understood, could intervention in Asia Minor be tolerated. According to the Italian account of the meeting, Mussolini said: "It only remains to wait therefore." In reply, Chamberlain warned: "The Turkish question is a question of waiting. Not a minute too soon, not a minute too late."[69] On receipt of the Italian version, Chamberlain amended the last phrase to read more circumspectly: "The greatest discretion and caution are required."[70]

In both Ethiopia and Asia Minor, then, Great Britain served as a brake on Fascist Italy's impetuosity. In this way,

[67] *DDI*, IV, No. 352.
[68] For British recognition of Mussolini's part in winning Mosul for Iraq, see B.D., C3729/3729/22 (Annual Report, 1926, p. 22).
[69] *DDI*, IV, No. 444.
[70] *DBFP*, II, No. 255, n. 11.

Chamberlain supplemented the work of the Palazzo Chigi officials. When in 1926 the influence of Contarini and his fellow diplomats declined appreciably, the Anglo-Italian entente came to represent a substitute guarantee of Mussolini's good behavior.

The Essence of the Special Relationship: Sir Austen Chamberlain

The mystery is why Mussolini tolerated such restraint at British hands. He certainly was not an Anglophile. His attitude toward British imperialism resembled that of William II—something to be resented, envied, and, if possible, emulated. Until the creation of the Anglo-Italian entente, which was deemed to bring emulation within sight, the tone of Mussolini's comments in the *Documenti diplomatici italiani* recall the Kaiser's Anglophobe marginalia on the prewar record of German foreign policy. "Chicanery" was Mussolini's epithet for Britain's Dodecanese policy; apropos of the British role in the Corfu affair, he referred sarcastically to "the record of altruistic policy practiced by Great Britain in this grey postwar period." The Labour government's explanation of its sudden recognition of Soviet Russia "passed the bounds of all impudence," and MacDonald's slowness in coming to grips with foreign policy was castigated: "I cannot neglect the defence of Italian interests entrusted to me in order to suit the exclusive convenience and opportunity of English policy, which is inspired as always by narrow, egotistical sentiments." "Italy is not a British dominion," he wrote on hearing that certain Labour MPs wished to visit Italy in the spring of 1924 to observe the first elections held under a Fascist administration.[71]

Significantly these comments antedated the Matteotti affair and the coincident accession to the British foreign

[71] *DDI*, II, Nos. 160, 345, 620; III, Nos. 3, 99.

secretaryship of Sir Austen Chamberlain. The two events changed Mussolini's demeanor toward Great Britain. From the start, British Conservatives had been well disposed ideologically to Italian Fascism. But at first their favor seemed of little importance to Mussolini. In 1923 Lord Rothermere's press was willing to carry Fascist publicity for a fee, but no Italian money was forthcoming, and the project lapsed.[72] Lord Curzon considered Fascism a useful social movement, yet he incurred Mussolini's intense dislike. It was the murder of Matteotti that seemed to teach him the value of British Conservative sympathy. It has been observed above to what extent British Conservatives rallied world opinion to Mussolini's side in the dark days of late 1924. Nor did the proclamation of the Fascist dictatorship on January 3, 1925, diminish British Conservative support. For example, on January 7, Winston Churchill, so Italy's finance minister reported to Mussolini, expressed "sympathy for Your Excellency and appreciation of Your Excellency's energetic work in the repression of bolshevism."[73] Churchill continued in this vein during 1925, confiding to Ambassador Della Torretta his admiration for the "discipline . . . firmness and severity" of Fascist Italy.[74] He expressed this admiration tangibly by helping to arrange a war-debt settlement favorable to Italy. In early 1927 Churchill visited Rome privately and made a speech at the British embassy to a group of journalists, once more extolling Mussolini.[75]

Other prominent Conservative ministers were undeterred by Mussolini's growing dictatorship from showing their regard for Fascism and its leader. In March 1925 the secretaries of state for air and for colonies requested an interview, which Mussolini was only too delighted to grant.[76]

72 It.D. (Ministry of Popular Culture), 30/428/014445-48.
73 *DDI*, III, No. 662.
74 *DDI*, IV, No. 194.
75 *Corriere della Sera*, Jan. 21, 1927.
76 *DDI*, III, Nos. 746, 750.

Two months later Mussolini's ego was flattered a little more when the counsellor at the British embassy in Rome, Howard Kennard, was transferred as a result of Mussolini's complaint that he showed sympathy for the Italian opponents of Fascism.[77] In sum, the Matteotti affair and the subsequent dictatorial experiment proved a test of allegiances within and without Italy. British Conservatives emerged from the ordeal ranged more clearly than before among the staunchest supporters of Mussolini. Both Mussolini and his movement were upstarts. Their overwhelming acceptance by respectable British Conservatives in 1925-26 ultimately appealed to the Fascist leader's always sensitive vanity.

In the last resort, the Anglo-Italian entente was held together by the personal friendship of Mussolini and Chamberlain. This warm relationship was regularly refurbished by Chamberlain's frequent visits to Italy. Fortunately, the foreign secretary loved to travel in the Mediterranean, since Mussolini was not inclined to repeat his one trip to England. Once the two men met, in Rome in December 1924 for the first time, a bond was established. In private both liked to pose as simple and reasonable beings, and so found each other congenial. With each meeting the mutual pleasure and esteem grew. After the encounter at Locarno, Chamberlain wrote to Ambassador Graham in glowing terms: "All my pleasant impressions of [Mussolini] gained in Rome were renewed and confirmed. It is not part of my business as Foreign Secretary to appreciate the action in the domestic politics of Italy, but if I ever had to choose in my own country between anarchy and dictatorship, I expect I should be on the side of the dictator. In any case, I thought Mussolini a strong man of singular charm and I suspected not a little tenderness and loneliness of heart. Meeting me but seldom and quite alone and find-

[77] *DDI*, III, No. 700.

ing me sympathetic, I expect that he shows me a side of his character which the public is never allowed to see, and even his most intimate friends but seldom if ever. I believe him to be accused of crimes in which he had no share, and I suspect him to have connived unwillingly at other outrages which he would have prevented if he could. But I am confident that he is a patriot and a sincere man; I trust his word when given and I think we might easily go far before finding an Italian with whom it would be as easy for the British Government to work."[78]

From Rapallo, where he met Mussolini at the end of 1925, Chamberlain wrote to his foreign office: "The more one knows the Italian prime minister, the more one appreciates and loves him." The message opportunely was passed on to the Italian embassy in London, and thence to Mussolini himself.[79] The high point of cordiality was reached, however, when Mussolini was entertained by the Chamberlain family aboard the yacht on which they were traveling off Leghorn in September 1926. Lady Chamberlain, especially, outdid herself, even to wearing the Fascist insignia. On the Duce's departure the Fascist salute was given by all the British party, save Chamberlain himself who was inhibited by his position as minister of the crown. Mussolini was captivated, noting exultantly: "Chamberlain is, deep down, rather a sympathizer with Fascism."[80]

The emphasis in the Anglo-Italian entente on a vague ideological affinity and on the personal friendship of two individuals disguised the fact that it was short on concrete political cooperation. On the Italian side, in particular, the returns in the colonial world in the middle 1920s could only be regarded as meager. This gave to the entente an air of

---

[78] Quoted in C. Petrie, *Life and Letters of Sir Austen Chamberlain* (London, 1939-40), II, 295-96. Cf. Chamberlain's similar phraseology apropos Mussolini in his address to the Imperial Conference in October 1926 (*DBFP*, II, p. 925).
[79] *DDI*, IV, No. 220.   [80] *DDI*, IV, No. 443.

brittleness. For Mussolini was not blind to the scarcity of positive accomplishment. Despite his personal affection for Chamberlain and other individual Conservatives, his pristine jealousy and distrust of the British empire lingered on and was occasionally given voice. In November 1929 at a Council of Ministers meeting, of which no communiqué was issued, he said bluntly: "It is a great illusion to think that the English Conservative government is a sincere friend of Italy."[81] Yet the British tie in the mid-twenties was still tolerable: "Don't antagonize the English," Mussolini remarked at the time of Locarno.[82] Possibly the Anglo-Italian entente might be exploitable in the future. Mussolini was not to put it to the test until 1935.

[81] It.D. (Ministry of Interior, Italian Social Republic), 329/1295/112726. Kirkpatrick, *Mussolini*, pp. 166-67, testifies, largely on the basis of his sojourn at the British embassy in Rome 1930-1933, to Mussolini's constant irritation with Britain barely concealed beneath the surface.

[82] B.D., C4231/2261/22 (Annual Report, 1925, p. 7).

16. Decisions in the Balkans

Yugoslavia and a Balkan Locarno

CHAMBERLAIN was able to presume on his friendship with Mussolini to curb Fascist Italy in colonial questions. In addition, outside Europe British naval power gave London the whip hand. But it was hardly to be expected that in Continental affairs the Anglo-Italian entente would exercise a similar restraining influence on Mussolini. In other words, if Mussolini felt frustrated in Africa and Asia Minor, he might turn to Europe in search of a diplomatic coup, and do so unhampered by Britain. In fact, in 1925-26 he conceived and tried to execute some far-reaching schemes in the Balkans.

In the sphere of Italy's relationship with Yugoslavia the long contest between the proponents of rapprochement and the ultranationalists was reaching a climax, with the catalyst Albania. Any campaign to establish Italian hegemony there would certainly wreck the Italo-Yugoslav understanding reached in the Pact of Rome. During the Matteotti affair Mussolini had followed a policy of nonintervention in Albania's civil war. By the spring of 1925 he had acceded to Ahmed Zogu's invitation to counterbalance Yugoslavia in Albania to the extent of speeding up Italy's economic penetration. In the summer he was ready to seek a political agreement with Zogu.

The negotiations were entrusted first to Lessona, the unofficial emissary whom Mussolini had used earlier to make contact with Zogu. Lessona entered wholeheartedly into the spirit of things, and tried, not always successfully, to hide his approaches to Zogu behind a veil of secrecy. Once the two men met on the Albanian seacoast north of Durazzo at the dead of night in the best cloak-and-dagger fashion. Through Lessona the Albanian president received supplies of cash with which to keep his troops and police paid and loyal.[1] Despite these favors and despite Zogu's insistence that he wanted a political accord, negotiations hung fire because Rome and Tirana had fundamentally incompatible ideas about the nature of the desired agreement.

Broadly speaking, within the ranks of Italian officialdom there were three schools of thought on the Albanian question. At one extreme, the ultranationalists and Fascist party zealots wanted to establish an Italian protectorate as swiftly as possible, at any cost and on any terms; Lessona was typical of this group. At the opposite pole were the heirs of Sforza in the Palazzo Chigi, led by Secretary General Contarini. They supported economic penetration of Albania, but maintained that any political action should depend on prior agreement with Yugoslavia. They feared that the negotiations under way with Zogu spelled the ruination of the Pact of Rome. Probably Lessona did not exaggerate much when he contended that from the start Contarini "was determined to see that negotiations should come to nothing."[2] A third faction consisted of those career diplomats who approved of a political arrangement which would tie Zogu to Italy, even at the risk of a breach with Belgrade. But they also feared that the diplomatic naïveté of Mussolini and such emissaries as Lessona would produce a treaty that would pledge blanket Italian support of Zogu's expansionist schemes. To forestall this they advocated a plan named after their spokesman in the Palazzo Chigi, Vincenzo Lojacono, head of the department of general affairs and also of a recently created Albanian office within the foreign ministry. Lojacono's plan called for the insertion in any treaty with Zogu of a clause making the Italian obligation to come to Albania's aid dependent on

[1] Lessona, *Memorie*, pp. 101-106. See also *DDI*, IV, No. 63.

[2] Lessona, *Memorie*, p. 96. Also on Contarini's attitude see Pastorelli, *Italia e Albania*, pp. 101-103, 157-58.

a prior appeal to the League of Nations. This was in accord with the Conference of Ambassadors decision at Paris in 1921, which entrusted Albania's integrity to the League and postulated that Italy act as the League's agent in Albania.[3] With this precaution it was even possible to believe that an Italo-Albanian treaty could be made palatable to Yugoslavia if its announcement was properly timed.

The Lojacono formula was in fact an essential ingredient of the Italian offer of a public treaty and convention to be accompanied by a secret military accord held out to Ahmed Zogu in the summer of 1925.[4] Zogu, however, had no inclination to emasculate a promise of Italian aid by a reference to the Conference of Ambassadors decision of 1921. Undoubtedly aware that he was committed to Italy, Zogu was nonetheless determined to delay and force as hard a bargain as possible. Lessona resorted to a variety of tricks to wring the long-promised treaty from him. He threatened melodramatically to lead his own band of Fascist blackshirts in an invasion of Albania, then tried coercion with a fictitious letter to Mussolini describing Zogu as faithless and recommending that he be abandoned to his fate.[5] But it seems to have been the need for more Italian money that forced Zogu to meet Italy halfway. Suddenly on August 19 Zogu announced his readiness to sign a secret military accord, leaving the public treaty to be negotiated later. Rome accepted this, and Lojacono made a quick trip to Durazzo to assist Lessona in drafting the pact.[6]

The accord was embodied in an exchange of letters between Zogu and Mussolini, dated, respectively, August 23 and 26. There were seven clauses in the agreement, which provided in the main for military cooperation against third

[3] Pastorelli, *Italia e Albania*, pp. 158, 162-65.
[4] *Ibid.*, pp. 170-74.
[5] Lessona, *Memorie*, pp. 107-111.
[6] *Ibid.*, pp. 111-12; Pastorelli, *Italia e Albania*, pp. 178-80.

parties. The crux of the bargain struck was in Clauses 4 and 5:

4. In the event that Italy is attacked by a Balkan state, Albania undertakes to declare war on that state upon Italy's request.

5. If joint military action should result in territorial compensation, Italy undertakes to obtain for Albania territory inhabited by people, the majority of whom speak Albanian.[7]

It was the latter clause which seemed potentially explosive. Under it Zogu might enlist Italy in the cause of Albanian irredentism, which could only be appeased at Yugoslavia's expense. The incompatibility with the Pact of Rome hardly needed to be stressed.

The secret military pact was anathema to the Contarini group in the Palazzo Chigi.[8] On the other hand, it was intended to be the prelude to a more important public treaty which would regularize Italo-Albanian relations in the eyes of the world. Indeed, until the public treaty was concluded, the validity of the secret military pact itself was questionable. Therefore Contarini and his followers swallowed the secret agreement and concentrated their attention on the prospective public treaty. If the latter could be made to depend on the Conference of Ambassadors decision of 1921, something of the Pact of Rome might yet be salvaged.

In the fall of 1925 Lessona was back in Tirana exploring the possibility of a treaty to be registered with the League of Nations.[9] He found Zogu as evasive and uncompromising as ever.[10] Italy and Albania remained far apart until November 14 when Lessona and Juk Koci, Zogu's private

---

[7] Pastorelli, *Italia e Albania*, pp. 180-81.
[8] Lessona, *Memorie*, pp. 111-12.
[9] *DDI*, IV, No. 157; *DBFP*, I, No. 165.
[10] Pastorelli, *Italia e Albania*, pp. 182-95.

secretary who also acted as Lessona's interpreter, reported to Mussolini in Rome. Without warning the Duce revealed that he was no longer unalterably committed to the Lojacono plan. A draft treaty was quickly drawn up. It comprised three articles by which Italy guaranteed Albania's independence and frontiers, while in return Albania recognized that her integrity was a matter of Italy's own security. Although the preamble referred to the Conference of Ambassadors decision of 1921, in no way did execution of the pact depend on a prior appeal to the League of Nations.[11] Mussolini actually signed two copies of the agreement; but on the very morning in December 1925 that Lessona was to leave for Tirana to obtain Zogu's countersignature, the Duce revoked his instructions. Much to Lessona's consternation, Mussolini announced that he had decided not to formalize the treaty at the moment. The explanation given was a report of the Italian army general staff that Zogu had already negotiated a similar accord with Yugoslavia.[12]

Mussolini's *volte-face* was apparently due to information from the Italian military attaché in Belgrade, who had just provided the outline of a draft agreement between Zogu and the Yugoslav government made in August 1924 while Zogu was in exile in Yugoslavia. The arrangement was probably never validated, and by the end of 1925 was a dead letter; nevertheless, it was advanced skillfully as proof of Zogu's untrustworthiness by the opponents of an Italo-Albanian treaty. Lessona asserts positively that the fine hand of Contarini directed the maneuver.[13] At any rate, the shelving of the treaty was an unmistakable victory for the proponents of the Pact of Rome.

11 *Ibid.*, pp. 214-18.

12 Lessona, *Memorie*, p. 114.

13 *Ibid.*, p. 116. Pastorelli, *Italia e Albania*, pp. 219-23, also holds Contarini mainly responsible for the treaty's suspension.

The suspension of negotiations with Zogu brought into the open again the possibility of reinvigorating the Italo-Yugoslav rapprochement. During the winter of 1925-26 two forms of Italo-Yugoslav agreement were explored. The first was for a direct understanding on Albania. The authorities in Belgrade, on finding that Zogu was not the Yugoslav puppet he had once seemed, resolved that their interests in Albania would be best served now by cooperation with Italy. King Alexander bluntly proposed that the two powers partition Albania between them. Ninčić talked more circumspectly of economic collaboration there.[14] It seems reasonable that when on July 20, 1925 Belgrade signed the Nettuno Conventions, which guaranteed the rights of Italians living in Dalmatia, it was intended as an inducement to Italy to share the spoils in Albania.[15] Unfortunately, although the Yugoslav government had signed the Nettuno Conventions cheerfully enough, the Yugoslav parliament obstinately refused to ratify them. Security for Italian *optanti* in Dalmatia promised in the conventions had come to represent in Rome a virtual prerequisite for extending the Pact of Rome to cover Albania. On the other hand, there were other factors keeping the hope of Italo-Yugoslav cooperation alive. Mussolini's post-Locarno propaganda blasts at German nationalism on the Brenner were welcomed in Belgrade, for Italy and Yugoslavia were agreed on opposing any signs of irredentism in southern Austria.[16] Further, Mussolini was conscious of the need to avert the signing of a Franco-Yugoslav pact. By holding out the prospect of enlarging the Pact of Rome to embrace Albania, he hoped to keep Belgrade out of the French orbit. In February 1926 Ninčić visited Rome, as Contarini had been urging and planning. Although Ninčić was un-

---

[14] *DDI*, III, Nos. 671, 672, 694, 764.
[15] *DDI*, IV, Nos. 71, 76.
[16] G.D., 2784H/1386/538118-19, 538168.

able to commit Mussolini to anything concrete, the two men had an amicable exchange of views.[17]

The other method that was broached of bringing Italy and Yugoslavia together was the ambitious plan of a Balkan Locarno. The Rhine pacts of October 16, 1925 bred a vogue for analogous regional security pacts. Contarini and his colleagues in the Palazzo Chigi were enthusiastic in principle for Locarno-type security agreements, but they had a specific reason for wanting Italy to join a Balkan Locarno. Belgrade could not fail to be impressed by the amount of Italian economic activity in Albania during the autumn of 1925. By the end of the year the seal had been set on Italy's economic control of Albania for the foreseeable future.[18] While the Yugoslav government pressed for an Albanian understanding with Italy, until the understanding was forthcoming Yugoslavia could be relied on to take steps to counter Italy. One Yugoslav tactic devised in late 1925 was to turn to Albania's other neighbor, Greece.[19] Thus there arose the prospect of a Yugoslav-Greek détente which might provide the nucleus for a Balkan Locarno. Without Italian participation any agreement dedicated to the preservation of the Balkan status quo would constitute a formidable obstacle to Italy in Albania and elsewhere. In effect Contarini's stratagem was to draw any anti-Italian sting by patronizing and joining such a pact.[20]

But Mussolini did not like the Locarno Pacts. He had put his signature on them only under pressure; his candid opinion was that they were a futile exercise in international conciliation. He could not, then, be expected to favor a Balkan facsimile. Admittedly he muted his criticism, but at

[17] *DDI*, IV, Nos. 240, 250, 269; De Dampierre, *Revue des Deux Mondes*, Nov. 1, 1953, pp. 22-23.

[18] Swire, *Albania*, pp. 461-66.

[19] Zogu contended that Belgrade and Athens together were fomenting yet another revolution in Albania to get rid of him (*DDI*, III, Nos. 815, 833; IV, Nos. 109, 113).

[20] *DDI*, IV, No. 122; Lessona, *Memorie*, pp. 112-13.

the same time gave no encouragement to the Contarini faction endeavoring to include an Italo-Yugoslav rapprochement in a Balkan Locarno. Early in 1926 Mussolini expressed his opinion that a Balkan Locarno was "extremely premature," and with such phraseology quietly but emphatically dismissed the project.[21]

While a separate Italo-Yugoslav agreement on Albania and a Balkan Locarno languished, another shift occurred in the story of Italy's tortuous negotiations with Ahmed Zogu. Throughout the winter of 1925 Lessona chafed restlessly, waiting for the lapsed negotiations to be resumed. Then in February 1926, as Lessona records ruefully in his *Memorie*, Mussolini was persuaded "to bring back negotiations with Albania into normal diplomatic channels."[22] For this purpose, Baron Pompeo Aloisi was transferred from the Bucharest legation to Durazzo. One of Aloisi's first acts was to invite a former colleague, Francesco Jacomini di San Sevino, then serving on the Italian delegation discussing war debts in London, to join him in Albania. (It is from Jacomini that we have an account of Aloisi's stewardship of the Durazzo legation during 1926, less graphic but more dependable than Lessona's Albanian narrative.) Aloisi and Jacomini were old-guard diplomats who in their conduct might be counted on to reflect some of Contarini's qualms about an association with Zogu. In addition, Aloisi's initial instructions were to avoid too close an entanglement. He was to concentrate "on economic questions, putting aside for the moment strictly political problems."[23] This was as great a triumph for the cautious element in the Palazzo Chigi as the suspension of negotiations some months earlier.

[21] *DDI*, IV, No. 237.
[22] Lessona, *Memorie*, p. 120.
[23] F. Jacomini di San Sevino, "Il Patto di Tirana del 1926," *Rivista di Studi Politici Internazionali*, XX (April 1953), 236-37.

It was at this juncture that Secretary General Contarini submitted his resignation. The immediate cause of his departure was Mussolini's verbal assault on Stresemann over the Alto Adige, coupled with the threat to send Italian armies across the Brenner Pass. However, the assertion has also been made that Contarini's discontent arose in the main from the increasingly anti-Yugoslav temper of Mussolini's policy. Guariglia, writing from his position within the Palazzo Chigi, stresses the secretary general's distaste for the "double game" played by Fascist Italy in the Adriatic. Contarini's biographer refers more explicitly to Fascist intrigues, not only with Zogu of Albania but also with the Croatian autonomists of Dalmatia.[24]

As to the charge that Mussolini estranged Belgrade with his rash support of the Croatian separatists, it is certain that he did not lack encouragement, particularly from disgruntled Italians living in Dalmatia, to exploit Yugoslavia's internal divisions. Undoubtedly, at times Mussolini verbally sympathized with proponents of the idea, and he may have corresponded with Croatian leader Stjepan Radić.[25] However, there was even more to divide Italy and the Croatian autonomists than to unite them. In Dalmatia great mutual enmity existed between Croat and Italian. Croatian politicians continued to give currency to the rumor that in the Pact of Rome Mussolini had promised to assist the Serbs quell any Croatian uprising. The price paid by Belgrade was supposed to be both Fiume and a free hand for Italy in Albania. Italy returned the accusation, charging that in Italian Venezia Giulia, Radić and his followers were engaged in fomenting disaffection among the Slav popula-

[24] Guariglia, *Ricordi*, pp. 14, 50; Legatus, *Vita di Contarini*, pp. 121-22, Secondary authorities who ascribe Contarini's resignation primarily to Mussolini's Adriatic policy include Di Nolfo, *Mussolini e la politica estera*, p. 184, and Seton-Watson, *Italy from Liberalism to Fascism*, pp. 695-96.

[25] *DDI*, III, Nos. 517, 615, 696, 791, 793, 795.

tion.[26] Then in November 1925, Radić composed his differences with the Serb-dominated government in Belgrade
to the extent of joining the cabinet. In other words, in the
weeks before Contarini's resignation, the Yugoslavs
achieved a measure of ethnic harmony. The opportunity for
Mussolini to intrigue with the Croatian separatists had
never been worse. Evidence that Belgrade was affronted at
this time by Italian collusion with them does not exist.

No doubt the general drift of Mussolini's Adriatic policy
disturbed Contarini. The secretary general was plainly disappointed at Mussolini's dismissal of a Balkan Locarno.
He deplored the mere contemplation of an open alliance
with Zogu, which would alienate Yugoslavia. But on the
score of Albania, which had become the criterion of Italo-
Yugoslav relations, Contarini had only limited grounds for
pessimism and despair in March 1926. He had tolerated
without resigning the secret military pact with Zogu of the
previous August, and his school of thought had won a considerable victory in December with the shelving of a public
treaty. Furthermore, with Aloisi's appointment to Durazzo, Albanian affairs were restored to the Palazzo Chigi's
domain. It seems logical to suppose that Contarini, having
determined to resign out of personal pride, found the moment opportune, not because Mussolini threatened to do
something rash in Albania but because there appeared some
assurance of Fascist moderation in the Adriatic for the immediate future.

If Contarini viewed the Adriatic situation in February
1926 with pessimism, it was probably due less to Fascist
recklessness than to Yugoslav obduracy. The Nettuno Conventions continued unratified. Although the Yugoslav government was willing to join Italy in a Balkan Locarno,

26 It.D. (Mussolini's private secretariat), 3/407/001134-36; *DDI*, IV,
No. 535.

whenever the question of a specific Albanian agreement was raised, Belgrade always seemed to foresee a partition of the country—which ran against the grain of Contarini's thinking. Moreover, Contarini had suspicions about the anti-Italian influence exercised by the Quai d'Orsay over Yugoslav officials. Yet all this indicated only that Italo-Yugoslav relations early in 1926 were in a state of unusual fluidity.[27]

Much of what Contarini feared and opposed in the Adriatic came to pass after his resignation. To anticipate these developments in order to account for his departure from office is an understandable temptation, and one not resisted by some writers. But the record is clear. When Contarini resigned, the policy of rapprochement with Yugoslavia begun by Sforza, although plainly in jeopardy, was not yet completely overthrown. Instead, that policy's demise was hastened by the secretary general's departure.

The Capture of Albania

Mussolini returned to the idea of an Albanian treaty within a short while after Contarini's resignation. The occasion was unwittingly provided by the British. All along, Italian headway in Albania had been made over the objections and opposition of the British legation in Durazzo in charge of Sir Harry Eyres.[28] With the arrival in May 1926 of a new and even more energetic British minister, William O'Reilly, Italy's campaign for further economic penetration of Albania ran into an increasing number of British roadblocks. When Aloisi returned to Rome to inform Mussolini of this, the Duce resolved that drastic measures were called for and that it was necessary to tie Zogu firmly to Italy by a treaty. So early in June, Aloisi went back to Durazzo with instructions to reopen the sus-

---

[27] Pastorelli, *Italia e Albania*, pp. 279-81.
[28] *DDI*, III, Nos. 60, 105, 262; IV, No. 198.

pended negotiations for a public treaty. The influence of Lojacono and his Albanian office was still strong within the Palazzo Chigi at this time, for the proposal Aloisi was authorized to offer was based on the Lojacono plan of July 1925. That is, the prospective treaty with Zogu would clearly stipulate that any Italian promise to defend Albania be executed only after an appeal to the League of Nations, as predicated in the Conference of Ambassadors decision of 1921.[29]

But Zogu's attitude had not changed since the summer of 1925. He still had no intention of subordinating Albania's security to an appeal to the League of Nations. Therefore he now suggested that an Italo-Albanian political accord without reservations be signed, after which he would meet with Mussolini to discuss an additional agreement based on the 1921 decision. Italy, however, was not to be caught this way, refused further loans to Zogu, and claimed that the secret treaty of the previous year presupposed an appeal to the League of Nations before going into effect. A meeting between Zogu and Mussolini would have to come after a treaty containing a reference to the Paris decision of 1921 was signed. If Zogu wished, the treaty could remain secret until the two heads of government met.[30] But Zogu was unmoved, and the Italians were the first to crack.

Aloisi feared lengthy negotiations, news of which would sooner or later leak out and weld all parties interested in Albania into an anti-Italian bloc. If a treaty was to be signed, he argued, it should be done quickly to present the world with a fait accompli: "At the moment it is necessary to bind the Albanian government at once in an intergovernmental accord, even if this accord departs from the well-known Paris declaration." Desperately Aloisi clung

29 Jacomini, *Rivista di Studi Politici Internazionali* XX (1953), pp. 238-43; Pastorelli, *Italia e Albania*, pp. 295-300.
30 *DDI*, IV, Nos. 334, 337, 340, 341, 345.

to the hope of securing at a later date Zogu's reaffirmation of the 1921 decision, or of a formula which "would indirectly comprehend" the Paris declaration without specifically mentioning it. In reality, Aloisi had become dazzled by the prospect of an Italian protectorate in Albania, and now looked forward to arrangements that "would completely monopolize in Italy's favor the internal and foreign actions of Albania." On June 26 he went to Rome to review strategy with Mussolini. Given Aloisi's mood and Contarini's absence, the result was perhaps a foregone conclusion. According to Jacomini's memoir, it was during this visit that the final determination was taken to sign a treaty without a specific reference to either the League of Nations or the Conference of Ambassadors decision of 1921. Lojacono wanted to hold fast to his own formula, but Mussolini was adamantly set on a political accord with Zogu, whatever the cost. Consequently the proposal that Aloisi took back to Albania this time referred in its preamble to the Conference of Ambassadors decision, but nowhere mentioned a prior appeal to the League of Nations.[31]

There remained one hurdle, however. Aloisi returned to Durazzo on July 6, and on the 10th held a "long and laborious" discussion with Zogu. But Zogu offered only "a project of an accord devoid of any political content whatever." Mussolini promptly ordered the treaty negotiations broken off, if only to save face.[32] The real reason was to give Mussolini time to tackle the problem of British opposition in Albania, which was the origin of Zogu's prevarication. Not only was he under pressure from the British legation not to conclude a treaty with Italy, but he might wring concessions from both Italy and Britain by playing off one against the other. As part of this game he had informed

[31] Jacomini, *Rivista di Studi Politici Internazionali* XX (1953), pp. 243-45; Pastorelli, *Italia e Albania*, pp. 309-310, 323-24.
[32] *DDI*, IV, Nos. 365, 367.

O'Reilly in Durazzo about the beginning of June of his
negotiations for an Italian treaty, and had represented
Italy's insistence on a reference to the 1921 decision as an
ultimatum. Predictably O'Reilly rose to the bait, and an
alarmed Whitehall instructed its ambassador in Rome to
question Mussolini on the propriety of Italy's Albanian
diplomacy.[33] It was not altogether surprising that Mussolini felt the need to soothe Britain before resuming negotiations with Zogu. In the interim, while dealing with
London, it was also necessary to keep Zogu quiet. Therefore Aloisi was allowed to assure him that when treaty
talks resumed the 1921 decision would not be raised. To
sweeten him further, Aloisi was to hint that Rome considered the secret treaty of 1925 to be valid, using the formula:
"Italy, by interrupting the political negotiations, does not
intend to honor less any of the engagements previously
contracted."[34]

It was not difficult at the time to persuade London to
leave Italy a clear field in Albania. Chamberlain owed Italy
a favor; Mussolini's belligerence toward Turkey contributed to Britain's victory in the Mosul question which
came about in June 1926. But Italian belligerence in the
Near East had shown signs of getting out of hand, and Mussolini had made his bellicose trip to Libya in April. It was
logical British strategy to turn Mussolini away from Asia
Minor by encouraging him in Albania, where Italian
penetration had a species of international sanction. Thus
Chamberlain was prepared to recognize Albania as "Italy's
Belgium."[35] On July 29 Della Torretta held a conversation
with Chamberlain in London, in the course of which the

---

[33] *DBFP*, II, Nos. 69, 73, 75; *DDI*, IV, No. 357; Jacomini, *Rivista di
Studi Politici Internazionali XX* (1953), pp. 245-47.

[34] *DDI*, IV, Nos. 369, 370; Jacomini, *Rivista di Studi Politici Internazionali XX* (1953), pp. 247-48.

[35] This apposite phrase is used by the British scholars, Macartney
and Cremona, *Italy's Foreign and Colonial Policy*, p. 96.

British foreign secretary expressed his distrust of Zogu and denied any intention of obstructing Italy in Albania.[36] Then in mid-August O'Reilly was transferred from Durazzo, giving rise to some unseemly Italian rejoicing which, in turn, embarrassed London.[37] The Italians had reason to be pleased, for Chamberlain's instructions to William Seeds, the new British minister to Albania, read: "I have endeavoured to make it plain that I do not desire you either to question, or to interfere in, Italian activities in Albania so long as they conform to her legitimate aspirations. It is not easy to define the word 'legitimate' in this connection." Elucidating further, Chamberlain appeared to rule out flagrant Italian intervention in Albania's domestic affairs and the incitement of an Italo-Yugoslav war.[38] But there was sufficient scope left for Italy's immediate plans. On September 10, with Zogu no longer able to turn to the British for tactical help, negotiations for an Italo-Albanian treaty were resumed in earnest. There was irony in the situation; the Anglo-Italian entente, to which the Palazzo Chigi wholeheartedly subscribed, had finally opened the door to a treaty which many of Italy's professional diplomats had worked to prevent.

With British benevolence assured, the negotiations with Zogu now had a fairly easy road.[39] At one point the plan was to sign the pact at a meeting of Mussolini and Zogu, but this did not materialize. Albania hoped to conclude simultaneously a series of economic accords, which, however, required negotiations of too great a length. Therefore the treaty signed at Tirana on November 27, 1926 by Aloisi and Albanian Foreign Minister Elias Vrioni was a plain political accord of five articles.[40] Its heart lay in the first two:

[36] *DBFP*, II, No. 118; *DDI*, IV, No. 383.
[37] *DDI*, IV, No. 409. [38] *DBFP*, II, No. 167.
[39] The Lojacono faction in the Palazzo Chigi raised some mild objections which were brushed aside (Pastorelli, *Italia e Albania*, pp. 346-54).
[40] Jacomini, *Rivista di Studi Politici Internazionali* XX (1953), pp. 248-53.

ARTICLE 1. Italy and Albania recognize that any disturbance directed against the political, juridical, and territorial status quo of Albania is opposed to their reciprocal political interest.

ARTICLE 2. To safeguard the above-mentioned interest, the High Contracting Parties undertake to give their mutual support and cordial collaboration. They likewise undertake not to conclude with other Powers political or military agreements prejudicial to the interests of the other Party.[41]

On the surface, these were vague promises. Unlike the secret treaty of August 1925, there was no allusion to the liberation of those populations speaking Albanian. But on the other hand, the treaty lacked a safety device such as a prior appeal to the League of Nations. The operation of the treaty, in reality, turned on the gloss put on the Albanian status quo which Italy was pledged to uphold. Was this Albania's integrity in the international sphere? Or did it mean the preservation of Zogu's regime within Albania? If the latter, then the treaty had far-ranging connotations. It might justify Italy's military intervention in Albania on the excuse of protecting Zogu. Or in reverse fashion, like the secret treaty, it left the door open for Zogu to drag Italy into his quarrel with Yugoslavia on the grounds that Belgrade gave aid to his political enemies.

Mussolini was perfectly conscious of this broad interpretation and was prepared to live with it. A letter to the chief of the army general staff, General Pietro Badoglio, on October 2 revealed Mussolini's willingness to fight Yugoslavia at a moment's notice. In this, he expounded on the deteriorating state of Italo-Yugoslav relations. He was particularly indignant over the dismissal of the Yugoslav minister in Rome, Antoniević, "a sincere friend of Italy," and his

41 Quoted in Swire, *Albania*, pp. 478-79.

replacement by "so perfidious an ENEMY of Italy, of the Fascist regime and of myself personally *that I shall refuse to receive him.*" The nonratification of the Nettuno Conventions was mentioned more than once; but even if they were to be approved, "they will remain merely a pact between governments and will not change the basic relationship between the peoples, which is what it is: *bad (cattiva).*" Mussolini came to the peak of belligerence in the conclusion:

> The moral, dear Marshal [*sic*], is this.
>
> We have to prepare—without losing a minute of time—the twenty mobilized divisions of which our program disposes.
>
> We have to give our officials an offensive and aggressive mentality. Stimulate their *amour propre* by making known the slanderous infamies of the Kingdom of the Serbs, Croats, and Slovenes.
>
> Fortunately, Italy today is capable of inflicting on the Kingdom of the Serbs, Croats, and Slovenes one of those lessons which suffice to correct the mental and political perversity of any people.
>
> But once more: there is not a moment's time to be lost.[42]

Knowing the Fascist propensity for words over deeds, it is quite probable that precise military plans for an attack on Yugoslavia were never made, but Mussolini's frame of mind was plain enough. Surprisingly, in view of the letter's date, it contains no reference to Albania. Yet during the fall of 1926 the possibility of an armed clash with Yugoslavia over Albania was never far from Mussolini's mind. As Italy and Zogu moved closer to a formal agreement rumors of incursions into Albania by anti-Zogu forces based in Yugoslav territory multiplied. This was the sort

[42] *DDI*, IV, No. 446.

of fighting in which, once the treaty was signed, Italy might easily become involved. Mussolini, however, had no qualms about this. Although he protested formally about the border forays to Belgrade, privately he welcomed them because they could be used to justify the impending Pact of Tirana.[43] Patently, those in and outside Italy who saw the treaty as an expression of aggressive intent against Yugoslavia were not without justification.

Despite its sinister implications, Italy was able to represent the Tirana pact to most of the world's governments as a simple and innocent reaffirmation of Italy's special interest in Albania, already recognized by the Conference of Ambassadors in 1921. In support of this view, a letter from Aloisi to Vrioni was published on December 5, specifically refuting the charge that the treaty gave Italy the right of intervention in Albanian domestic politics.[44] But Rome could not accomplish this task of international salesmanship alone. Britain and, to a lesser extent, Greece were called on and constrained by their Mediterranean entente with Italy to join in assuaging suspicions.[45]

Of course, whatever propaganda success Italy won elsewhere, Yugoslavia was irreconcilable. Presented with the treaty on November 30, a few days before it was made public, Ninčić greeted the news with complaints on two counts. On the procedural side, Italy had not only kept Yugoslavia in the dark but had indulged in outright deception. Ninčić referred to a message from the Italian legation only a day before the signing of the Tirana pact; this had led him to believe that negotiations between Mussolini and Zogu were at most at the beginning stage. Second, Ninčić castigated the treaty on substantive grounds. Belgrade had always abjured such an accord with Zogu out of considera-

[43] *DDI*, IV, Nos. 496, 502.
[44] For text, see Swire, *Albania*, pp. 479-80.
[45] B.D., C12845/391/90; *DBFP*, II, Nos. 357, 388; *DDI*, IV, Nos. 508, 514, 519, 522, 530, 536.

tion for Italy. Now Rome had established "a veritable protectorate over Albania," and, the Yugoslav foreign minister
continued, "I do not see how it can be fitted into the framework of our good relationship." Italy's protestations of innocence were dismissed as "mere words."[46]

Ultimately the vehemence of the Pašić cabinet arose from
the fact that it had staked its foreign policy and tenure of
office on the Pact of Rome. The only way for it to escape
the odium of a bankrupt foreign policy was to reassert
quickly Italo-Yugoslav cooperation in the Adriatic by converting the Tirana pact into an accord *à trois*. The tactic
was tried, and the British, showing some concern at what
their blank check to Mussolini in Albania had produced,
seconded Belgrade. It was a forlorn hope. Just as Italy and
Yugoslavia had collaborated almost three years earlier to
prevent France or Czechoslovakia from joining the Pact of
Rome, so now Mussolini was in no mood to share his Albanian gains with anyone. He bluntly informed the British
ambassador and the world of this.[47] On December 10 Italy
and Albania ratified the Pact of Tirana. On the 16th
Ninčić resigned, and was followed by the rest of the Yugoslav cabinet. Three days later former Premier Pašić died.
With Antonievič gone from Rome, the total collapse of the
Pašić government left King Alexander alone of the Yugoslav architects of the Pact of Rome in power.

The king was hardly an inconsequential figure. The
Italo-Yugoslav détente of 1924 had been built largely on
the mutual esteem and common attachment to authoritarian government of Mussolini and the king. King Alexander,
in spite of everything, seemed anxious to perpetuate this
personal rapport. Although he did not hide his chagrin at
the Pact of Tirana, significantly his criticisms were directed

[46] *DDI*, IV, No. 512. For the Italian version of what Ninčić was told
in advance of the Tirana pact, see *DDI*, IV, No. 498.
[47] *DBFP*, II, Nos. 329, 362, 372, 385; *DDI*, IV, Nos. 531, 548, 554, 562;
Corriere della Sera, Dec. 9, 1926.

at the suddenness, not the terms of the treaty.[48] Rather, it was Mussolini who decided that the Tirana pact should result in a clean break. The original intermediary between Mussolini and Alexander had been General Bodrero, who, after the Pact of Rome, had become minister to Belgrade. However, like all others associated with the policy of Adriatic goodwill, by the end of 1926 Bodrero was discredited, at least in Mussolini's eyes. He retained his ministerial post, but his usefulness as a go-between was finished. Nor was Mussolini in any hurry to find a substitute envoy to the king. Such was the import of a disquisition on Italo-Yugoslav relations after Tirana provided later by a certain Count Guido Malagola Coppi for his friend, the United States minister to Hungary.[49] According to Malagola, Mussolini deliberately let his special relationship with King Alexander languish in the late 1920s, while he anticipated the demise of the Yugoslav state as the result of a revival of Croatian separatism. (It was after rather than before the Treaty of Tirana that Mussolini's intrigues with the Croats flourished.[50]) The Tirana pact itself was calculated to arouse Croatian unrest if only because it exposed the fallacy of cooperation with Italy, which had been fundamentally a Serbian policy.

With the disappearance from the scene of Pašić and Ninčić and the lapse of the cordial relationship between Mussolini and King Alexander, the new cabinet in Belgrade could not fail to be responsive to the wave of popular Italophobia which the Tirana pact evoked throughout Yugoslavia. Only an immediate and obvious gesture of good will by Fascist Italy might have checked the deteriorating situation. But not only did Rome reject the Yugoslav request for a pact *à trois*; it also refused any token return to

---

[48] *DDI*, iv, No. 592.
[49] State Dept. files, 760H.65/673, 677, and 678.
[50] Carocci, *Politica estera dell'Italia fascista*, pp. 168-81.

the Pact of Rome. In truth, following alarmist reports from Belgrade, a proposal was drawn up in the Palazzo Chigi in January 1927 for a joint Italo-Yugoslav declaration reaffirming allegiance to the principles of the Pact of Rome, which was to be in exchange for Yugoslav assurances regarding the treatment of Italians living in Dalmatia. Whether Mussolini ever seriously considered any such overture must be doubted, and in the event, the offer was filed in the Italian foreign ministry and never sent to Belgrade.[51] In the absence of an overture from Rome the new Yugoslav government set out in 1927 to find a riposte to the Pact of Tirana. Continued encouragement of anti-Zogu and anti-Italian elements within Albania was one possibility.[52] But it was more important for Yugoslavia to strengthen her diplomatic position against Italy. Britain was willing to arbitrate between Rome and Belgrade, but Yugoslavia needed a counterweight to Italy, not a mediator.[53] An attempt was made once more to secure Greek support.[54] However, neither Britain nor Greece was the logical source of help for Yugoslavia. The Pact of Rome had moved Yugoslavia away from her partners in the Little Entente and from the entente's patron, France. The breakdown of the Italo-Yugoslav rapprochement automatically sent her in the reverse direction. More specifically, the Rome pact had been employed by the Belgrade government to resist pressure from Prague and Paris to sign a treaty of friendship and arbitration with France. With the decline of the Pact of Rome, Belgrade gravitated toward a treaty with France. Since the terms of an agreement had been drafted as early as March 1926, the surprise is that it took so long after the Pact of Tirana to come into formal existence. Apparently Briand, the pacifier, tried as long as

[51] *DDI*, IV, No. 563 and notes.
[52] *DDI*, IV, Nos. 589, 596.
[53] *DDI*, IV, Nos. 571, 572, 578, 581, 583.
[54] *DDI*, IV, Nos. 576, 597, 598.

possible to include Yugoslavia and Italy in one treaty with France. But Mussolini consistently maintained his resistance to any such pact.[55] An exclusive Franco-Yugoslav accord was ultimately signed on November 11, 1927, and Italy responded on the 22nd with the second Treaty of Tirana. The latter was a defensive alliance, serving to formalize rather than add to Italy's far-reaching commitments to Zogu implied in the first Tirana pact.[56] In reality, for Italy and Yugoslavia the parting of the ways had been reached in November 1926.

Albania proved to be the testing ground of relationships, not only between Italy and Yugoslavia but also between Mussolini and the Palazzo Chigi. Where Corfu had appeared a passing aberration which the professional diplomats had been called in to correct, Mussolini's Albanian policy evolved slowly and the disparagement of the old guard's opinion became a permanent feature. Yet it must be admitted that the professionals brought much of this on themselves. In trying to exploit Fascism for nationalistic ends they were playing with fire; in the Adriatic they were burned. Here the Anglo-Italian entente did not act as a shield behind which the professionals could shelter. More specifically, they encouraged Mussolini in Fiume at the risk of alienating Belgrade. What consistency was there in the position that Fiume was a lawful target of Italian expansion but not Albania? After all, Italy's special interest in Albania had the stamp of international approval. Not surprisingly, some of the career diplomats themselves rejected this logic and followed Mussolini all the way in his Adriatic imperialism and challenge to Yugoslavia. Even the tactic of promoting Croatian separatism received at least consideration among some Italian diplomats. Those who occupied the Durazzo legation tended ultimately to enter into

---

[55] G. Suarez, *Briand*, VI, 244-45.
[56] Pastorelli, *Italia e Albania*, pp. 496-502; Swire, *Albania*, pp. 508-14.

the spirit of colonial competition and to urge Mussolini on to quicker and deeper penetration of Albania. Marquis Durazzo in 1924 and Baron Aloisi in 1926 were notable in this respect. In Rome, Lojacono encouraged Mussolini, although eventually his own Albanian recommendations were rejected. These enthusiasts were perhaps a minority within the Palazzo Chigi to begin with, but their numbers would grow with time and the Duce's apparent successes. Thus Mussolini's forward policy in the Adriatic not merely widened the gulf between himself and the old guard, but caused a clear division among the Palazzo Chigi officials themselves.

17. Revisionism on the Danube

A Novel Quadruplice

THE CAPTURE of Albania was not the only coup in southeastern Europe planned by Mussolini in 1926. What happened in Albania was a logical culmination of the process begun in 1921 when the Conference of Ambassadors entrusted Albania's protection to Italy. In short, it was not an exclusively Fascist triumph. On the other hand, a wholly Mussolinian and more far-ranging venture would be a radical realignment of forces in the Danube valley. And this Mussolini envisaged, using Rumania as the focal point of his scheme.

In an earlier chapter we saw that Rumania's legal title to Bessarabia awaited only Italian ratification of the Allied protocol of 1920, which understandably became a touchstone of Italo-Rumanian relations. In 1924 Mussolini had promised to use Italy's good offices in Moscow to persuade the Soviet Union to accept the loss of Bessarabia, but he had met with no success at all. In the wake of this failure, progress toward an Italo-Rumanian entente came to a standstill; as far off as ever were both Italy's participation in Rumania's economy and a political accord. This was the burden of a lengthy review of the position by the Marquis Durazzo on taking over the Bucharest legation in December 1925. He urged on Mussolini some initiative in the Bessarabian question to get things moving again. One possibility was to take up a Rumanian suggestion for "an assurance to be kept secret that . . . should Russia raise the question of Bessarabia by resort to arms or diplomatic discussion, the [Italian] government would afford Rumania all its moral and diplomatic support"; Durazzo allowed that this was fraught with "not a few difficulties and dangers." An alternative idea was further persuasion of Moscow to relinquish Bessarabia, "which might be given the character, not so much of a definite démarche made only once, as of continuous pressure" exerted hopefully in conjunction with other powers; France and Poland were suggested as possible partners.[1]

What broke the deadlock was not an Italian initiative but a significant change within Rumania. This was the entry into office in the spring of 1926 of a new cabinet headed by General Alexander Averescu. Averescu had been educated in Italy and was reputed to be both an Italophile and pro-Fascist. Yet one of his government's first acts was to override Italian objections and sign a friendship pact with France. On the other hand, Mussolini would take this rebuff from an ideological sympathizer without becoming incensed; in fact, it stimulated Italy to reach some accord with Bucharest lest Rumania slip completely into the French orbit. Averescu was willing to balance his Francophile gesture by an agreement with Italy, so he set no preconditions regarding Bessarabia. Negotiations were conducted on the Italian side by Dino Grandi, and on the Rumanian by Averescu himself and the Rumanian minister in Rome, Alexander Lahovary.[2] Three months after the accord between France and Rumania, an Italo-Rumanian friendship pact was concluded on September 16, 1926. On first seeing the draft treaty offered by Italy, the Rumanian foreign minister had commented ruefully on the treaty's "platonic character."[2a] In the course of the negotiations, Italy was persuaded to accept a secret clause regarding future military cooperation. But this involved no specific commitment, and the published clauses of the treaty were couched in the most general language.[3] Above all, there was no reference to Bessarabia. To emphasize further the innocuousness of the accord, Italy insisted at the ceremonial sign-

---

[1] *DDI*, IV, No. 197.   [2] *DDI*, IV, No. 295.   [2a] *DDI*, IV, No. 378.
[3] Carocci, *Politica estera dell'Italia fascista*, p. 59.

ing attended by both Mussolini and Averescu that there be a public exchange of letters carefully explaining that Italian ratification of the Bessarabian treaty "will take place only when this can be done without prejudicing Italy's interests of a general nature." It was, conceded Averescu, "a question of time and opportunity."[4]

Superficially then, the Italo-Rumanian pact was no more substantial than most of the other arbitration agreements that followed Locarno. For that matter, it said no more than the inconsequential Italo-Czech treaty of 1924. Yet it was vastly more important, partly because the Rumanian and Italian governments intended that it should be so, partly because events quickly brought out its true portent. For Fascist Italy the pact with Rumania was linked in a preparatory way with the first Treaty of Tirana with Albania just over two months later. Aloisi left Bucharest for Albania to preside over the negotiations leading up to the Tirana pact, while Durazzo, who had held the Albanian post, took Aloisi's place in Bucharest in time for the Italo-Rumanian pact. Moreover, while France and Czechoslovakia rushed to Yugoslavia's side in denouncing the Treaty of Tirana, Bucharest honored the spirit of the recent friendship pact and hailed the treaty.[5] But one good turn deserves another, and Averescu now felt free to raise the Bessarabian question again. He called for one more mediatory overture to Moscow, certain to be rejected, and then Italian ratification of the protocal of 1920.[6]

All along, Mussolini had anticipated that the Italo-Rumanian pact would sooner or later, in however roundabout a way, compel him to a firm decision on Bessarabia, and he had made it well in advance. Even before the signing of the pact he had confidentially informed the Italian ambassador in Moscow: "I have come to the decision to ratify the

---

[4] *OO*, XXII, 406-407.   [5] *DDI*, IV, Nos. 536, 547.
[6] *DDI*, IV, No. 573.

Bessarabian treaty as soon as Rumania provides suitable compensation."[7] Also early in September Mussolini had sketched in a memorandum what he considered an adequate quid pro quo; substantially the same requirements were presented to Averescu early in 1927.[8] The Duce's demands were in three parts. First was the usual request for commercial privileges in Rumania, "to assist Italy overcome difficulties with Russia of an economic nature as a result of ratification." It had been nearly three years since Fascist Italy had accorded the Soviet regime de jure recognition in the expectation of vast amounts of mutual trade which had long ago proved illusory, but it was still a useful bargaining ploy.[8a] Then came a minor point, but one of concern to a hypernationalist like Mussolini—the teaching of Italian in Rumania's secondary schools. The sting lay in the third, and political, category: "The honest counterweight to balance the risks and dangers of a rupture of diplomatic relations between Italy and Russia must be offered us by Rumania in the field of Danubian politics. Under the aegis and eventually with the participation of Italy, Rumania must strive to reach an accord with Hungary on the one hand and Bulgaria on the other. Only by realizing under Italian inspiration and guidance an Italo-Magyar-Rumanian-Bulgarian quadruple alliance [*quadruplice*] could the Italian government face with equanimity the inevitable crisis with Russia."

In this proposed new grouping was the essence of Mussolini's strategy in the Danube valley. The French advance into the region would be halted, or impeded, by dismemberment of the Little Entente, which was to be accomplished by the detachment of Rumania. Yugoslavia might have been wooed away earlier by the Pact of Rome, but

---

[7] *DDI*, IV, No. 408.

[8] *DDI*, IV, Nos. 401, 580.

[8a] Of particular concern was the threatened loss of Russian oil supplies to Italy (Carocci, *Politica estera dell'Italia fascista*, pp. 63-64).

Mussolini had declined the chance for the sake of Albania. He had never genuinely considered a détente with the Czech parliamentary democracy. Therefore Yugoslavia and Czechoslovakia were allowed to drift into Italophobia, and all the eggs were put in the Rumanian basket. As for the alienation of Russia by ratification of the Bessarabian protocol, this was entirely satisfactory to Mussolini's ideological mind. The whole idea, of course, ran counter to the school of thought in the Palazzo Chigi represented by Contarini; it was obviously more than coincidence that Mussolini's Danubian experiment was tried out in the year after his resignation. The followers of Sforza and Contarini urged friendship with Czechoslovakia, Yugoslavia, and even the Soviets, ideology notwithstanding, on the ground of a common interest in checking the proclivities of the defeated nations of World War I. By far the most radical departure from conventional Italian diplomacy in Mussolini's strategy was the proposal to cut across the line between victor and vanquished by associating Italy and Rumania with Hungary and Bulgaria. On Mussolini's ability to convince Bucharest to follow this new and radical path turned the entire scheme.

What, in effect, Rumania was offered was the final assurance and legal sanction in Bessarabia, but at the hazard of reawakening another irredentist bogey in Transylvania, for such was the inference of an association with Hungary. In trying to sell this enterprise Mussolini made special allocations of money to win the favor of the Rumanian press.[9] But in reality he staked everything on Averescu. "Averescu is a sincere friend of Italy," he wrote confidently to King Victor Emmanuel.[10] Indeed, the general was cast in the same role the Duce was playing in Italy: a Fascist dictator with the power and inclination to change

9 It.D. (Ministry of Popular Culture), 40/437/021548-52.
10 *DDI*, IV, No. 428.

342

the direction of his country's foreign policy. But this turned out to be another fantasy. Averescu was only an embryonic dictator with little scope to make radical foreign policy decisions, even if he wanted to; and there is every indication that he did not want to. In Durazzo's words, Averescu was "taken somewhat by surprise" at Mussolini's proposition, and "replied to me in a rather evasive fashion." Nonetheless, the negative response was clear. "He had seen in the Little Entente first and foremost a means for Rumania to exercise a major weight in international councils and to avoid the isolation which had threatened in the period immediately after the war. And from this point of view, at least, the Little Entente still rendered Rumania a signal service. Could a different grouping serve her equally well?"[11] Plainly not, the general implied.

Mussolini's reaction was unclear. He marked the news from Bucharest enigmatically "important" and "interesting." Undoubtedly Averescu's reply was a decisive setback for a policy which could not easily be reversed. Mussolini had, so to speak, burned his Czech and Yugoslav bridges behind him. But he was not the sort to admit and rectify past mistakes. Italy still had not ratified the Bessarabian protocol, and the frayed relationship with Russia might be repaired; but any ties which Italy and the Soviets might form were sure to be limited and of little avail to Italy in the Danube valley. The only recourse for Mussolini, short of renouncing his Danubian aspirations, was to go forward in the direction he had chosen. But after Rumania's emphatic refusal to break up the Little Entente, what remained of Mussolini's quadruple alliance was an Italian combination with the Balkan revisionists, Hungary and Bulgaria. Once again the revisionism implicit in Fascism's foreign policy had risen to the surface.

For most of three years after taking office Mussolini had

[11] *DDI*, IV, No. 586; see also *DDI*, IV, p. 464, n. 1.

steadfastly rejected all overtures from Hungary and Bulgaria. But at the same time a certain ideological affinity had developed between Fascist Italy and ruling circles in Budapest and Sofia. In Hungary the powerful, reactionary Magyar aristocracy found much to praise in postwar Fascism. In Bulgaria, after Stambuliski's death in 1923, governments were generally right-wing and authoritarian—not unlike the Duce's. This may have helped the defeated states to bear Mussolini's early rebuffs with equanimity. At any rate, lacking other European friends, they remained receptive to the slightest hint of assistance from Italy.

It was during 1925 that Mussolini began to edge in the direction of the Danubian revisionist states. The immediate cause and opportunity was the developing Italo-Yugoslav quarrel in the Adriatic. Because Bulgaria's irredentism was aimed at Yugoslavia, the Albanian contest brought together Italy and Bulgaria in particular. Mussolini began to change his previous habit of ascribing all disturbances on the Yugoslav-Bulgarian border to Sofia's machinations; instead, Yugoslavia was charged now with harboring and assisting disaffected Bulgarian exiles. But Mussolini was proceeding cautiously, and he asked the Bulgarian government to appreciate his delicate position; but Italy did not dare appear to be fomenting or exploiting the rivalry between Bulgaria and Yugoslavia.[12] The year 1925 also saw the first signs of greater warmth between Rome and Budapest. Italy began to show belated signs of interest in the international Hungarian rehabilitation loan as a means of gaining a foothold in the country. And Mussolini proposed a meeting with Bethlen the next time the Hungarian premier visited northern Italy, to which Bethlen responded warmly.[13]

[12] *DDI*, III, Nos. 805, 811, 823. Similarly, when in October 1925 a skirmish on the Greek-Bulgarian border invoked League of Nations intervention, Mussolini refused to show any open favoritism to Sofia (J. Barros, "The Greek-Bulgarian Incident of 1925," *Proceedings of the American Philosophical Society*, CVIII [Aug. 1964], 354-85).

[13] *DDI*, III, No. 814.

But it was not until 1926 and Contarini's resignation in the spring that Italy made serious overtures to Hungary and Bulgaria. At the March session of the League of Nations Council, while Beneš canvassed the idea of a Balkan Locarno so beloved of the Contarinians in the Palazzo Chigi, Grandi was busy preparing the ground for a different kind of Balkan pact. He obtained from the Bulgarian foreign minister, Atanas Burov, and the Hungarian Count Bethlen a commitment to join in "an agreement among the states of the Danubian-Balkan region . . . under the aegis of Italy."[14] The novel design of a *quadruplice* of Italy, Rumania, Hungary, and Bulgaria was taking shape. In September the Italo-Rumanian friendship pact was, so it was optimistically assumed in Rome, the prelude to Rumania's participation in the scheme. The following month Burov visited Rome to discuss the crucial subject of reconciliation between Rumania and the Danubian irredentists.[15] However, what impressed Budapest and Sofia more than these academic schemes and paper preparations was the Treaty of Tirana of November 27, for the spectacular breach between Rome and Belgrade, which the treaty represented, made Mussolini's overtures to the revisionist states more a matter of necessity and less of choice. Fascist Italy now had a genuine need for Hungarian and Bulgarian friendship in order to encircle a hostile Yugoslavia. As Grandi annotated an account of Belgrade press speculations on "the chain of alliances" which Italy might construct around Yugoslavia: "That is exactly what has to be done."[16]

Mussolini's plan for a Danubian bloc made up of four states was torpedoed by Rumania's refusal to join in January 1927. What remained was a half-developed Italian

[14] *DDI*, IV, Nos. 274, 279.
[15] *DDI*, IV, Nos. 453, 468.
[16] *DDI*, IV, No. 425 and note. For the record, of course, Italy denied any intention of encircling Yugoslavia (*DDI*, IV, Nos. 523, 526).

rapprochement with Hungary and Bulgaria. Having no alternative policy in the Danube valley, Rome set about bringing the relationship with the two countries to fruition. As far as Bulgaria was concerned, this was done without any overt flourish, largely because Rome's quarrel with Belgrade made it unnecessary. Common hostility to Yugoslavia was a surer Italo-Bulgarian tie than any treaty. But Hungary was different. The Magyar irredentists were independent and unpredictable. Moreover, Mussolini was busily engaged in cultivating the friendship of the Magyar's archenemy, Rumania. In these circumstances, Italy, to be sure of Hungary's allegiance, had to buy it with a formal agreement. Indeed, in early 1927, while Mussolini's hopes of including Hungary and Rumania in a radical Danubian alignment were still alive, arrangements were made for Bethlen to visit Italy again; an Italo-Hungary treaty was clearly in the offing.[17]

In the spring Mussolini continued to try to balance between Rumania and Hungary. Italy's ratification of the Bessarabian protocol, which was supposed to win Rumania's adherence to Mussolini's grand design, now had to be used to mollify the Rumanian reaction to the impending accord with Hungary. So in March ratification was given and may have muted, if it did not silence entirely, Rumanian criticism of what followed on April 5. This was the signing in Rome by Mussolini and Bethlen of a pact of amity, conciliation, and arbitration, valid for 10 years instead of the customary five. It was accompanied by another accord of no little consequence to Italy for the channeling of Hungarian trade through Fiume.[18]

This was the first bilateral agreement Hungary had achieved with any of the victors of World War I. It revived many suspicions of Mussolini's intentions which had

[17] *DDI*, IV, Nos. 579, 582, 584.
[18] *DDI*, V, Nos. 56, 121, 123, 134.

been voiced when he took office.[19] Mussolini contributed to the uneasiness by glowing and extravagant words at the signing ceremony: "Today more than ever Italy views with pleasure and confidence Hungary moving toward that better future of which she is well worthy."[20] In the course of the next year his actions suited the meaning of these words. It was in June 1928 that the League of Nations received evidence that Italy was smuggling arms to Hungary in violation of the Treaty of Trianon.[21]

It is often supposed that it was the Hungarian treaty of 1927 that launched Mussolini on his revisionist course.[22] This is not factually true; for some years he had been consorting with the German nationalists. But it certainly led him on to expose his revisionism with less restraint. Furthermore, by associating Italy with irredentism on the Danube, Mussolini went a long way to committing his country to a new European alignment under the patronage of Germany. This was so, even though it may have been the opposite of what Mussolini intended. Guariglia asserts that the Duce's Danubian policy was anti-German. To provide a barrier against German penetration of the Balkans, he was prepared not only to sponsor a Hungarian revival but even to contemplate an Austro-Hungarian reunion and Habsburg restoration.[23] If indeed this was Mussolini's strategy, it was impractical. At the least, it was inconsistent to back

---

[19] Carocci, *Politica estera dell'Italia fascista*, pp. 80-82; Di Nolfo, *Mussolini e la politica estera*, pp. 197-99. The Hungarians naturally regarded the treaty as an unmitigated victory for revisionism (M. Horthy, *Memoirs* [New York, 1957], pp. 134-35).

[20] *OO*, XXII, 336-38.

[21] *LNOJ*, IX (1928), 906-909. Also on Mussolini's encouragement of Magyar irredentism in the late 1920s, see Carocci, *Politica estera dell'Italia fascista*, pp. 82-83, 124-27; L. Kerekes, "Italien, Ungarn und die Österreichische Heimwehrbewegung, 1928-1931," *Österreich in Geschichte und Literatur*, IX (Jan. 1965), 1-13.

[22] For instance, see Di Nolfo, *Mussolini e la politica estera*, pp. 199-205.

[23] Guariglia, *Ricordi*, pp. 86-87.

Germany against France on the Rhine, but not against France and her allies on the Danube. Once Mussolini took to attacking the Little Entente and French influence therein by recourse to the irredentists of Budapest and Sofia, he presented Germany with a standing invitation, when able and inclined, to join in the fray against France and the Danubian status quo. Here again we encounter the fatal flaw in Fascist Italian diplomacy: a blind self-confidence in the ability to manipulate revisionism without a qualm about becoming its pawn.

Bessarabia and Soviet Russia

Mussolini's plan for a Danubian *quadruplice* seriously affected relations between Rome and Moscow. Italy's concomitant ratification of the Bessarabian treaty of 1920 was bound to put an intolerable strain on Russo-Italian friendship, already badly bruised by the reemphasis of ideological distinctions in the Matteotti affair. On the other hand, although Mussolini's early expectations of what was to be gained through Soviet friendship had evaporated, Russo-Italian relations had remained reasonably cordial during 1925-26, the memory of Matteotti notwithstanding. In the main, this was due to events over which neither Moscow nor Rome had much control.

Late in 1924 the British Conservatives had regained office, using the election slogan that a vote for Labour was a vote for communism. One of the new government's first actions was to abrogate the Anglo-Soviet trade treaty. In Moscow the value of the Italian tie increased at once. Soviet officials, despite Matteotti, began to speak in friendlier accents and to renew the time-honored promises of commercial favors for Italy.[24] Mussolini, for his part, however disillusioned he might have been about Soviet promises, was in no hurry

24 *DDI*, III, No. 592.

to admit the failure of his policy of friendship toward Russia. Moreover, Rome and Moscow still found themselves on the same side in certain diplomatic questions, notably in their common desire to gatecrash any Tangier conference. Mussolini decided to respond in kind to the Soviet protestations of goodwill and to curb somewhat the rising current of anti-bolshevism among his supporters. Giving a résumé of his recent diplomacy to the Senate on May 20, 1925, he discussed the threat of Bolshevik subversion at some length. But he minimized the danger in Italy and insisted his government had the matter well in hand. Above all, he distinguished between the Comintern's activity and the "absolutely correct" posture of the Soviet diplomats in Italy. Moscow was duly appreciative of this carefully worded statement.[25]

A few months later, however, Russo-Italian friendship underwent another trial. Moscow, understandably, viewed the Locarno Conference in October 1925 as an attempt to woo Germany away from Russia and into the Anglo-French camp—as an attempt to reisolate Russia, in fact. In this sense, Mussolini's signature on the Locarno Pacts ranged Italy unequivocally with an anti-Soviet bloc. On the other hand, Italy's adherence to Locarno had been a last-minute affair, and Moscow's first reaction was to try to win Italy back from her new allegiance. Chicherin asked to visit Rome and talk with Mussolini, to which Mussolini had no objection. Russian and Italian diplomats talked in terms of a friendship pact of the sort common in the post-Locarno years. Contarini, for one, believed strongly that Russian friendship was necessary to the West in order to counter the threat of German revisionism.[26] But for unknown reasons, Chicherin chose not to make a trip to Italy, and, as the months went by, Moscow and Rome charged each other

<hr/>

[25] *OO*, XXI, 317-19; *DDI*, IV, No. 5.   [26] *DDB*, II, No. 54.

with reneging on a pact of friendship.[27] Indeed, the longer
the delay, the less chance there was for such an accord. A
year or so after Locarno, Mussolini began to discover the
pleasure of a special relationship with the British Conservative,
Chamberlain. No legal incompatibility was involved,
but certainly Mussolini's association with the Soviets went
against the grain of the Anglo-Italian entente. There could
be little doubt that in a pinch Mussolini would choose
London over Moscow.[28] That he was inclined to do so was
indicated by his tolerance of a revival of anti-Bolshevik
propaganda in Italy. When in April 1926 Mussolini was
wounded by a demented Irish woman who had no connection
with the Comintern, a mob automatically demonstrated
outside the Soviet embassy in Rome. The Italian
government then refused to receive a Soviet protest of the
incident.[29] At this moment it became apparent to Moscow
that Locarno had not succeeded in driving a wedge between
Berlin and Moscow. On April 24, 1926 the Russo-German
Treaty of Berlin was signed, and the Soviet appraisal
of the importance of Mussolini's good will declined
accordingly.[30]

There remained one criterion of Russo-Italian relations,
which overrode ideology, Matteotti, and Locarno, and
which in the last resort determined whether the détente
that had begun with recognition continued or lapsed. This
was Italian ratification of the Bessarabian protocol. So long
as Mussolini withheld it, and thereby also withheld Rumania's
full legal title to the region, the Soviets would endure
much at Italian hands and preserve at least the semblance
of friendship between Moscow and Rome. But

27 *DDI*, IV, Nos. 175, 305.

28 At his Leghorn meeting with Chamberlain in September 1926, for
instance, Mussolini seemed to go out of his way to paint as black a
picture as possible of Russo-Italian relations (B.D., C11092/9326/22).

29 *Corriere della Sera*, April 11, 1926; *DDI*, IV, No. 294.

30 On the Russo-German treaty of April 1926 with reference to
Italy, see *ADAP*, II (1), Nos. 120, n. 5, and 146.

Mussolini was less concerned with nonratification as a means of maintaining a tie with Russia than he was with ratification as a bribe to entice Rumania to join his grand design in the Danube valley. On September 16, 1926 the conclusion of the Italo-Rumanian friendship pact implied that a shift in Italy's stand on Bessarabia was imminent. All along, Moscow had insisted that it would be "absolutely intransigent in the Bessarabian question"; and the Italian ambassador in Moscow, Gaetano Manzoni, warned that "the crisis will be most serious: I would say mortal: the Bessarabian question is, in fact, the only open political question between Italy and Russia at the moment."[31] Mussolini encouraged Moscow to hope that Italian ratification of the Bessarabian protocol could be averted, and hinted at a treaty of friendship, neutrality, and arbitration as his price. To delay ratification, he wrote to King Victor Emmanuel, "permits Italy still to play the Russian card."[32] But the Soviets refused to be mollified. On November 20 Manzoni reported: "The Italo-Rumanian pact, the Bessarabian situation (*fatto Bessarabico*) have, then, occasioned the manifestations of Soviet political frigidity toward Italy, and at the same time they have brought to the surface the already existent but hitherto latent feeling of coldness."[33]

The Soviets were correct in distrusting Mussolini. Since September 1926 he was resolved on ratification of the Bessarabian protocol; his talk of a Russo-Italian political accord was so much camouflage. This emerged clearly on March 7, 1927, when Italy at long last ratified the Bessarabian protocol—and this despite Rumania's refusal to join Mussolini's league of Balkan states. Mussolini's prime concern was still to reconcile Bucharest to Italy's growing

[31] *DDI*, III, No. 98; IV, No. 412.   [32] *DDI*, IV, Nos. 417, 428.
[33] *DDI*, IV, No. 492.

rapprochement with revisionist Hungary.[34] Mussolini quite consciously, then, provoked a breach with the Soviets. Obviously he now considered the utility of the Russo-Italian rapprochement to be at an end. It was time to return to a consistent anti-Bolshevik ideology.

[34] *DDI*, v, Nos. 54, 55, 57, 109.

18. Mussolini's Quarrel
with France

The Scope of the Dispute

MUSSOLINI'S policies in 1926 in southeastern Europe had a wider, continental dimension. His plan to inveigle Rumania into a quadruple alliance presaged the disintegration of the Little Entente, which by the mid-1920s had become a crucial link in the French security system to contain Germany and the Balkan revisionists. To destroy the Little Entente, then, was to destroy the main agency of French influence in the Danube valley. Mussolini's *quadruplice* was nothing less than an attempt to supplant French with Italian influence there. The tactic was self-defeating. The more Italy challenged France's client states, the more they sought refuge in a close association with France. The first Treaty of Tirana, for example, was followed by a Franco-Yugoslav pact. Nevertheless, Mussolini's grand design on the Danube was an excellent illustration of the anti-French spirit which infused so much of his diplomacy.

By 1926 Mussolini, to hurt France, was prepared to use defeated Hungary and Bulgaria against the Little Entente, brushing aside the argument of the Sforza-Contarini school in the Palazzo Chigi that the Little Entente was a barrier to pan-German expansion southward. Not surprisingly, Mussolini's links with the German nationalist right, established in 1923-24, but minimized during the Matteotti affair, were refurbished in the mid-1920s. The Nazis were cultivated in particular; even Neurath, the trusting German ambassador in Rome, became convinced of Mussolini's liaison with Fascist sympathizers in Germany.[1]

---

[1] G.D., 529K/4154/152086. For a description of the activities in Germany of two Fascist agents, Biseo and Renzetti, in 1926, see G.D.,

Almost certainly Hitler was the recipient of Italian money. André François-Poncet, French envoy to Berlin in the 1930s, and SS General Karl Wolff, who served with the German army in Italy during World War II, both have made this charge.[2] Salvemini cites the trial in Rome of an Italian official accused of embezzlement. When it became clear that the missing funds had been intended for Hitler, the trial was concluded in secret. Further, Salvemini relates the assurances of Prussian Minister President Otto Braun, conveyed through Hermann Ullstein of the German publishing house, that Mussolini assisted financially in Hitler's early electoral successes.[3] In addition, it is extremely likely that Hitler was given more than money. Guariglia, from his vantage point within Italian officialdom in the inter-war years, alleges that certain of the secret shipments of Italian arms across the Alps in the 1920s were destined for the Nazis of Austria and southern Germany.[4]

Mussolini's intrigues with the Nazis and other German nationalists were based on his premise that Italian and German nationalism had a common enemy in France. The inevitability of Franco-German hostility, however, was called into question by the Locarno Pacts—one reason why Mussolini accepted them so reluctantly. Nor could Mussolini be expected to applaud the Franco-German honeymoon that followed Locarno. The seal to be set on the Franco-German bargain reached at Locarno was Germany's entrance into the League of Nations. Mussolini did not dare veto this, but he did upbraid the Italian delegation at Geneva for seeming to promote it, insisting, "we must be the

---

24K/3617/003165-66; 28K/3617/003322-24. For actual reports by such Italian agents, see It.D. (Farinacci files), 330/1296/113305-307; (Mussolini's private secretariat), 287/1193/087721, 170/491/050253.

2 François-Poncet, *The Fateful Years*, tr. J. Leclercq (New York, 1948), p. 238; R. Wichterich, *Benito Mussolini* (Stuttgart, 1952), p. 197.

3 Salvemini, *Mussolini diplomatico*, p. 61.

4 Guariglia, *Ricordi*, pp. 76-77.

last to contribute to this [German] success."[5] After Germany's entry into the League, the famous private conversations between Briand and Stresemann at Thoiry in the fall of 1926 bespoke still closer Franco-German cooperation. At Leghorn, Mussolini confided to Chamberlain "a little anxiety lest [the talks] should be carried too far."[6] So, "in view of the presumed accords between France and Germany," Mussolini decided to offer Stresemann some alternative to his pro-French course by taking up a German overture for an arbitration pact on the lines of the numerous arbitration treaties spawned by Locarno.[7] This was despite Fascist Italy's constant public denigration of the spirit of Locarno and international arbitrament in general.[8] Thus, on December 29, 1926, less than a year after the verbal duel between Mussolini and Stresemann over the Alto Adige, an Italo-German arbitration treaty was signed. It aroused some stir, particularly in British leftist circles that suspected Mussolini's affinity for German revisionism. But as Mussolini truthfully protested, the pact was limited in scope and importance.[9] It gave rise to an attempt to couple Italianization of the Alto Adige with pacification of the German minority there.[10] In May 1927 Mussolini asked for the assistance of the German military in strengthening Italy's air force, a request reluctantly granted by Berlin.[11]

These measures, however, did nothing to dissuade Stresemann from pursuing his rapprochement with Briand. On the other hand, Stresemann's position in the triangular relationship among Germany, France, and Italy was relatively unimportant to Mussolini. He was staking all on the ac-

---

[5] *DDI*, IV, No. 276. [6] B.D., C11092/9326/22.
[7] *DDI*, IV, No. 436. On the actual negotiation of the pact, see *ADAP*, III, Nos. 193, 195, 229, 233, 234, 250, 253.
[8] Rumi, *Movimento di Liberazione in Italia*, No. 80 (1965), pp. 50-55; Salvemini, *Mussolini diplomatico*, pp. 100-103.
[9] *DDI*, IV, Nos. 565, 569; *Corriere della Sera*, Jan. 2, 1927.
[10] It.D. (Mussolini's private secretariat), 250/1091/068171-77.
[11] G.D., L223/4207/067156-57.

quisition of power by the extreme German nationalists; in this scheme of things Stresemann's policy of fulfillment in the west was a passing German phenomenon which could be ignored and outlived. A telegram to Romano Avezzana once asked rhetorically: "On what foundation could a Franco-German alliance be built?" The Duce answered himself comfortingly: "On the basis of Locarno? No, because Locarno precludes any sort of alliance. On the basis of Versailles? Still less because this treaty is accepted by no German, not one I say, not even by the ambiguous Stresemann."[12]

In the meantime, Mussolini went out of his way to demonstrate to the world his own implacable hostility toward France. In his elementary view each nation state was either rising or waning, and Fascist dogma held that, among the so-called Latin sisters, Italy was destined to prevail over France. "Truly decadent, such is my opinion of the French people," he once confided to one of his Fascist cronies.[13] Moreover, traditional French contempt for Italy only strengthened the Duce's compulsion to assert Italian superiority. "In the eyes of every Frenchman," he complained, "we are only 'sales macaroni.' "[14] Like many Italian nationalists, Mussolini's attitude to France was tinged with a personal rancor. This has to be taken into account in appraising the difficulties that overtook Franco-Italian relations after 1925.

North African Problems

The twin North African problems, Tangier and Tunisia, were naturally in the forefront of Franco-Italian differences. Early in 1925, as we have seen, an accord balancing French concessions in the former question against Italian in the lat-

<hr/>

12 *DDI*, IV, No. 363.
13 It.D. (Mussolini's private secretariat), 287/1193/087685.
14 Quoted in Kirkpatrick, *Mussolini*, p. 167.

ter appeared to be taking shape. But it did not materialize, largely because the French went back on their implied promise to allow Italy some say in negotiating an international statute for Tangier. In April 1925 a cabinet change occurred in Paris. Ambassador Romano Avezzana was first assured by the new premier, Paul Painlevé, and by Aristide Briand, now foreign minister, that France still desired to assuage Italian pride in Tangier.[15] On the other hand, recently restored to the post of secretary general in the French foreign ministry was Philippe Berthelot. Romano Avezzana anticipated trouble from this "collaborator in the policies of Clemenceau," known for his Italophobia.[16] Berthelot was, perhaps more than anyone else, the authentic voice of the Quai d'Orsay; it was his point of view that would prevail over the vague pro-Italian sentiments of Painlevé and Briand. Romano Avezzana discovered this the first time he talked to Berthelot on the specific subject of Tangier. The ambassador's gloomy account to Mussolini ran: "I have held a conversation with Berthelot about the Tangier Statute. I must, with regret, inform Your Excellency that it was far from satisfactory. Berthelot . . . told me that he had studied the question and discussed it with Briand. Both had come to the conclusion that our request could not be granted. 'I consider,' he told me, 'that by adhering even partially to Italy's point of view, we should create a vague, dubious situation which far from being serviceable could be the source of new difficulties. To avoid these it is better to be frank and sincere. We must stick to the accord of 1912 whereby France disinterested herself in Libya and Italy in Morocco, comprehending by that term all territory subject to the Sultan's sovereignty, even in places like Tangier where France, through cir-

[15] *DDI*, III, Nos. 692, 775.

[16] *DDI*, III, No. 856; IV, No. 11. Berthelot's anti-Italian sentiments are confirmed by P. Flandin, *Politique française, 1919-1940* (Paris, 1940), pp. 94-97; H. Lagardelle, *Mission à Rome* (Paris, 1955), p. 13.

cumstances extraneous to Italy, had come to arrangements with England and Spain.' "[17]

It is not clear why France suddenly resumed so hard a line in the Tangier issue. No doubt it was to some extent due to the contest between professionals and politicians within the Quai d'Orsay. (The situation was the reverse of that in the Italian foreign ministry; in Rome it was the professionals who were milder and more conciliatory than their Fascist chief, while in Paris the career diplomats were more rigid and chauvinistic than the conciliatory foreign minister, Briand.[18]) Romano Avezzana ascribed France's reversal to the vicissitudes of the war against the Moroccan Riff. But there was another factor of the utmost importance in the background. Only a few weeks earlier Romano Avezzana, in a grandiose attempt to heal the rift between Italy and France, had proposed a broad colonial entente covering a variety of issues and places.[19] Mussolini did nothing to disavow this step. Of its very nature, such a project in the beginning was bound to be vague. Paris may well have perceived an opportunity to win from Italy desiderata in Tunisia in return for spectacular but general promises which probably could never be realized, in which case there was no need to make immediate and precise payment to Italy in Tangier. Thus the humiliation of Italy's exclusion from the Tangier negotiations continued. Romano Avezzana won from Briand an assurance that "Berthelot's reply in this regard was not definitive and that the question would be re-examined when the situation in Morocco became clearer."[20] The question, then, remained technically open. Rome, formally, neither en-

[17] *DDI*, IV, No. 3.
[18] On the situation inside the Quai d'Orsay at this time, see R. D. Challener, "The French Foreign Office: The Era of Philippe Berthelot," in *The Diplomats*, pp. 49-85.
[19] *DDI*, III, Nos. 829, 842, 845.
[20] *DDI*, IV, No. 18.

dorsed nor repudiated the 1923 statute about to be implemented.

Meanwhile, Romano Avezzana, apparently receiving no countermand from Rome, went ahead with his suggestion for a broad Franco-Italian colonial understanding. To Painlevé he expatiated on the notion of a Tunisian accord satisfying the demands of French nationality within the framework of an overall agreement: "Painlevé asked me what my ideas were in this respect. I replied to him, speaking always on a personal basis, that the solution, it appeared to me, should be sought in a revision of colonial mandates, and in a preferential right to the Portuguese colonies, colonies which have been falling into decadence through the irremediable weakness of the metropolitan country. I also referred to the need to settle the relationship between Italy and the colonial territories of France, observing that the occupation of the whole of Africa by England and France herself could not maintain its character of exclusive domination without provoking reactions sooner or later." Patently tailored to suit Mussolini was the mention of an Italian mandate. Nor was the idea altogether alien to the spirit of the professionals in the Palazzo Chigi for, as Romano Avezzana took care to point out, an Italian option on Portugal's colonies was an ambition already endorsed by Secretary General Contarini.[21]

The attraction to France was obvious. To obtain something tangible and quick from Italy in Tunisia, Paris would make any number of promises for the future, doubtful of fulfillment if only because Britain's approval of such colonial transactions was far from certain. Consequently Romano Avezzana's overtures were greeted warmly in the Quai d'Orsay. Joseph Caillaux, Anatole De Monzie, and even the formidable Berthelot—all talked amiably of the

[21] *DDI*, IV, No. 129.

need to solve Italy's "demographic" problem with a mandate and colonies, principally at Portugal's expense.[22]

By far the most enthusiastic French reception came from Briand. Although he had little personal sympathy for Mussolini or his regime, he was above all dedicated to international good will among all types of men and states. Moreover, his political mind ran in the direction of sweeping, general agreements. During the summer of 1925 he pushed eagerly for as extensive a European security pact as possible. In the field of Franco-Italian relations Briand, with Romano Avezzana's support, hoped to unite colonial and continental arrangements into one gigantic package. France would give Italy a Brenner guarantee, thus enrolling Mussolini decisively in the antirevisionist camp. Outside Europe Italy would satisfy France in Tunisia in return for loosely defined prospects in Portugal's colonies.[23]

Of course, tying European and colonial affairs together meant that a breakdown in one part of the deal could upset arrangements in the other. So it was that Romano Avezzana's plan for a Franco-Italian entente was undercut by Mussolini's refusal to see European security in the same light as Briand and the Italian ambassador. Mussolini's rejection of a French guarantee of the Brenner and his obvious disdain for the Locarno Pacts effectively destroyed hopes for a global agreement.

Furthermore, when belatedly Mussolini came to pronounce on the colonial side of the Briand-Romano Avezzana negotiations, he did so negatively. He was decidedly skeptical of the vague colonial propositions which emanated from Paris. Although he was offered substantially what he had sought at the Lausanne Conference in 1922, he had learned at Lausanne the scant value of promises couched in generalities. On one report apropos of an Italian lien on Portugal's colonies he scrawled: "Interesting

22 *DDI*, III, Nos. 845, 846.   23 *DDI*, IV, Nos. 126, 284.

but too distant and costly."[24] Nor did Mussolini feel that the Tunisian situation demanded urgent negotiations. France's pledge not to abrogate unilaterally the 1896 conventions still held, and Briand repeated it when Poincaré returned to the cabinet.[25] "It is not suitable for the moment to insist on Tunisian questions. There is no need to seem to be begging for mediocre concessions," Mussolini wrote in September 1926.[26]

By this time the Tangier question had reawakened. The new international statute had been officially declared effective on June 1, 1925, and immediately the effect of Italy's noncooperation was felt.[27] More to the point, the difficulties Italy was able to create encouraged Spain to suggest a revision of the whole statute. Primo de Rivera had never liked the international status of Tangier; he dreamed of incorporating the city into Spanish Morocco or turning it into a Spanish mandate. He opened negotiations with France for this purpose; by the summer of 1926 there were persistent rumors of a separate Franco-Spanish deal. Even if these were exaggerated, Spain's actions had given currency to the notion of revising the 1923 statute. Plainly another Tangier conference was in the offing. These events, in turn, gave Mussolini the opening to repeat his call for participation in all Tangier negotiations.[28] This time circumstances were propitious, and Fascist Italy was ultimately enabled to recover face.

At first, the French government, again overriding the opinion of its embassy in Rome, refused to entertain Italy's fresh demand. In Paris Berthelot once more was the official to give Romano Avezzana a negative response. Berthelot went further and insisted that Spain, too, was

[24] *DDI*, IV, p. 215, n. 1.   [25] *DDI*, IV, No. 385.
[26] *DDI*, IV, No. 402.
[27] G. Stuart, *The International City of Tangier*, 2d ed., rev. (Stanford, 1955), pp. 88-90.
[28] *Ibid.*, pp. 91-93; *DDI*, IV, Nos. 390, 396, 399, 403.

set on excluding Italy.[29] But this proved to be the first
chink in France's armor. For Paris had turned down the
Spanish bid to gain sovereignty over Tangier, and Primo
de Rivera did not want to do France any favors. On the
contrary, the Tangier dispute facilitated the conclusion on
August 7, 1926, of an Italo-Spanish treaty of friendship and
arbitration, which evoked discreet grumbles from Paris.
However, Mussolini was at pains not to exaggerate the
treaty's scope, and explicitly denied that it sanctioned a
Spanish mandate over Tangier.[30] Indeed, too much should
not be read into the Italo-Spanish pact.[31] Fascist Italy had
already learned how weak a prop Spain was to lean on in
any conflict with France. Nevertheless, the arbitration treaty
provided a backdrop for limited Italo-Spanish cooperation
in the Tangier question. As a result, Spain promised France
to help exclude Italy merely from the "preliminary" negotiations for another Tangier conference. As to "Italy's intervention in the definitive deliberations on Tangier,"
Madrid raised no objection.[32]

Of much greater consequence, however, was British help,
which was also made available to Italy in 1926. In view of
the Anglo-Italian entente it was the least that Chamberlain
could do to aid Mussolini in a question where his demand
was not for concrete gain but prestige alone. In addition,
London had become alarmed at the exclusive Franco-
Spanish talks, and Chamberlain resolved to bring Italy
into the game on Britain's side.[33] In June he encouraged
Italy to restate her conditions for acceding to the current
Tangier Statute. Rome drew up a nine-point memorandum

[29] *DDI*, IV, No. 421. See also De Dampierre, *Revue des Deux Mondes*,
Nov. 1, 1953, pp. 19-20.
[30] *DDI*, IV, No. 407; *OO*, XXII, 199.
[31] The rumors of secret military clauses (Salvemini, *Mussolini diplomatico*, pp. 155-56) have never been justified by concrete evidence.
[32] *DDI*, IV, No. 437; Stuart, *International City of Tangier*, pp. 93-96.
[33] B.D., C3729/3729/22 (Annual Report, 1926, pp. 12-13).

similar to that which Mussolini had asked to be appended to the statute two years earlier. None of the particular demands for participation in the Tangier administration was unacceptable, but the ninth point laid down "the right of Italy to be consulted on any future changes in the Tangier regime."[34] Nothing definite developed until Chamberlain met Mussolini off Leghorn at the end of September. There Chamberlain pledged himself to support a formula for Italian participation in the pending Tangier negotiations: "First preliminary conversations between France and Spain, and then at a later date discussions *a quattro*, that is to say, with the presence of Italy and England."[35] After this, however stubbornly France might resist, Italy was certain of a seat at the next conference table. To ensure the triumph, Rome hastened to adjust to the British position. Out of deference to Chamberlain, Italy treated with cold formality a Soviet Russian request to join in the new Tangier talks, held aloof from all proposals to reconvene a full Algeciras conference, and refrained from provocatively authorizing the opening of an Italian post office in Tangier.[36]

With Britain's assurance, Mussolini now had victory in his pocket, although it was not realized for some time. The "preliminary" negotiations between France and Spain dragged on, and Mussolini received some advice to revert to an independent policy. The Italian diplomatic agent in Tangier, Count Luigi Vannutelli Rey, expounded the argument that Italy's economic interests in Morocco were better served by playing a free-lance role than by limiting opportunities through adhesion to an international Tangier statute. Mussolini marked these reports "interesting" and "important."[37] But Mussolini always found it difficult to sub-

[34] Stuart, *International City of Tangier*, p. 97.
[35] *DDI*, IV, Nos. 444, 461.   [36] *DDI*, IV, Nos. 458, 488.
[37] *DDI*, IV, No. 550 and note.

ordinate prestige to anything. So Italy persevered in seeking admission to the conference room, and at last her patience was rewarded. On July 25, 1928 a revised Tangier statute was concluded and signed by France, Spain, Britain—and Fascist Italy.[38]

Once France began to move under combined Anglo-Spanish pressure toward accommodating Italy in Tangier, Briand again raised the matter of a French quid pro quo in Tunisia. In October 1926, as earlier, Briand and Romano Avezzana together tried to comprehend a new Tunisian statute within a broader settlement. This time France held out the offer of support for Italy in East Africa and Asia Minor; Mussolini's recent interest in the disintegration of both Ethiopia and Turkey had been duly noted in Paris.[39] The Franco-Italian bargain was to be sealed by promoting a personal relationship between Briand and Mussolini which might be founded in a meeting of the two, either tête-à-tête or in company with Chamberlain and Stresemann.[40] This formula of colonial entente and personal tie was exactly that being employed contemporaneously by Chamberlain and Mussolini to promote an Anglo-Italian entente. Unfortunately Mussolini had no desire to establish a personal rapport with Briand whom he despised, along with Stresemann, as a utopian and pusillanimous internationalist. Furthermore, the Duce was being pilloried in the French press for his intrigues within France against the anti-Fascist expatriates. The consequent and mounting Franco-Italian press war left him in a savage mood. So he rebuffed the overture brusquely: "A Mussolini-Briand meeting *a due* seems completely useless in the state of things and certainly it is not necessary to meet to stabilize for five

38 Stuart, *International City of Tangier*, pp. 99-102.

39 Romano Avezzana had pointedly inquired of Berthelot what would be France's attitude in the event of an Italo-Turkish war (B.D., C3729/3729/22 [Annual Report, 1926, p. 22]; *DBFP*, II, No. 448).

40 *DDI*, IV, Nos. 434, 471, 503-504; De Dampierre, *Revue des Deux Mondes*, Nov. 1, 1953, p. 19.

years the Tunisian conventions [of 1896]. . . . I do not intend that Fascist Italy should be presented as a kind of
supplicant for meetings *a due* or *a quattro* as though in
need of political or moral rehabilitation."[41] Romano Avezzana remonstrated gently that Briand's proposal might bear
more consideration, and suggested that Italy adopt an attitude of "reserved expectation." Whereupon Mussolini replied sharply: "I am convinced that expectation will have
to be still more reserved."[42] In public, he simply restated
his insistence on the priority of a Tunisian convention
guaranteeing Italian rights for three or five years.[43] With
this rebuff, negotiations, for both a Tunisian settlement
and an all-encompassing colonial entente lapsed again.[43a]

Italian rights in Tunisia constituted a long-standing and
persistent Franco-Italian difficulty. (The problem was not
resolved until the notorious Laval-Mussolini agreement
of January 1935, based on what had been prospected a
decade earlier: the application of delayed French nationality to the Tunisian Italians in a context of a comprehensive
European and African agreement.) But if Tunisia was the
most substantive subject of discord between Rome and
Paris in the mid-1920s, it did not rank as the most serious
and highly charged, at least in Mussolini's eyes. This distinction was reserved for the dispute over the exiles from
Italy who settled in France.

The fuorusciti

The problem of the *fuorusciti* escalated to a point of high
tension as a result of the Matteotti affair and the proclamation of the Fascist dictatorship. This produced a sudden increase in emigration across the Alps. Hitherto, most

[41] *DDI*, IV, No. 505.
[42] *DDI*, IV, Nos. 513, 516.
[43] *Corriere della Sera*, Oct. 30, 1926.
[43a] In February 1927 Paris was still pressing for a Franco-Italian
accord and a Briand-Mussolini meeting, but still to no avail (*DDI*, V,
No. 3).

of those who had left Mussolini's Italy had done so for economic reasons (French agriculture always welcomed Italy's surplus population). Among those with political motives, the anarchists had predominated. Little leadership had come from the few known names in this first wave of émigrés; ex-premier Nitti and ex-foreign minister Sforza had held aloof from the other *fuorusciti* in Paris, while Don Luigi Sturzo, former leader of the Popular party, had settled in the secondary *fuorusciti* center of London. But the new exiles were of an entirely different caliber. They included the cream of the Italian intelligentsia and left-of-center political life. Giovanni Amendola, Giuseppe Donati, Piero Gobetti, Gaetano Salvemini, later the brothers Carlo and Nello Rosselli—these were only a sample of the quality of Italians who after 1925 fled to France to exercise their right of free speech. Such men set about at once to coordinate the voice and activities of the Parisian *fuorusciti*. In particular, they possessed the talent to improve on the rather unsophisticated anti-Fascist journalistic ventures of the pre-1925 period. At one time or another in the next decade, *Corriere degli Italiani*, *La Libertà*, and *Giustizia e Libertà*! achieved large circulations and modest influence within and without France.[44] Mussolini, resuming an assertive brand of diplomacy in 1925, was in a mood to respond to the new thrust and bite of his adversaries.

In so volatile a question as the *fuorusciti* the influence of an individual on Mussolini could be vital. It seems not without significance that at the crucial moment a change occurred within the French embassy in Rome. This was the resignation in September 1924 of Camille Barrère. Barrère had always been on friendly terms with Mussolini since 1914 when his embassy was probably one of the sources of French money for Mussolini's interventionist campaign.[45]

[44] Delzell, *Mussolini's Enemies*, Chap. 1, *passim*; A. Garosci, *Storia dei fuorusciti* (Bari, 1953), Chaps. 1, 2, *passim*.
[45] Serra, *Barrère*, p. 333.

He was known to be sympathetic to the Fascist experiment, and since Mussolini's accession to power he had consistently shown a more conciliatory attitude to Italian pretensions —in Tunisia and Tangier, for example—than the Quai d'Orsay. Mussolini was understandably displeased with the replacement of the congenial Barrère by René Besnard with his freemasonic background.[46] Actually Mussolini read into the move more of an affront than Paris intended.[47] At all events, the chances that Besnard might restrain him from making an issue of the post-Matteotti *fuorusciti* were slim.

After 1924 Mussolini stepped up his objections to the *fuorusciti*, and based them on two specific counts. From the diplomatic point of view, he argued that, in league with the left-wing Parisian press, they set the tone for much of French opinion, thereby creating an atmosphere totally alien to a Franco-Italian rapprochement.[48] On the other hand, a more sincere complaint, one may suspect, was that the *fuorusciti* stirred up trouble for Mussolini in Italy. His extinction of practically all but clandestine domestic opposition in 1925 and 1926 made the efforts of the *fuorusciti* to reach an Italian audience all the more intolerable. Of course egotism forbade too frank an admission that they might shake the Fascist regime, but much could be made of *fuorusciti* plans to invade Italy from French soil and of their involvement in assassination attempts on Mussolini.[49] As *fuorusciti* activity increased with the accumulation of exiles, Fascist Italy's demands for French police action

[46] *DDI*, III, No. 550.

[47] See an anonymous report for Mussolini from a source within the French embassy in Rome (*DDI*, III, No. 95). The Duce marked the observation that Barrère's resignation was due to his need for rest with three exclamation points. Cf. Charles-Roux, *Une grande ambassade*, pp. 277-79.

[48] See, for instance, *DDI*, IV, Nos. 290, 429.

[49] *DDI*, III, Nos. 675, 745; IV, No. 415; Suarez, *Briand*, VI, 241-42; G. Wagnière, *Dix-huit ans à Rome* (Geneva, 1944), Chap. 25.

against them grew more pressing. By 1926 Mussolini linked the *fuorusciti* question with that of Tunisia; there was no solution of one without the other, he implied.[50] Thus the *fuorusciti* were "recognized"; they represented as important a diplomatic problem as the most traditional colonial dispute to divide France and Italy.

Over the years and regardless of cabinet changes in Paris, the French response to Mussolini's protests was consistent. Romano Avezzana, whenever he presented the Fascist case, always received from French officials a courteous hearing and vague promises to see what could be done. But when pressed, they could and did fall back on the pointed argument that in democratic France the citizenry in general and the press in particular could not be controlled as they were in Mussolini's Italy. It was Poincaré's favorite line that the question was one of French party politics because "the great majority of Radical-Republicans were in principle averse to the Fascist regime," and no French government dared seem to be negotiating on a domestic issue under duress by Mussolini.[51] This is not to say the French authorities were altogether idle. Occasionally they would openly impede the *fuorusciti*; a big meeting to be addressed by Nitti and Sturzo, among others, was canceled, and when the *Corriere degli Italiani* advocated Mussolini's assassination, the police stepped in and suspended the paper.[52] But for the most part, insofar as an attempt was made to restrain the *fuorusciti*, it was preferred French policy to work behind the scenes. This unobtrusive action lacked spectacular result, but Romano Avezzana appreciated it and now and again tried timidly and obliquely to bring it to Mussolini's attention.[53] But success by stealth was not the manner of Fascist Italy. Prestige was as precious as sub-

---

[50] *DDI*, IV, Nos. 285, 290.
[51] *DDI*, III, No. 507; IV, Nos. 420, 434.
[52] *DDI*, III, No. 786; Delzell, *Mussolini's Enemies*, p. 50.
[53] *DDI*, III, No. 608; IV, No. 209.

stance, and the Duce's demands not only had to be met but had to be seen to be met. This was the one thing no French government could provide and stay in office.

Failing to obtain satisfaction from Paris, Mussolini was thrown back on his own devices for an answer to the *fuorusciti*. He adopted two lines of counterattack. One was to use his control of the Italian press and his own talent for polemical journalism to reply in kind to the anti-Fascist propaganda emanating from Paris. This began as a rejoinder to the *fuorusciti* and the French left-wing papers, but quickly moved on to criticism of the tolerant French democratic system and French policy in general. With the escalation of verbal sniping into a full-scale press war, as fast as Mussolini complained to Paris of the *fuorusciti*, the French would fire back protests about the Francophobe tone of the Italian press.[54] But the other method followed by Mussolini against the *fuorusciti* was even more explosive. He had always been prepared to meet the *fuorusciti* on their own ground by sending his own agents across the Alps. Now he resolved to increase the activity of such agents drastically. Their task was twofold: first, to promote pro-Fascist propaganda and to rally sympathetic Frenchmen to Mussolini's cause; second, to infiltrate and report on the *fuorusciti* groups. Action in either capacity smacked of espionage, and certainly by all international precedents constituted unlawful interference in French internal affairs. Naturally there was a major risk of an incident plunging Paris and Rome to fresh depths of mutual recrimination. The Bonservizi murder in 1924 had hinted at what might lie in store.

Not much progress was made on the job of proselytism, at least not in the twenties. A pro-Fascist newspaper in French was started, and some royalists were attracted.[55] In 1925 Georges Valois founded his *Faisceau* movement in direct

---

[54] *DDI*, IV, Nos. 284, 419, 420, 543, 552.
[55] It.D. (Mussolini's private secretariat), 287/1193/087700-706. See also *DDI*, III, No. 713.

imitation of Mussolini's experiment. But none of this promised much. The situation was summed up by the philo-Fascist counsellor at the French embassy in Switzerland when he adjudged Fascism in France to lack program, leadership, and prospects.[56] On the other hand, the Fascist government in Rome was considerably more successful in placing spies within the *fuorusciti* network, and in this fashion did hamper its enemies abroad.[57] So there arose a sort of Italian civil war between Fascist and anti-Fascist fought out on the soil of France; it was this aspect of Mussolini's measures that provoked international repercussions.

The affair which disclosed the nature and extent of Mussolini's intrigues within France concerned the Garibaldi brothers, Ricciotti and Peppino. Grandsons of the legendary Garibaldi, they were accordingly well-known among Italian republicans and freemasons. Perhaps because of their famous surname, they achieved a prominent position among the Parisian *fuorusciti*. Ricciotti was the more activist politico and a leading conspirator in plans for a *fuorusciti* invasion of Italy. However, as early as 1923 Ricciotti was in touch with both Bonservizi and Ambassador Romano Avezzana, and he entered the pay of Fascist Italy. Others, probably including Peppino, were similarly bought.[58] After Bonservizi's death and with Mussolini's growing lack of confidence in Romano Avezzana, the paymaster of these double agents became an Italian "inspector of public security" named LaPolla. In the fall of 1926 Ricciotti Garibaldi was instructed by his Italian paymasters to concoct a fake plot to invade Italy, and to implicate the *fuorusciti* and the French government in it. Then on Octo-

[56] *DDI*, IV, No. 196.

[57] Delzell, *Mussolini's Enemies*, pp. 43-44; Garosci, *Storia dei fuorusciti*, pp. 294-95. For a firsthand account of this activity, see A. Dumini, *Diciasette colpi* (Milan, 1951), Chap. 1, *passim*.

[58] It.D. (Mussolini's private secretariat), 287/1193/087707-708, 087710-11; *DDI*, II, Nos. 163, 170.

ber 24 the French police arrested LaPolla. On November 4 Garibaldi was apprehended in Nice where he was gathering recruits for his army. Volunteers were told they were bound for either Italy or Spanish Catalonia. LaPolla's correspondence with Garibaldi came to light, and Garibaldi admitted to the police his role as Mussolini's *agent provocateur.* The French papers blazoned the story. In fact, they were encouraged to do so by the Quai d'Orsay which, "in a fit of excitement" as Romano Avezzana termed it, resolved once and for all to put Mussolini publicly in the wrong. It has already been indicated how this helped to torpedo Briand's recent overture for a Franco-Italian colonial entente, which may have been in the mind of the anti-Italian members of the French foreign ministry from the first. At any rate, the French press, given its head, had a field day featuring Mussolini's use of *agents provocateurs* and subversion generally. The Duce's disclaimers, apart from being completely untrue, were feeble by comparison.[59]

The Garibaldi affair came as the climax to a period of mounting Franco-Italian tension. It followed hard on Gino Lucetti's attempt on Mussolini's life, which Mussolini had blamed on the *fuorusciti* and lax French security. Consequently Mussolini had stepped up Italian press attacks on France, and some Fascist hotheads had taken this as a cue to attack various French consulates. Now Garibaldi's revelations and France's understandable exploitation of them added fuel to the blaze. René Besnard, the French ambassador in Rome, feared the Duce might no longer be able to control his party extremists whom he had unleashed. Although Besnard was neither Italophobe nor jingoist, he advised Briand "to take military and naval precautions."[60] Indeed, in the coming weeks an unusual concentration of

[59] *DDI,* IV, Nos. 479-81; *Corriere della Sera,* Nov. 7, 1926. On the Garibaldi plot itself, see Delzell, *Mussolini's Enemies,* pp. 51-52, and Garosci, *Storia dei fuorusciti,* pp. 21-24, 271-73.

[60] Suarez, *Briand,* VI, 243-44.

French troops and warships was observed around Nice, close to Italy's frontier. These moves were made to the accompaniment of a fresh wave of French criticism directed this time on Yugoslavia's behalf at the first Pact of Tirana signed on November 27. Mussolini growled in a circular drafted to Italian diplomats in his own hand: "France . . . remains the most militarist nation in Europe and the world."[61] For a few days the situation appeared ominous; even Mussolini was chastened by the lengths to which the Franco-Italian war of insults was stretching. Briefly reversing his usual conduct, he took steps to prevent further incidents, affording French consulates police protection and declining to let the Italian press respond to the latest insults of the Paris papers.[62] In the event, what Romano Avezzana called "the acute phase" of the Franco-Italian crisis was over by Christmas 1926.[63] But the problem of the *fuorusciti* and Mussolini's long-term methods of countering them did not change. The issue remained barely below the surface, likely to erupt in new, ugly incidents. Above all, it continued to be a staple of press editorials and emotional public opinion, poisoning the atmosphere for a resolution of more substantive Franco-Italian differences.

The rub was that the *fuorusciti* question itself was not at all substantive. The *fuorusciti* did not threaten Fascism. They had relatively little influence within Italy. Abroad, although they kept world opinion aware that opposition to Mussolini still existed, no government seemed likely to adopt an attitude of diplomatic hostility to Fascist Italy under *fuorusciti* pressure alone. Mussolini himself implicitly conceded the lack of substance in the quarrel. "It was at the least stupid," he once remarked to Besnard, "to compromise the relations and perhaps the fate of 80 million

61 *DDI*, iv, No. 535.
62 *DDI*, iv, Nos. 477, 595; *Corriere della Sera*, Nov. 16, 1926.
63 *DDI*, iv, Nos. 556, 558.

men for the license allowed a dozen extortionists."[64] And in December 1927 when for a short time Mussolini was considering a Franco-Italian agreement, it was found possible to reach a compromise on the *fuorusciti*, at least on paper.[65] In other words, the *fuorusciti* problem was an artificial one; it could be brushed under the rug or exaggerated, according to taste. Mussolini deliberately chose the latter alternative.

There is no simple explanation of Mussolini's choice. Undoubtedly his own personality accounted for much. Before coming to office, he had shown in the nether reaches of Italian politics a talent and relish for intrigue. After attaining power, he displayed the same taste for undercover maneuver in his relations with the German nationalists and Ahmed Zogu. So we may assume that he derived an actual thrill from the subversion and intrigue in which his challenge to the *fuorusciti* involved him. In addition, both Mussolini's character and the movement he embodied displayed a dogmatism that would brook no contradiction. Insofar as Fascism was considered a doctrine for universal application—and there is evidence that Mussolini did entertain such ambitions—anti-Fascist propaganda, even outside Italy, could not be ignored, but had to be fought by all and every means at whatever the risk.

But when all is said and done, it is hard to escape the conclusion that Mussolini magnified the *fuorusciti* question in order to pick a quarrel with France. As though, having once decided that a future Social Darwinian conflict lay between France and a nationalist Italy, it was necessary to make this plain by emphasizing as many points of difference as possible. It was in this vein that he summarily dismissed even the contingency that France might sincerely desire improved relations with Italy. "Mere rhetoric," he

[64] *DDI*, IV, No. 290.
[65] Suarez, *Briand*, VI, 242.

inscribed one telegram in which Romano Avezzana argued that Paris genuinely desired an accommodation with Italy. Less than a year after Briand had offered Italy a Brenner guarantee, Mussolini could write: "The truth is that France has not yet made a single gesture—I repeat a single gesture—of concrete friendship toward Italy."[66] Franco-Italian discord was a basic assumption of Mussolini's diplomatic vision. The *fuorusciti*, Tunisia, and Tangier were, then, not so much causes as symptoms of a predetermined rivalry.

The French persistently underestimated the depth of Mussolini's Francophobia. Paris held firm to the conviction that sooner or later Italy would have to turn to France for protection against pan-Germanism. The logic of this view was buttressed by the record of Italian diplomacy since 1900 and, above all, by Italy's intervention on the Entente side in World War I. Unfortunately for these calculations, Mussolini was no traditionalist. Rather than join France against Germany, he was ready to turn German nationalism against the Rhine in order to allow Italy to usurp France's position in the western Mediterranean and the Balkans. Mussolini thus felt no compulsion to resolve outstanding differences with France, while French policy was based on the misconception that he did.

Romano Avezzana shared the illusion that the German danger must reconcile Paris and Rome; no doubt the belief encouraged him to remain at the Paris embassy as long as he did. His tenure began propitiously enough for a Franco-Italian rapprochement. The year 1923 saw Franco-Italian cooperation at the outset of the Ruhr crisis and in the Corfu affair. But these were plainly ad hoc understandings, and Romano Avezzana did not feel really optimistic until 1925 when Briand tried to build on the supposed joint fear of Germany. As far as we can tell, Romano Avez-

[66] *DDI*, IV, Nos. 65, 285.

zana was not aware of Mussolini's association with the German nationalists and inclination to use them. Consequently Mussolini's refusal to respond to Briand's overtures left him rather bewildered. But he continued, somewhat pathetically in the circumstances, to lecture Mussolini on the merits of a Franco-Italian accord. As best he could, he tried to take the sting out of the *fuorusciti* issue by minimizing in his reports the influence wielded by the exiles. At the same time he showed himself painfully aware of the dangers inherent in the press war that raged around the *fuorusciti*, and more than once urged Mussolini to call a truce.[67] But by and large, his advice was ignored and Mussolini showed progressively less interest in his opinion. By the end of 1926 his ineffectiveness and general uneasiness recalled that of De Bosdari in Berlin a year earlier on the eve of his resignation. Appropriately, after staying at his post long enough to ride out the storm over the Garibaldi affair, Romano Avezzana resigned in February 1927, a dispirited man. The Italian journalist Giuseppe Borgese describes how "he retired with a young wife somewhere in the Campanian countryside, there to vanish."[68]

During his term at the Paris embassy Romano Avezzana proved an ardent Francophile; it is doubtful that his sentiments were shared to the full by his professional colleagues in the Palazzo Chigi.[69] For instance, the schemes for a broad Franco-Italian colonial agreement espoused by Romano Avezzana seem to have aroused a mixed reaction in the foreign ministry. On the other hand, there can be no

[67] *DDI*, IV, Nos. 297, 361, 474, 478, 684.

[68] G. A. Borgese, *Goliath: March of Fascism* (New York, 1937), p. 257.

[69] For example, Contarini complained to Ambassador Graham of "the French policy of pin-pricks directed against Italy, a State which France apparently regarded as being a secondary power" (B.D., C3729/3729/22 [Annual Report, 1926, p. 11]). Contarini also expressed his irritation with France to the Belgian ambassador in Rome (*DDB*, II, No. 54).

doubt that Romano Avezzana's discontent with the general drift of Mussolini's French policy, especially as it took shape in 1926, was seconded by the rest of the old-guard diplomats. One and all, they could approve Mussolini's obduracy in the Tangier and Tunisian questions because they had helped Fascism into office to avenge the disparagement that Italy had suffered at Allied hands in the postwar years. But the emphasis the Duce put on the *fuorusciti* appalled the Palazzo Chigi along with Romano Avezzana. The issue concerned no national interest that the professionals were aware of. They could not conceive that national prestige demanded the virulence of the Fascist press campaign against France, which reached its zenith after Contarini's resignation as secretary general in the spring of 1926. Above all, they never remotely considered that avenging past slights should extend to a breakdown of the Franco-Italian wartime alliance. On this point a vast gulf was fixed between Mussolini and the professionals of the Palazzo Chigi.[70]

[70] For Palazzo Chigi opinion on the *fuorusciti* and general Franco-Italian relations, see Guariglia, *Ricordi*, pp. 61-62, 65-74, 110-11, 120-22.

19. Ideology and Foreign Policy

Fascism for Export

LIKE MOST modern dictators, Mussolini claimed, truthfully or not, to base his rule on mass support. By analogy, to spread Fascism abroad presupposed a measure of public support, or at least tolerance, beyond Italy's frontiers. In Mussolini's eyes the foreign reputation of Fascist Italy was closely linked to the propagation of Fascist ideas, which his approach to the *fuorusciti* well demonstrated.

Mussolini's concern for opinion outside Italy was sharpened by the Matteotti affair. Even after the crisis was over and the need to solicit support was no longer urgent, he kept up a lively interest in any incident which reflected on foreign estimates of his regime.[1] Italy's diplomats abroad soon learned to keep him supplied with appropriate information, and in return were more than likely to receive a directive personally drafted by Mussolini. Often he liked to pretend that his concern stemmed from the effect of adverse publicity on the international value of the lira.[2] Of course, his real interest lay less in the narrow world of the bourses, whose denizens were safe conservatives well-disposed to Fascism anyway, than in a broader world opinion susceptible to the arguments of the *fuorusciti* whose numbers and activities had been increased markedly by the Matteotti affair. The public appearances of distinguished Italian exiles were carefully observed and obstructed if a foreign government would cooperate. Sturzo, Salvemini, and above all, Nitti were singled out for special scrutiny.[3]

[1] This concern he expressed quite openly in the Chamber of Deputies on March 27, 1925 (*OO*, XXI, 268).

[2] *DDI*, III, Nos. 664, 667, 673, 749; IV, Nos. 33, 358.

[3] *DDI*, III, Nos. 677, 717, 782; IV, Nos. 55, 103, 144, 306, 489, 559. See also Nitti's letters to King Victor Emmanuel protesting this persecution (Nitti, *Rivelazioni*, pp. 581-600).

Two attempts on Mussolini's life in November 1925 and April 1926 brought a fresh spate of instructions to the diplomats to remove any impression of turmoil within Italy and to reemphasize the unanimity of Italians behind Mussolini.[4] With the growth of the cult of the leader in Italy, the status of Fascism came to depend increasingly on that of the Duce himself. So all slurs on Mussolini's reputation had to be vigorously rebuffed. News that his enemies were searching in Switzerland for evidence of Mussolini's discreditable youth there was enough to cause alarm in Rome.[5] Any hint that he was in poor health met with instant contradiction; physical and political virility were presumably weighed in the same scale.[6] The extremes to which this sensitivity could reach were demonstrated after Locarno, when it was learned that Chamberlain, Briand, and Stresemann collectively were to be awarded the Nobel peace prize. For a time the Fascist government considered demanding equal recognition as a peacemaker for Mussolini, who just before Locarno had boasted: "I consider the Italian nation to be in a permanent state of war."[7] But perhaps the most gauche response to criticism, if only because it was a public gesture, concerned some mild censure of the Fascist dictatorship that appeared in the London *Times*. Despite the paper's normal sympathy for Fascist Italy and despite Ambassador Della Torretta's warning, Mussolini sent a personal rebuttal which duly appeared in the letters-to-the-editor column.[8]

All this frenetic activity in the field of public relations suggested that Mussolini might be edging toward a new and vigorous drive to sow Fascist ideology abroad. Significantly the ideologically embarrassing détente with the Soviet

---

[4] *DDI*, IV, Nos. 167, 178, 201, 490.
[5] *DDI*, III, Nos. 611, 669.
[6] *DDI*, IV, No. 69.
[7] *DDI*, IV, No. 532; *OO*, XXII, 37.
[8] *DDI*, III, No. 857; IV, No. 46; *Times* (London), June 23 and 26, 1925.

Union was now at an end, while at home the attempt was under way to enunciate and practice a coherent Fascist philosophy in the guise of the corporative state. In 1922 Mussolini had explained to Roberto Cantalupo his intention to disseminate his own political and social ideas, via Italian emigrants, in successive stages. Refutation of adverse publicity by letters to the editor and the like was at most a negative labor to keep the terrain clear until the seeds of universal Fascism could be planted. It was time to begin this latter, more positive, task.

The year 1926 saw the *Segreteria dei fasci all'estero* start to assume greater prominence. In September its secretary general, Bastianini, proposed that his office take a more active role in forestalling plots hatched abroad. In particular, he wanted to assure Mussolini's personal safety by creation of a praetorian guard, part of which would serve on Italy's frontiers. Acting on information from Italian consuls abroad, it would prevent the infiltration of subversives into Italy. To supplement this precaution, 150 of Bastianini's agents would be attached to Italian embassies and legations to scent out *fuorusciti* intrigues. In more general terms, Mussolini was urged "to bring into being agreement among the Fascist movements (*fascismi*) of the various nations."[9] It is impossible to say how far Bastianini's specific recommendations were implemented, but certainly they were reflective of the temper of Fascist officialdom in Rome.

Within a short while the *Segreteria dei fasci all'estero* itself underwent reform and streamlining. It received a new statute which increased Rome's central control of all Fascist groups outside Italy, and acquired a new secretary general. Although Bastianini's enthusiastic optimism about the spread of Fascism abroad never flagged, he was apparently not the most efficient administrator. His successor, Piero Parini, was expected to invigorate and escalate

9 *DDI*, IV, No. 426.

the office's activity.[10] In the meantime, Mussolini in his
public statements began to suggest tentatively that Fascism
might be adaptable to the needs of other nations: "The
method will be different in different countries, but the
spirit will be the same." And he did not dispute the contention of others that Fascism, "anti-democratic, anti-liberal,
anti-socialist, and anti-Masonic," was engaged in a "war of
doctrine."[11]

It has already been observed that, because so many Italo-
Americans were well disposed toward Mussolini, the United
States in the 1920s provided a laboratory in which to test
the propagation of Fascism. Moreover, by the middle of
the decade two inhibiting factors were removed. In 1925
the thorny problem of Italy's war debt to the United
States was settled. And if Italo-American differences on immigration were not resolved, Washington's firmness had
made the issue so dead that Mussolini, to save face, took
the position that now Italy neither needed nor desired a
population outlet in the United States.[12] In other words,
Italy no longer expected to suffer in the war-debt and immigration questions by repercussions from a stepped-up
promotion of Italo-American Fascism. So in 1927 Count
Ignazio Thaon di Revel crossed the Atlantic to build the
fasci into a national organization to be called the Fascist
League of North America. On arrival in New York he
made no secret of his purpose, nor of the fact that he was
an authorized emissary of the Italian government.[13]

Thaon di Revel's activities, which ultimately turned the
whole matter of Italy's encroachment on the American
scene into a formal issue between the governments in Rome

---

10 For the new statute, see *OO*, XXIII, 89-91; for Bastianini's sunny
appraisal of the *fasci* abroad just before leaving his post, see It.D.
(Mussolini's private secretariat), 263/1122/074442-45. On Parini's reputation see Donosti, *Mussolini e l'Europa*, pp. 17-20, and *USFR, 1928*, III,
107-109.

11 *OO*, XXII, 286-88, 386.   12 *OO*, XXII, 150-51, 363-67.

13 *New York Telegram*, July 23, 1927.

and Washington,[14] lies beyond the scope of this work. Nonetheless, Mussolini's intentions in America manifested his inclination to inject ideology into foreign policy. Perhaps it would be wrong to characterize him as a total ideologue. He was too much of a nationalist for that. Indeed, there existed always in his policy a conflict between the pull of Italian self-interest and that of a supranational Fascist ideology. To Italy's ultimate sorrow, it was to be the latter which would prevail in the era of the Rome-Berlin Axis.

The Fascist Party and the Palazzo Chigi

Fascism never aroused the enthusiasm of the Italian masses, as Mussolini liked to pretend. But he held power as long as he kept the allegiance of the hard core of Italy's power structure. In foreign policy, above all, Mussolini enjoyed for the better part of two decades the unwavering support of the powerful institutions that framed public opinion. King Victor Emmanuel repaid Mussolini for his late conversion to monarchical principles by accommodating his visits, invitations, and general relations with foreign royalty to suit Fascism's diplomacy. At one time or another, the foreign ministries of Spain, Britain, Yugoslavia, and Greece were all wooed vicariously through the royal medium. Much the same was true of the Vatican. Mussolini renounced his youthful atheism, rebuked and tried to curb his more anticlerical followers, and as early as 1923 entered into those negotiations with Cardinal Pietro Gasparri, the Papal secretary of state, which were to result in the Lateran Accords six years later. In return, Fascist sympathizers among the clergy were given free rein to endorse Mussolini's program. Monsignor Alessandro Testi Rasponi undertook to stimulate the national consciousness of the Italian

[14] See my article, "Fascism for Export: Italy and the United States in the Twenties," *American Historical Review*, LXIX (April 1964), 710-12.

episcopate. Cardinal Vincenzo Vannutelli in an important speech in February 1923 did much to allay foreign doubts of the new Italian premier.[15] The Vatican evidenced some qualms at Fascist brutality during and after the Matteotti affair.[16] But the demise of Mussolini's entente with the Soviets and the prospect of a definitive church-state rapprochement in Italy, for which negotiations began in earnest in 1926 under the auspices of the Palazzo Chigi, were inducement enough for the Vatican to resume its cordiality to Fascism. Pope Pius XI twice sent warm congratulations to Mussolini on the latter's escape from an assassin's bullet. The Duce was thus reassured that his regime's status and endeavors abroad could still expect the beneficence of the vast network of international Catholicism.[17]

Parliament was another institution on which Mussolini found he could rely for consistent support of his foreign policy. Even while the Chamber of Deputies contained representatives of a variety of political parties, foreign policy received curt treatment. The *Atti parlamentari* divulge that, while Mussolini presented a series of summaries of world affairs, there was little debate on what he said of Italian diplomacy. The extreme left offered occasional criticism but understandably neglected foreign policy in the face of the ominous domestic situation. Those deputies who made interpellations of their own initiative did so to encourage Mussolini in the paths he had already chosen—the preservation of Italy's coal supply from the Ruhr, the protection of Italian citizens abused in the Austrian Tyrol, colonial expansion, and reorganization of the machinery of emigration.[18] Hence, it was more a

[15] *DDI*, I, Nos. 500, 535, 544.

[16] *DDI*, III, No. 706; IV, No. 86.

[17] On the Vatican's relations with the Fascist state in 1926 see especially *DDI*, IV, Nos. 293, 448, 473, 499, 564, 575.

[18] Italy, *Atti dello parlamento*, Leg. 26, Camera dei deputati, *Discussioni*, IX, 8394-8469, 8965-67; X, 9037-39, 9139-42; XI, 10091-92, 10510-12; XII, 11088-11114, 11124-33. See also L. Gasparotto, *Diario di un deputato* (Milan, 1945), pp. 188-89.

change in degree than in kind when in January 1925 the Aventine opposition to Mussolini was barred from the chamber. The Duce had little to fear on the score of foreign policy from any conceivable parliament.

The conscience of Italy, however, had for long resided, not in parliament, but in the press; Mussolini, as a journalist, knew it. As soon as he took office, the opposition press became the object of a campaign of covert violence, the results of which were not unnoticed by the foreign diplomats in Rome. One tells of being forced to buy the radical *Il Mondo* carefully concealed within a pro-government journal.[19] In mid-1923 a press censorship law was prepared, although it was not passed and applied until 1925 as a result of the Matteotti affair. Its effect was instantaneous, especially on a paper like Milan's renowned *Corriere della Sera* which was accustomed to treat foreign affairs in some depth. It was not so much that the *Corriere* began to print the party line, but that within a matter of weeks any real discussion of the momentous diplomatic issues of the day disappeared from its columns entirely. In January 1925 a rumor that Luigi Albertini, the editor-in-chief, was planning to publish the paper in Lugano, Switzerland, provoked one of Mussolini's personally drafted telegrams of inquiry.[20] Either the story was false or Albertini was dissuaded. With the establishment of his dictatorship, Mussolini proceeded to bring the entire Italian press into the Fascist fold. Owners were cowed into dismissing independent editors. In November 1925 the Albertini brothers were eased out of the editorial office of the *Corriere della Sera* and replaced by a Fascist. Censorship was less strictly applied to comment on foreign affairs than it was to the reporting of events within Italy, but this was a relative freedom at best.[20a] "Journalism should collaborate with the nation,"

[19] Wagnière, *Dix-huit ans à Rome*, Chap. 14: "La presse muselée."
[20] *DDI*, III, No. 650.
[20a] Carocci, *Politica estera dell'Italia fascista*, p. 29.

Mussolini once declared.[21] Given his premise that the Italian nation was identified with Fascism, Mussolini achieved full collaboration.

Because of the acquiescence, voluntary or otherwise, of monarchy, church, parliament, and press in Fascist policies, added emphasis was given to the Palazzo Chigi's role as watchdog on Mussolini. In this capacity the old-guard diplomats served on behalf of both the Italian establishment, which hoped simultaneously to use and tame Mussolini, and of the European chancelleries which had laid aside their first misgivings about international Fascism. Charged with carrying out Fascist foreign policy, it was presumed that they would be the first to perceive and the best placed to thwart any Mussolinian rashness.

The relationship between Mussolini and his diplomats could not help but be distant. The Duce was an upstart, while they belonged to an aristocracy which cooperated with Fascism only to save itself. Significantly, the tradition dating from Cavour's day of long, confidential letters exchanged between Italy's foreign minister and his chief ambassadors came to an abrupt halt at the end of 1922.[22] In more positive fashion, the mistrust between the new order and the old was expressed in the surveillance the Fascist party exercised over Italy's diplomatic representatives abroad. It has already been remarked how freely the party enthusiasts of the American *fasci* criticized the Italian consulates and embassy in the United States. Nor was this exceptional. Bonservizi, the first of Mussolini's agents in Paris, did not hesitate to indict members of both the Italian delegation to the Reparations Commission and the Italian embassy for their lack of Fascist zeal. Count Vannutelli Rey, the counsellor and sometimes chargé of the em-

[21] Gasparotto, *Diario*, p. 191.
[22] A. Rosso, "Quatro momenti della diplomazia italiana," *Rivista di Studi Politici Internazionali*, XXI (July 1954), 420.

bassy, was Bonservizi's special bête noire. But the ambassador himself was not immune; while praising his diplomatic skill, Bonservizi also managed to impugn his loyalty.[23] As early as June 1923, Bastianini, secretary general of the *fasci all'estero*, accused the entire diplomatic corps of anti-Fascism because they believed "the government of Mussolini will pass away soon."[24] The Fascist party agents kept up the attack, sometimes from unlikely places. One report held that the Italian diplomats in Egypt were addicted to freemasonic ideas, another that they were hostile to the *fasci* in Australia.[25] Not all such charges were taken at face value in Rome. Grandi, for one, seems to have been unimpressed.[26] But their impact was occasionally devastating, as the case of Mazzone, an Italian consul in Malta, demonstrated. Mazzone was instructed by Rome to encourage the Maltese to demand union with Italy, but he was rash enough to doubt Maltese affection for Fascist Italy and to warn of probable repercussions from the British authorities. When the Maltese failed to show much evidence of their *italianità* as the consul had forecast, he was accused by Fascist party officials of deliberate dereliction of duty and forced to resign. A colleague who testified to Mazzone's ability and probity axiomatically found his own loyalty called into question.[27]

These were minor figures, however, and, in contrast, suspicion of lukewarmness in the upper echelons of Italy's

[23] It.D. (Mussolini's private secretariat), 287/1193/087690-91, 087702, 087707.

[24] It.D. (Mussolini's private secretariat), 286/1200/087173-74. See also It.D. (Mussolini's private secretariat), 286/1200/087160-69; It.D. (Ministry of Popular Culture), 31/429/014649. Bastianini's strictures were later extended to the personnel of the colonial ministry (It.D. [Mussolini's private secretariat], 286/1200/087178-216).

[25] *DDI*, IV, Nos. 281, 329.

[26] *DDI*, III, No. 797; IV, p. 301, n. 1. See also Bastianini's complaint that business was transferred from his secretariat to other ministries (It.D. [Mussolini's private secretariat], 286/1200/087217).

[27] It.D. (Ministry of Popular Culture), 26/425/012582-601, *passim*; *DDI*, IV, No. 22.

diplomatic service did not bring on more than a verbal squib or a disquieting rumor. In the midst of the Matteotti crisis, Romano Avezzana found himself accused in one of Mussolini's own messages of making "highly inopportune and even tendentious statements about my government and about me personally." The ambassador denied this and offered his resignation; but Mussolini declined to accept it and the incident came to nothing.[28] Della Torretta was not accused directly, but in March 1926 he felt disturbed enough to call to Mussolini's attention a dispatch in a London paper that his ambassadorial position was in jeopardy "because I am not a Fascist."[29] Again, the episode reflected the perpetual tension between the party and the professional diplomats, and may have had something to do with Della Torretta's resignation in February 1927. But Mussolini himself showed no disposition to make an open issue of the lack of Fascist zeal displayed by his senior diplomats.

In like manner, he was cautious in tackling the institution of the foreign ministry itself. A reform, promulgated in January 1924, aimed at increasing the element of competition for entrance into the foreign service and providing quicker promotions on merit; and Mussolini's reformist spirit was welcomed by some of the younger members of the Palazzo Chigi as "a breath of fresh air." But his measures were far from radical and did little to facilitate infiltration by party representatives.[30] Nor did the introduction of Dino Grandi as undersecretary in 1925 contribute much to the overt *fascistizzazione* of the foreign ministry, whatever Mussolini might have intended by the appointment.[31] The *Documenti diplomatici italiani* do not

[28] *DDI*, iii, Nos. 349, 354, 358, 361.

[29] *DDI*, iv, No. 287.

[30] *OO*, xx, 158; Donosti, *Mussolini e l'Europa*, pp. 14-15; the quotation is from Varé, *Laughing Diplomat*, p. 237.

[31] Beginning in 1927 some Fascists were appointed to diplomatic posts, although only to positions of lower rank (Carocci, *Politica estera dell'Italia fascista*, p. 25).

indicate that he tried to promote a peculiarly Fascist foreign policy. In his first diplomatic endeavors we have observed him assisting Mussolini's revisionist policy in the Balkans and Adriatic quarrel with Yugoslavia. But shortly, Grandi was to be found not infrequently siding with the professionals against Mussolini and the party. For instance, it has been mentioned that he had little use for the *fasci all'estero* and their ideological crusade. But what gratified the Palazzo Chigi traditionalists more than anything was his total acceptance of the need to maintain the entente with Britain.[32] Contarini's judgment of Grandi as "malleable" was amply borne out.

As remarkable as Grandi's adoption of Palazzo Chigi manners and principles, however, was the fact that Mussolini tolerated it. (In 1929, when the Duce relinquished the foreign minister's post, he made Grandi his successor.) It was typical of his reluctance in the mid-twenties to insist on the *stile fascista* in his own foreign ministry, in sharp contrast to his eagerness to propagate Fascist ideas in the world at large. Yet it is not hard to explain. The Italian diplomatic corps belonged almost to a man to that conservative establishment whose support Fascism needed to stay in power. Moreover, the continued presence of well-known career diplomats in the Palazzo Chigi helped to allay disquiet in foreign capitals. There was no reason for Mussolini to alienate these influential and useful officials by a clearcut campaign to make the foreign ministry unimpeachably Fascist. It was much safer and simpler to ignore them when it suited Mussolini's purpose. Hence the Palazzo Chigi's orthodox opinion on the general direction that Italian policy should take, particularly with regard to the Balkans and to France, was cavalierly disregarded. When Mussolini entertained designs which might offend the professionals' moral scruples or diplomatic convictions, he had

---

[32] Guariglia, *Ricordi*, pp. 48-50.

recourse to his own private and sometimes secret agents: Bonservizi and LaPolla in France, Capello in Germany, Lessona in Albania, Thaon di Revel in the United States, and so on. Those of the old guard who resigned in 1926 and 1927—De Bosdari, Contarini, Romano Avezzana, Della Torretta—were not victims of a campaign to clear the Palazzo Chigi of non-Fascists. They all left of their own accord, finding for one reason or another Mussolini's indifference to their views to be insupportable.

Contarini's departure was the crucial one because it left the Palazzo Chigi officials leaderless. Chiaramonte Bordonaro, who took Contarini's place as secretary general, was transferred to the London embassy the following February, after which the secretary generalship remained vacant.[33] Indeed, 1927 saw quite a changing of the guard. Not only did Romano Avezzana and Della Torretta resign from their positions in Paris and London, respectively, but also Barone Russo, Mussolini's traditionalist *chef de cabinet*, was dispatched in March to Geneva to join the Italian delegation to the League of Nations.[34] This meant that most of the senior diplomats who in 1922 had undertaken to control Mussolini were no longer numbered among his immediate advisers. It was testimony to the extent that Mussolini, even without the direct *fascistizzazione* of the foreign ministry, was now free of Palazzo Chigi guidance.

The resignations of Contarini and other prominent diplomats did not mean that Mussolini had lost the confidence of the entire foreign ministry. The Palazzo Chigi had offered itself to Mussolini because it wanted a nationalist foreign minister, and he did not disappoint them. While some senior officials began to have doubts about where Mussolini was leading after 1925, there remained a strong nationalist sentiment which approved of a great part

[33] Ferraris, *L'amministrazione del Ministero degli esteri*, pp. 66-67.
[34] *DDI*, IV, p. vii; Guariglia, *Ricordi*, p. 50.

of Mussolini's program for national aggrandizement. Montagna, who represented Italy at the Lausanne Conference, in Athens, and in Constantinople, was a highly placed spokesman for the ultranationalists from the start. Later, the Italian ministers to Albania, Durazzo and Aloisi, and also Lojacono, head of the Albanian office in the Palazzo Chigi, seemed to fall into this category. Such diplomats backed Mussolini's struggle to restore Italian prestige, even if it involved occasional vulgar and ridiculous boasting; they admired his expansionist Adriatic policy in Fiume and Albania, despite the belligerent hostility to Yugoslavia it entailed; and they favored his drive for Near Eastern and East African empire, especially if it could be conducted in unison with Britain. Whatever the apologists may suggest in their memoirs, the nationalist temper of Mussolini's diplomacy gratified many of the career diplomats and more than made up for Mussolini's neglect of the Palazzo Chigi leaders. And nationalist spirit would keep the bulk of Italy's foreign service loyal to the Fascist regime until the dangers inherent in its foreign policy became too obvious to ignore. However, it took most of 20 years to disabuse the Palazzo Chigi. On the whole, the Italian diplomats, despite their privileged observation post, proved not much more perspicacious than the rest of the Italian power structure.

20. The Napoleonic Year, and Stocktaking

In his ANNUAL report at the end of 1925 Sir Ronald Graham, the British ambassador in Rome, wrote: "The Fascist party is now so strong at home that, in the search for fresh fields to conquer, it is tempted to turn its attention to the domain of foreign policy."[1] In the new year 1926 Mussolini announced in the P.N.F. journal, *Gerarchia*, that the Fascist revolution was embarking on its "Napoleonic year."[2] By this he referred primarily to the consolidation of the Fascist dictatorship within Italy. But domestic and foreign politics were conjoined in Mussolini's mind, and the phrase is certainly applicable to the year in which he imposed his own unmistakable stamp on Italian diplomacy.

Mussolini began the Napoleonic year of 1926 by plunging into his verbal quarrel with Stresemann over the Alto Adige. This provided the occasion of Contarini's resignation which was followed, not accidentally for sure, by a series of adventurous diplomatic moves. An unreserved campaign was launched to transform Albania into a veritable Italian protectorate; Italian expansion was menacingly directed toward Ethiopia and Turkey; a positive attempt was made to break up the Little Entente; and the ideological crusade was intensified, both by challenging the *fuorusciti* on French soil and by exporting Fascism on a worldwide scale. After all this—early in 1927—the old guard at the Palazzo Chigi were further decimated by resignations and new assignments.

Mussolini's flurry of activity during 1926 met with mixed fortune—success (by Fascist standards) in Albania, failure to construct a novel Danubian bloc, and in the colonial sphere the prospect of distant rather than immediate gains.

[1] B.D., C4231/2261/22 (Annual Report, 1925, p. 2).
[2] *OO*, XXII, 67.

On the other hand, Mussolini was perhaps more concerned with the general task of imposing a Fascist identity on Italian foreign policy, regardless of short-term results. Hitherto he had been restricted in his diplomacy—by the Palazzo Chigi, by the Matteotti affair, and even by his own lack of self-confidence. Not until 1926 was Mussolini able to pursue his own designs without hindrance from within Italy. At the same time his broad diplomatic strategy crystallized around two main points. In Europe, France—and by extension France's allies in central and southeastern Europe—emerged as Italy's chosen enemy and prey. In the colonial world, national glory and living space for Italy's surplus population were to be won on the shores of the eastern Mediterranean and in East Africa.[3] Such a program was hardly new in the history of Italian diplomacy. Toward the close of the nineteenth century Francesco Crispi, with whom Mussolini has aptly been compared, had dabbled in authoritarian rule at home while expressing Italian nationalism abroad in rivalry with France and in an attack on Ethiopia. Whatever the merits of this foreign policy, Mussolini by 1926 arrogated the Crispian tradition to provide a fairly consistent pattern for his diplomatic exploits, a pattern not always admitted by his detractors.[4]

That Mussolini regarded the Napoleonic year as a culminating point of early Fascist diplomacy would seem to be indicated by his subsequent conduct. The frenzied diplo-

[3] Indeed, beginning with Grandi's appointment as undersecretary in 1925, a conscious effort was made to coordinate the work of the Ministry of Colonies with that of the Ministry of Foreign Affairs, and to integrate colonial enterprise into the broader framework of Fascist foreign policy (Carocci, *Politica estera dell'Italia fascista*, pp. 25-26).

[4] See, for example, Salvemini, *Mussolini diplomatico*, p. 61: "He [Mussolini] had no definite plans, but was only trying out different devices day by day according to changing moods. Like the knights-errant of old, he was roaming the world in search of adventure." Also Hughes in *The Diplomats*, p. 225: "Rather than a considered plan, the whole thing looks more like a random and unco-ordinated striking-out in all directions in the hope of scoring points on the cheap."

macy of 1926 died away and no startlingly fresh maneuvers were undertaken in the next few years. In his annual report for 1927 the British ambassador concentrated on the ramifications of the Italo-Albanian Treaty of Tirana of November 1926, and had little else of consequence to report. The following year he wrote: "The year 1928 has been a comparatively uneventful one so far as Italian foreign policy is concerned. There have been no spectacular events, no dramatic gestures, no flamboyant speeches or sabre-rattlings."[5] It was almost as though Mussolini, having asserted his own dominance over Italian foreign policy and delineated the essential outlines of Fascist diplomacy during the Napoleonic year, had achieved his principal goal. Now he was prepared for a time to sit back and take stock of the international situation.[6]

Mussolini's satisfaction after 1926 presumably also stemmed from the fact that the international community (with the possible exception of France) came to accord Italy the status of a major power. Mussolini was assured of consultation on all major issues, from Locarno to Tangier, thus upholding what an interwar German commentator called the "principle of continual presence."[7] The international deference paid Mussolini was, of course, largely a reflection of his friendship with powerful Britain. And the Anglo-Italian entente served not only Italy but also Europe's chancelleries. For the entente, filling the vacuum left by the declining professionals of the Palazzo Chigi, represented a guarantee of the Duce's tolerable behavior. This impression was actively encouraged by Whitehall, which

[5] B.D., C2925/2925/22 (Annual Report, 1927, p. 3); C4108/4108/22 (Annual Report, 1928, p. 3).

[6] The concept of a post-1926 stocktaking is conveyed in the title of Chap. 6 of Di Nolfo's *Mussolini e la politica estera*—"Un bilancio." Di Nolfo refers specifically to Mussolini's Senate speech of June 5, 1928, which surveyed several years of Fascist diplomacy (*OO*, XXIII, 158-92).

[7] E. Eschmann, *Die Aussenpolitik des Faschismus* (Berlin, 1934), pp. 16-17.

was convinced that Corfu had been "a salutary lesson."[8] Rumors of Mussolini's overture for a German alliance were summarily dismissed. The blame for the Franco-Italian dispute was laid more on Paris than Rome, and Mussolini's word was considered sacrosanct.[9] The tendency to see Mussolini in the most favorable light possible was widespread in the English-speaking world. The American viewpoint in the 1920s was expressed by Secretary of State Henry Stimson: "He was in those years, in his foreign policy, a sound and useful leader, no more aggressive in his nationalism than many a democratic statesman."[10]

The Anglo-Italian entente, moreover, has colored the historical judgment of Italy's early diplomacy. Significantly, within the foreign ministry, Bureau V of the General Department for European and Near Eastern Affairs, which handled the routine business of the Anglo-Italian entente, was headed at this time by Raffaele Guariglia. Guariglia, in his *Ricordi*, emphasizes the entente's moderating influence on Mussolini. As such, it helped to justify the Palazzo Chigi's cooperation with Fascism.[11] One cannot but wonder whether the picture Guariglia conveys of the first years of Fascist foreign policy—as by and large circumspect and traditional—is not the product of his preoccupation with the Anglo-Italian entente. It seems pertinent to raise the question since, prior to the publication and opening of documentary sources, Guariglia's was the only firsthand comprehensive account of early Fascist di-

---

[8] B.D., C2661/2661/22 (Annual Report, 1923, p. 3).

[9] See, for example, *DBFP*, I, Nos. 335, 422; II, No. 108, and p. 925; B.D., C415/77/22, C10797/391/90, and Chamberlain papers, Vol. 258, Nov. 2, 1925.

[10] H. Stimson and M. Bundy, *On Active Service in Peace and War* (New York, 1948), pp. 269-70.

[11] Guariglia, *Ricordi*, pp. 64-65; cf. Legatus, *Vita di Contarini*, pp. 87-88. Di Nolfo, *Mussolini e la politica estera*, pp. 50-51, unkindly suggests that some Italian diplomats have exaggerated Mussolini's early moderation either out of naïveté or in justification of their own collaboration.

plomacy which scholars had to work from. In other words, the Anglo-Italian entente lies behind the conventional verdict that Mussolini's diplomacy in the 1920s was "a decade of good behavior."[12]

Britain, without doubt, did restrain Mussolini from precipitate action—in the Near East and East Africa. On the other hand, the Anglo-Italian entente had distinct limitations. For one thing, it depended heavily on the personal relationship between Mussolini and Chamberlain, and thus existed at the mercy of a change of personnel in Whitehall. There is not a little irony in the fact that, while it was Chamberlain's part to placate Mussolini, it was to be that of his stepbrother, Neville, to try to appease another Fascist, Hitler, in the next decade. There is this distinction that, unlike Neville, Austen succeeded at least in the short run and surrendered little substantial in the process. But here—in the lack of immediate concrete gain on Fascist Italy's part—lay another important weakness of the Anglo-Italian entente of the twenties. London won for Italy admission to the Tangier Conference, but this was strictly a matter of honor. Churchill's lenient war-debt settlement

[12] S. W. Halperin, *Mussolini and Italian Fascism* (Princeton, 1964), pp. 72-73. The idea of "a decade of good behavior," during which Mussolini remained under the benign influence of the Palazzo Chigi, is quite widespread. It is expressed, for instance, in the following diverse works: R. Albrecht-Carrié, *Italy from Napoleon to Mussolini* (New York, 1950), pp. 198-200, and the same author's *A Diplomatic History of Europe*, pp. 432-36; Anchiere, *Il Politico*, xx (1955), 212; G. Craig, "Totalitarian Approaches to Diplomatic Negotiation" in *Diplomatic History and Historiography*, ed. A. Sarkissian (London, 1961), pp. 109-110; H. S. Hughes in *The Diplomats*, pp. 216-17, 229-30, and Gilbert, *ibid.*, pp. 512-14, 534; S. Hughes, *The Fall and Rise of Modern Italy* (New York, 1967), p. 167; Kirkpatrick, *Mussolini*, pp. 191-92; Moscati, *Studi Politici*, II (1953-54), 408-409, and the same author in *La politica estera italiana dal 1914 al 1943*, pp. 110-11; E. Nolte, *Three Faces of Fascism*, tr. L. Vennewitz (New York, 1966), pp. 225, 347; A. Rosso, *Rivista di Studi Politici Internazionali*, xxi (1954), 418-19; F. Siebert, *Italiens Weg in den Zweiten Weltkrieg* (Frankfurt, 1962), p. 14; E. Wiskemann, *Fascism in Italy* (London, 1968), pp. 50-51.

was in part simply a recognition that Italy was too poor to pay heavily. And Chamberlain's carte blanche in Albania granted Italy control of a poor country where Rome already held international approval to establish a preeminent position. Altogether, these amounted to a meager catalogue of British favors. The status that accrued to Mussolini from his special relationship with the British was important in assuaging his own ego and the Italian nationalists' wounded pride. But obviously the Duce would not rest content interminably with prestige in lieu of material profit.

The break came after 1933 when the growth of German power took the luster off an association with Britain. To keep up with his fellow Fascist, Hitler, Mussolini required of the Anglo-Italian entente more than it could supply. Then Mussolini reverted to other policies which, as we have seen, he had already explored during his first four and a half years in office.

First and foremost was Mussolini's flirtation with revisionism on the Rhine and the Danube. To endorse the principle of revisionism, which Mussolini did not do publicly until 1928, could not be termed a reckless action. Selective revisionism was internationally acceptable by the mid-1920s. For example, Britain's entire reparations policy was an exercise in revisionism. But Mussolini's tolerance of a German revival and of Balkan irredentism went far beyond anything the British imagined. Where London looked for revisionism by negotiation, Fascist Italy, by supplying arms to the *Reichswehr* and the Magyars, seemed to contemplate changing the peace treaties by unilateral action of the defeated nations. To many, revisionism was a means of relieving international grievances. To Mussolini it was a weapon to use against France and the Little Entente.

The Rome-Berlin Axis of 1936 was born partly of Mussolini's longstanding illusion that the growth of German power could be made to serve Italy's interests and partly of

his taste for an ideological foreign policy. This latter characteristic, too, was present in Fascist Italy's early diplomacy.
It was most evident in the attempt to export Fascism and in
Mussolini's deliberate escalation of the *fuorusciti* issue. In
addition, over a wider terrain much of Mussolini's early
diplomacy was informed by ideological prejudices, although
he was often confounded in his expectations. His partiality
for authoritarian, conservative figures like General Primo
de Rivera of Spain and General Averescu of Rumania did
not produce an alignment of those countries with Fascist
Italy to the extent he wanted. Nor did his special relationship with King Alexander of Yugoslavia, which rested on a
common political philosophy, persuade the Belgrade cabinet to acquiesce in Italian control of Albania. On the other
side of the ledger, the Duce loathed Beneš because the
Czech spoke for democracy in Central Europe; and the accession to office in 1924 of British Labour and of the *Cartel
des gauches* in Paris filled him with foreboding. (Not only
were MacDonald, Briand, and Beneš parliamentary democrats; they were also proponents of the Wilsonian ideal of
international conciliation which affronted Mussolini's red-
blooded nationalism.) Yet the socialist MacDonald made
concessions in the Dodecanese and Jubaland, Briand offered a Brenner guarantee, and Beneš a general rapprochement with Italy. Nonetheless, Mussolini rejoiced in the fall
of the Labour government and spurned every overture
from Paris and Prague. Instead, he reserved his friendship
for his colleagues of the right. The two most significant associations he formed between 1922 and 1927—with the
German nationalists and the British Conservatives—clearly
owed much to a general empathy of political principles. If
Mussolini's diplomacy in the mid-twenties could be conditioned by his congeniality toward conservatives, it was perhaps almost predetermined that Fascist Italy would become
tied to an actual Fascist regime in Berlin a decade later.

In the 1930s Fascist Italy turned increasingly to the use of violence in international affairs, in imitation of Nazi Germany to some extent. But again Mussolini's early foreign policy had indicated his penchant for force to get his own way. Corfu was the most obvious example; but also Fiume became Italian virtually because of a Mussolinian coup; and a Fascist attack on Asia Minor or Ethiopia was a very real threat in 1926. Moreover, in the government-controlled Italian press scorn was heaped on the spirit of Locarno while martial virtues were constantly exalted.

There were, in fact, two distinct sides to Mussolini as foreign minister in the period 1922-27. On the one hand, there was the signatory of Locarno and confidant of Sir Austen Chamberlain, more or less content to bask in the aura of this relationship. On the other, there was the ideologue and trafficker in revisionism, and spokesman for discontented, aggressive nationalism. The latter characteristics, which were firmly implanted in Fascist diplomacy by the close of 1926, make the verdict "a decade of good behavior" a relative one at most. Despite the best efforts of the Palazzo Chigi and the British Conservatives, the Duce was never more than a superficial "good European."

Bibliographical Note

THE MAIN documentary evidence has been described at the start of this book, in the Preface and in the list of abbreviations used in the footnotes. In addition to the primary sources already cited, it seems worth mentioning that the international treaties into which Italy entered were registered with the League of Nations and are therefore contained in the League's *Treaty Series*, 205 vols. (Geneva, 1920-46). The Italian texts are to be found in the publication of the Ministero degli affari esteri, *Trattati e convenzioni fra il Regno d'Italia e gli altri stati*, 59 vols. (Rome, 1865-1958).

As for newspaper sources, the official organ of the *Partito nazionale fascista* was *Popolo d'Italia*. Published first in Milan and then Rome, it was, after the March on Rome, in nominal charge of Benito Mussolini's brother, Arnaldo, although the Duce himself always took a keen interest in the paper's contents. The bulk of Mussolini's *Opera omnia* is drawn from its columns. The most powerful non-Fascist press voice was undeniably that of the liberal Milanese daily, *Corriere della Sera*. However, with the establishment of the Fascist dictatorship in 1925 it lost its independence, although as an official mouthpiece of the government, it always remained second in importance to Mussolini's own *Popolo d'Italia*.

Among the memoirs of Italian diplomats which make a broad survey of Fascist foreign policy, Raffaele Guariglia's *Ricordi, 1922-1946* (Naples, 1950) stands out. The work avoids obvious special pleading and tries to preserve a measure of dispassionate observation. Guariglia's position within the Palazzo Chigi during the 1920s made him responsible for much of the business of the Anglo-Italian entente. Although this was an advantageous observation point, it led Guariglia to overestimate Mussolini's attachment to Italy's wartime alliance; this, in fact, is his memoir's chief weakness. Antonio Salandra in *Memorie politiche, 1916–1925* (Milan, 1951) presents his view from his post at the League of Nations. Unfortunately, Salandra is far too anxious to excuse his own cooperation with Fascism and on occasion is guilty of misrepresentation. Daniele Varé speaks for the pro-Fascist younger set at the Italian foreign ministry in *Laughing Diplomat* (New York, 1938). The title is indicative; this is strictly a lightweight work. Two other chatty memoirs, dealing mostly with diplomatic personalities, are by Pietro Quaroni—*Ricordi di un ambasciatore* (Milan, 1954) and *Valigia diplomatica* (Milan, 1956). A selection of essays drawn from both of these memoirs has appeared in English under the literal title *Diplomatic Bags* (London, 1966). Carlo Sforza resigned from the Italian diplomatic service on Mussolini's accession to power. Nevertheless, he still possessed his special sources of information on the situation in Rome. Of Sforza's many books, his *L'Italia dal 1914 al 1944 quale io la vidi* (Rome, 1945) is the nearest to a diplomatic memoir of the interwar years.

None of the foreign diplomats in Rome in the 1920s has left a comprehensive account of Fascist foreign policy at this time. Georges Wagnière, the Swiss minister, *Dix-huit ans à Rome: Guerre mondiale et fascisme, 1918–1936* (Geneva, 1944), and Baron Napoleon Beyens, the Belgian representative to the Vatican, *Quatre ans à Rome, 1921–1926* (Paris, 1934), are both uneven and episodic. *A Diplomat Looks at Europe* (New York, 1925) by Richard W. Child, the American ambassador at the time of the March on Rome, is symptomatic of the undiscriminating adulation of the Duce by some Anglo-Americans.

Secondary works that treat early Fascist diplomacy are not plentiful. Ennio Di Nolfo pursues a scholarly approach in *Mussolini e la politica estera italiana (1919–1933)*

(Padua, 1960). Despite the book's many merits, it has some flaws. When Di Nolfo wrote, only the *Documenti diplomatici italiani* for the period October 1922 to May 1925 were available; the lack of the diplomatic record of 1926, Mussolini's Napoleonic year, when his foreign policy really began to take shape, constitutes a serious handicap. Moreover, Di Nolfo has used no German sources, with the result that he misses much of Mussolini's revisionist activity. These shortcomings are not found in Giampiero Carocci's *La politica estera dell'italia fascista (1925–1928)* (Bari, 1969). Based on all the available Italian, German, and British documentary sources, this monograph is explicitly concerned with the imposition of Mussolini's control over Italian diplomacy. Of course Carocci, by restricting his work to the years 1925-1928, forswears any comparison in depth with the Duce's first three years in office, and also any consideration of the gradual evolution of Fascist foreign policy since the March on Rome. Gaetano Salvemini's *Mussolini diplomatico, 1922–1932*, rev. ed. (Bari, 1952), and its English version, *Prelude to World War II* (London, 1953), are lively and contain much useful information derived in part from the author's participation in Italian politics. An outspoken opponent of Fascism, he was a prominent *fuoruscito* after 1925. But Salvemini's accounts are unbalanced in that they depict Mussolini as so absolute a buffoon and his policy as so utterly thoughtless that the devil is given very much less than his due. Two brief summaries of Mussolini's diplomatic career are *Mussolini e l'Europa* (Rome, 1945) by Mario Donosti, a pseudonym for Mario Luciolli, who served in the Palazzo Chigi between the wars, and *Il fascismo nella politica internazionale* (Rome, 1946) by the prolific Italian historian, Luigi Salvatorelli. Both books, however, were written too soon after the event to allow much depth or perspective. Another survey, *Italy's Foreign and Colonial Policy, 1914–1937* (London, 1938) by

401

Maxwell Macartney and Paul Cremona, is of course also outdated, but it stands up as a factual narrative remarkably well for its years. For what it is worth, the pro-Fascist justification of Mussolini's diplomacy may be found in Muriel Currey's *Italian Foreign Policy, 1918–1932* (London, 1932), and Luigi Villari's *Italian Foreign Policy under Mussolini* (New York, 1956). Fascist Italian diplomacy appears in a Mediterranean setting in the works of the interwar geopolitical school, most notably, Margaret Boveri, *Mediterranean Cross-Currents*, tr. L. Sieveking (London, 1938), and Elizabeth Monroe, *The Mediterranean in Politics* (London, 1938).

In essay form Ruggiero Moscati's "Gli esordi della politica estera fascista—Il periodo Contarini—Corfù," and his "Locarno—Il revisionismo fascista—Il periodo Grandi e la nuova fase della politica estera," originally given as talks over the Italian radio-television network, have been published in *La politica estera italiana dal 1914 al 1943* ("Edizioni radiotelevisione italiani" [Turin, 1963]), pp. 77-117. They are competent résumés based on the *Documenti diplomatici italiani*, although, as in most Italian works, non-Italian sources are ignored. H. Stuart Hughes has grounded his "Early Diplomacy of Italian Fascism, 1922-1932," in *The Diplomats, 1919–1939*, ed. G. Craig and F. Gilbert (Princeton, 1953), pp. 210-33, on the writings of Guariglia and Salvemini mentioned above. His essay necessarily reflects the limitations of these mentors. Perhaps the best and most up-to-date short discussion of Fascism's early foreign policy is the concluding section of Christopher Seton-Watson's *Italy from Liberalism to Fascism, 1870–1925* (London, 1967), pp. 665-98. Despite its brevity, it is a sound, well-researched essay. Giorgio Rumi's complementary articles, "Il 'fascismo delle origini' e i problemi di politica estera" and " 'Revisionismo' fascista ed espansione coloniale (1925-1935)," *Il Movimento di Liberazione in Italia*, No. 75 (April

1964), pp. 3-29, and No. 80 (July 1965), pp. 37-73, are based largely on newspaper and secondary sources, and concern the general nature rather than the substance of Mussolini's diplomacy. Rumi sees restlessness and aggression built into Fascist foreign policy from the start, although he equates revisionism with imperial expansion.

Other than passing comment in the memoirs of the actors concerned, discussion of the method by which Fascist foreign policy was formulated is scarce. Luigi Ferraris, *L'amministrazione centrale del Ministero degli esteri, 1848–1954* (Florence, 1955), chronicles in a strictly factual manner the structural changes that took place within the Italian foreign ministry. In *Vita diplomatica di Salvatore Contarini* (Rome, 1947), Legatus (probably the journalist Roberto Cantalupo) purports to assess the role of the famous secretary general who stayed at his post until the spring of 1926; but the book hardly goes beyond superficial generalities. For the societal groups that have most influenced the making of Italian diplomacy in the twentieth century, Norman Kogan's *The Politics of Italian Foreign Policy* (New York, 1963) may be recommended.

On Mussolini himself, the best work to date is Sir Ivone Kirkpatrick's *Mussolini: A Study in Power* (London, 1964). It is far from definitive, but is especially pertinent to this study. Because the author was a professional diplomat and on the staff of the British embassy in Rome from 1930 to 1933, his information on Mussolinian foreign policy is often drawn from firsthand sources, above all from Sir Ronald Graham whose career as British ambassador to Italy antedated the March on Rome and lasted until 1934. The projected sociopsychological biography of Mussolini by Renzo De Felice in some ways will probably prove more penetrating than Kirkpatrick's conventional approach. On the other hand, the two volumes published so far, *Mussolini: Il revoluzionario 1883–1920*, and *Mussolini: Il*

403

fascista, 1921–1929 (Turin, 1965-   ) contain little on Mussolini's foreign policy. Mussolini's ghostwritten *My Autobiography* (New York, 1928) is platitudinous and worthless. Quinto Navarra, the Duce's valet, naturally supplies much to delight the tabloid press in his *Memorie del cameriere di Mussolini* (Milan, 1946), but the book is not devoid of shrewd political observation. The most reliable reference work on the events of Mussolini's career is by Luigi Salvatorelli and Giovanni Mira, *Storia d'Italia nel periodo fascista*, 5th ed. (Turin, 1964).

There are a variety of works, both secondary and of a memoir nature, on specific diplomatic topics covered in this book. Apropos Corfu, Commander Antonio Foschini of the Italian navy has provided two eyewitness accounts of the preparation and execution of the occupation: *La verità sulle cannonate di Corfù* (Rome, 1953), and "A trent'anni dall'occupazione di Corfù," *Nuova Antologia*, CDLVIII (Dec. 1953), 401-12. These have their value, although they are marred by the author's superpatriotism. A reliable monograph of the Corfu affair is Pierre Lasturel's *L'affaire gréco-italienne de 1923* (Paris, 1925), although it has been to some extent superseded by James Barros, *The Corfu Incident of 1923* (Princeton, 1965). Barros, however, for reasons unknown refuses to consider the obvious, namely that Mussolini intended to annex the island. That this, indeed, was his aim is the main point of Ettore Anchiere's "L'affare di Corfù alla luce dei documenti diplomatici italiani," *Il Politico*, xx (Dec. 1955), 374-95.

The strained relations between Fascist Italy and Czechoslovakia are exemplified by Vladimir Kybal in his "Czechoslovakia and Italy: My Negotiations with Mussolini, 1922-1924," *Journal of Central European Affairs*, XIII (Jan. 1954), 352-68 and XIV (April 1954), 65-76. Kybal describes the events leading up to the unsatisfactory Italo-Czech pact of friendship of July 1924. He is rather pro-

Mussolini and decidedly anti-Beneš. Italo-Czech tension tended to set the tone for the relationship between Fascist Italy and the Little Entente as a whole. Mussolini's mounting quarrel with another member of the Little Entente, Yugoslavia, is dealt with in several Italian works on Fascism's Balkan policies. Preeminent among them is Pietro Pastorelli, *Italia e Albania, 1924–1927: Origini diplomatiche del Trattato di Tirana del 22 novembre 1927* (Florence, 1967). This is a thoroughly reliable monograph, although it takes no account of the Italian domestic situation, which obviously affected Mussolini's response to events in Albania. The book's worth is considerably enhanced by the deployment of some useful, unpublished source material; the prize document revealed by Pastorelli is the text of the secret Italo-Albanian treaty of August 1925. Memoirs on this subject include Alessandro Lessona's *Memorie* (Florence, 1958); despite the author's egotism and Italian nationalist prejudice, the book is a valuable source for the first and largely clandestine contacts between Mussolini and Ahmed Zogu. Francesco Jacomini di San Sevino in his "Il Patto di Tirana del 1926," *Rivista di Studi Politici Internazionali,* xx (April-June 1953), 227-60, which also constitutes the first part of his *La politica dell'Italia in Albania* (Bologna, 1965), gives a more sober account of the negotiations for the formal Italo-Albanian tie expressed in the Treaties of Tirana. Albania was one problem that contributed to the decline of Italo-Yugoslav relations after 1924. Another was the situation of Italians living under Yugoslav rule in Dalmatia. The Dalmatian issue is the particular concern of a further Italian diplomatic memoir, Carlo Umiltà's *Jugoslavia e Albania* (Milan, 1947). Dennison I. Rusinow, *Italy's Austrian Heritage, 1919–1946* (New York, 1969), is a sound monograph on the problem of those territories inhabited largely by Slavs and Germans which Italy gained after World War I. Naturally, Fascist Italy's relations with Yugoslavia and Austria figure prominently in the book.

In the area of Fascist Italy's relationship with the major powers, two members of the French embassy in Rome in the 1920s have commented on the difficult task of coping with the Francophobe Duce. François Charles-Roux, *Une grande ambassade à Rome* (Paris, 1961), is discursive; Robert De Dampierre, "Dix années de politique française à Rome, 1925-1935," *Revue des Deux Mondes* (Nov. 1, 1953), pp. 14-38, concentrates on Briand's abortive efforts to strike a deal with Mussolini for cooperation against Germany in Europe in return for a broad colonial entente. One item on the Franco-Italian colonial agenda concerned Tangier, which is the subject of a good monograph by Graham Stuart, *The International City of Tangier*, rev. ed. (Stanford, 1955). The richest sources of information on the crucial question of the Italian *fuorusciti* in France are Charles Delzell, *Mussolini's Enemies* (Princeton, 1961), and Aldo Garosci, *Storia dei fuorusciti* (Bari, 1953).

Largely because it was deliberately kept clandestine, hardly anything on Mussolini's early liaison with the German nationalists has appeared in print. Kurt Ludecke, one of Hitler's first emissaries to Rome, tells—probably truthfully—what he knows in *I Knew Hitler* (New York, 1937), but it is far from the whole story. Walter Pese, "Hitler und Italien, 1920-1926," *Vierteljahrshefte für Zeitgeschichte*, III (April 1955), 113-26, and Edgar Rosen, "Mussolini und Deutschland, 1922-1923," *Vierteljahrshefte für Zeitgeschichte*, V (Jan. 1957), 17-41, approach the subject but, oddly eschewing German documentary sources, do not really come close.

Surprisingly the important and well-publicized Anglo-Italian entente constitutes even more virgin terrain. George W. Baer in the introductory chapter of *The Coming of the Italian-Ethiopian War* (Cambridge, Mass., 1967) touches on Britain and Italy in the 1920's. Giuseppe Vedovato, *Gli accordi italo-etiopici dell'Agosto 1928* (Florence, 1956), is also of necessity concerned somewhat with general Anglo-Italian relations. The entente is treated in passing by Guariglia in his memoirs and by Kirkpatrick in his biography of Mussolini. But really the subject has received no direct or consistent treatment. On relations between Italy and the United States in the twenties, there is a series of interesting articles by John P. Diggins, albeit on social and intellectual interchange more than diplomacy: "Flirtation with Fascism: American Pragmatic Liberals and Mussolini's Italy," *American Historical Review*, LXXI (Jan. 1966), 487-506; "Mussolini and America: Hero-Worship, Charisma, and the 'Vulgar Talent,'" *The Historian*, XXVIII (Aug. 1966), 559-85; "American Catholics and Italian Fascism," *Journal of Contemporary History*, II (Oct. 1967), 51-68.

IT SHOULD BE apparent from the foregoing bibliography that the treatment of early Fascist diplomacy has been by and large fragmentary and cursory. Only the books by Di Nolfo, Carocci, and Salvemini represent direct and substantial attempts to evaluate Mussolini's diplomacy in the 1920s. All the other works cited either dwell on one aspect of Mussolini's early foreign policy, or they discuss the subject only briefly and inevitably somewhat superficially. More often than not such an account of the twenties serves as a sketchy introduction to a more thorough examination of the spectacular and earth-shattering international politics of the following decade. This is understandable and intellectually quite legitimate. But the cumulative effect of the pattern repeated over and over has been to do violence to a degree of historical continuity in Fascist foreign policy, which it has been the purpose of this book to recognize.

Index

413